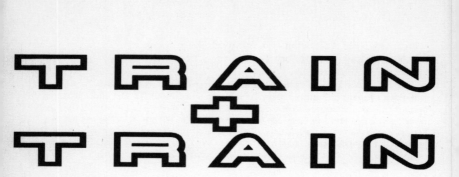

TRAIN + TRAIN

Volume 3

Original Story by

HIDEYUKI KURATA

Art by

TOMOMASA TAKUMA

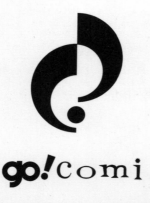

go!comi

Concerning Honorifics

At Go! Comi, we do our best to ensure that our translations read seamlessly in English while respecting the original Japanese language and culture. To this end, the original honorifics (the suffixes found at the end of characters' names) remain intact. In Japan, where politeness and formality are more integrated into every aspect of the language, honorifics give a better understanding of character relationships. They can be used to indicate both respect and affection. Whether a person addresses someone by first name or last name also indicates how close their relationship is.

Here are some of the honorifics you might encounter in reading this book:

-san: This is the most common and neutral of honorifics. The polite way to address someone you're not on close terms with is to use "-san." It's kind of like Mr. or Ms., except you can use "-san" with first names as easily as family names.

-chan: Used for friendly familiarity, mostly applied towards young girls. "-chan" also carries a connotation of cuteness with it, so it is frequently used with nick-names towards both boys and girls (such as "Na-chan" for "Natsu").

-kun: Like "-chan," it's an informal suffix for friends and classmates, only "-kun" is usually associated with boys. It can also be used in a professional environment by someone addressing a subordinate.

-sama: Indicates a great deal of respect or admiration.

Sempai: In school, "sempai" is used to refer to an upperclassman or club leader. It can also be used in the workplace by a new employee to address a mentor or staff member with seniority.

Sensei: Teachers, doctors, writers or any master of a trade are referred to as "sensei." When addressing a manga creator, the polite thing to do is attach "-sensei" to the manga-ka's name (as in Takuma-sensei).

Onii: This is the more casual term for an older brother. Usually you'll see it with an honorific attached, such as "onii-chan."

Onee: The casual term for older sister, it's used like "onii" with honorifics.

[blank]: Not using an honorific when addressing someone indicates that the speaker has permission to speak intimately with the other person. This relationship is usually reserved for close friends and family.

TRAIN

TRAIN + TRAIN
VOLUME 3

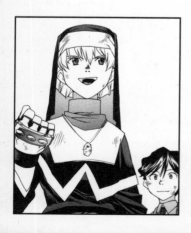

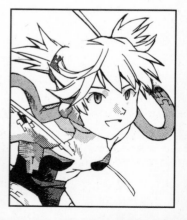

TRAIN

TRAIN
+
TRAIN

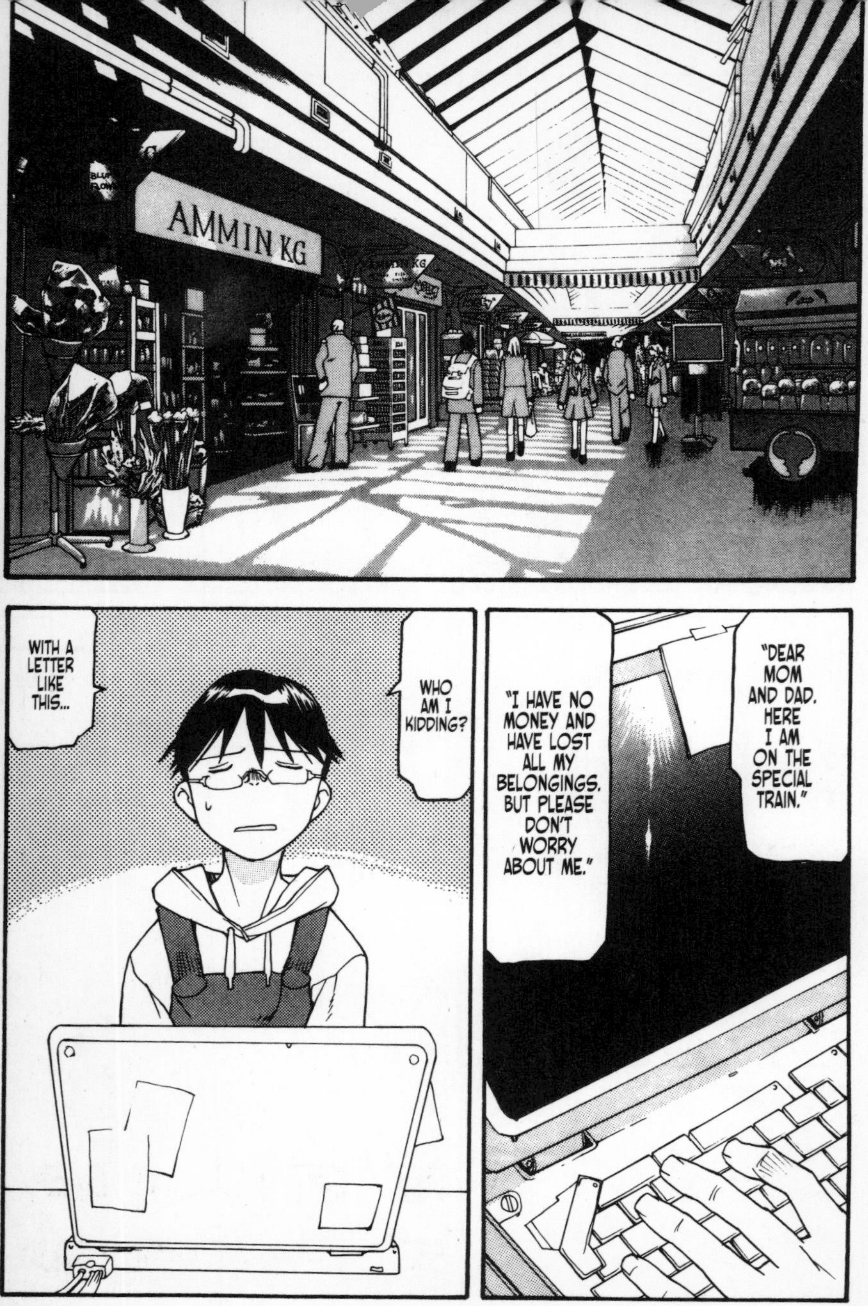
AMMIN KG
"DEAR MOM AND DAD. HERE I AM ON THE SPECIAL TRAIN."
"I HAVE NO MONEY AND HAVE LOST ALL MY BELONGINGS. BUT PLEASE DON'T WORRY ABOUT ME."
WHO AM I KIDDING?
WITH A LETTER LIKE THIS...

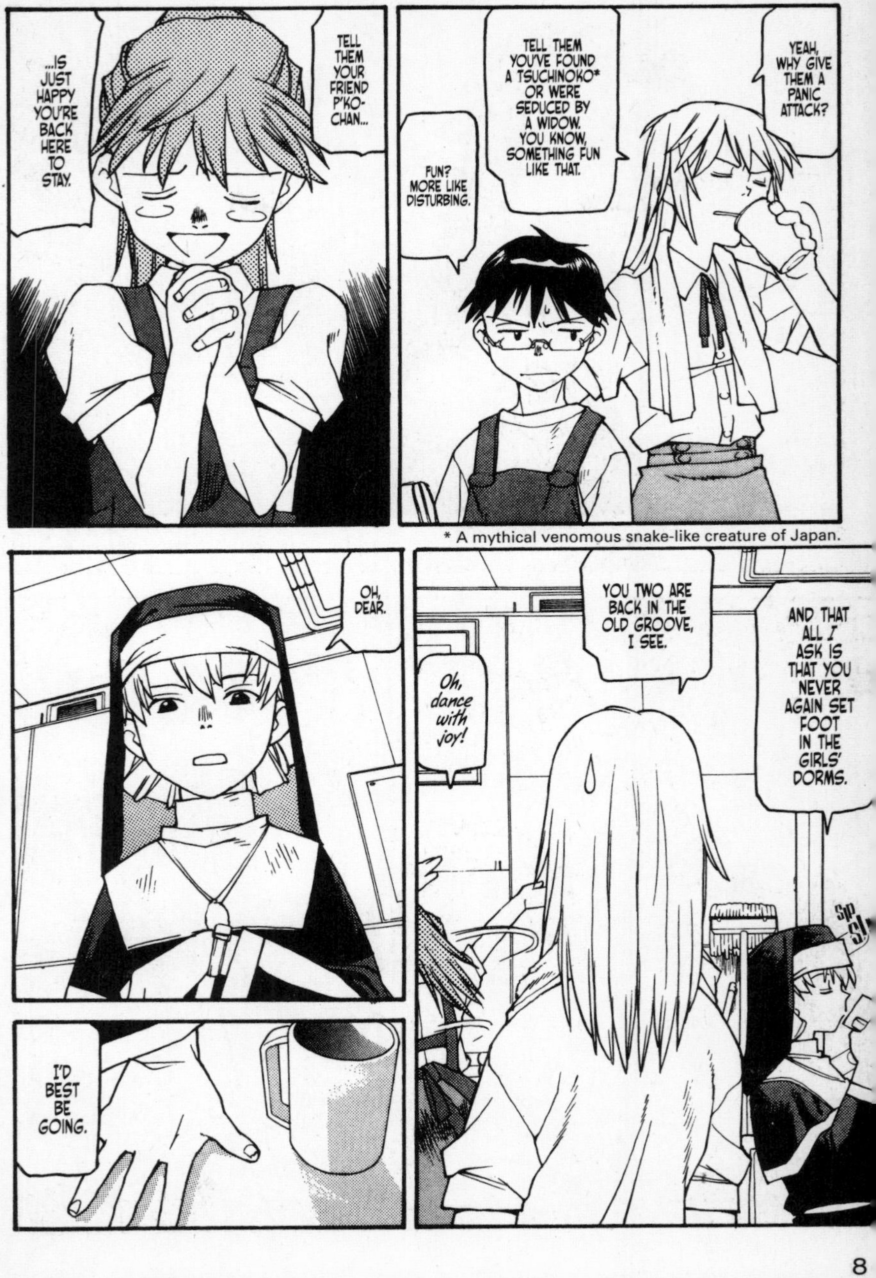
YEAH, WHY GIVE THEM A PANIC ATTACK?
TELL THEM YOU'VE FOUND A TSUCHINOKO* OR WERE SEDUCED BY A WIDOW. YOU KNOW, SOMETHING FUN LIKE THAT.
FUN? MORE LIKE DISTURBING.
TELL THEM YOUR FRIEND P'KO-CHAN...
...IS JUST HAPPY YOU'RE BACK HERE TO STAY.
AND THAT ALL *I* ASK IS THAT YOU NEVER AGAIN SET FOOT IN THE GIRLS' DORMS.
YOU TWO ARE BACK IN THE OLD GROOVE, I SEE.
Oh, dance with joy!
SIP SIP
OH, DEAR.
I'D BEST BE GOING.

* A mythical venomous snake-like creature of Japan.

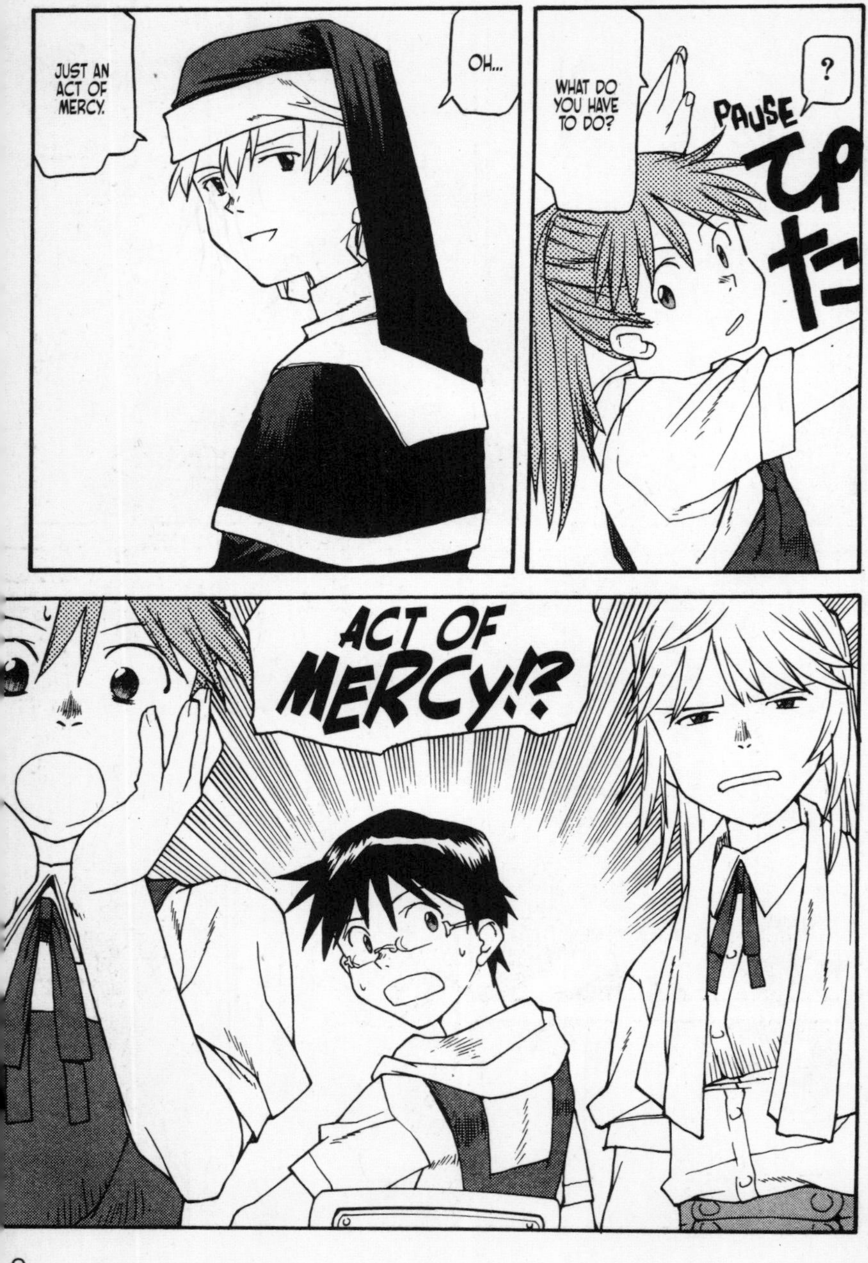
?
WHAT DO YOU HAVE TO DO?
PAUSE
ぴた
OH...
JUST AN ACT OF MERCY.
ACT OF MERCY!?

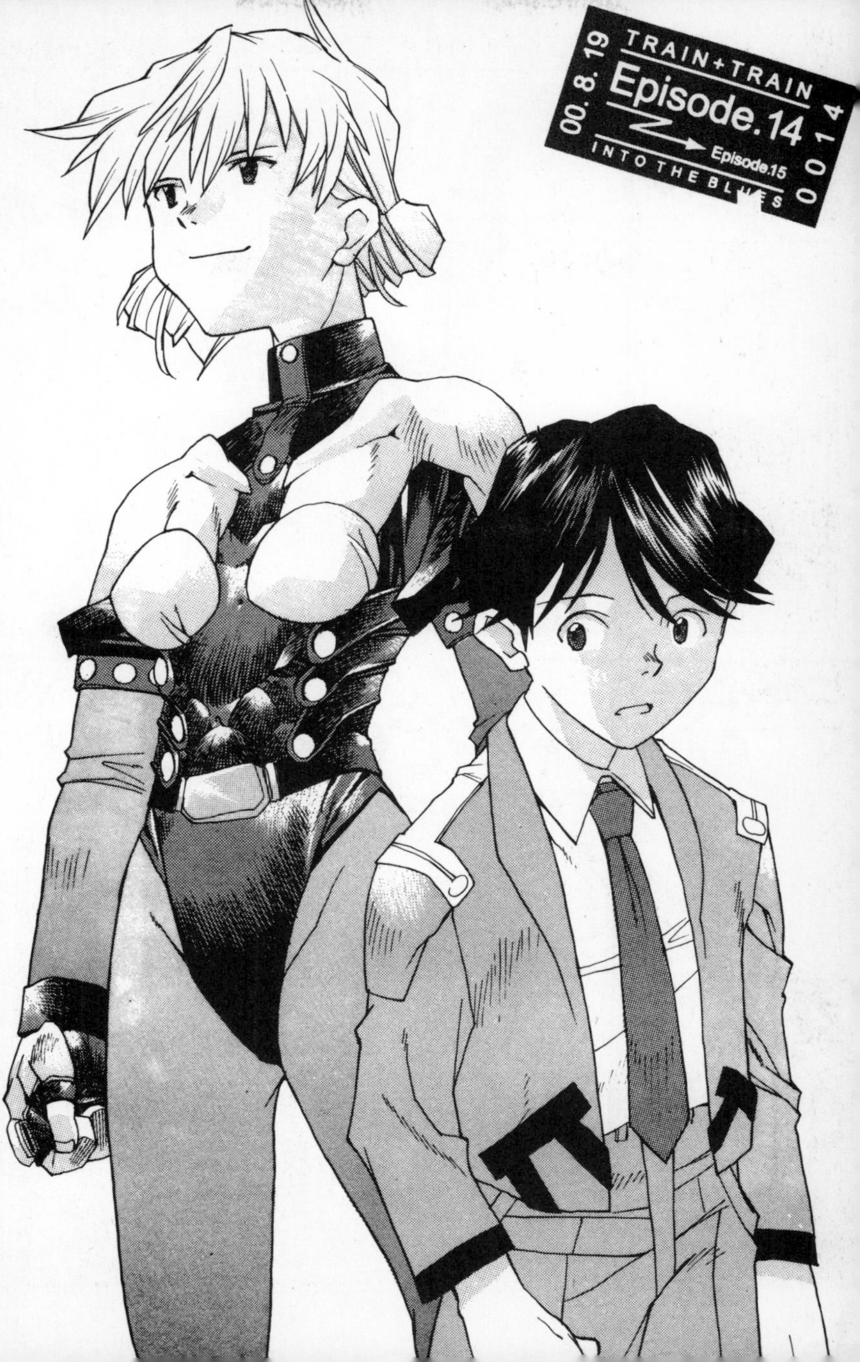
00. 8. 19
TRAIN+TRAIN
Episode.14
Episode.15
INTO THE BLUES
0014

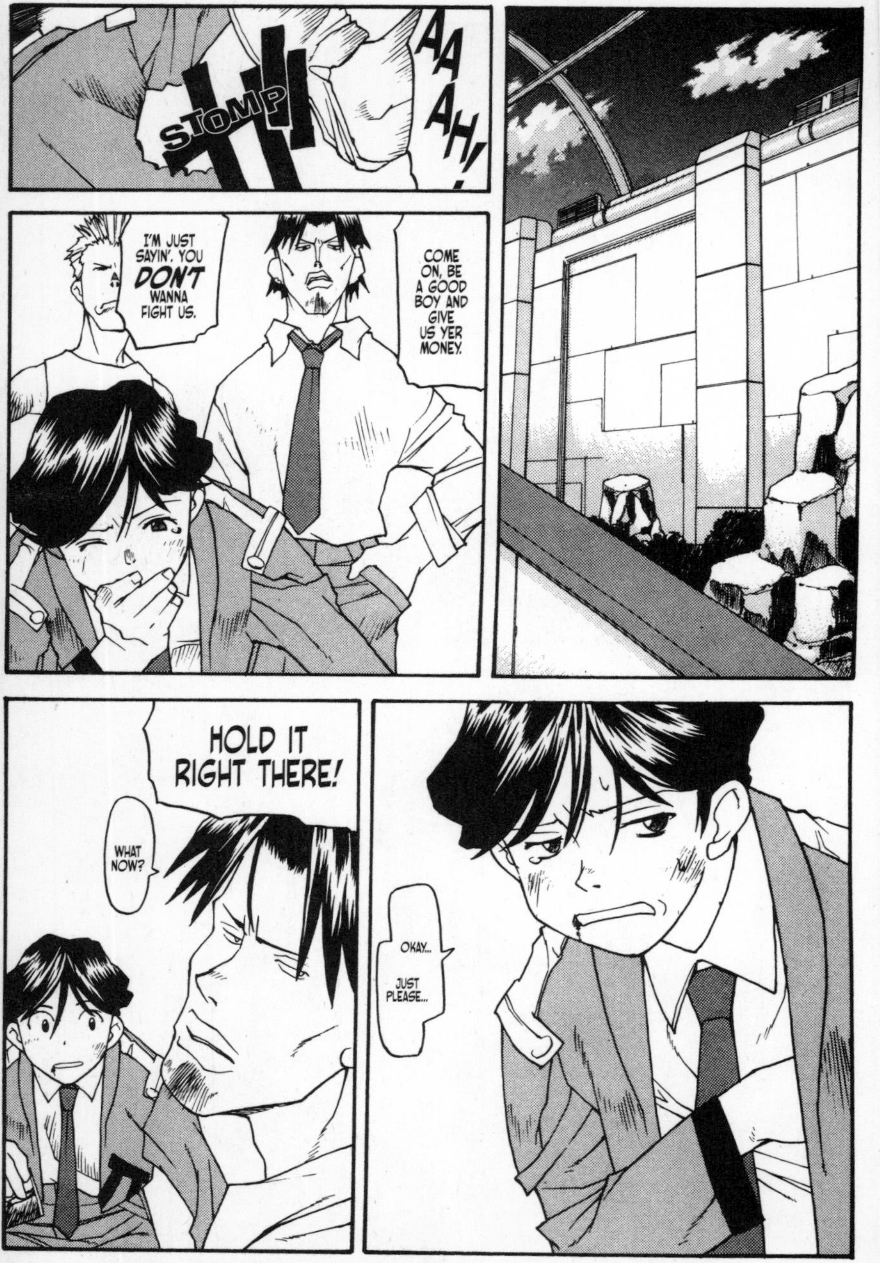
AAAAH!
STOMP
COME ON, BE A GOOD BOY AND GIVE US YER MONEY.
I'M JUST SAYIN'. YOU DON'T WANNA FIGHT US.
OKAY...
JUST PLEASE...
HOLD IT RIGHT THERE!
WHAT NOW?

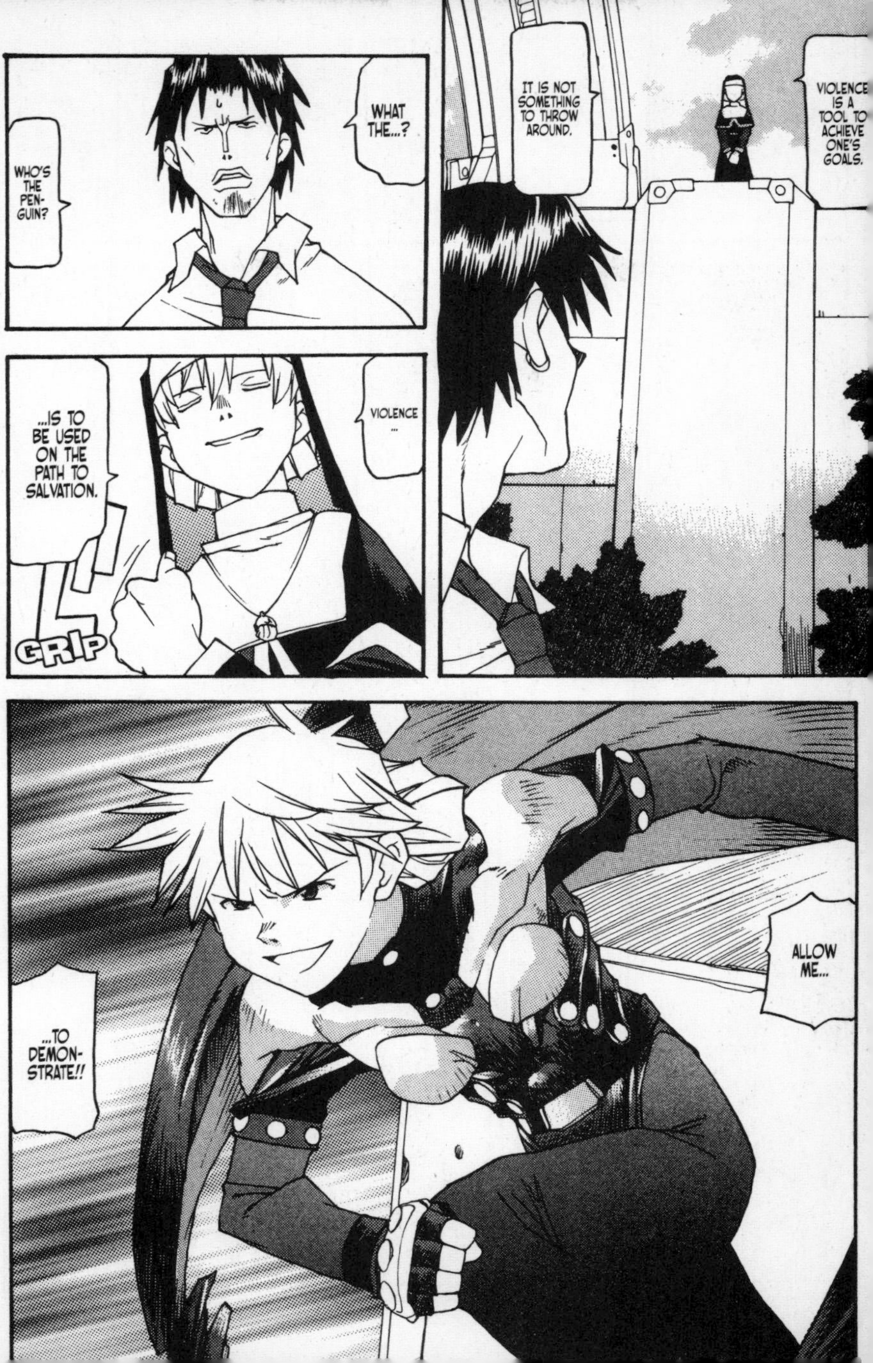
VIOLENCE IS A TOOL TO ACHIEVE ONE'S GOALS.
IT IS NOT SOMETHING TO THROW AROUND.
WHAT THE...?
WHO'S THE PEN-GUIN?
VIOLENCE ...
...IS TO BE USED ON THE PATH TO SALVATION.
GRIP
ALLOW ME...
...TO DEMON-STRATE!!

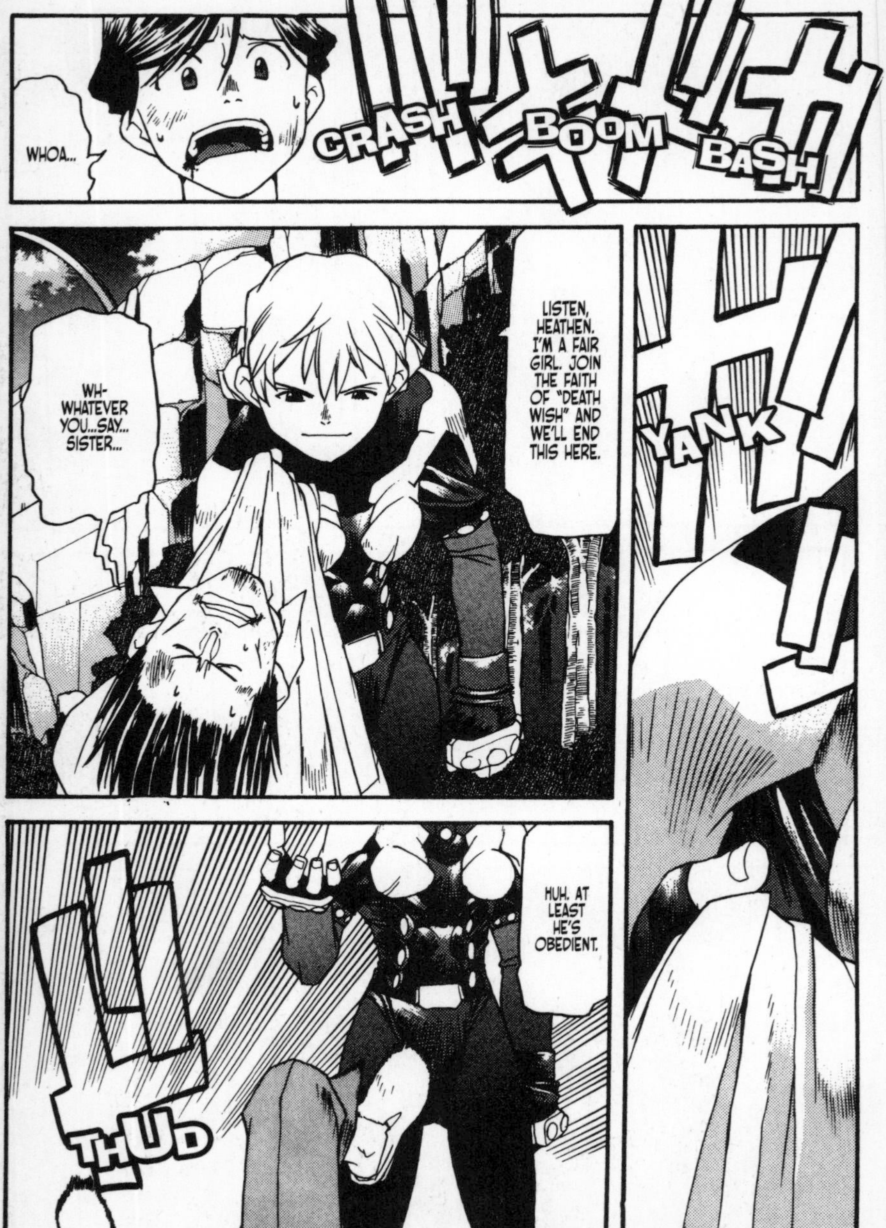

CRASH BOOM BASH
WHOA...
YANK
LISTEN, HEATHEN. I'M A FAIR GIRL. JOIN THE FAITH OF "DEATH WISH" AND WE'LL END THIS HERE.
WH- WHATEVER YOU...SAY... SISTER...
HUH. AT LEAST HE'S OBEDIENT.
THUD

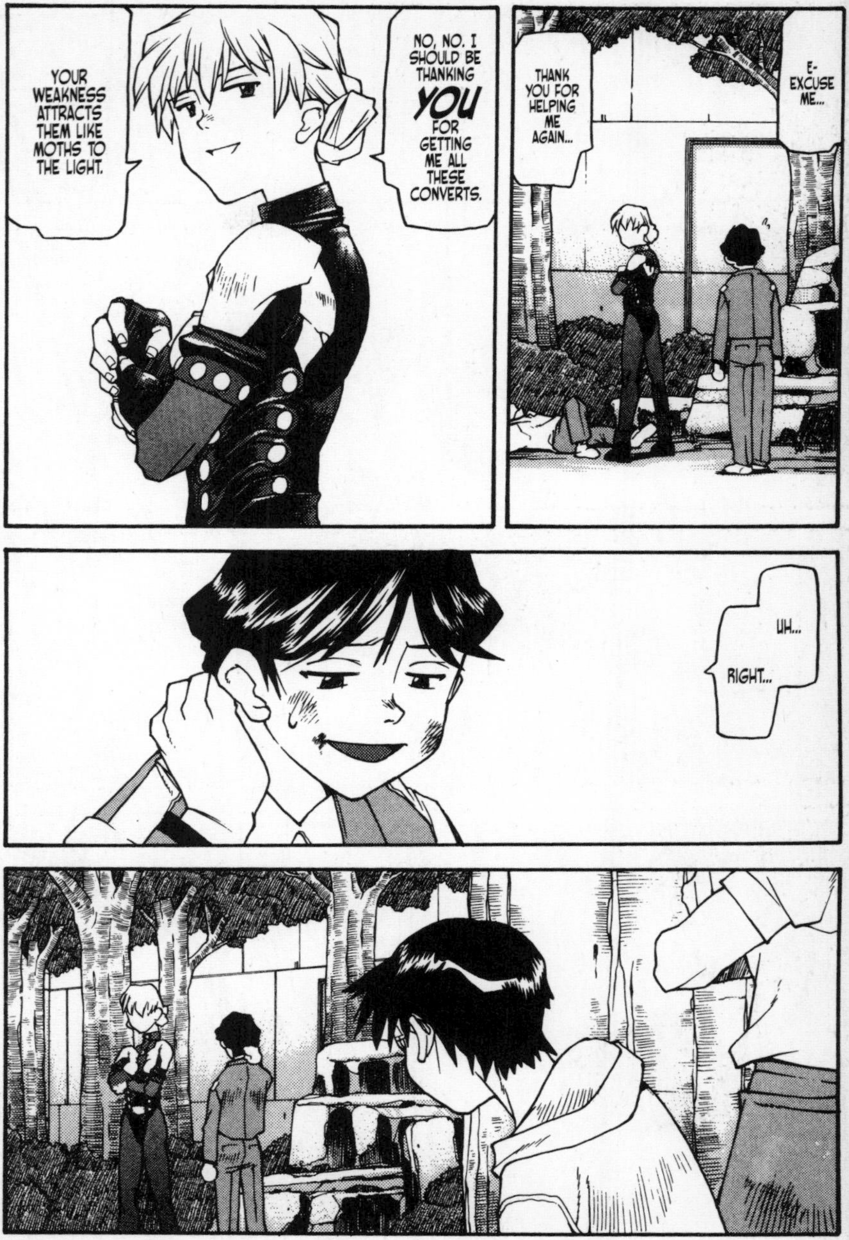
E-EXCUSE ME...
THANK YOU FOR HELPING ME AGAIN...
NO, NO. I SHOULD BE THANKING **YOU** FOR GETTING ME ALL THESE CONVERTS.
YOUR WEAKNESS ATTRACTS THEM LIKE MOTHS TO THE LIGHT.
UH... RIGHT...

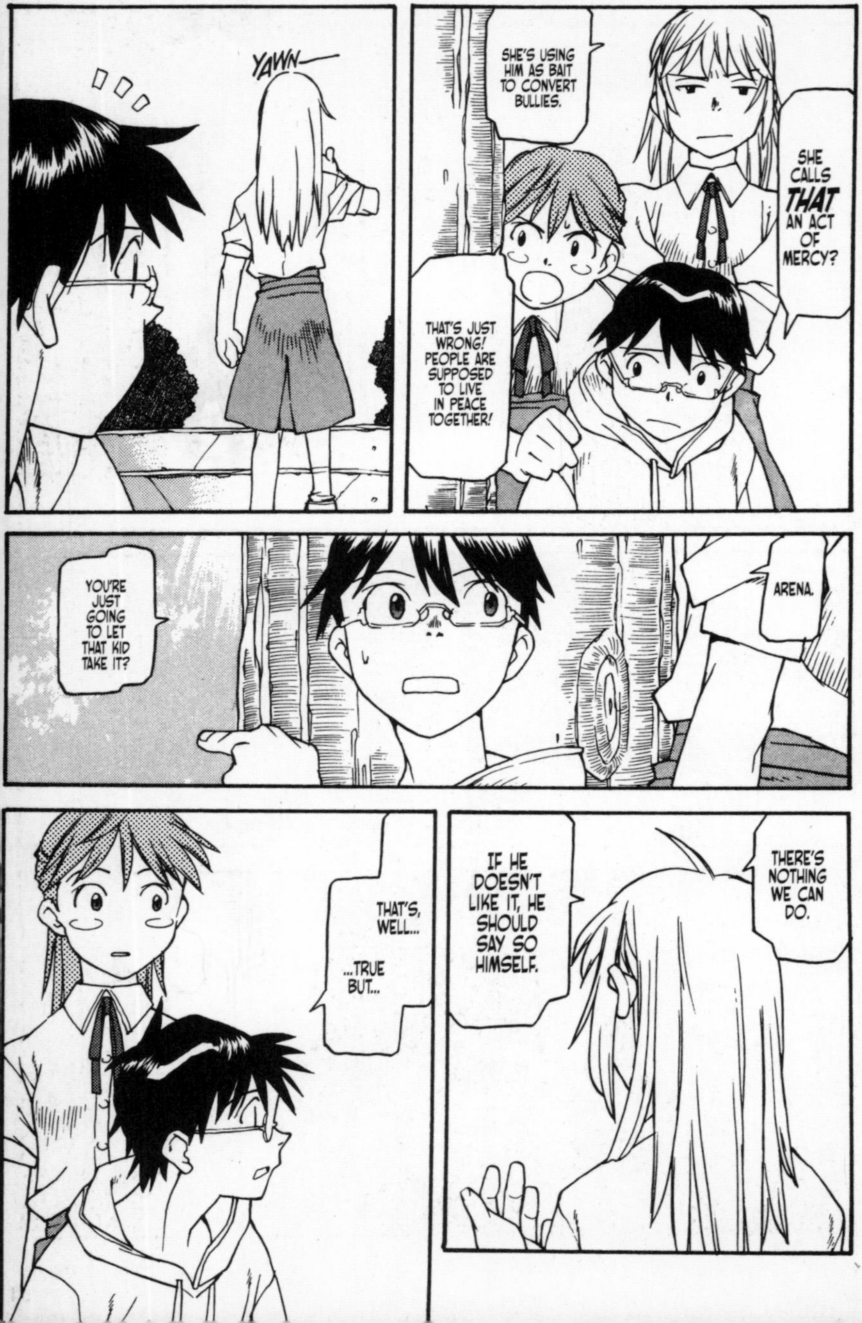
SHE'S USING HIM AS BAIT TO CONVERT BULLIES.
SHE CALLS THAT AN ACT OF MERCY?
THAT'S JUST WRONG! PEOPLE ARE SUPPOSED TO LIVE IN PEACE TOGETHER!
YAWN—
ARENA.
YOU'RE JUST GOING TO LET THAT KID TAKE IT?
THERE'S NOTHING WE CAN DO.
IF HE DOESN'T LIKE IT, HE SHOULD SAY SO HIMSELF.
THAT'S, WELL...
...TRUE BUT...

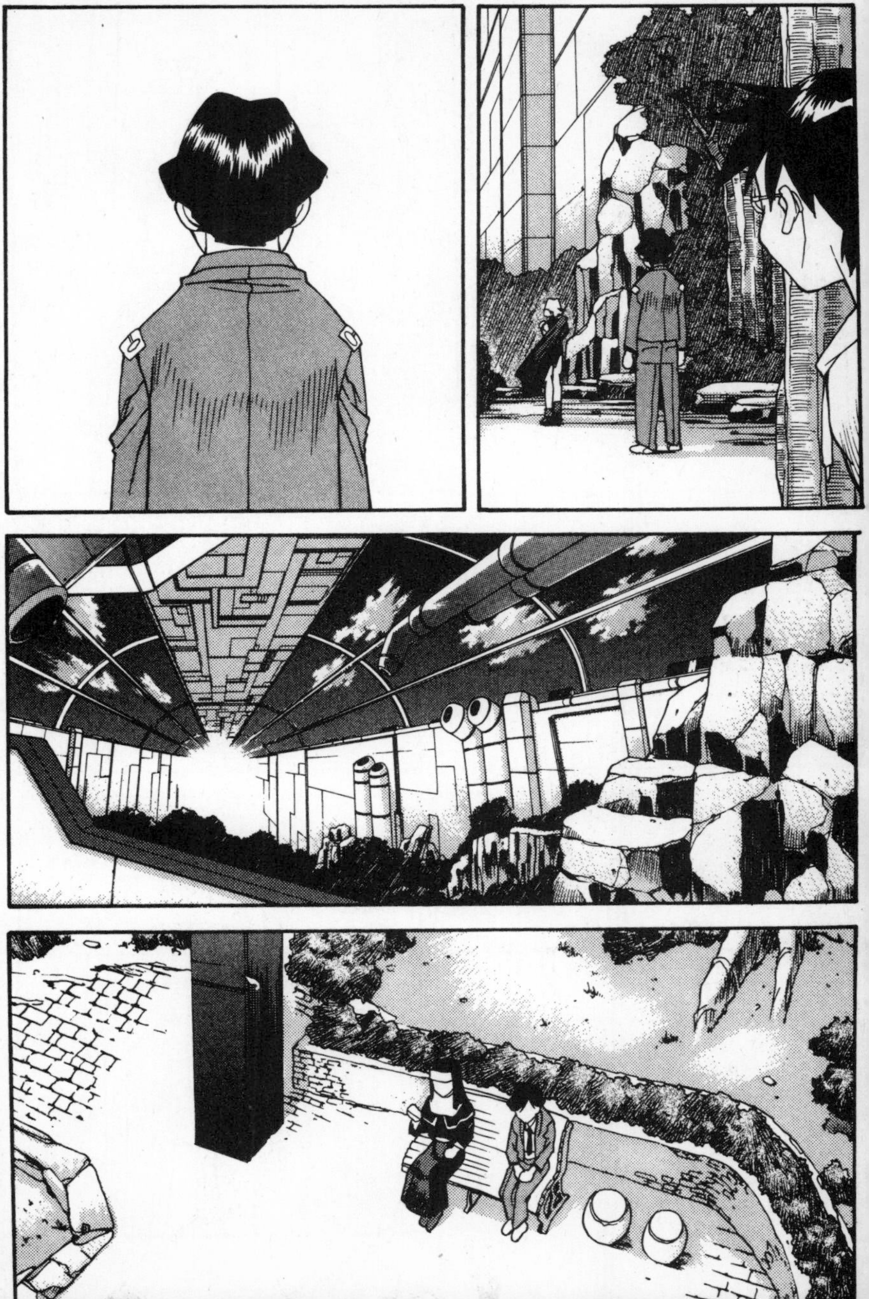

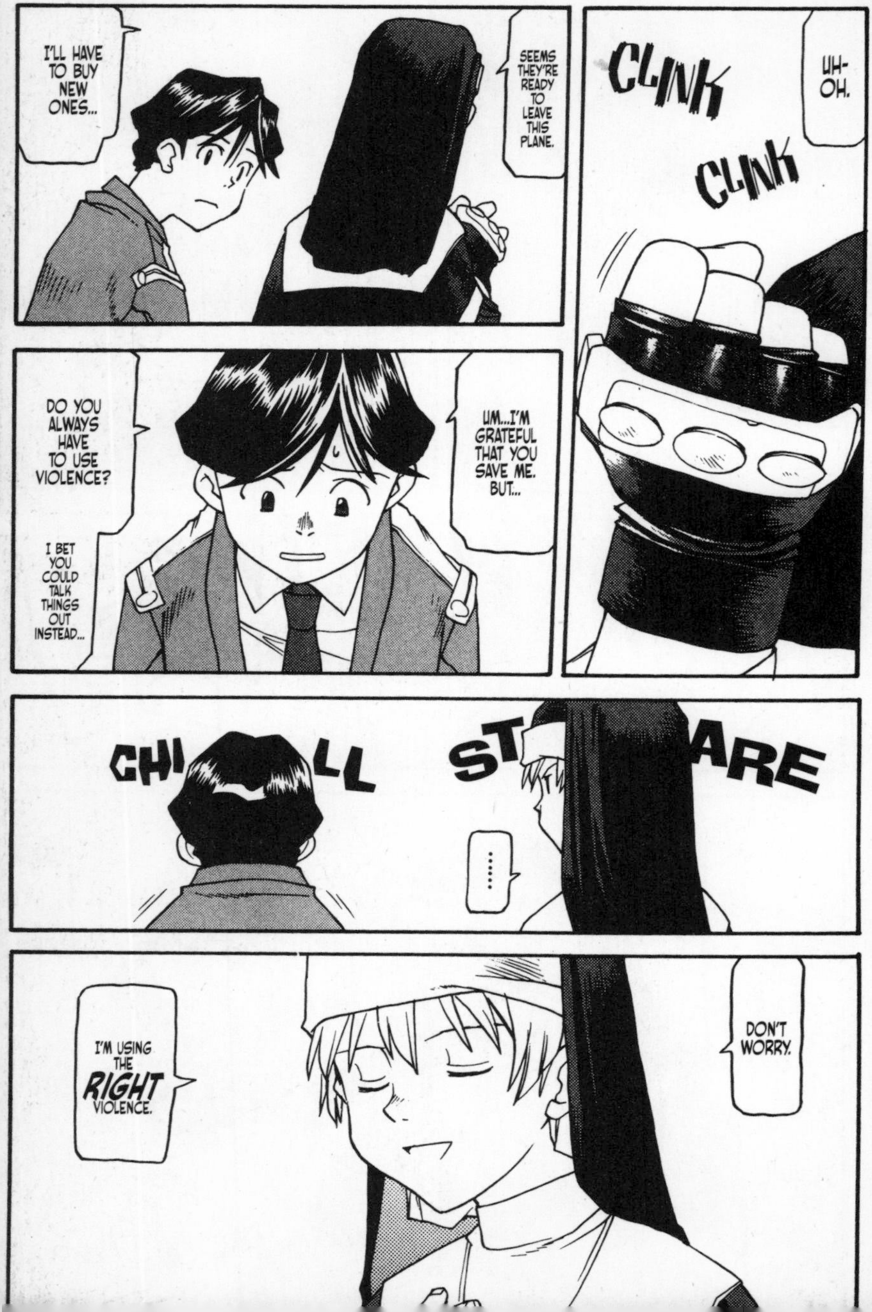
UH-OH.
CLINK
CLINK
SEEMS THEY'RE READY TO LEAVE THIS PLANE.
I'LL HAVE TO BUY NEW ONES...
UM...I'M GRATEFUL THAT YOU SAVE ME. BUT...
DO YOU ALWAYS HAVE TO USE VIOLENCE?
I BET YOU COULD TALK THINGS OUT INSTEAD...
ST ARE
......
CHI LL
DON'T WORRY.
I'M USING THE *RIGHT* VIOLENCE.

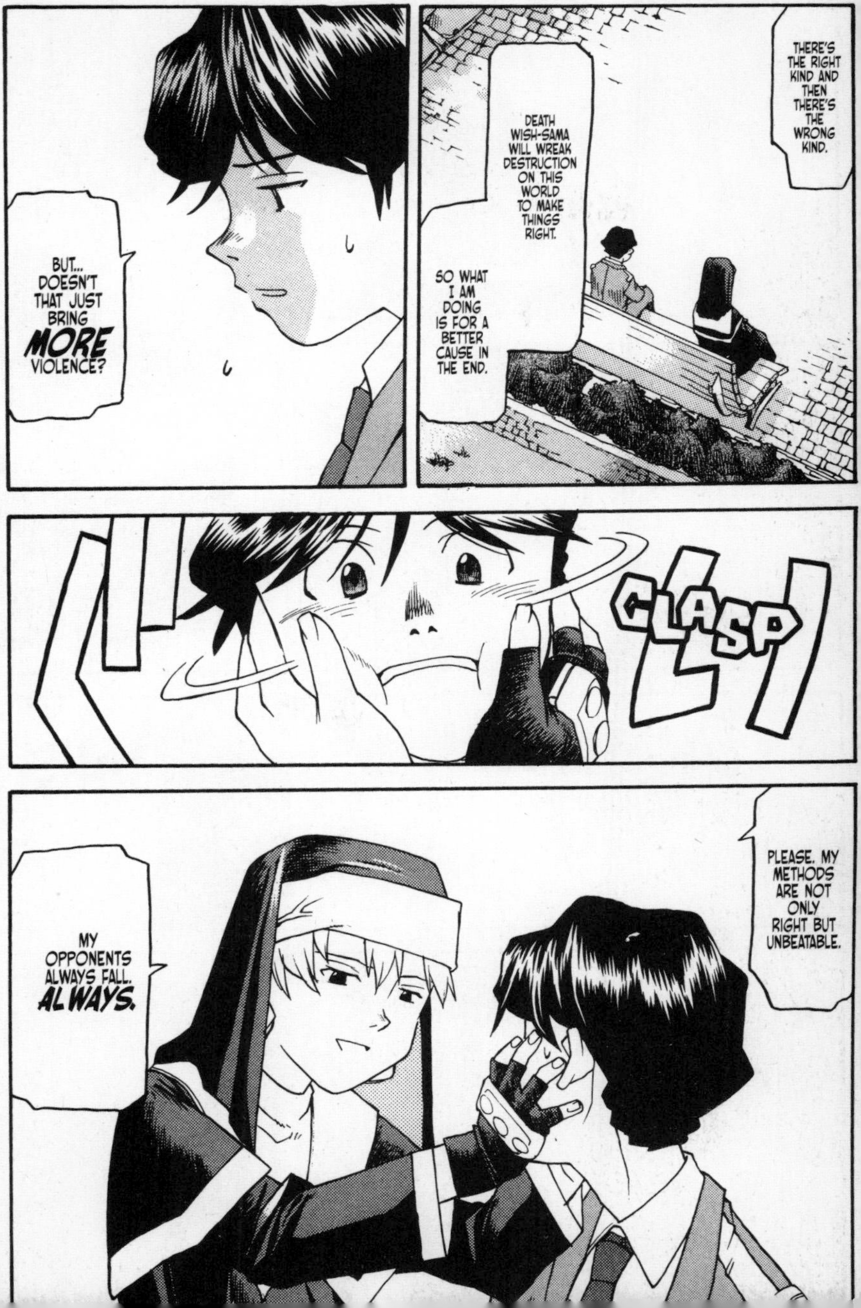
THERE'S THE RIGHT KIND AND THEN THERE'S THE WRONG KIND.
DEATH WISH-SAMA WILL WREAK DESTRUCTION ON THIS WORLD TO MAKE THINGS RIGHT.
SO WHAT I AM DOING IS FOR A BETTER CAUSE IN THE END.
BUT... DOESN'T THAT JUST BRING MORE VIOLENCE?
CLASP
PLEASE. MY METHODS ARE NOT ONLY RIGHT BUT UNBEATABLE.
MY OPPONENTS ALWAYS FALL. ALWAYS.

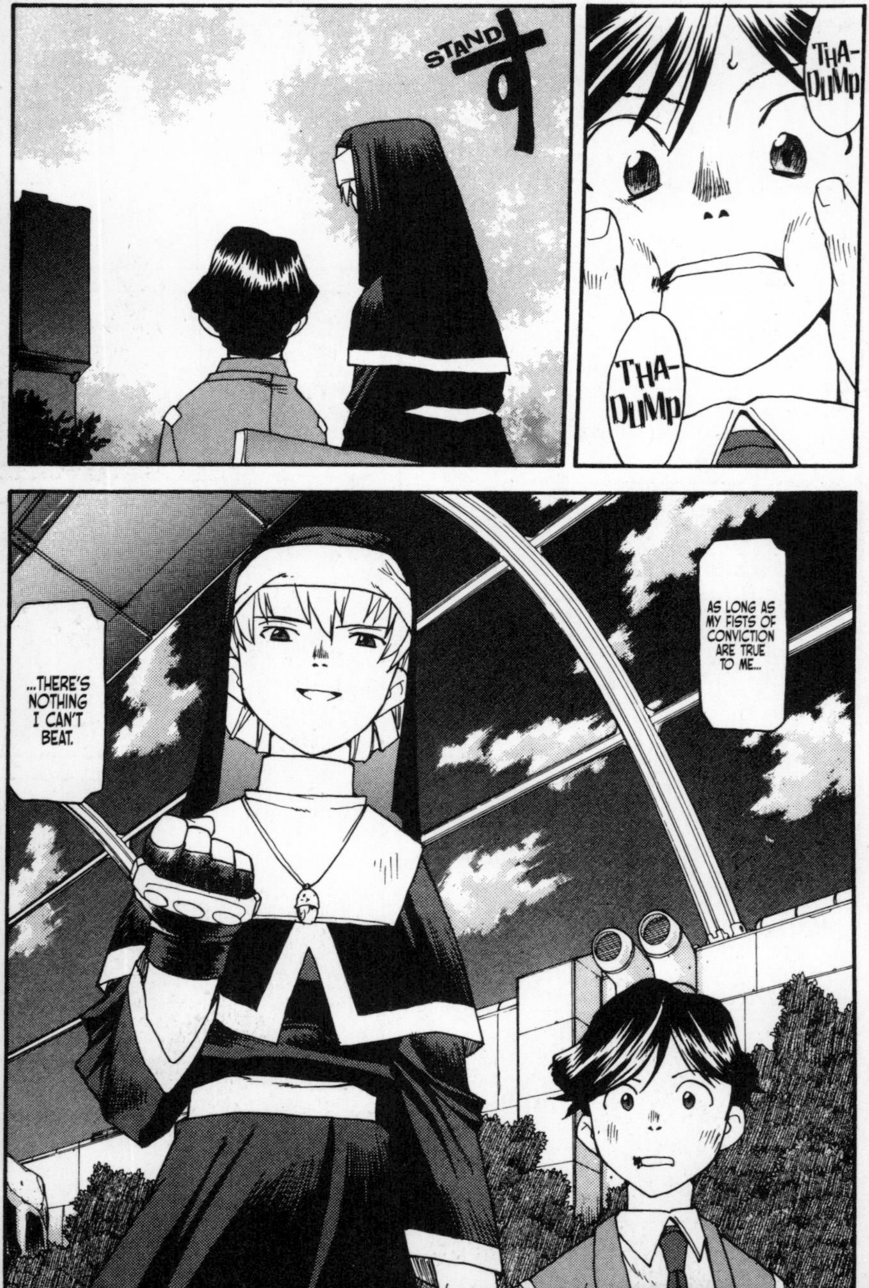
THA-DUMP
THA-DUMP
STAND
す
AS LONG AS MY FISTS OF CONVICTION ARE TRUE TO ME...
...THERE'S NOTHING I CAN'T BEAT.

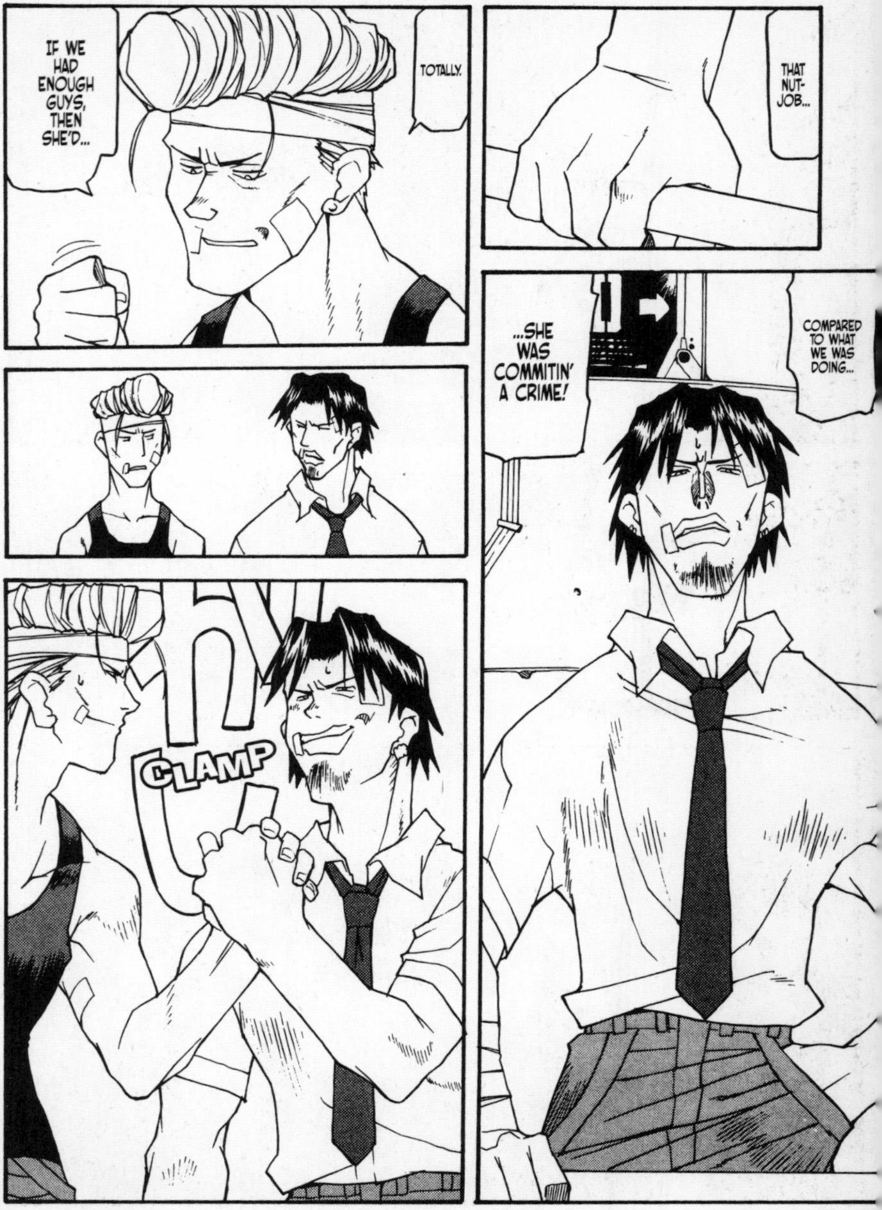
THAT NUT-JOB...
IF WE HAD ENOUGH GUYS, THEN SHE'D...
TOTALLY.
COMPARED TO WHAT WE WAS DOING...
...SHE WAS COMMITIN' A CRIME!
CLAMP

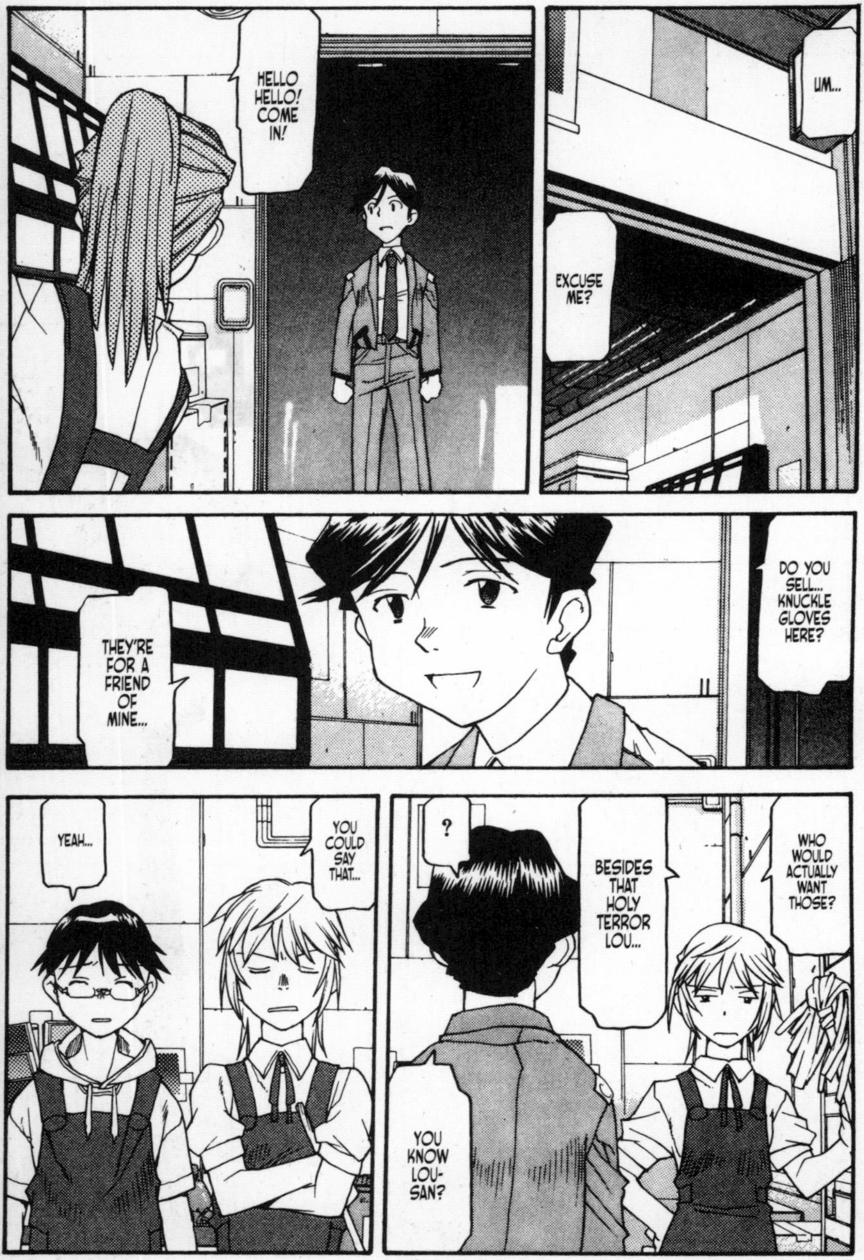
UM...
EXCUSE ME?
HELLO HELLO! COME IN!
DO YOU SELL... KNUCKLE GLOVES HERE?
THEY'RE FOR A FRIEND OF MINE...
WHO WOULD ACTUALLY WANT THOSE?
BESIDES THAT HOLY TERROR LOU...
?
YOU KNOW LOU-SAN?
YOU COULD SAY THAT...
YEAH...

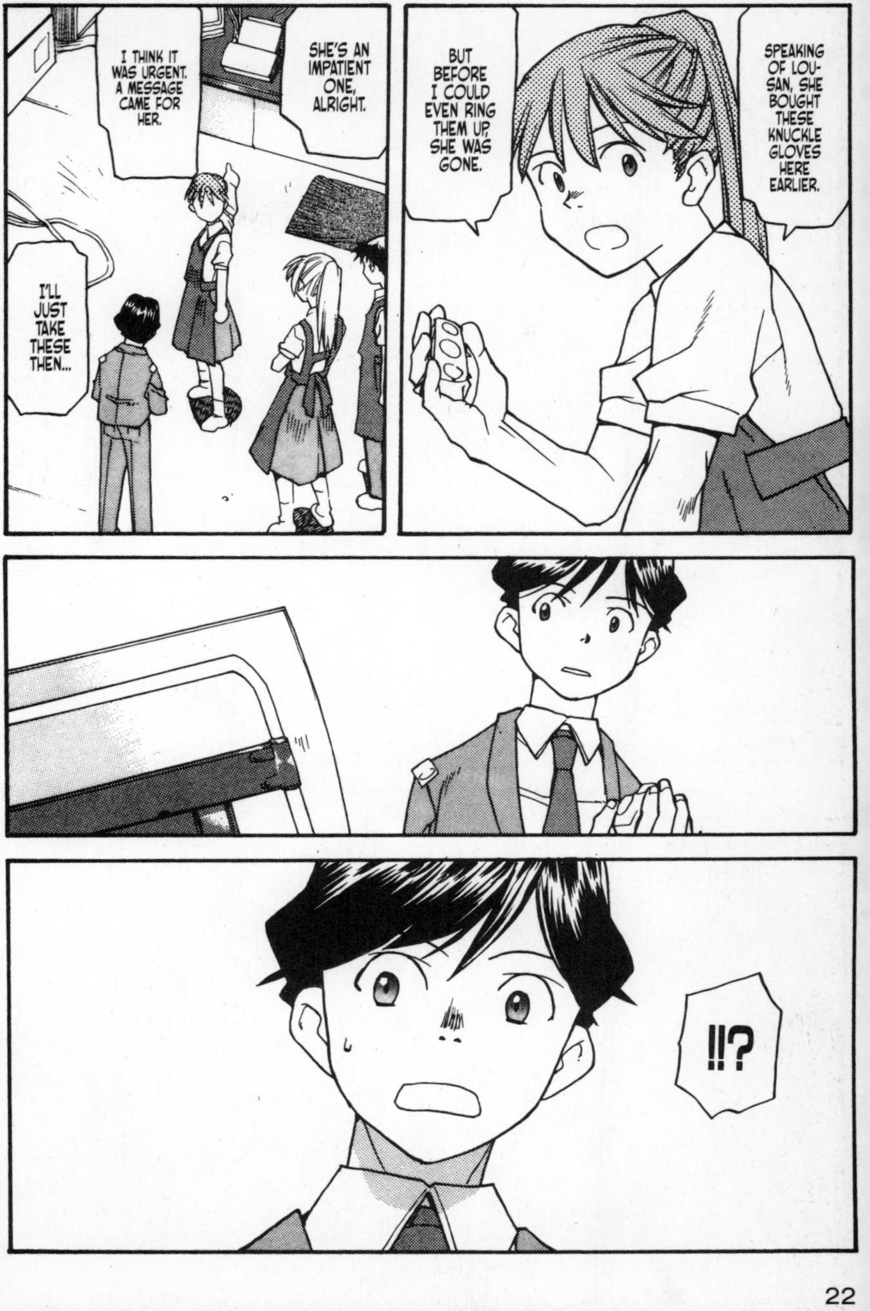
SPEAKING OF LOU-SAN, SHE BOUGHT THESE KNUCKLE GLOVES HERE EARLIER.
BUT BEFORE I COULD EVEN RING THEM UP, SHE WAS GONE.
SHE'S AN IMPATIENT ONE, ALRIGHT.
I THINK IT WAS URGENT. A MESSAGE CAME FOR HER.
I'LL JUST TAKE THESE THEN...
!!?

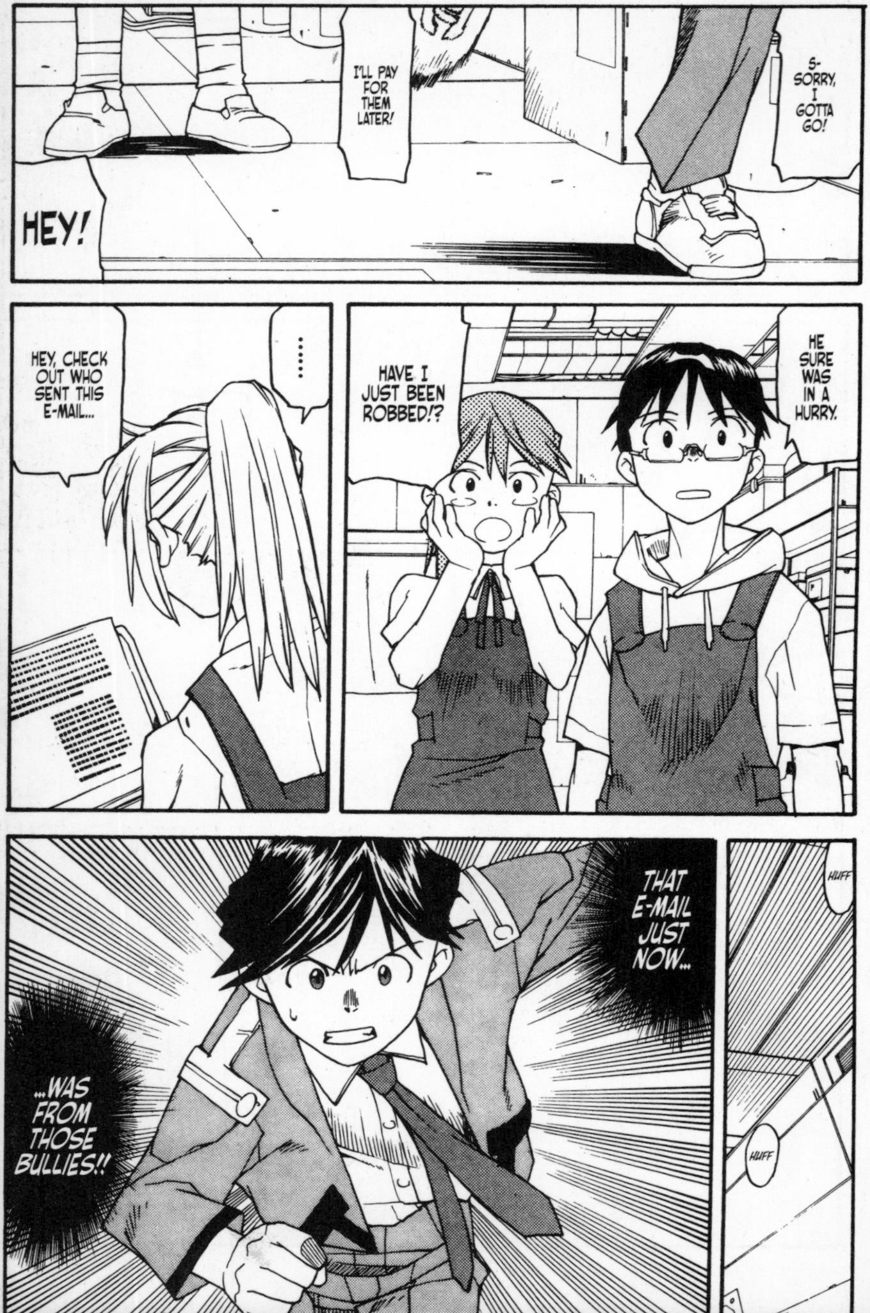
S-SORRY, I GOTTA GO!
I'LL PAY FOR THEM LATER!
HEY!
HE SURE WAS IN A HURRY.
HAVE I JUST BEEN ROBBED!?
......
HEY, CHECK OUT WHO SENT THIS E-MAIL...
HUFF
HUFF
THAT E-MAIL JUST NOW...
...WAS FROM THOSE BULLIES!!

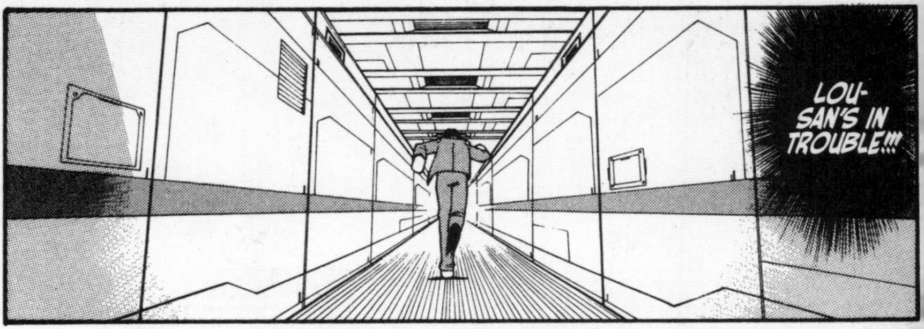
LOU-SAN'S IN TROUBLE!!!
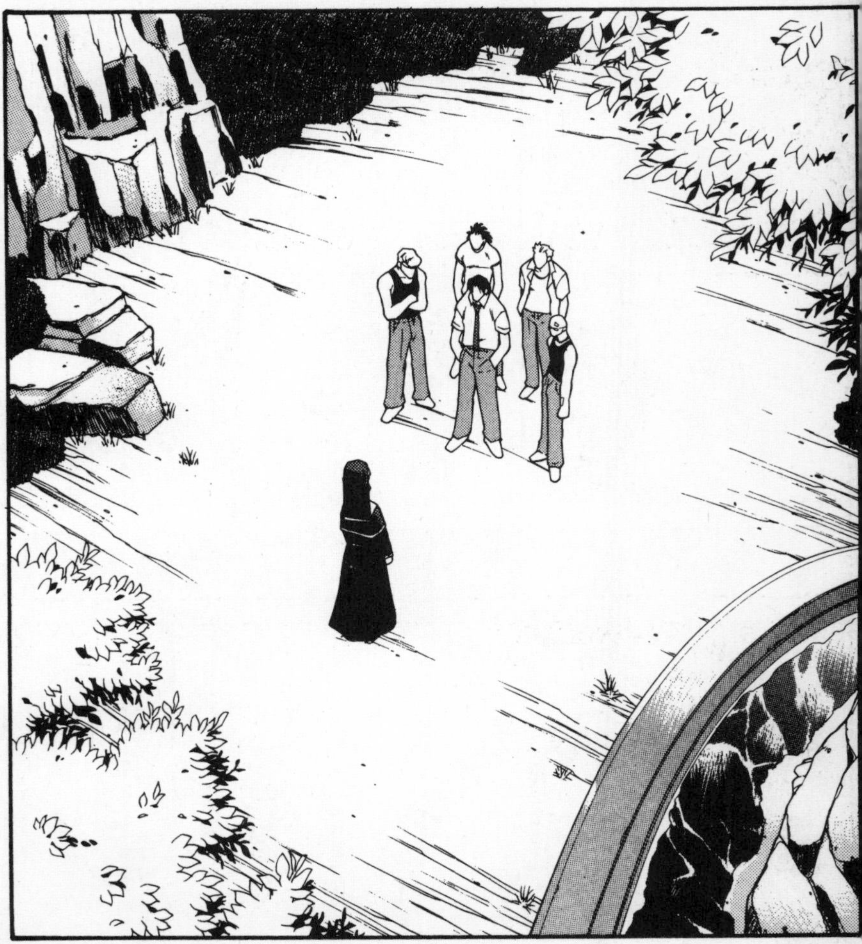

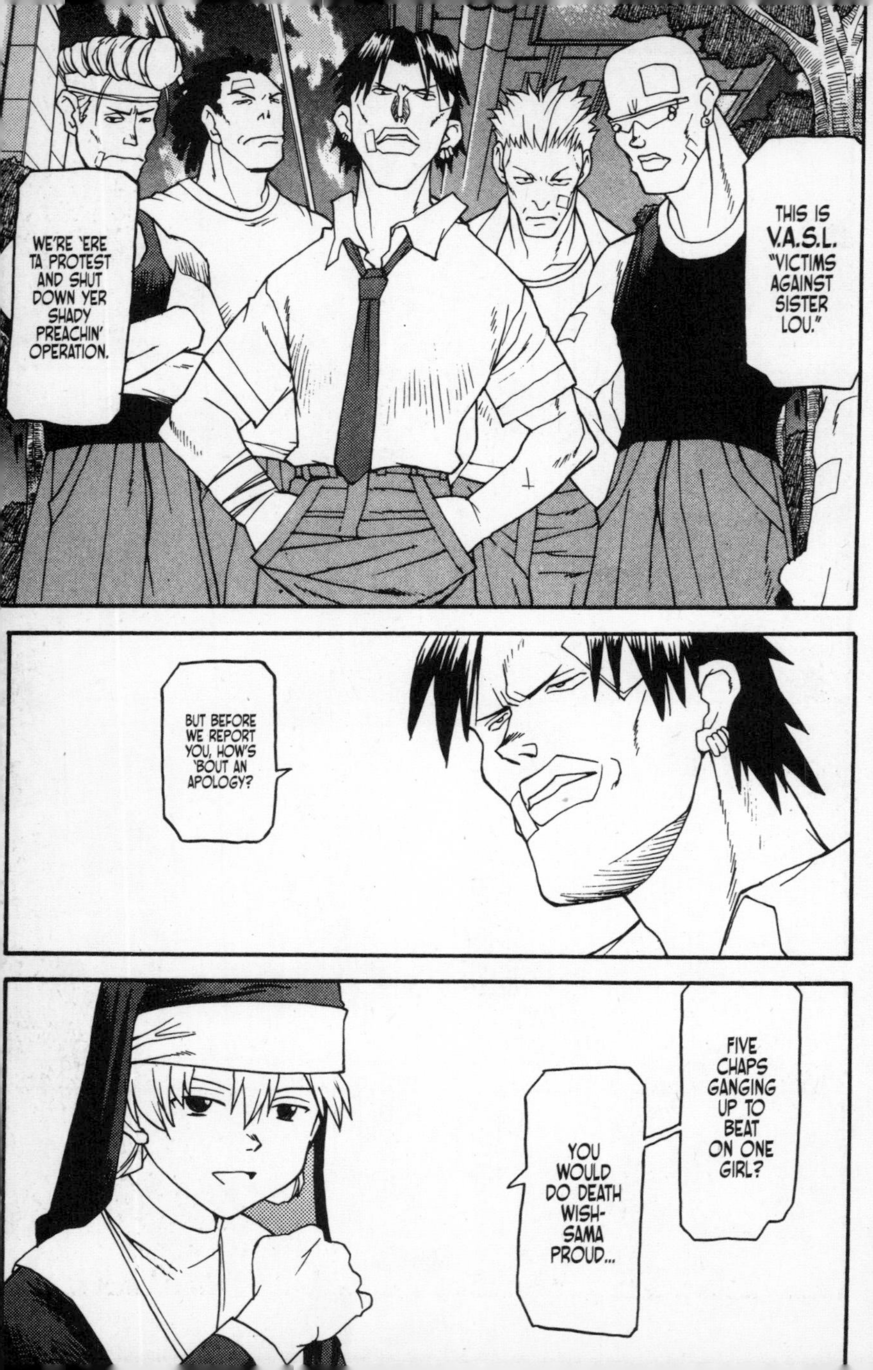
THIS IS V.A.S.L. "VICTIMS AGAINST SISTER LOU."
WE'RE 'ERE TA PROTEST AND SHUT DOWN YER SHADY PREACHIN' OPERATION.
BUT BEFORE WE REPORT YOU, HOW'S 'BOUT AN APOLOGY?
FIVE CHAPS GANGING UP TO BEAT ON ONE GIRL?
YOU WOULD DO DEATH WISH-SAMA PROUD...

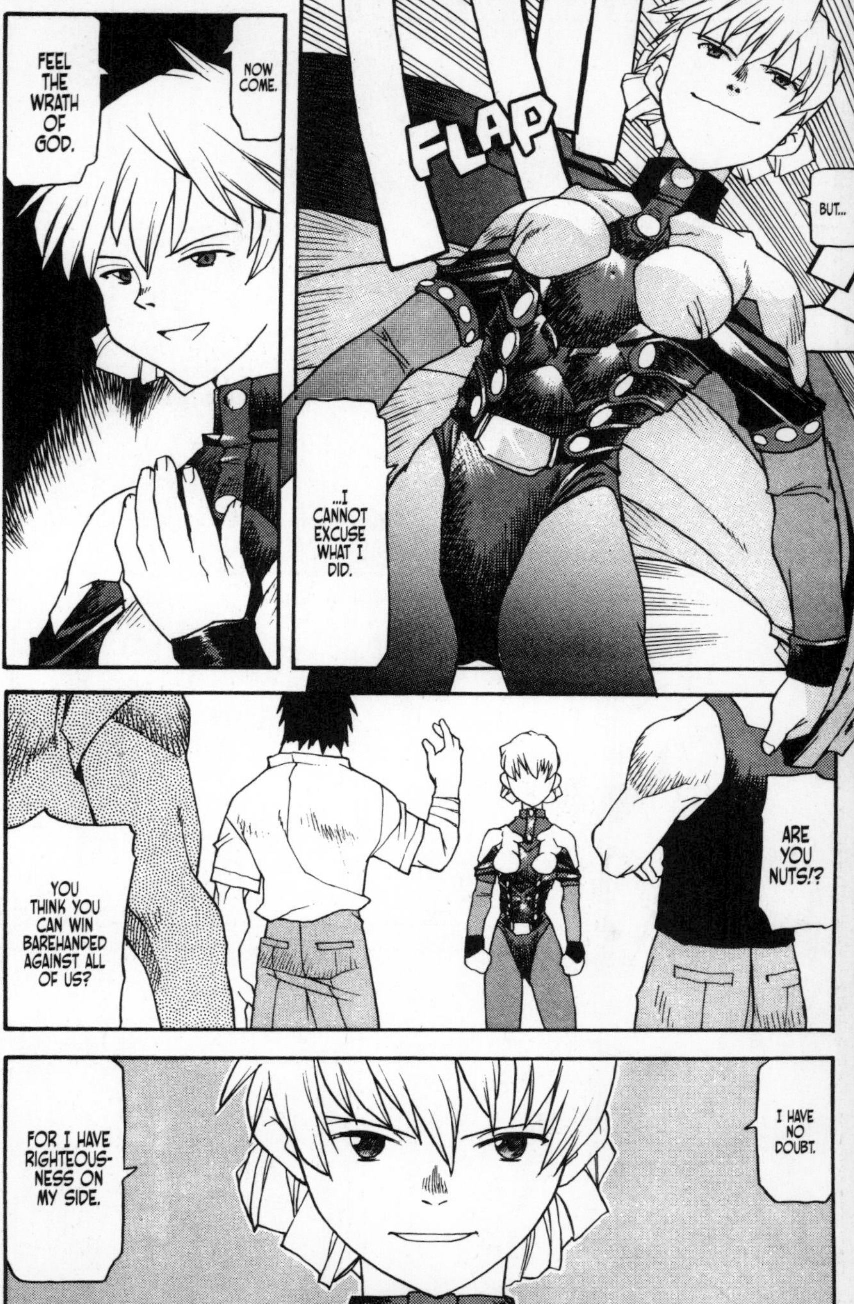
BUT...
FLAP
...I CANNOT EXCUSE WHAT I DID.
NOW COME.
FEEL THE WRATH OF GOD.
ARE YOU NUTS!?
YOU THINK YOU CAN WIN BAREHANDED AGAINST ALL OF US?
I HAVE NO DOUBT.
FOR I HAVE RIGHTEOUS-NESS ON MY SIDE.

HUFF
HUFF
!!
HUFF
HUFF

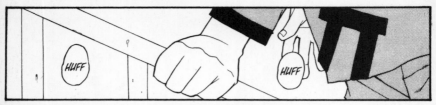

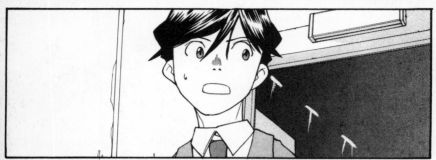

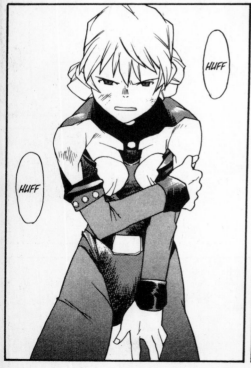

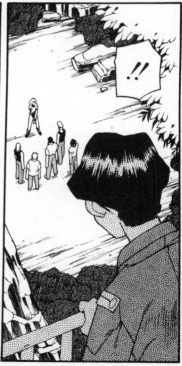

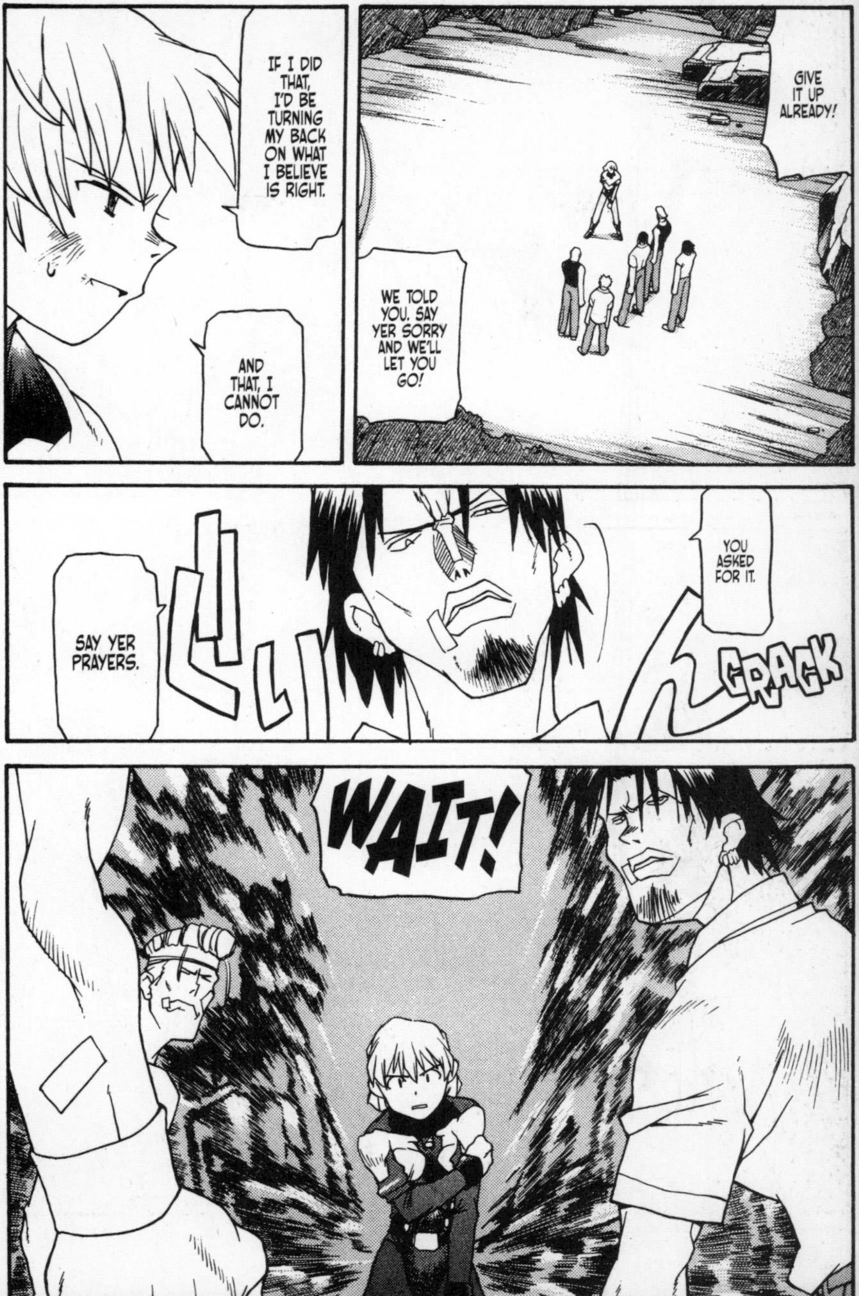
GIVE IT UP ALREADY!
WE TOLD YOU. SAY YER SORRY AND WE'LL LET YOU GO!
IF I DID THAT, I'D BE TURNING MY BACK ON WHAT I BELIEVE IS RIGHT.
AND THAT, I CANNOT DO.
YOU ASKED FOR IT.
CRACK
SAY YER PRAYERS.
WAIT!

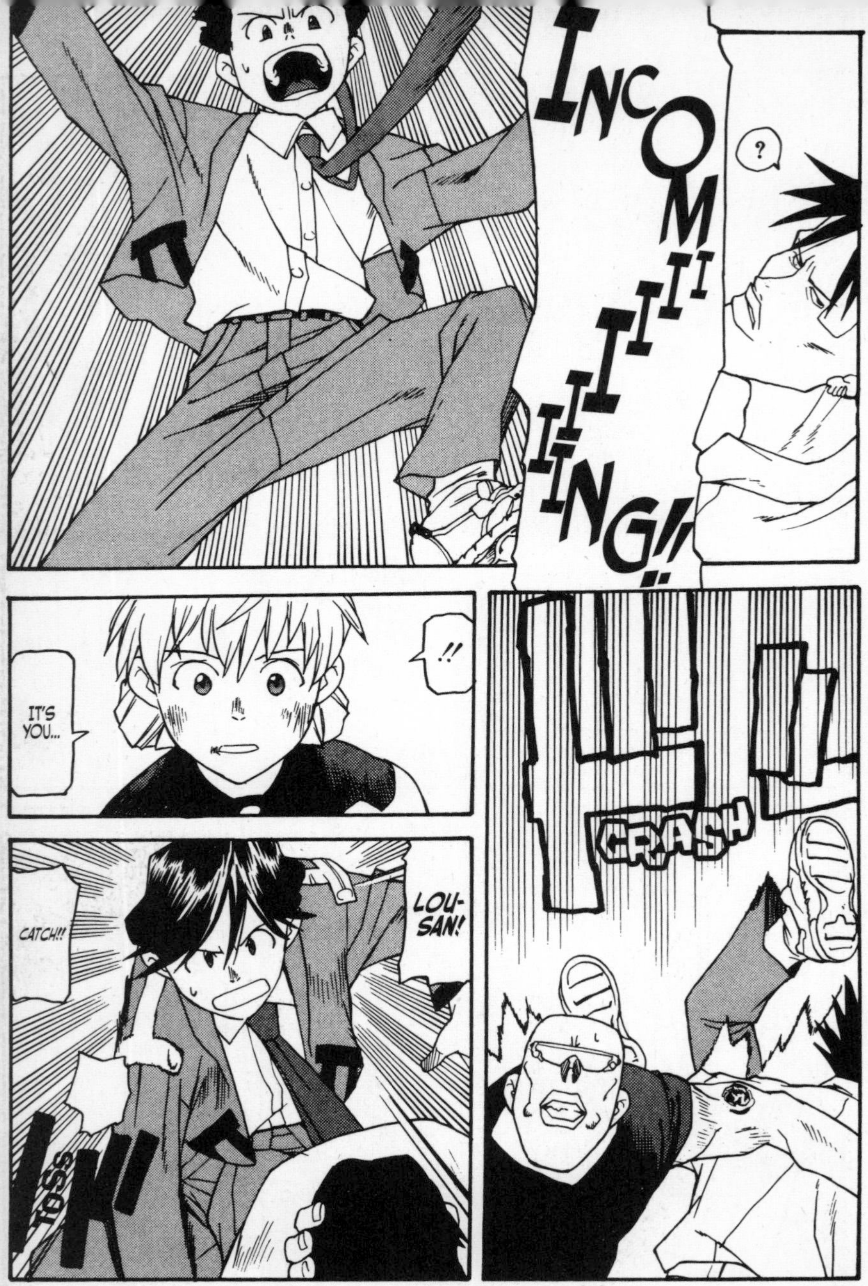

?
INCOMIIIIIIING!!
CRASH
!!
IT'S YOU...
LOU-SAN!
CATCH!!
TOSS

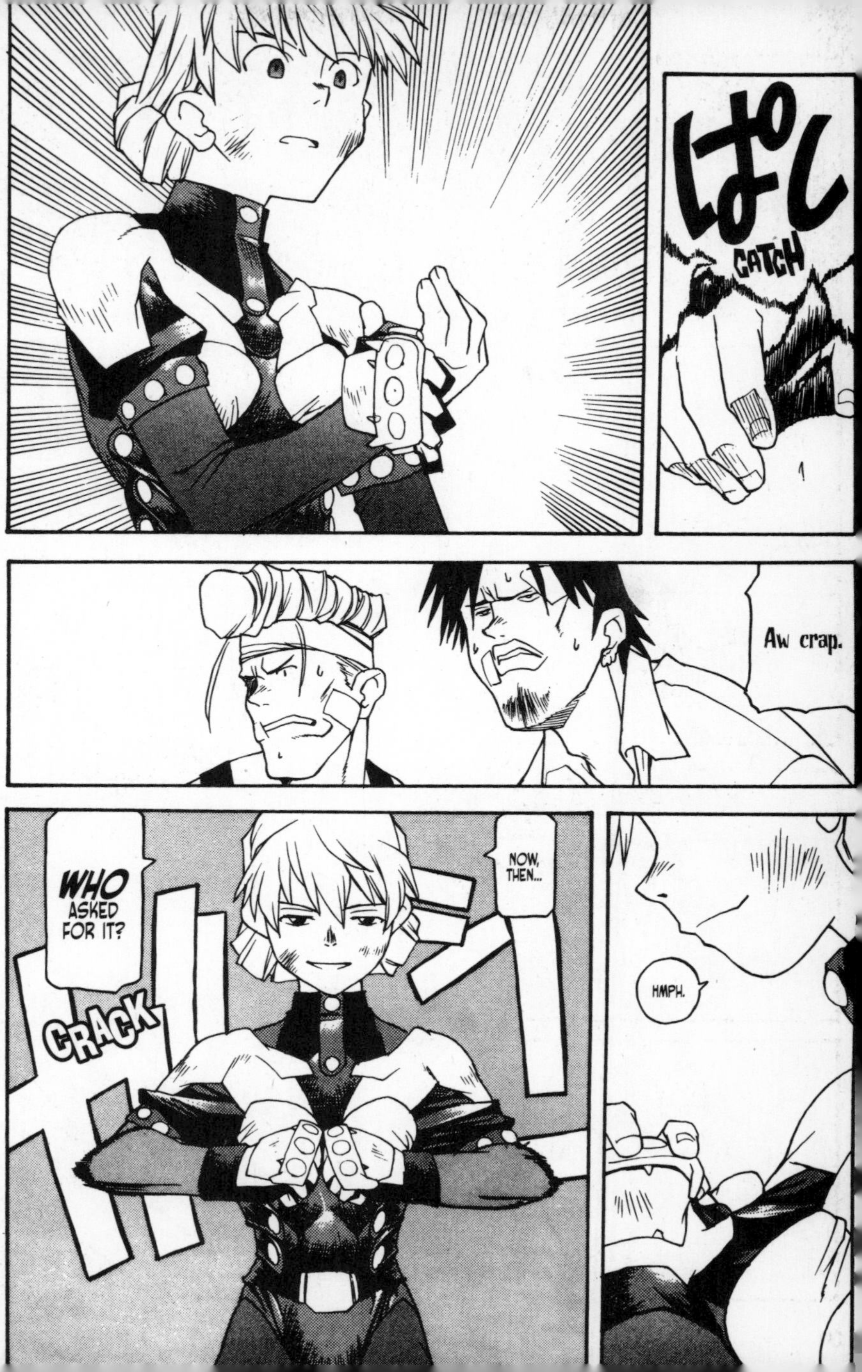
ぱし
CATCH
Aw crap.
HMPH.
NOW, THEN...
WHO ASKED FOR IT?
CRACK

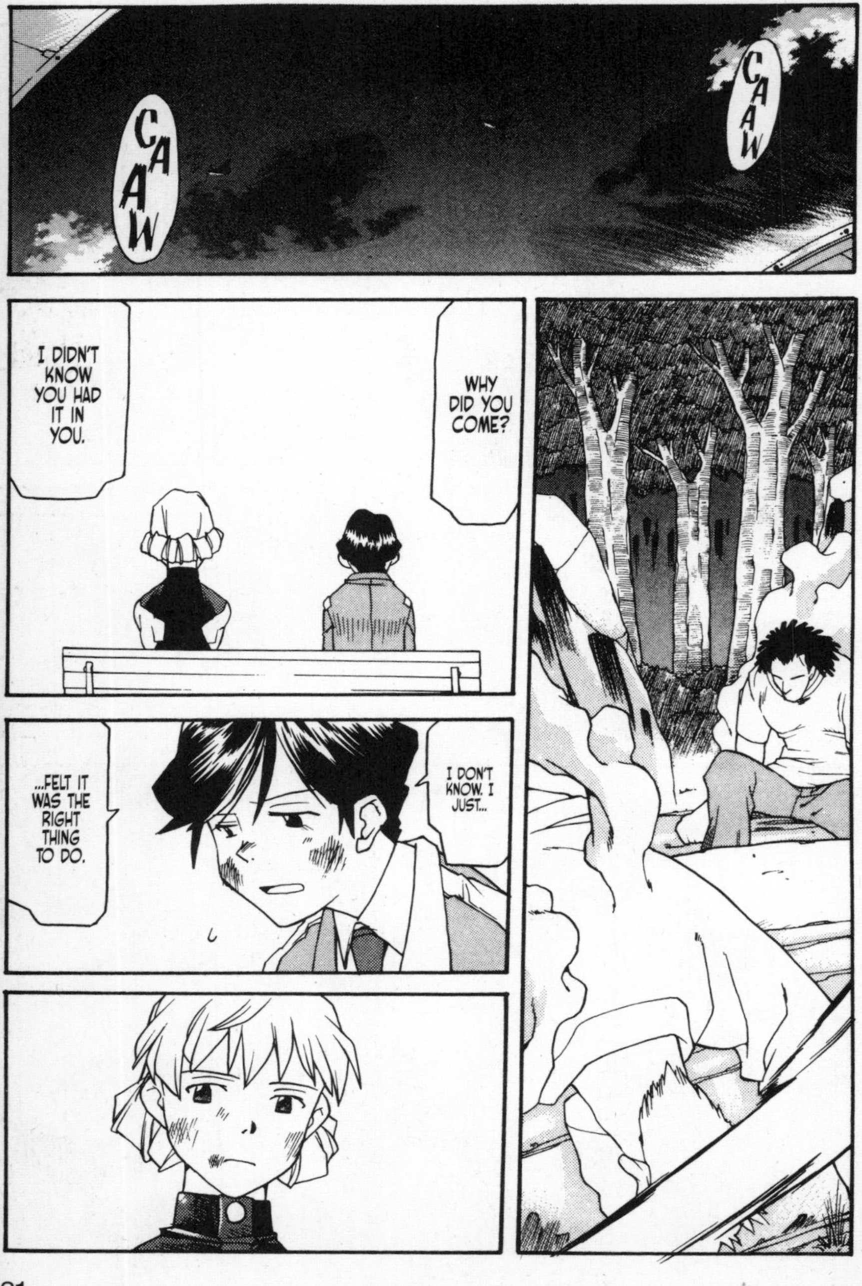
CAAW
CAAW
WHY DID YOU COME?
I DIDN'T KNOW YOU HAD IT IN YOU.
I DON'T KNOW. I JUST...
...FELT IT WAS THE RIGHT THING TO DO.

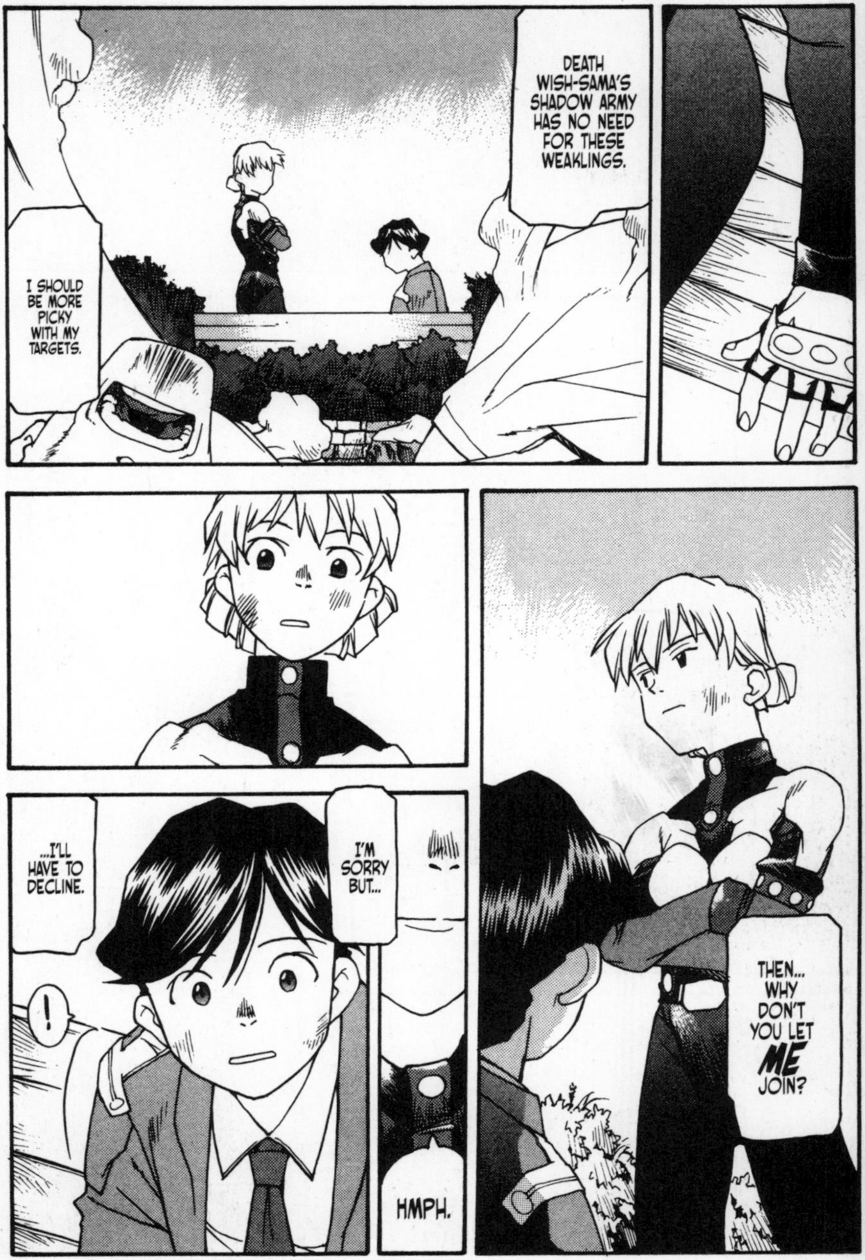
DEATH WISH-SAMA'S SHADOW ARMY HAS NO NEED FOR THESE WEAKLINGS.
I SHOULD BE MORE PICKY WITH MY TARGETS.
THEN... WHY DON'T YOU LET ME JOIN?
I'M SORRY BUT...
HMPH.
...I'LL HAVE TO DECLINE.
!

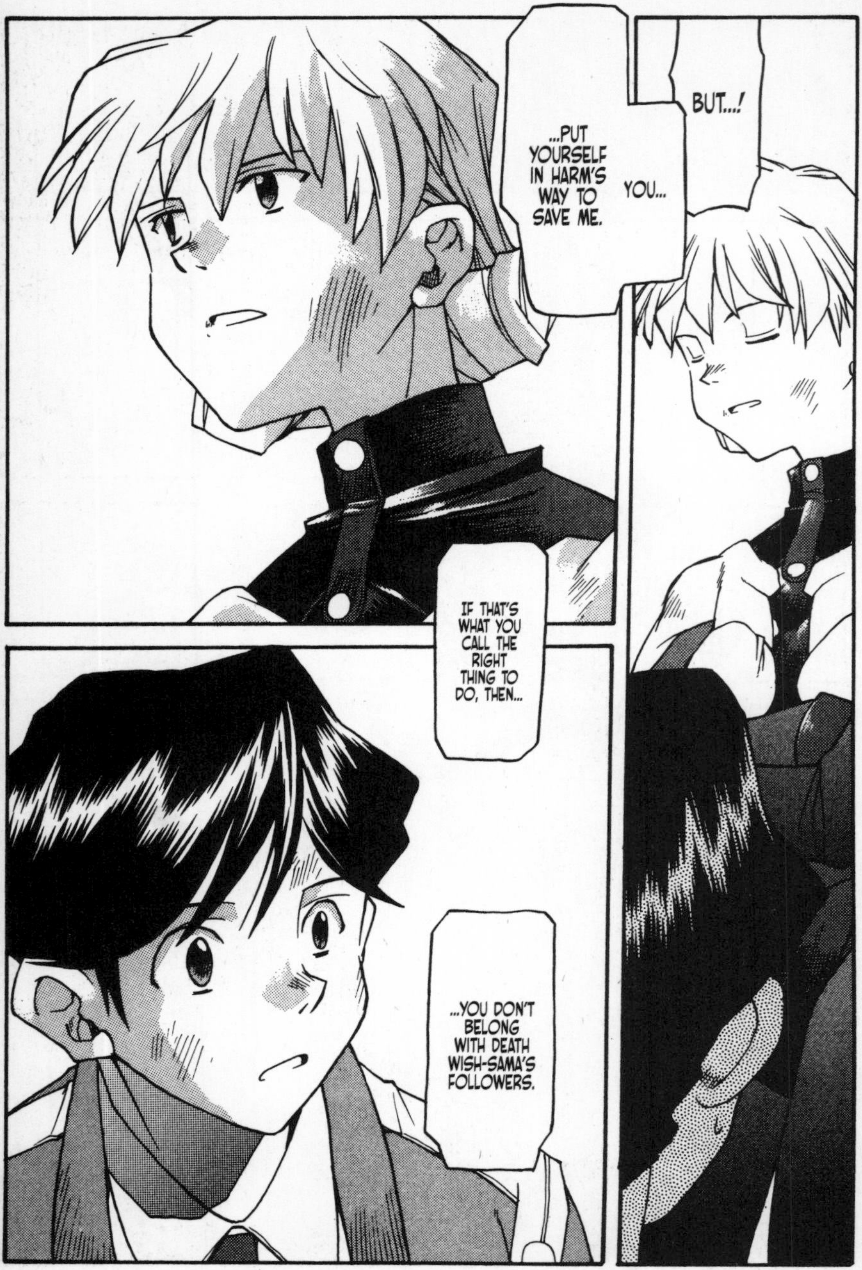
BUT...!
YOU...
...PUT YOURSELF IN HARM'S WAY TO SAVE ME.
IF THAT'S WHAT YOU CALL THE RIGHT THING TO DO, THEN...
...YOU DON'T BELONG WITH DEATH WISH-SAMA'S FOLLOWERS.

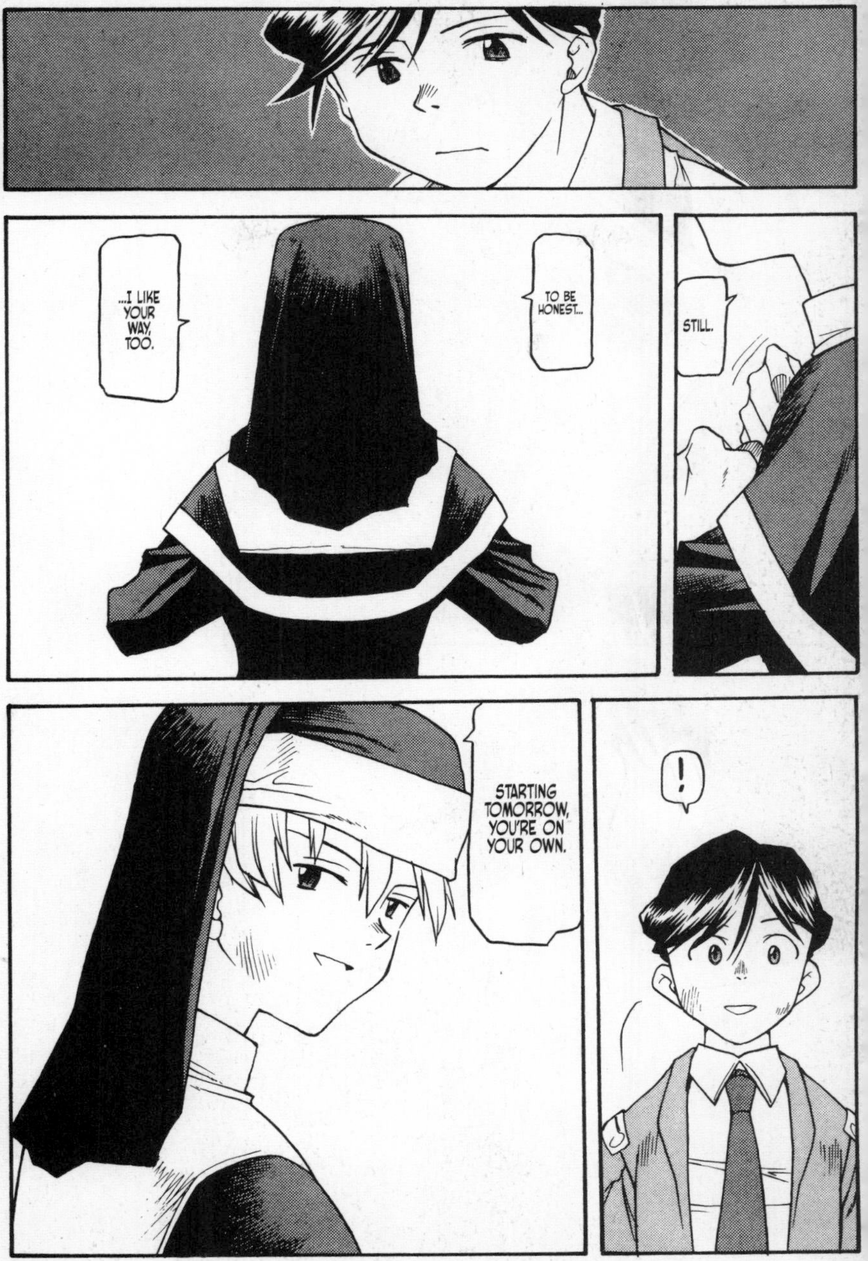
STILL.
TO BE HONEST...
...I LIKE YOUR WAY, TOO.
!
STARTING TOMORROW, YOU'RE ON YOUR OWN.

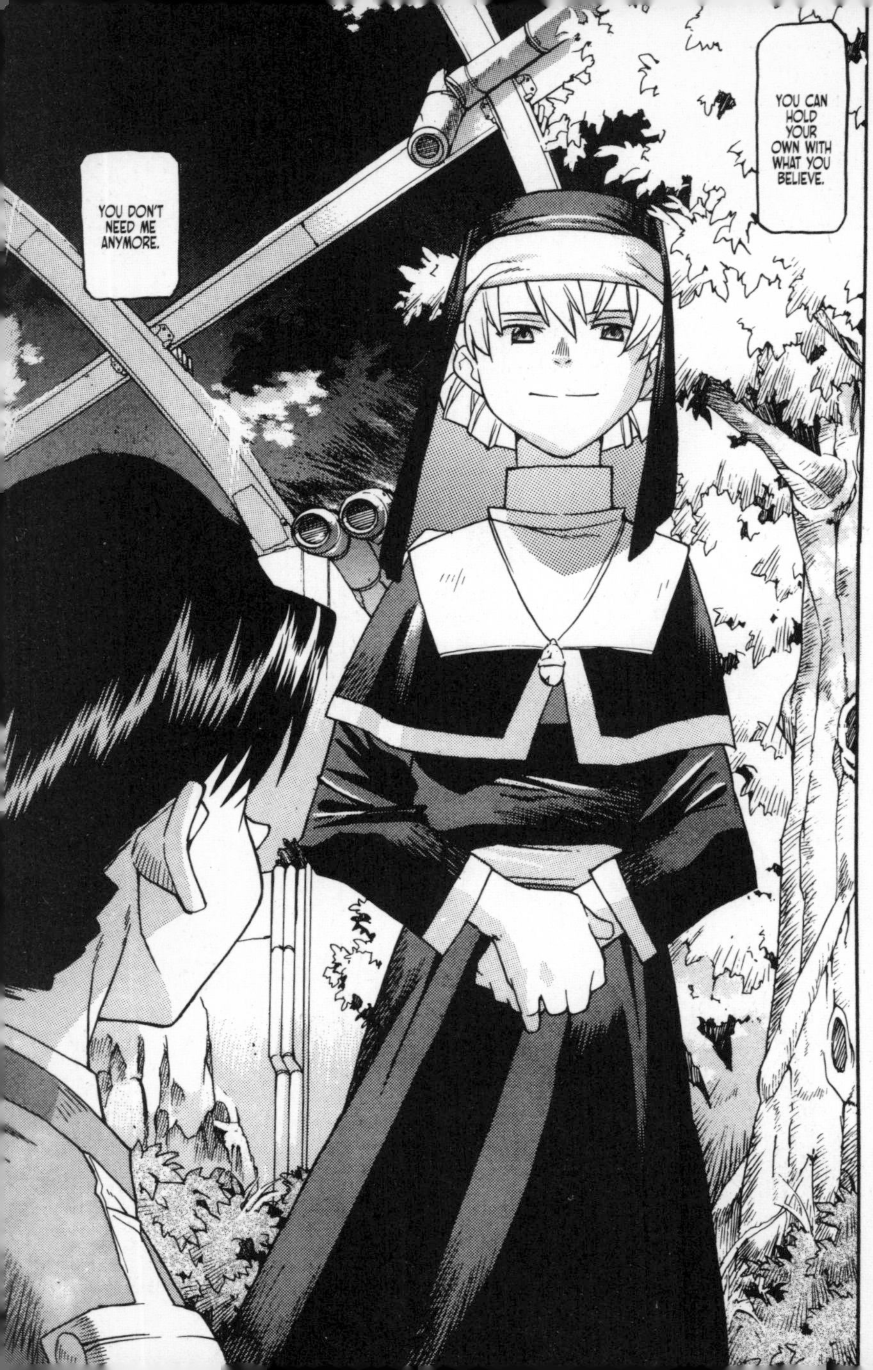
YOU CAN HOLD YOUR OWN WITH WHAT YOU BELIEVE.
YOU DON'T NEED ME ANYMORE.

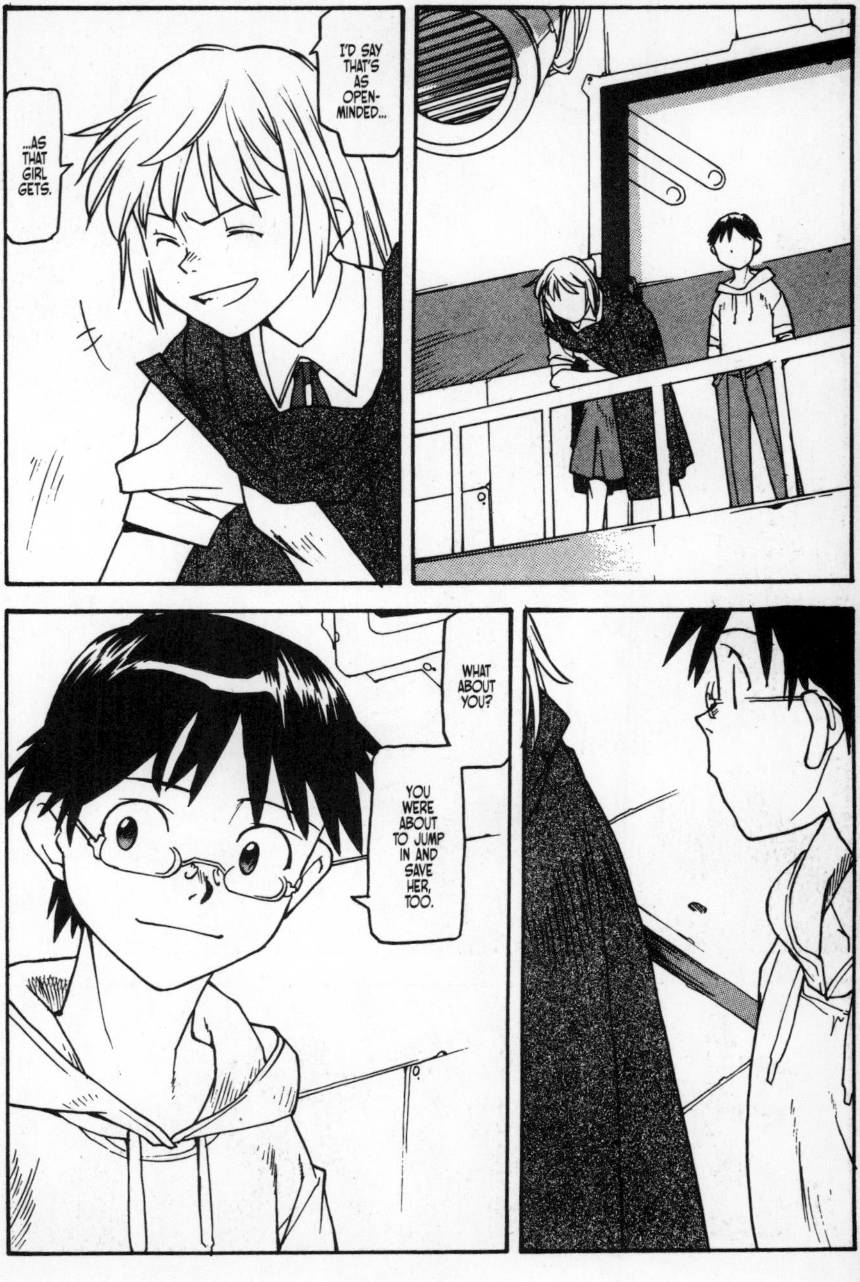
I'D SAY THAT'S AS OPEN-MINDED...
...AS THAT GIRL GETS.
WHAT ABOUT YOU?
YOU WERE ABOUT TO JUMP IN AND SAVE HER, TOO.

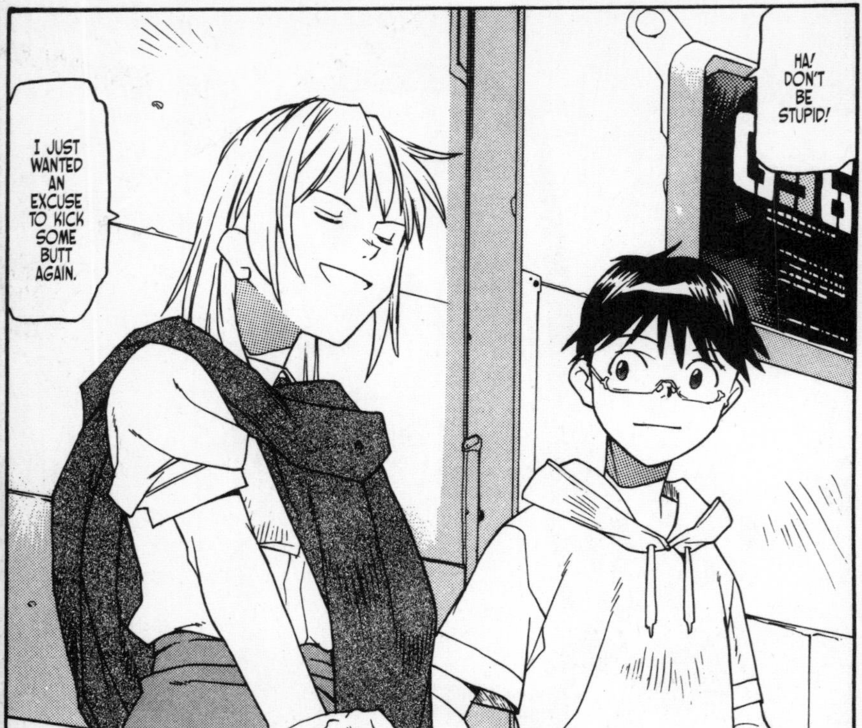
HA! DON'T BE STUPID!
I JUST WANTED AN EXCUSE TO KICK SOME BUTT AGAIN.

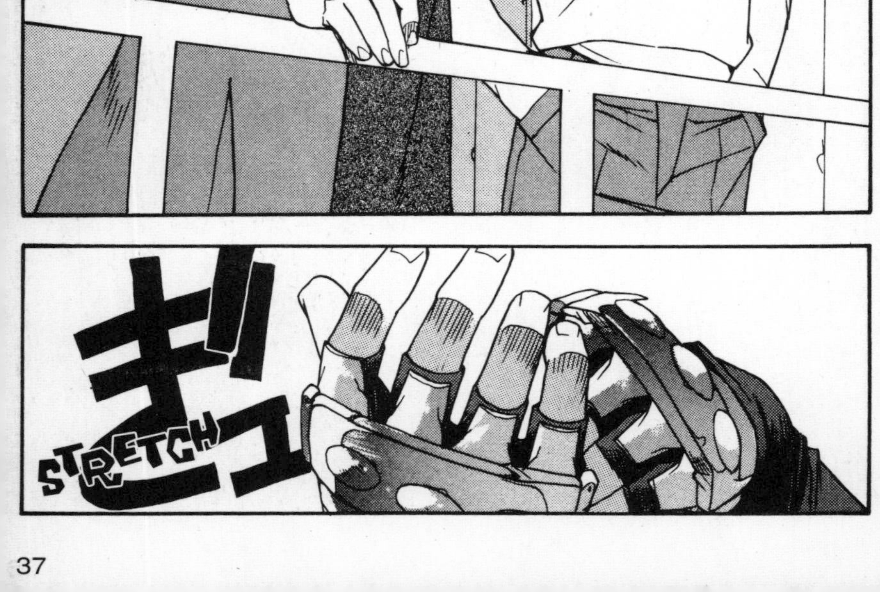
STRETCH

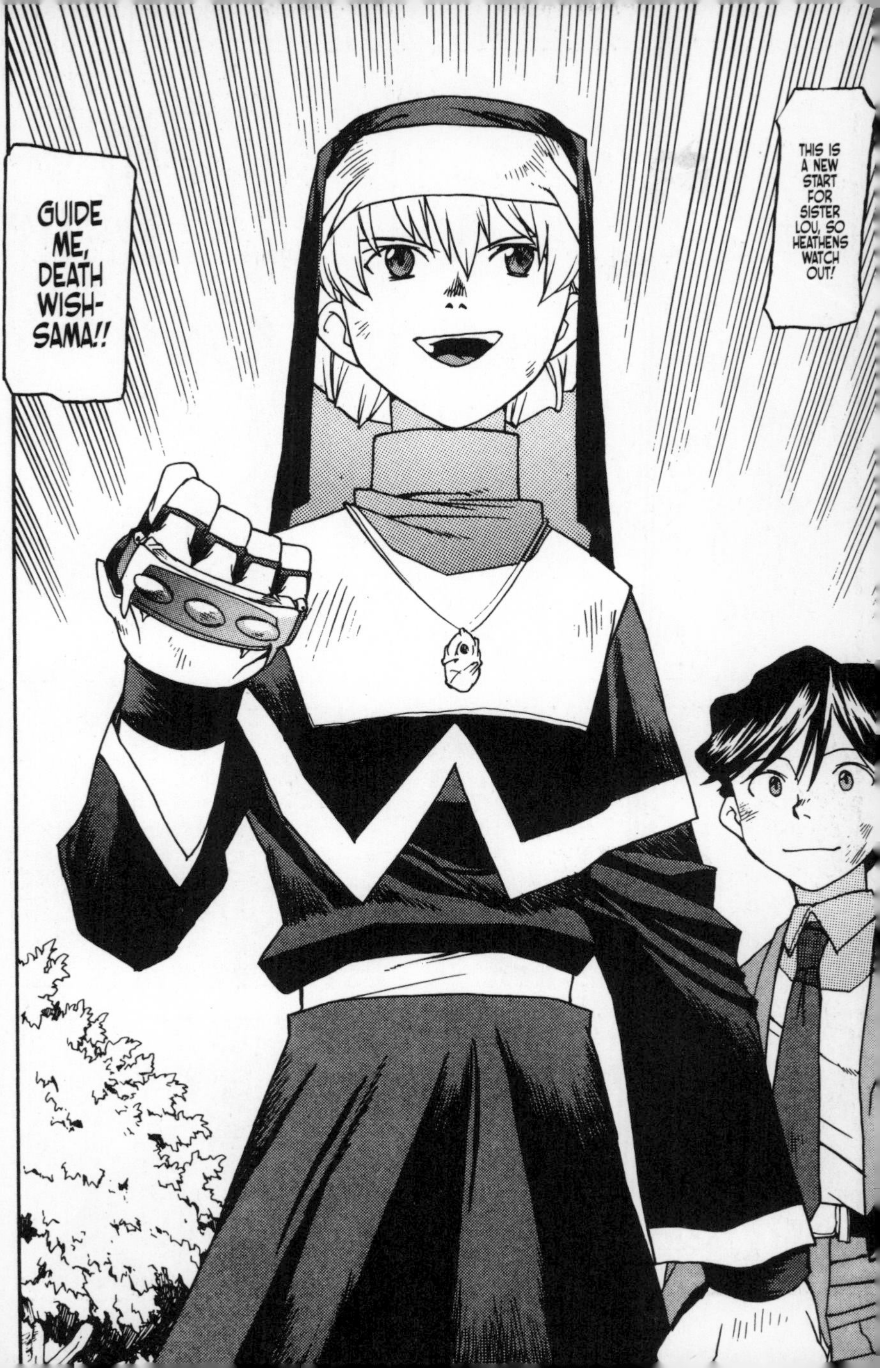
THIS IS A NEW START FOR SISTER LOU, SO HEATHENS WATCH OUT!
GUIDE ME, DEATH WISH-SAMA!!

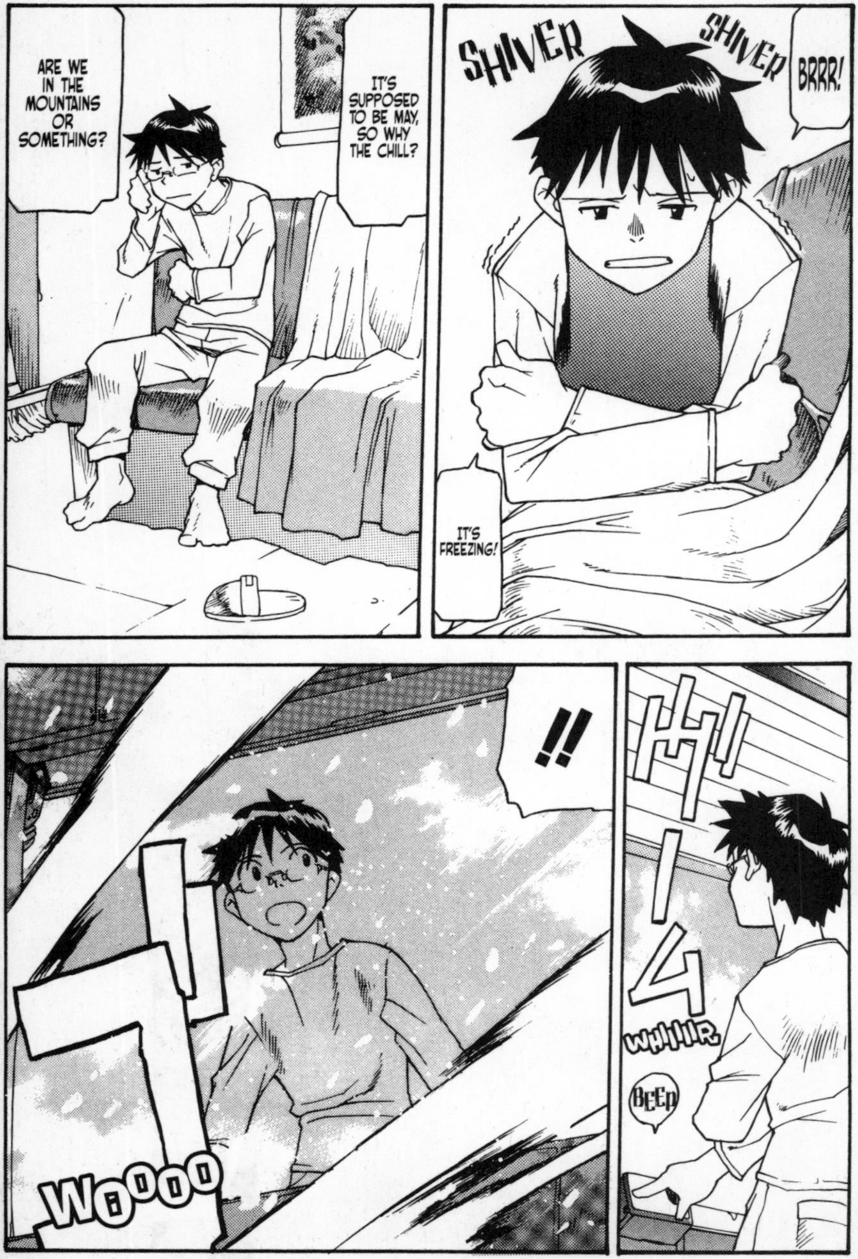
SHIVER
SHIVER
BRRR!
IT'S FREEZING!
IT'S SUPPOSED TO BE MAY, SO WHY THE CHILL?
ARE WE IN THE MOUNTAINS OR SOMETHING?
WHIIIR
BEEP
!!
WOOOO

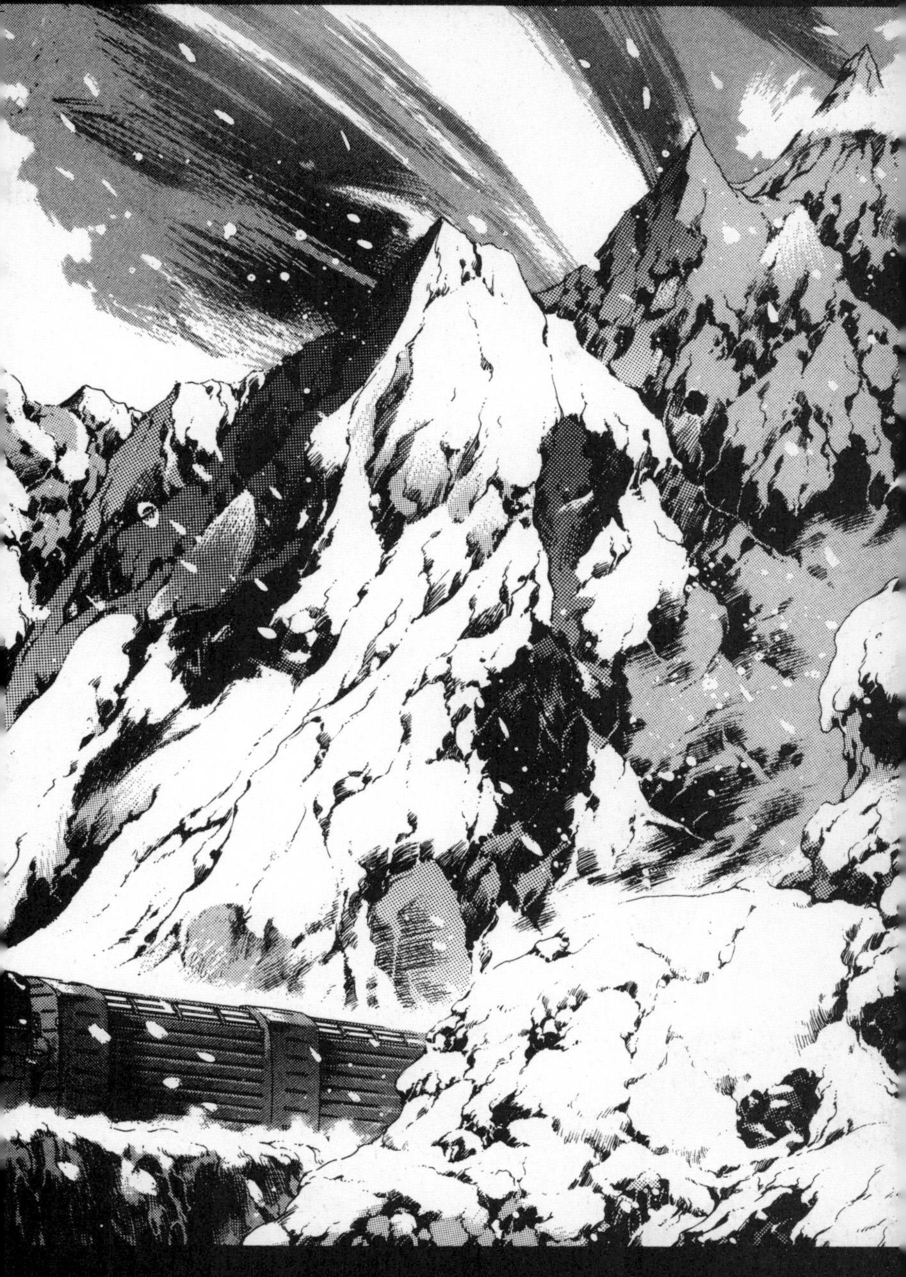

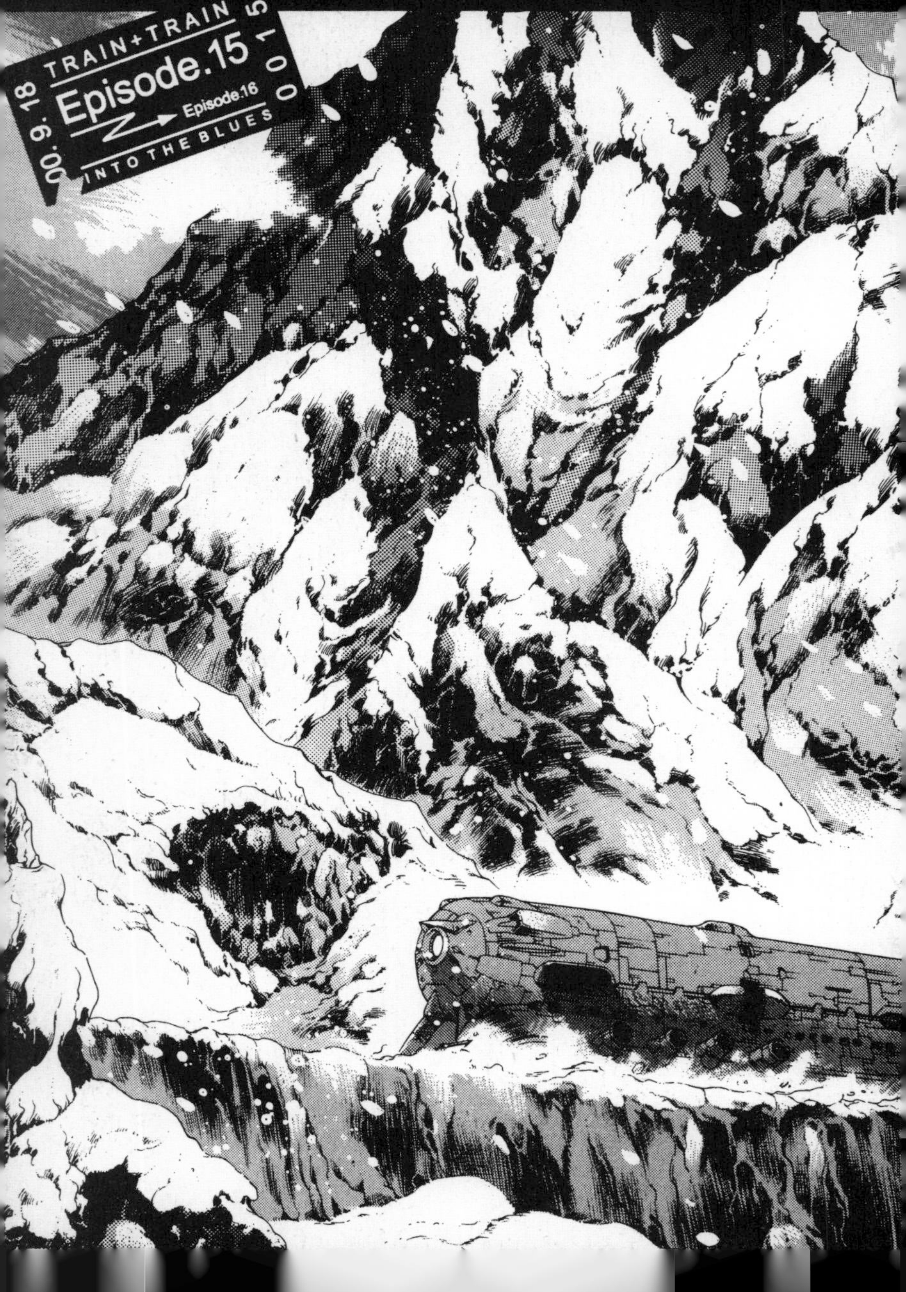
00. 9. 18
TRAIN+TRAIN
Episode.15
Episode.16
INTO THE BLUES
0015

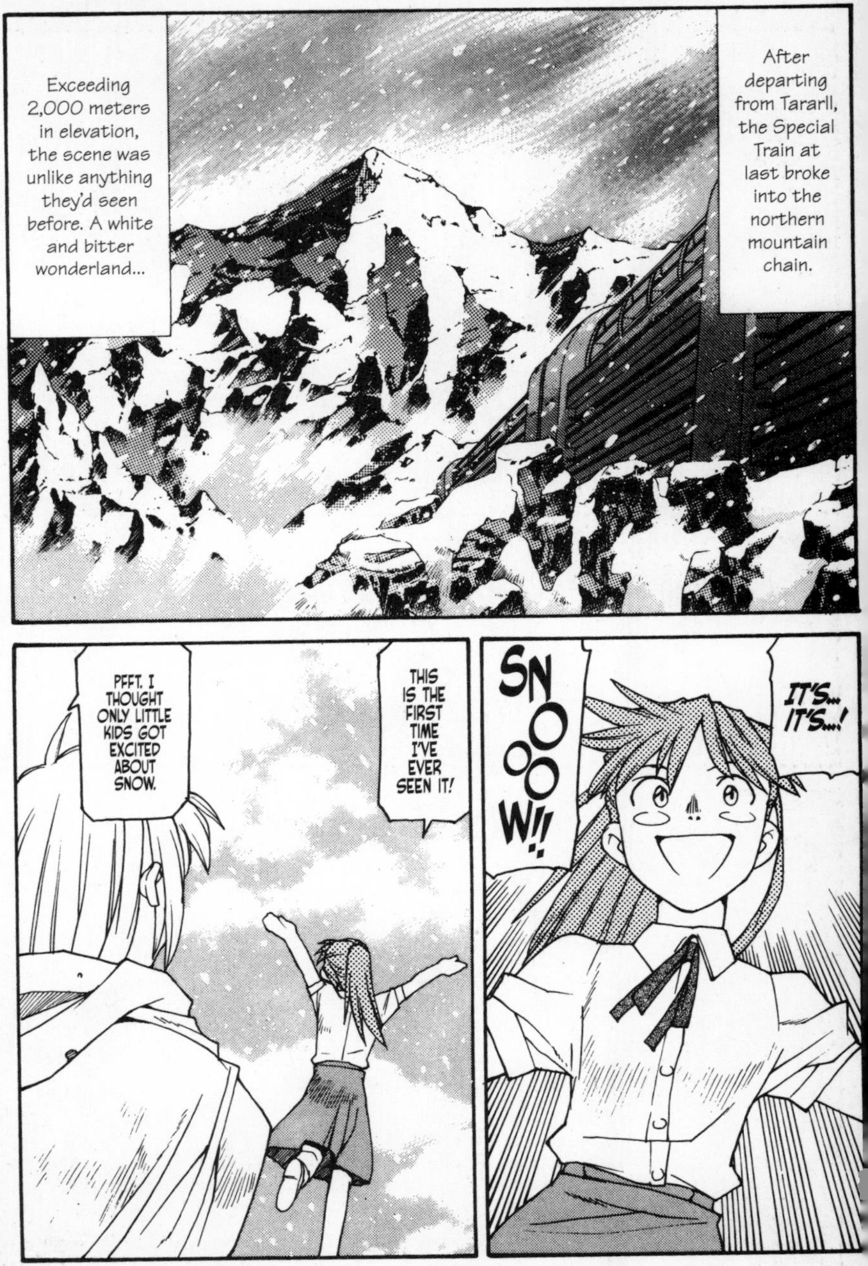
After departing from Tararll, the Special Train at last broke into the northern mountain chain.
Exceeding 2,000 meters in elevation, the scene was unlike anything they'd seen before. A white and bitter wonderland...
IT'S... IT'S...!
SNOOOOW!!
THIS IS THE FIRST TIME I'VE EVER SEEN IT!
PFFT. I THOUGHT ONLY LITTLE KIDS GOT EXCITED ABOUT SNOW.

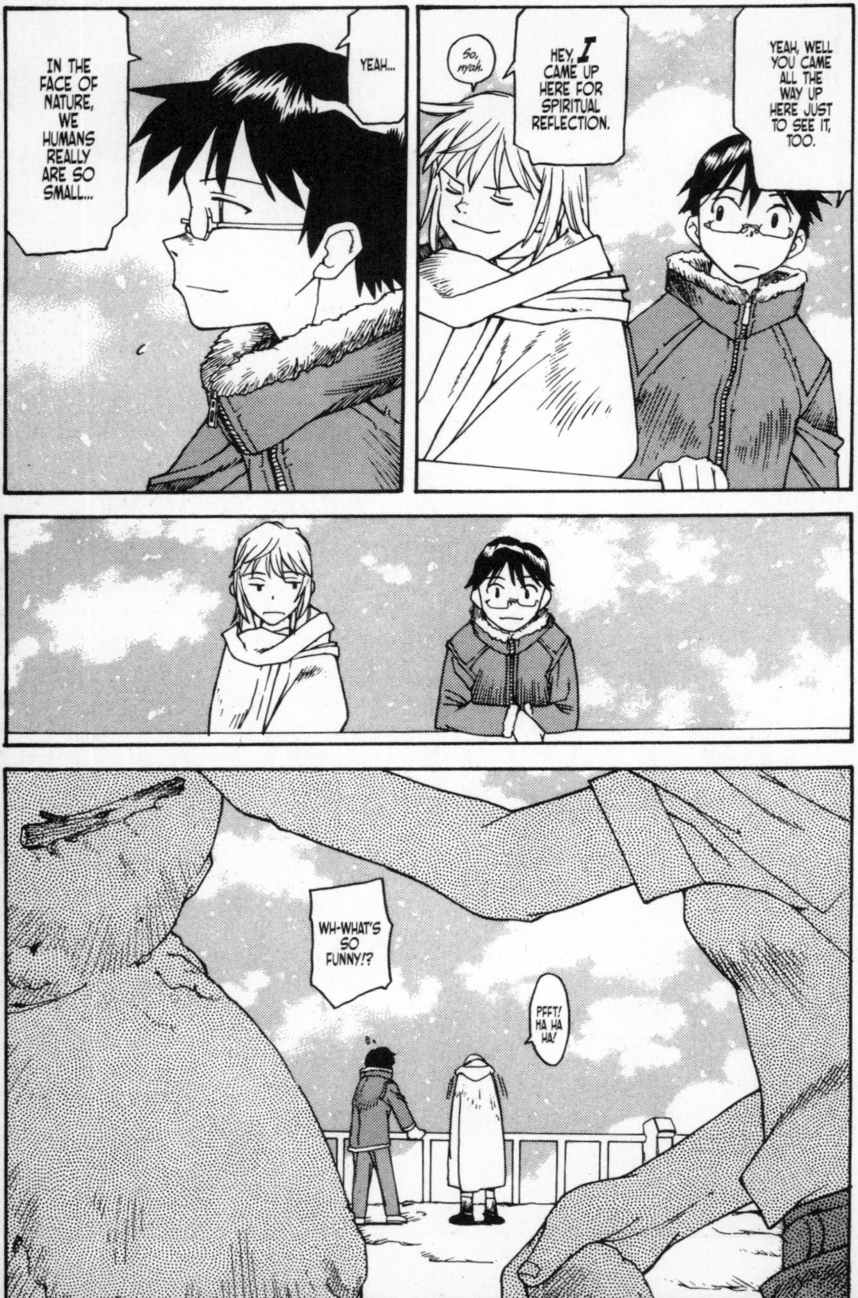

YEAH, WELL YOU CAME ALL THE WAY UP HERE JUST TO SEE IT, TOO.
HEY, I CAME UP HERE FOR SPIRITUAL REFLECTION.
So, nyah.
YEAH...
IN THE FACE OF NATURE, WE HUMANS REALLY ARE SO SMALL...
PFFT! HA HA HA!
WH-WHAT'S SO FUNNY!?

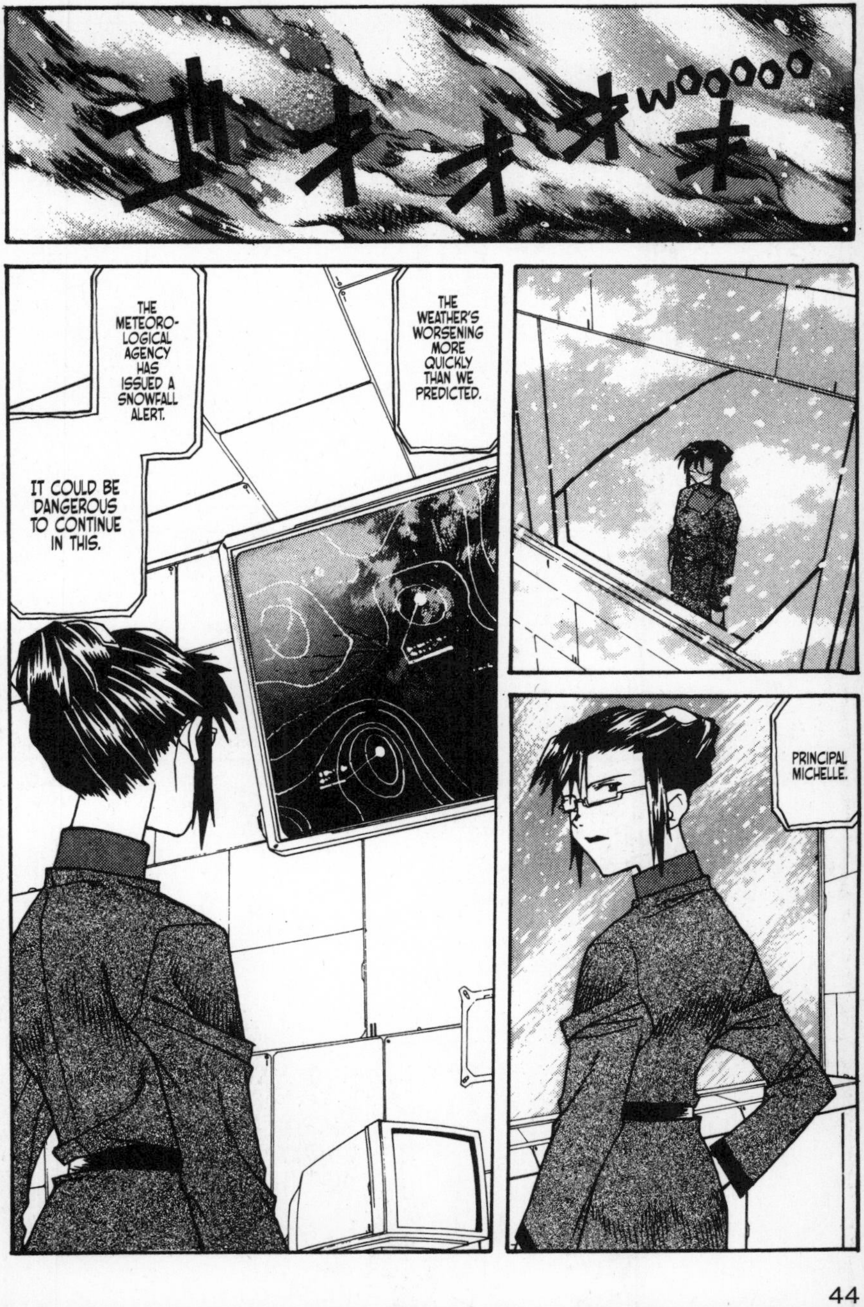
ゴオオオオ
WOOOOO
PRINCIPAL MICHELLE.
THE WEATHER'S WORSENING MORE QUICKLY THAN WE PREDICTED.
THE METEORO-LOGICAL AGENCY HAS ISSUED A SNOWFALL ALERT.
IT COULD BE DANGEROUS TO CONTINUE IN THIS.

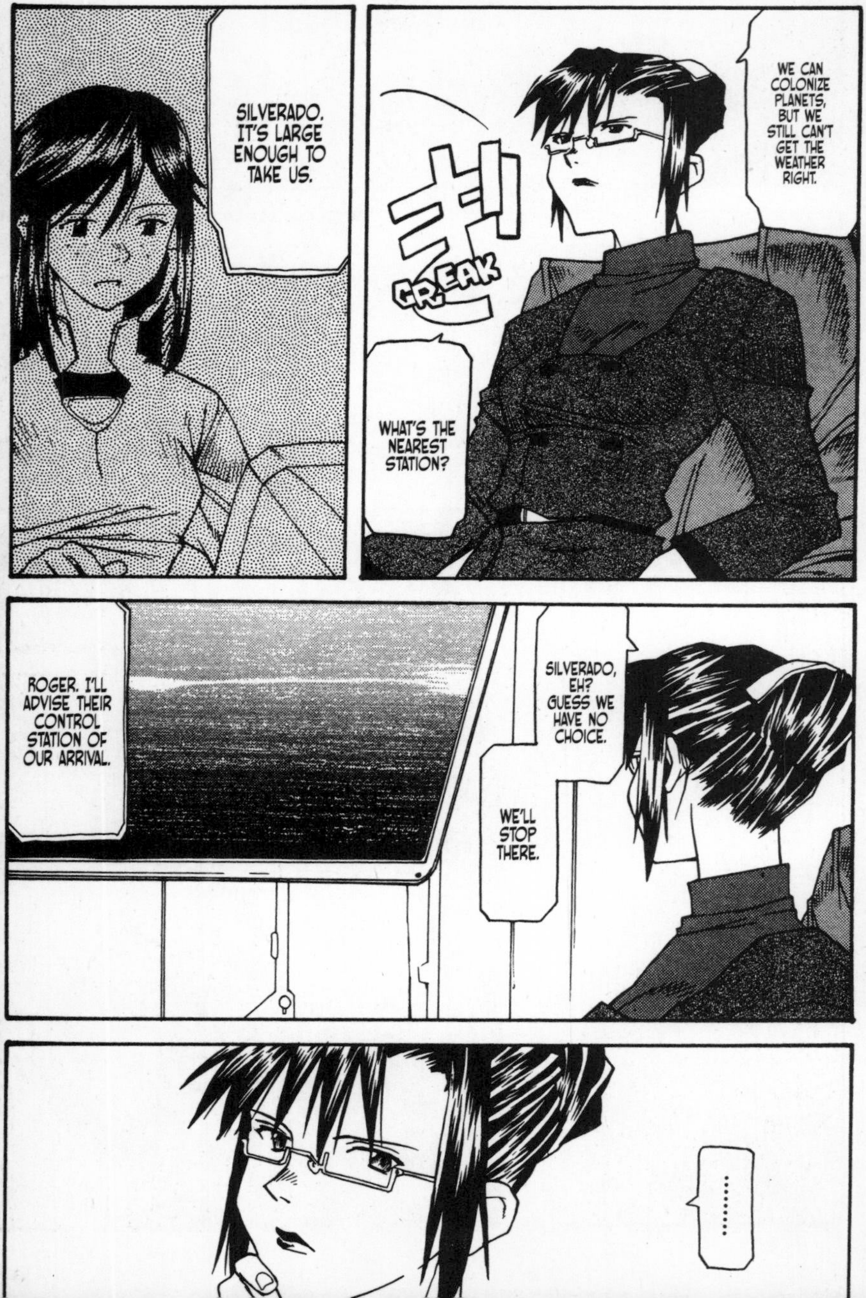
WE CAN COLONIZE PLANETS, BUT WE STILL CAN'T GET THE WEATHER RIGHT.
CREAK
WHAT'S THE NEAREST STATION?
SILVERADO. IT'S LARGE ENOUGH TO TAKE US.
SILVERADO, EH? GUESS WE HAVE NO CHOICE.
WE'LL STOP THERE.
ROGER. I'LL ADVISE THEIR CONTROL STATION OF OUR ARRIVAL.
....

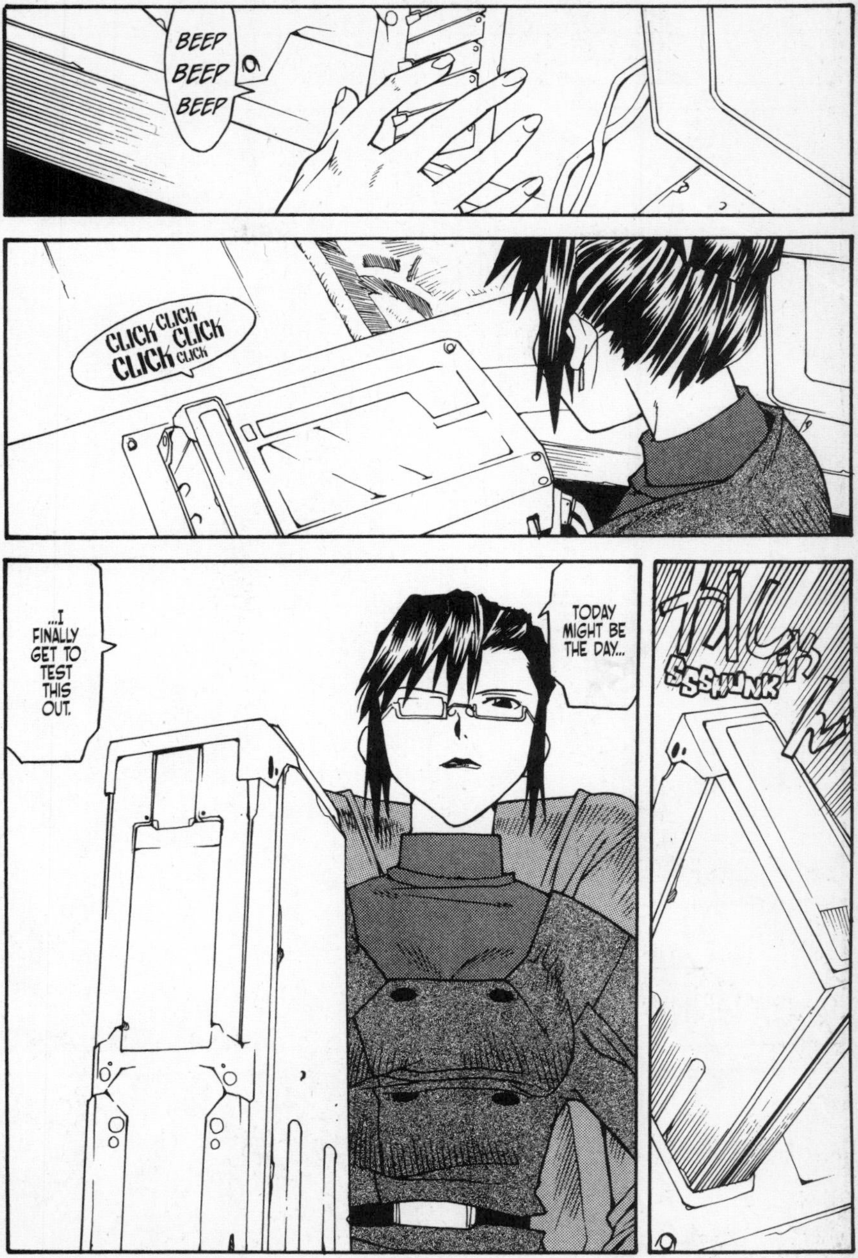
BEEP BEEP BEEP
CLICK CLICK CLICK CLICK CLICK CLICK
SSSHUNK
TODAY MIGHT BE THE DAY...
...I FINALLY GET TO TEST THIS OUT.

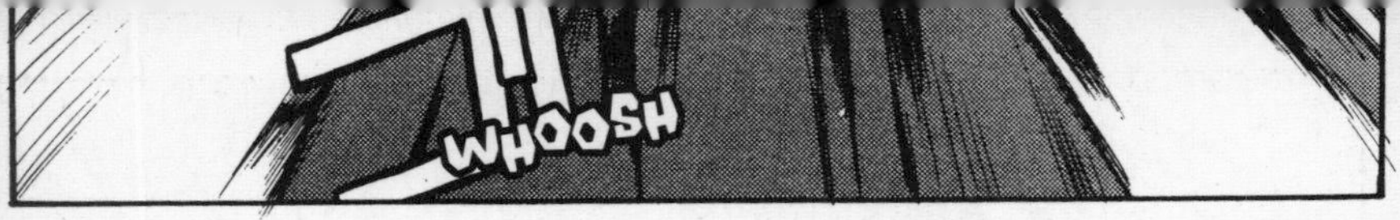
WHOOSH

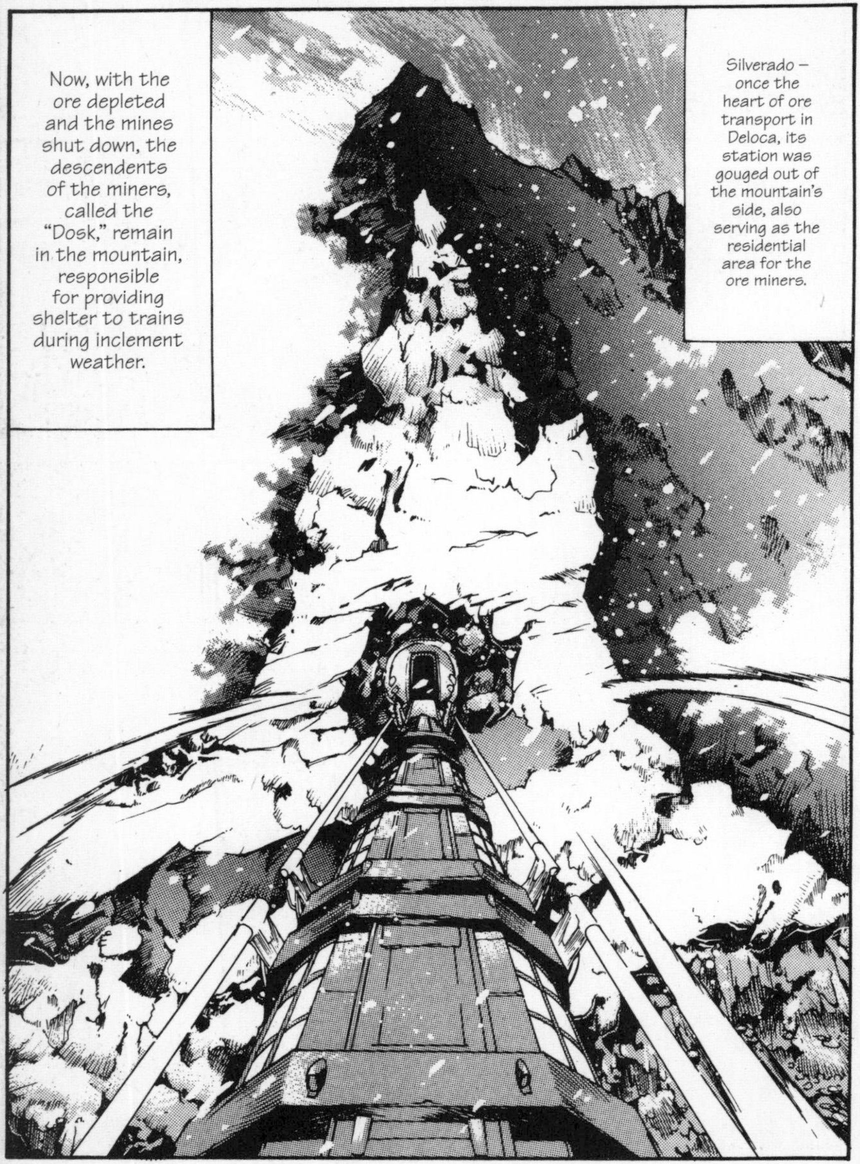
Silverado – once the heart of ore transport in Deloca, its station was gouged out of the mountain's side, also serving as the residential area for the ore miners.
Now, with the ore depleted and the mines shut down, the descendents of the miners, called the "Dosk," remain in the mountain, responsible for providing shelter to trains during inclement weather.

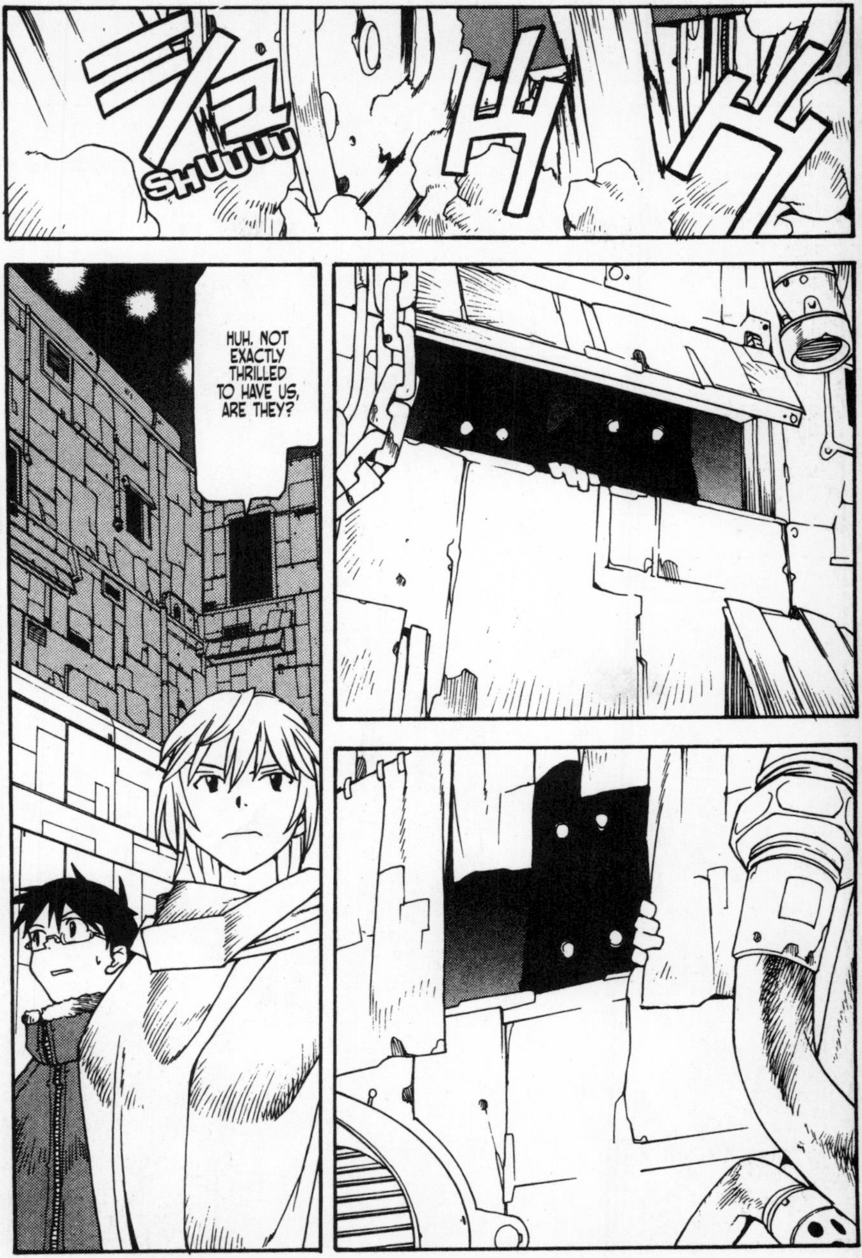
SHUUUU
HUH. NOT EXACTLY THRILLED TO HAVE US, ARE THEY?

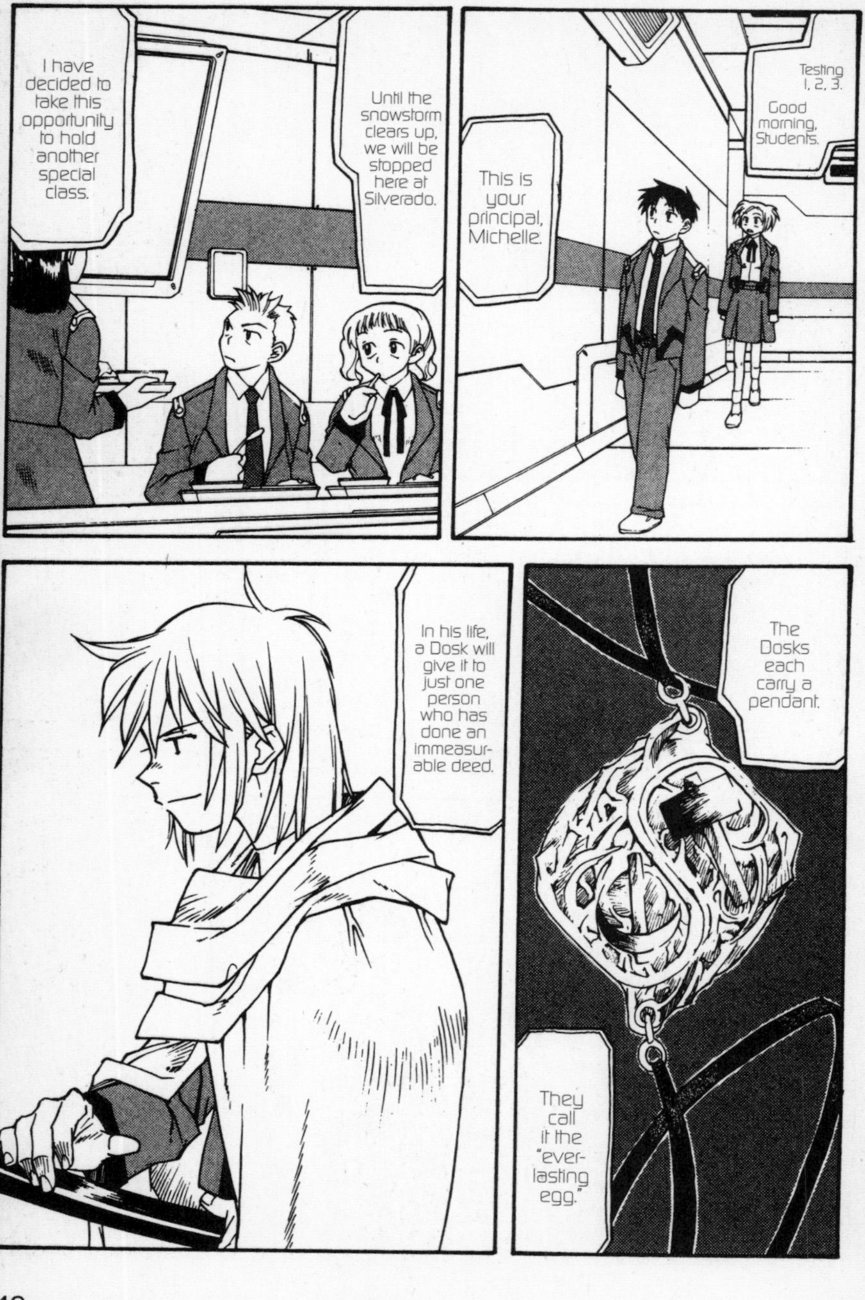
Testing 1, 2, 3.
Good morning, Students.
This is your principal, Michelle.
Until the snowstorm clears up, we will be stopped here at Silverado.
I have decided to take this opportunity to hold another special class.
The Dosks each carry a pendant.
They call it the "ever-lasting egg."
In his life, a Dosk will give it to just one person who has done an immeasur-able deed.

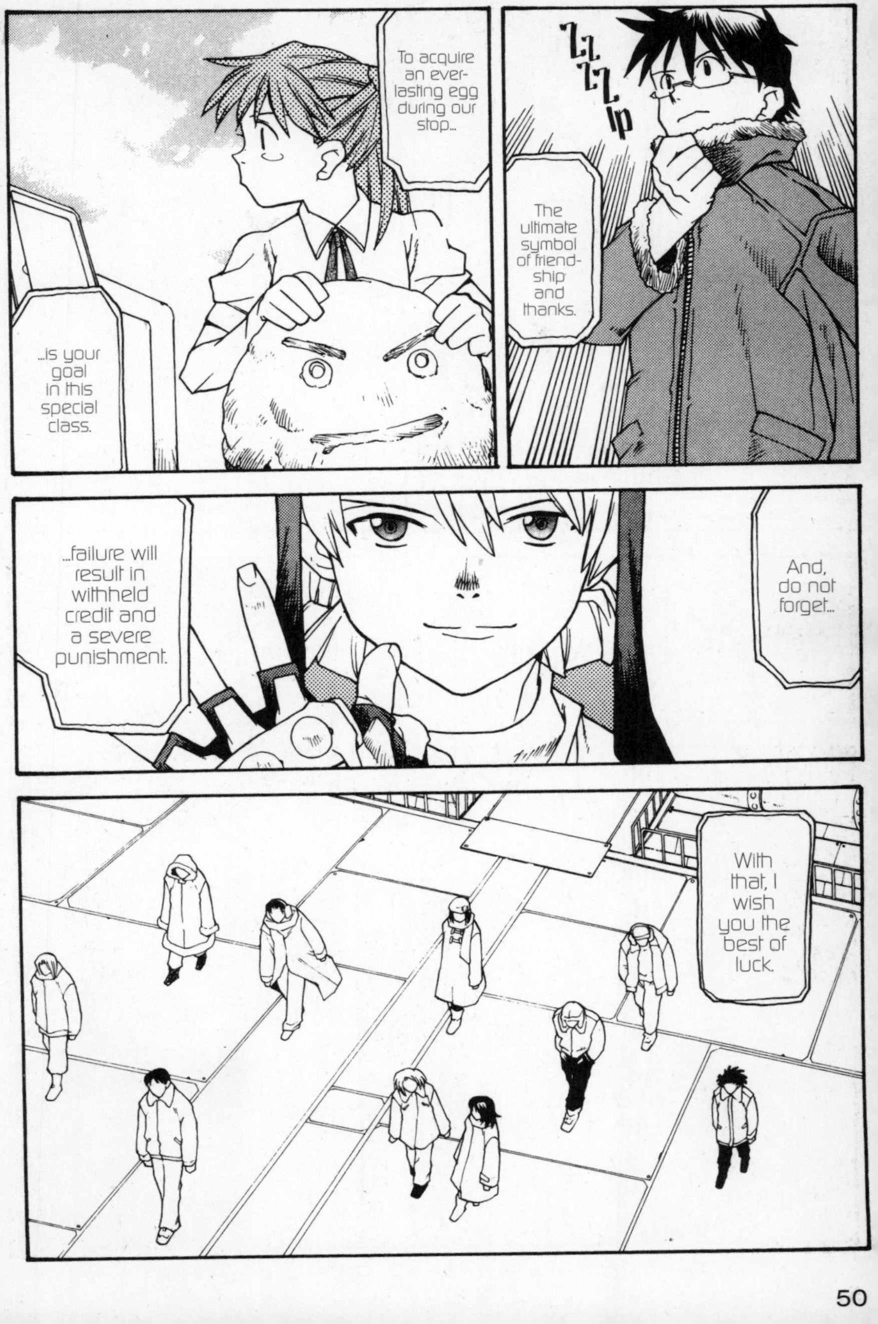
ZZZip
The ultimate symbol of friend-ship and thanks.
To acquire an ever-lasting egg during our stop...
...is your goal in this special class.
And, do not forget...
...failure will result in withheld credit and a severe punishment.
With that, I wish you the best of luck.

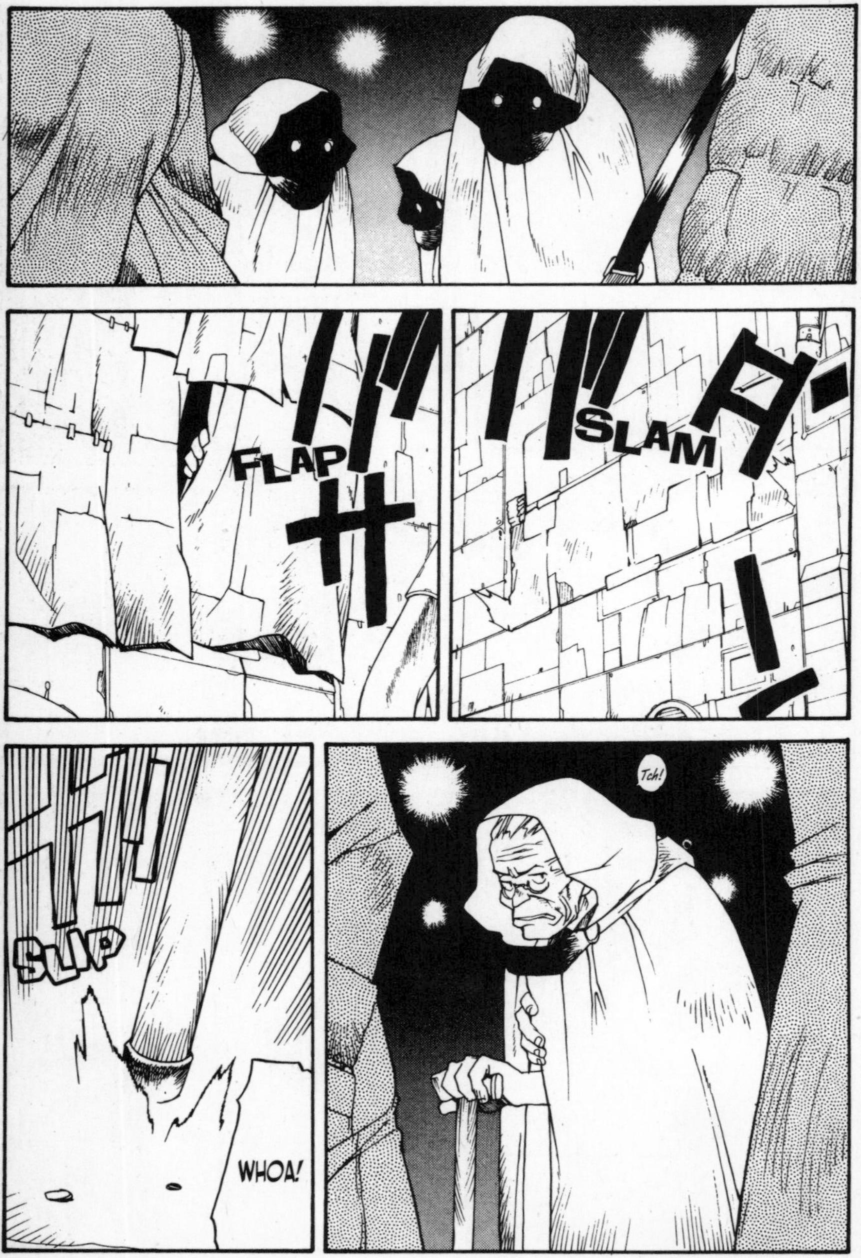
SLAM
FLAP
Tch!
SLIP
WHOA!

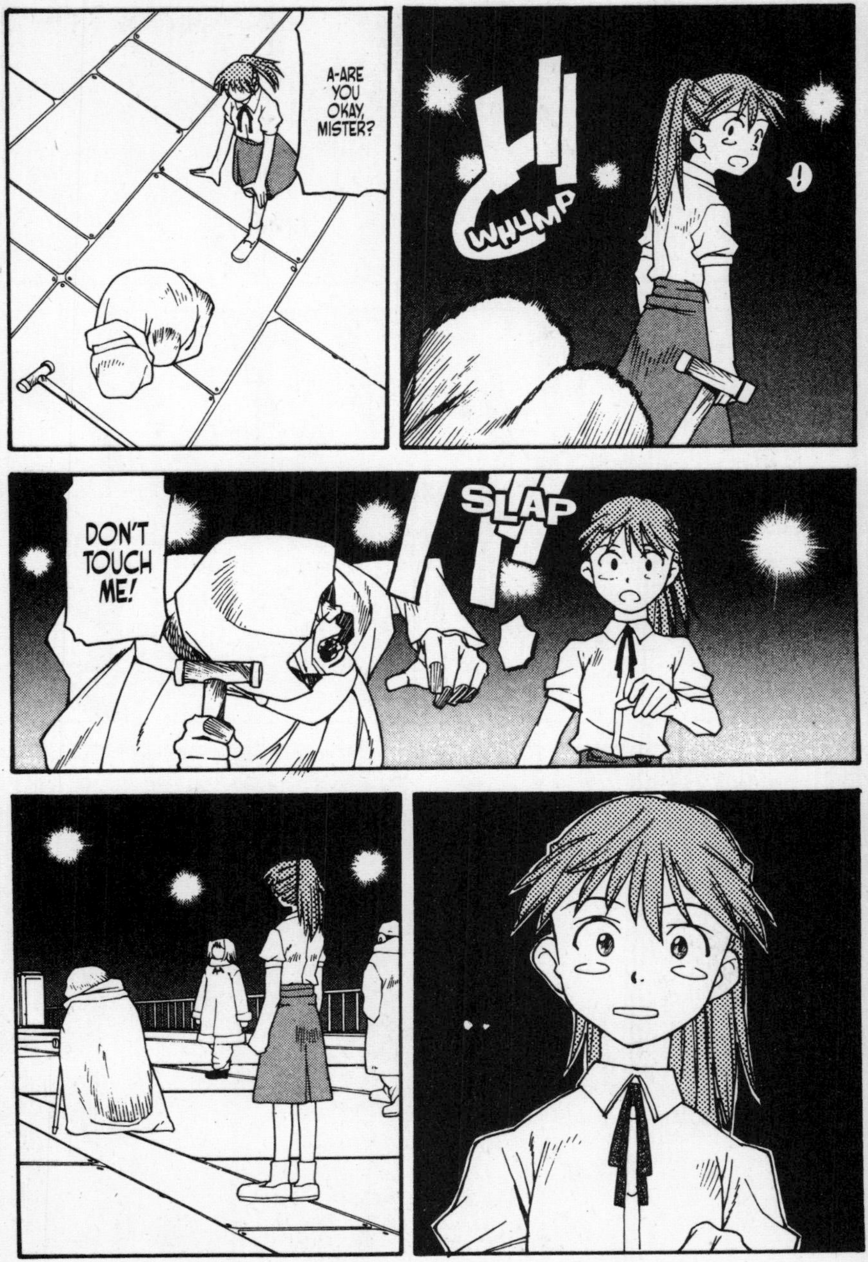
WHUMP
!
A-ARE YOU OKAY, MISTER?
SLAP
DON'T TOUCH ME!

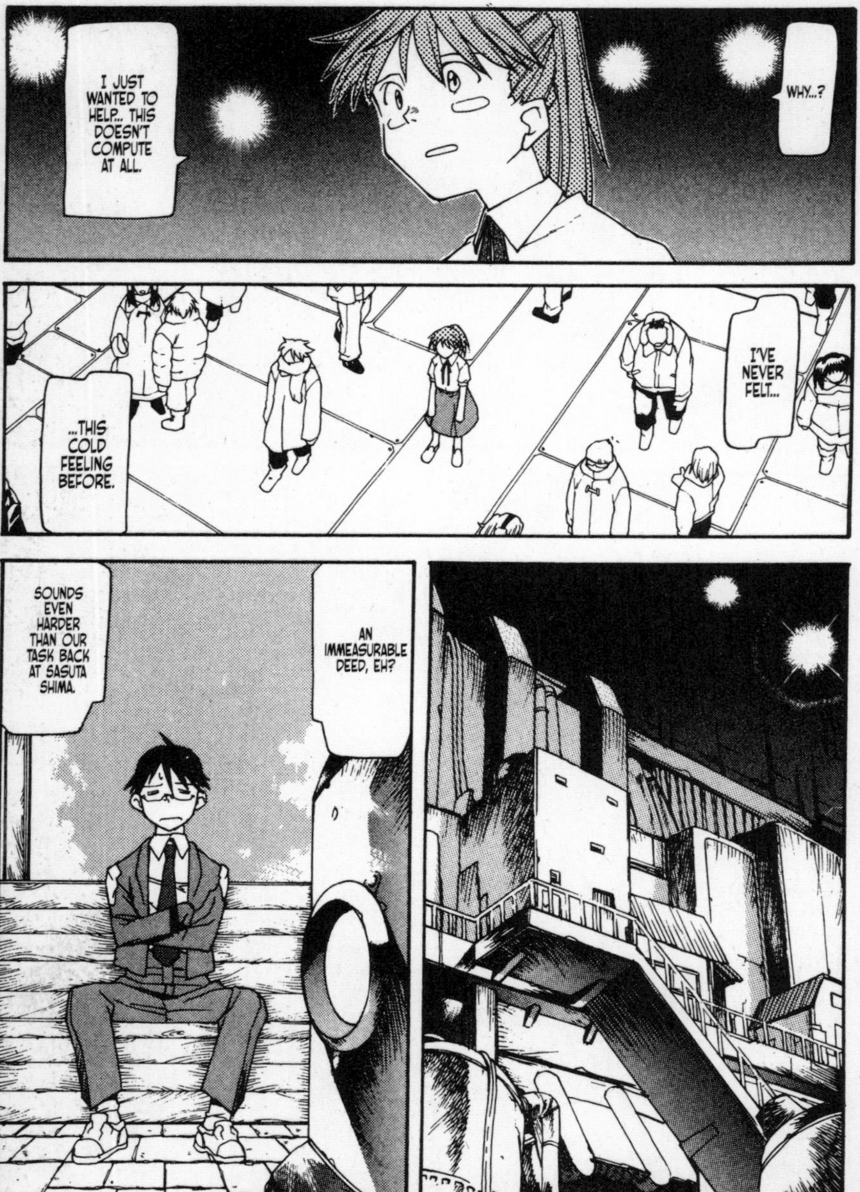
WHY...?
I JUST WANTED TO HELP... THIS DOESN'T COMPUTE AT ALL.
I'VE NEVER FELT...
...THIS COLD FEELING BEFORE.
AN IMMEASURABLE DEED, EH?
SOUNDS EVEN HARDER THAN OUR TASK BACK AT SASUTA SHIMA.

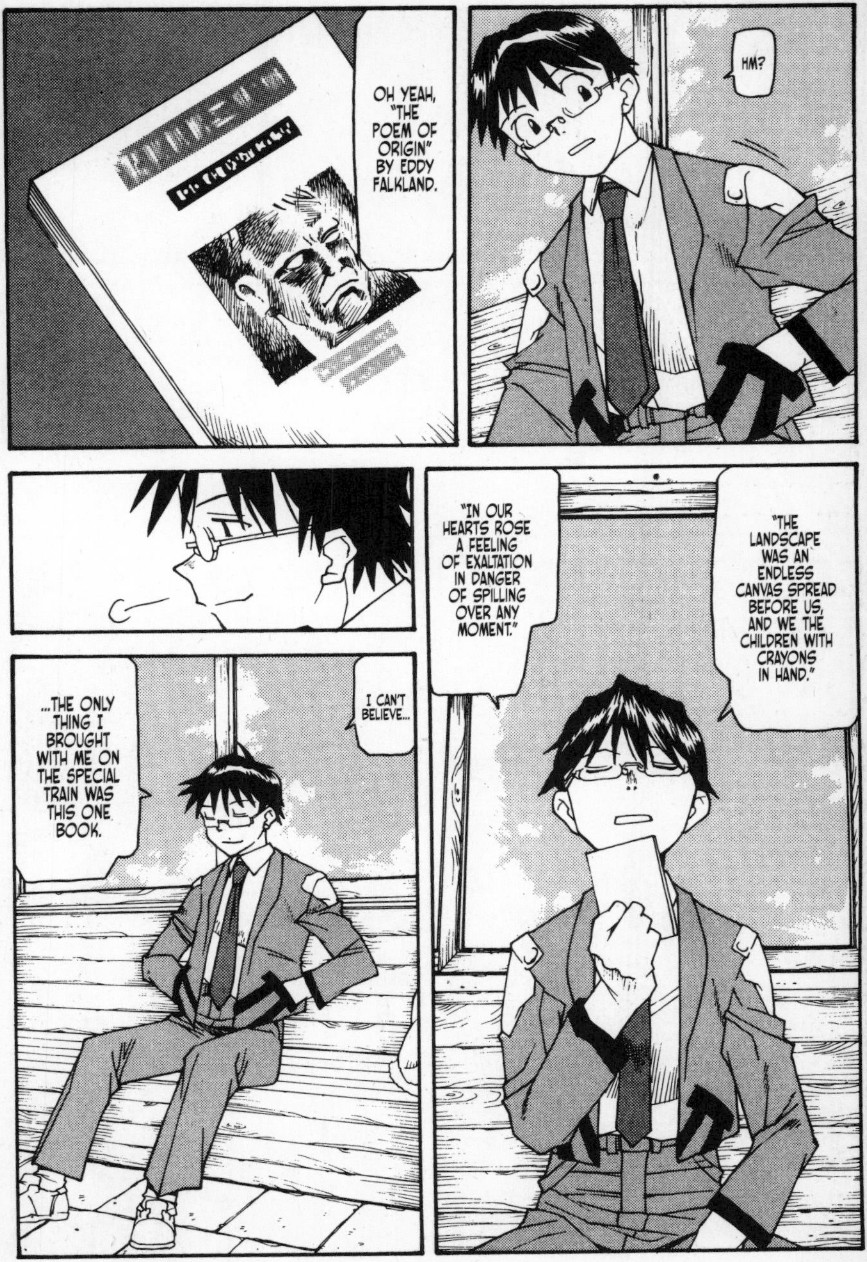
HM?
OH YEAH, "THE POEM OF ORIGIN" BY EDDY FALKLAND.
"THE LANDSCAPE WAS AN ENDLESS CANVAS SPREAD BEFORE US, AND WE THE CHILDREN WITH CRAYONS IN HAND."
"IN OUR HEARTS ROSE A FEELING OF EXALTATION IN DANGER OF SPILLING OVER ANY MOMENT."
I CAN'T BELIEVE...
...THE ONLY THING I BROUGHT WITH ME ON THE SPECIAL TRAIN WAS THIS ONE BOOK.

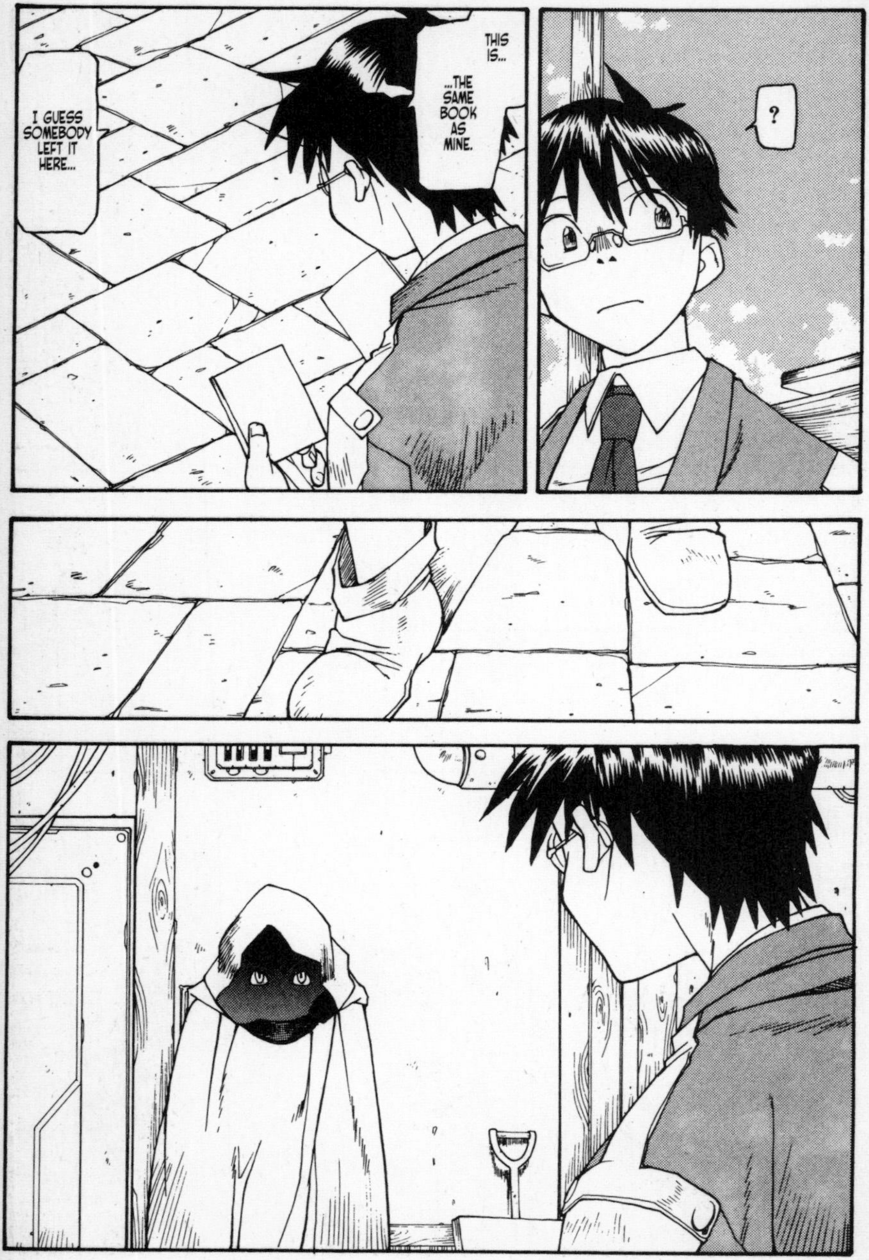
?
THIS IS...
...THE SAME BOOK AS MINE.
I GUESS SOMEBODY LEFT IT HERE...

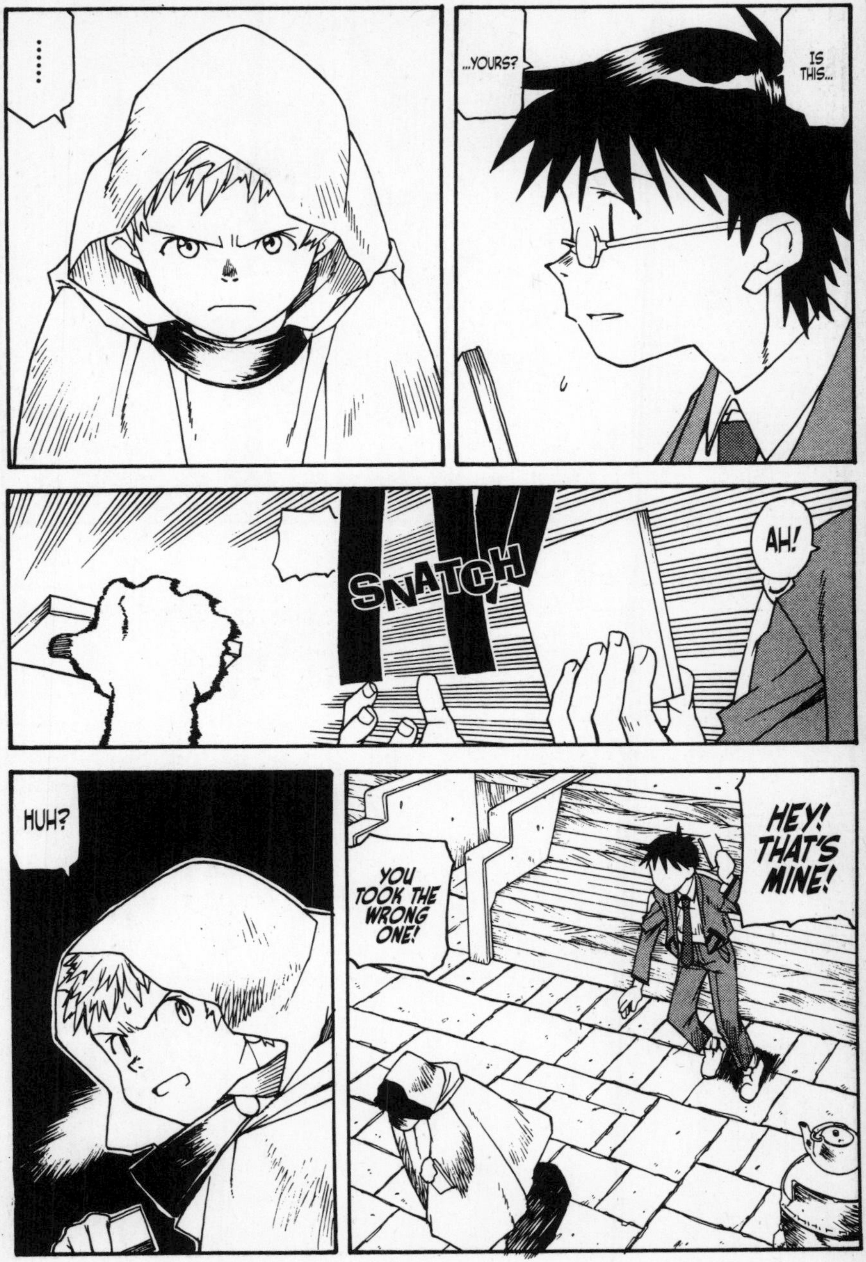
IS THIS...
...YOURS?
......
AH!
SNATCH
HEY! THAT'S MINE!
YOU TOOK THE WRONG ONE!
HUH?

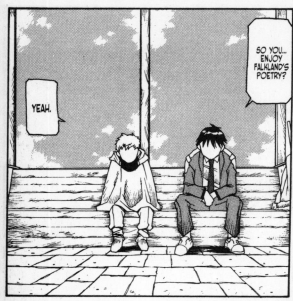

SO YOU... ENJOY FALKLAND'S POETRY?

YEAH.

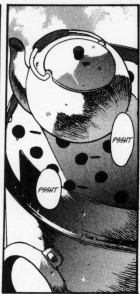

PSSHT

PSSHT

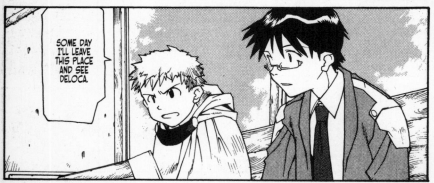

SOME DAY I'LL LEAVE THIS PLACE AND SEE DELOCA.

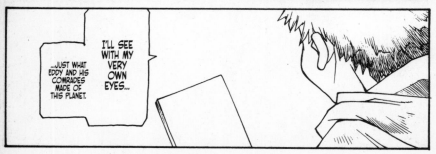

I'LL SEE WITH MY VERY OWN EYES...

...JUST WHAT EDDY AND HIS COMRADES MADE OF THIS PLANET.

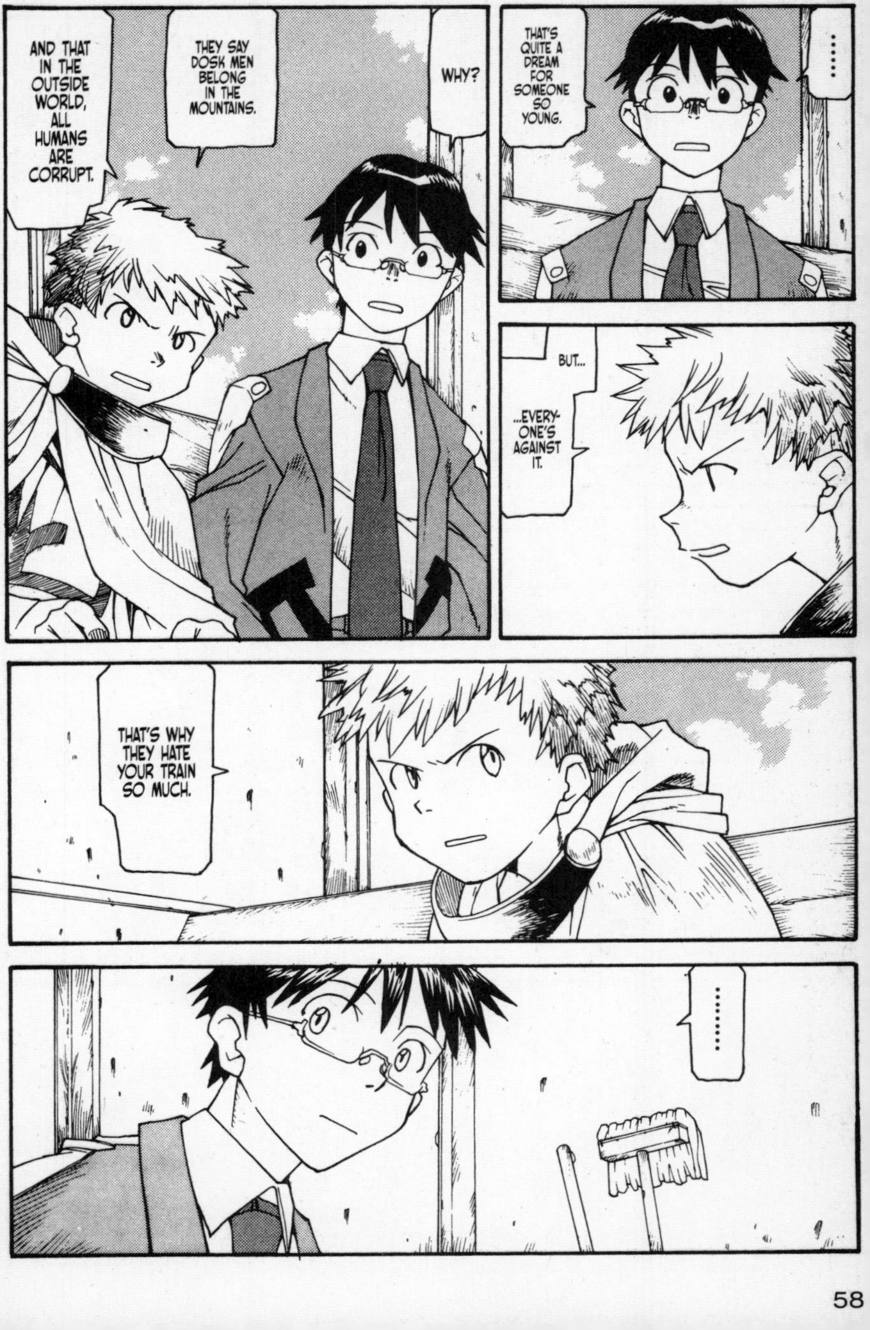
......
THAT'S QUITE A DREAM FOR SOMEONE SO YOUNG.
BUT...
...EVERY-ONE'S AGAINST IT.
WHY?
THEY SAY DOSK MEN BELONG IN THE MOUNTAINS.
AND THAT IN THE OUTSIDE WORLD, ALL HUMANS ARE CORRUPT.
THAT'S WHY THEY HATE YOUR TRAIN SO MUCH.
....

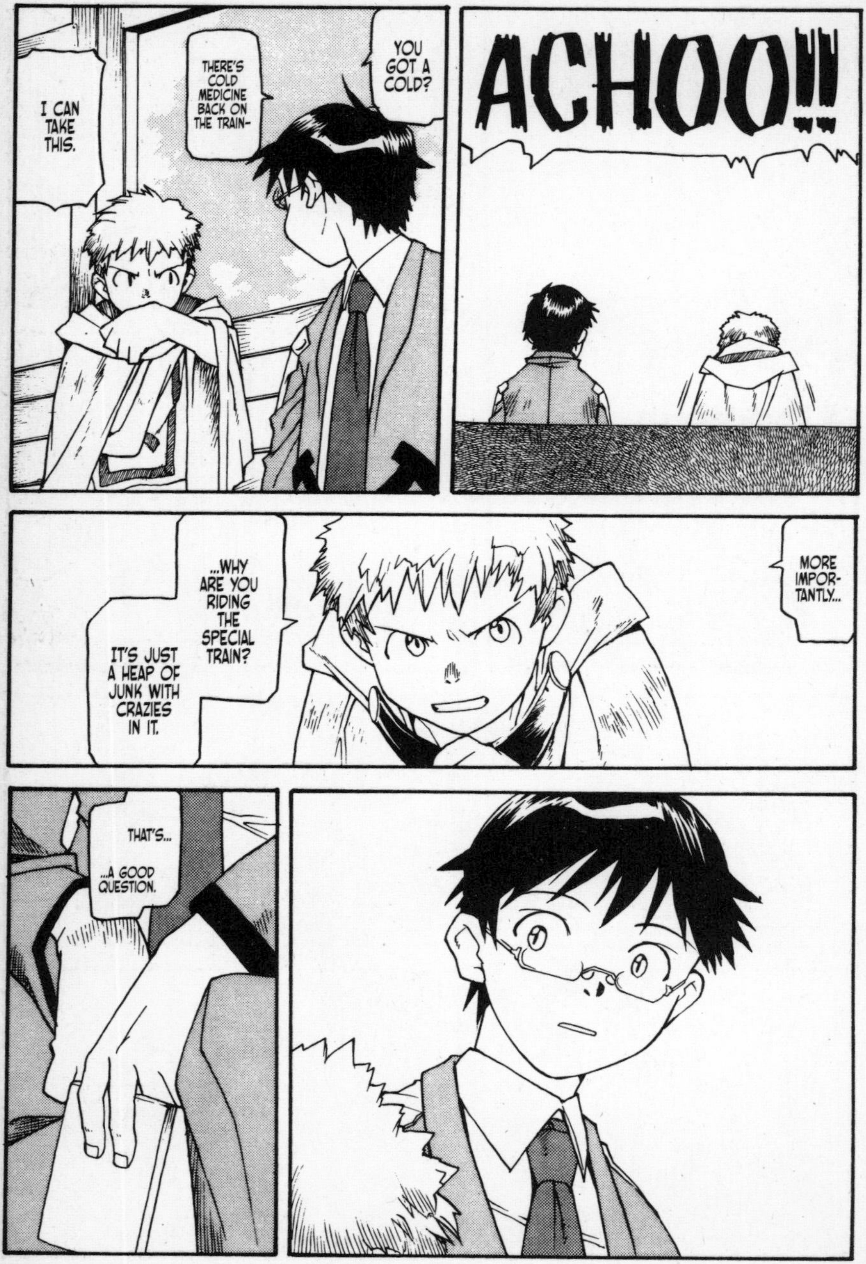
ACHOO!!
YOU GOT A COLD?
THERE'S COLD MEDICINE BACK ON THE TRAIN-
I CAN TAKE THIS.
MORE IMPORTANTLY...
...WHY ARE YOU RIDING THE SPECIAL TRAIN?
IT'S JUST A HEAP OF JUNK WITH CRAZIES IN IT.
THAT'S...
...A GOOD QUESTION.

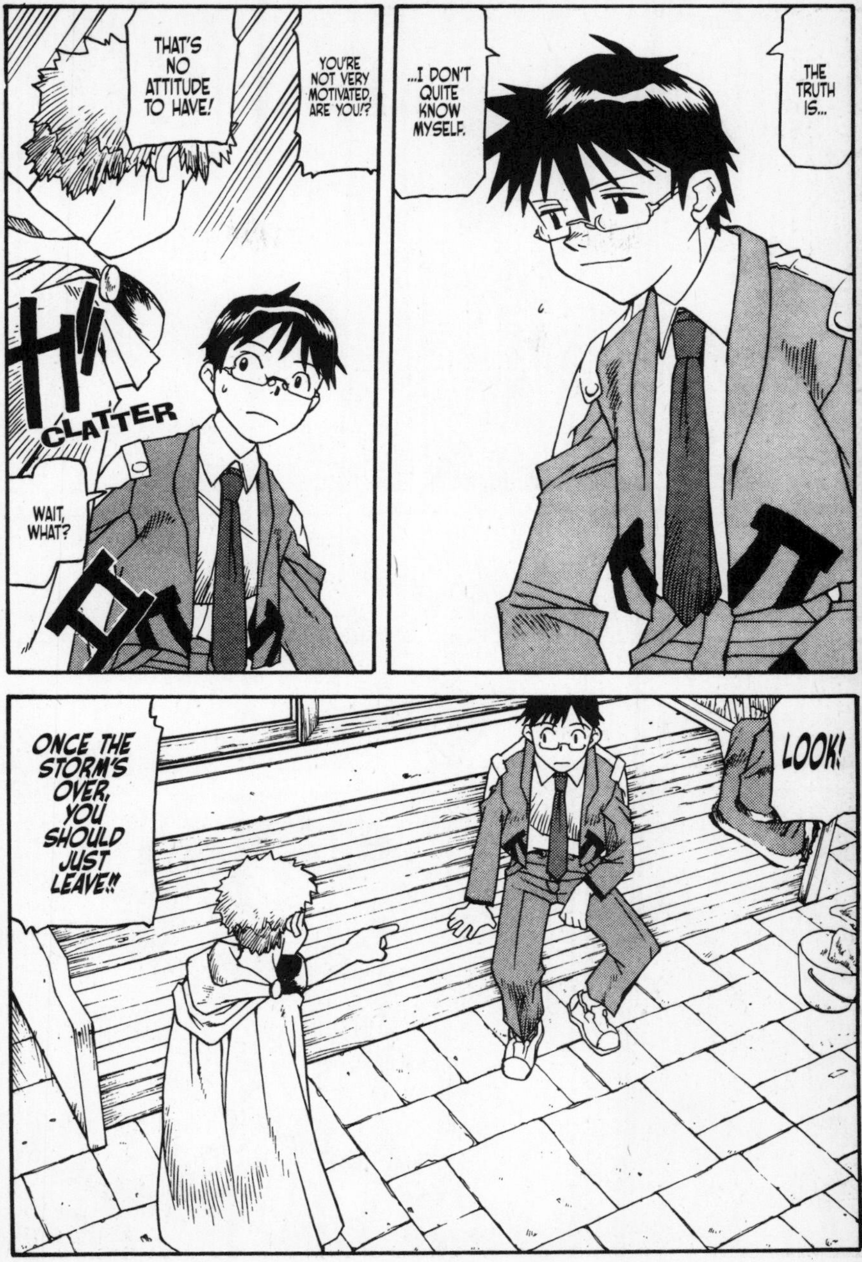
THE TRUTH IS...
...I DON'T QUITE KNOW MYSELF.
YOU'RE NOT VERY MOTIVATED, ARE YOU!?
THAT'S NO ATTITUDE TO HAVE!
CLATTER
WAIT, WHAT?
LOOK!
ONCE THE STORM'S OVER, YOU SHOULD JUST LEAVE!!

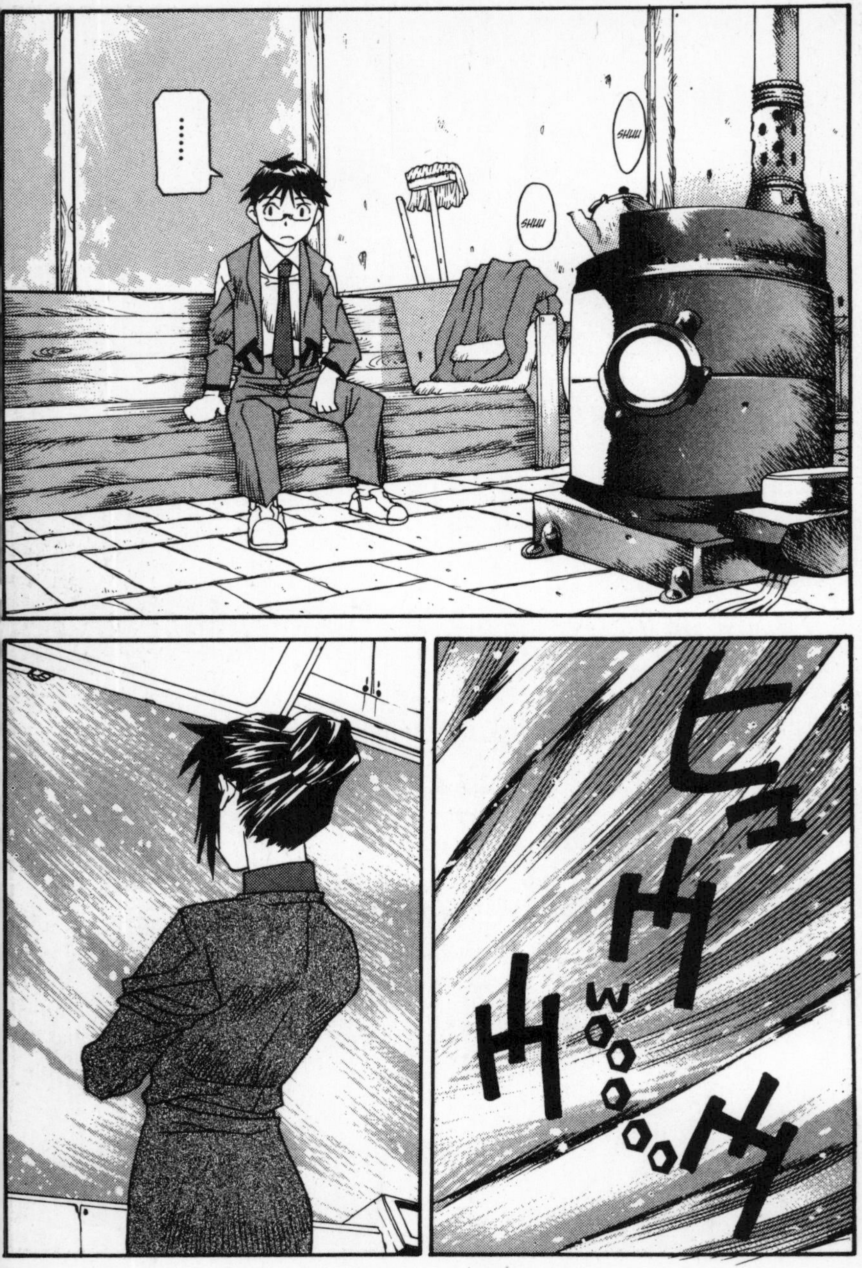

......
SHUU
SHUU
WOOOOO

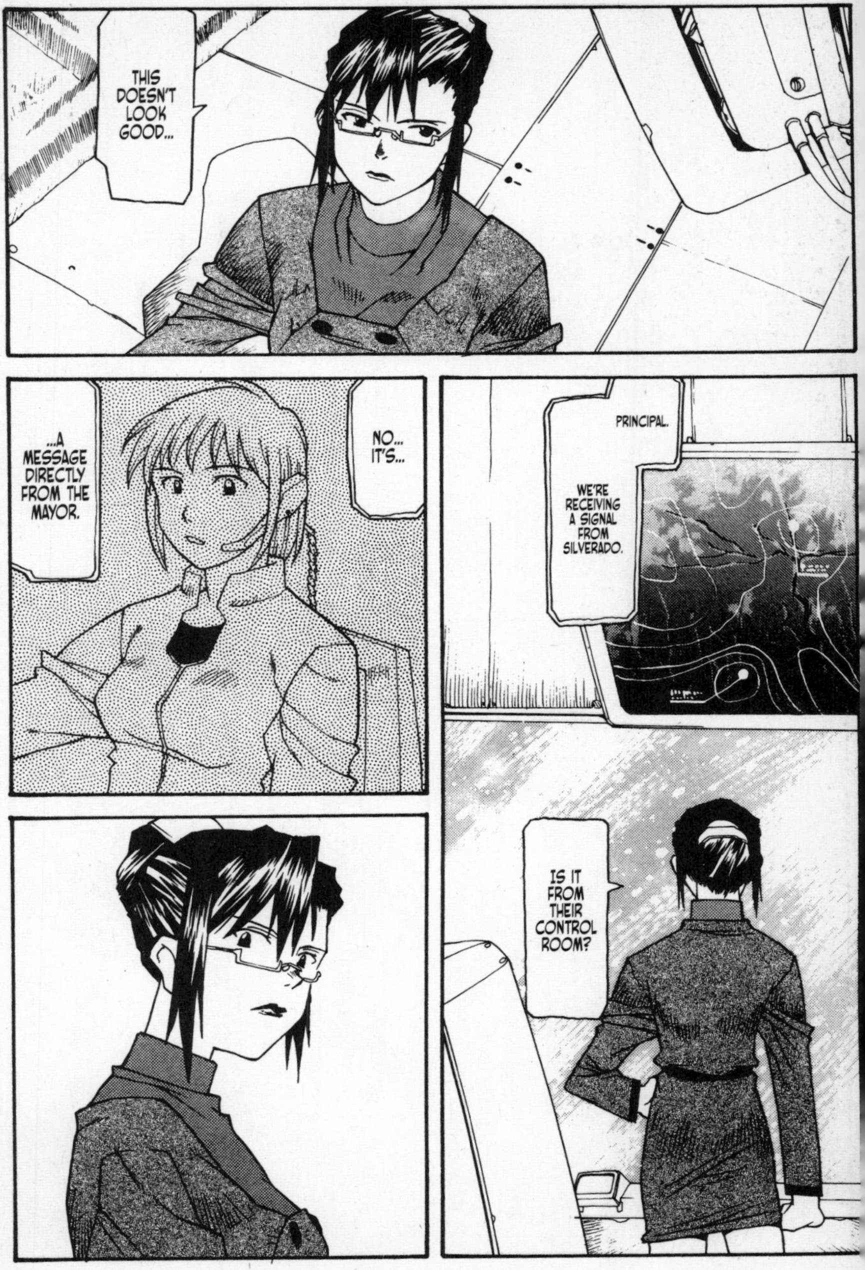
THIS DOESN'T LOOK GOOD...
PRINCIPAL.
WE'RE RECEIVING A SIGNAL FROM SILVERADO.
IS IT FROM THEIR CONTROL ROOM?
NO... IT'S...
...A MESSAGE DIRECTLY FROM THE MAYOR.

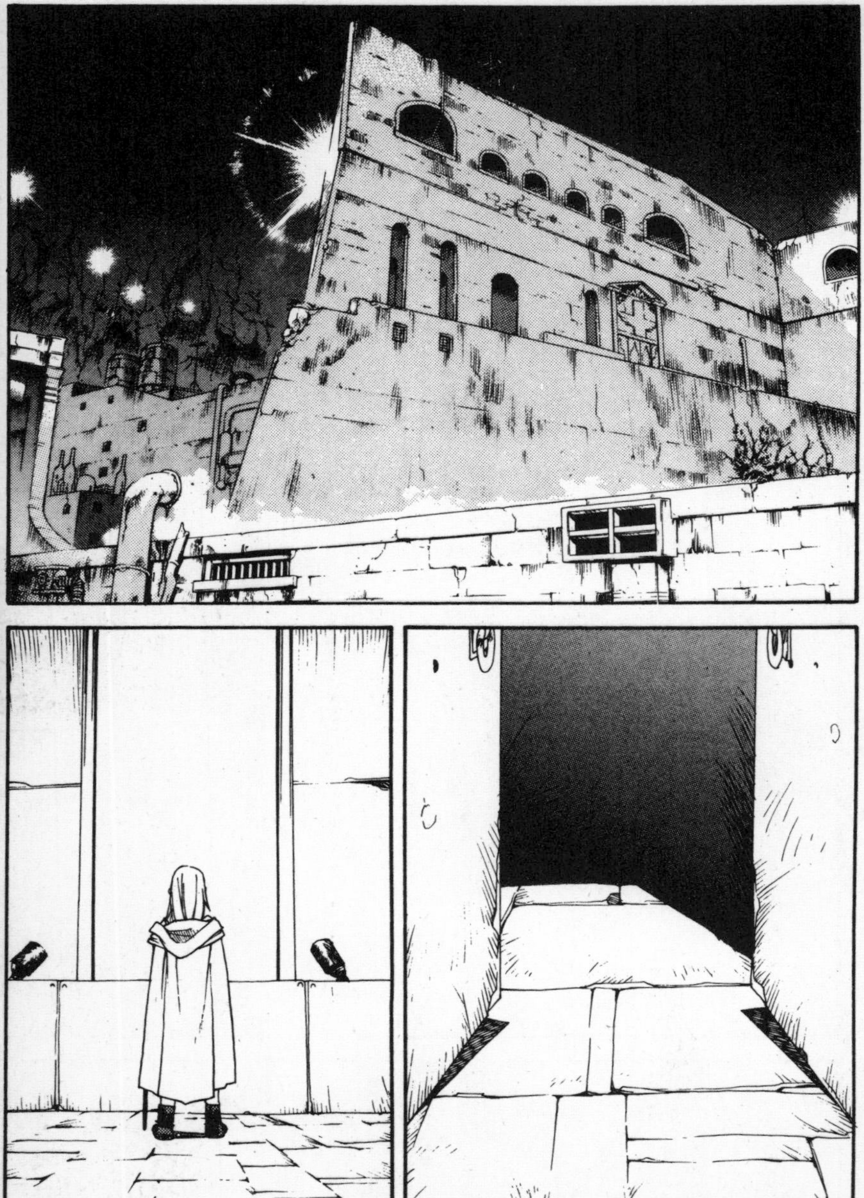

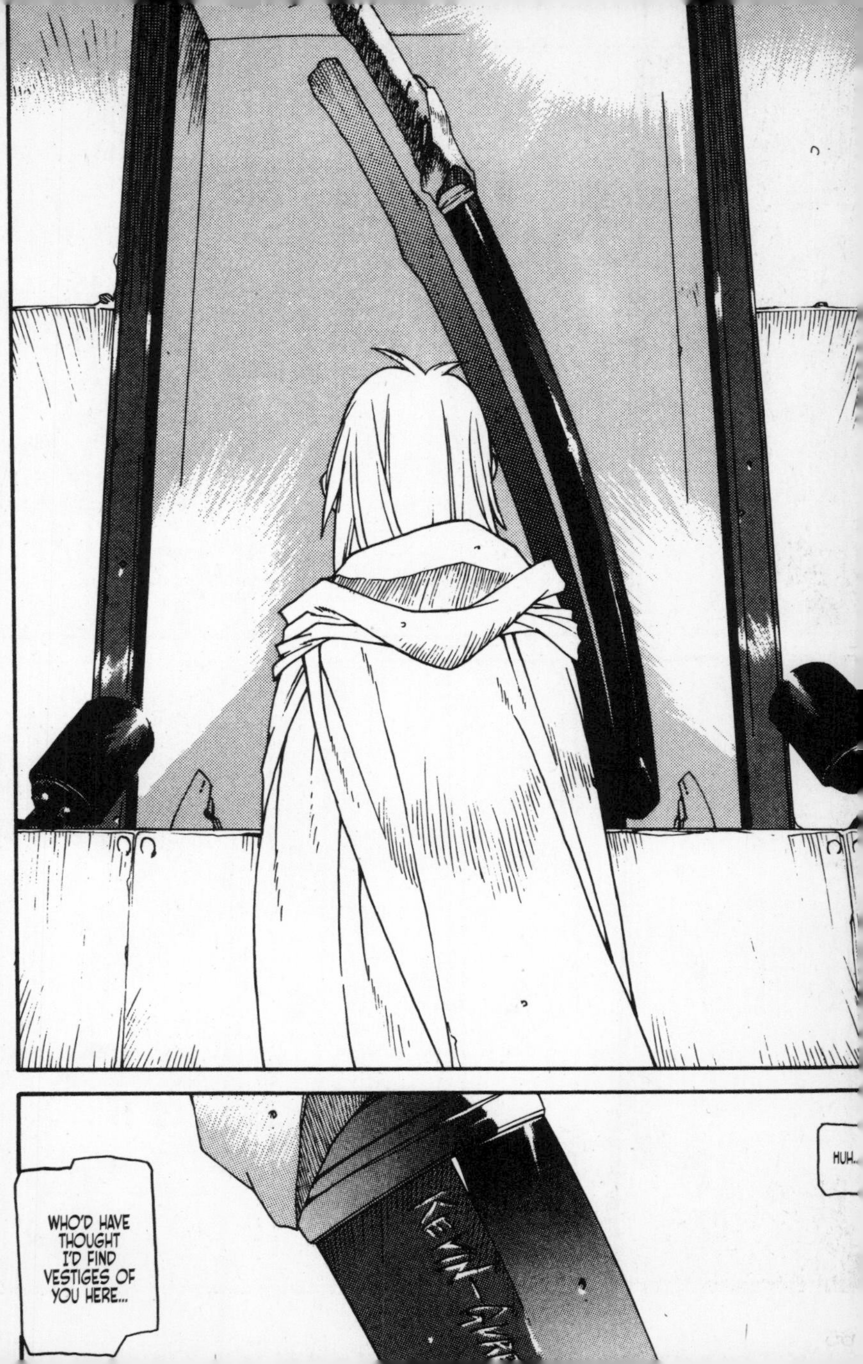
HUH...
WHO'D HAVE THOUGHT I'D FIND VESTIGES OF YOU HERE...

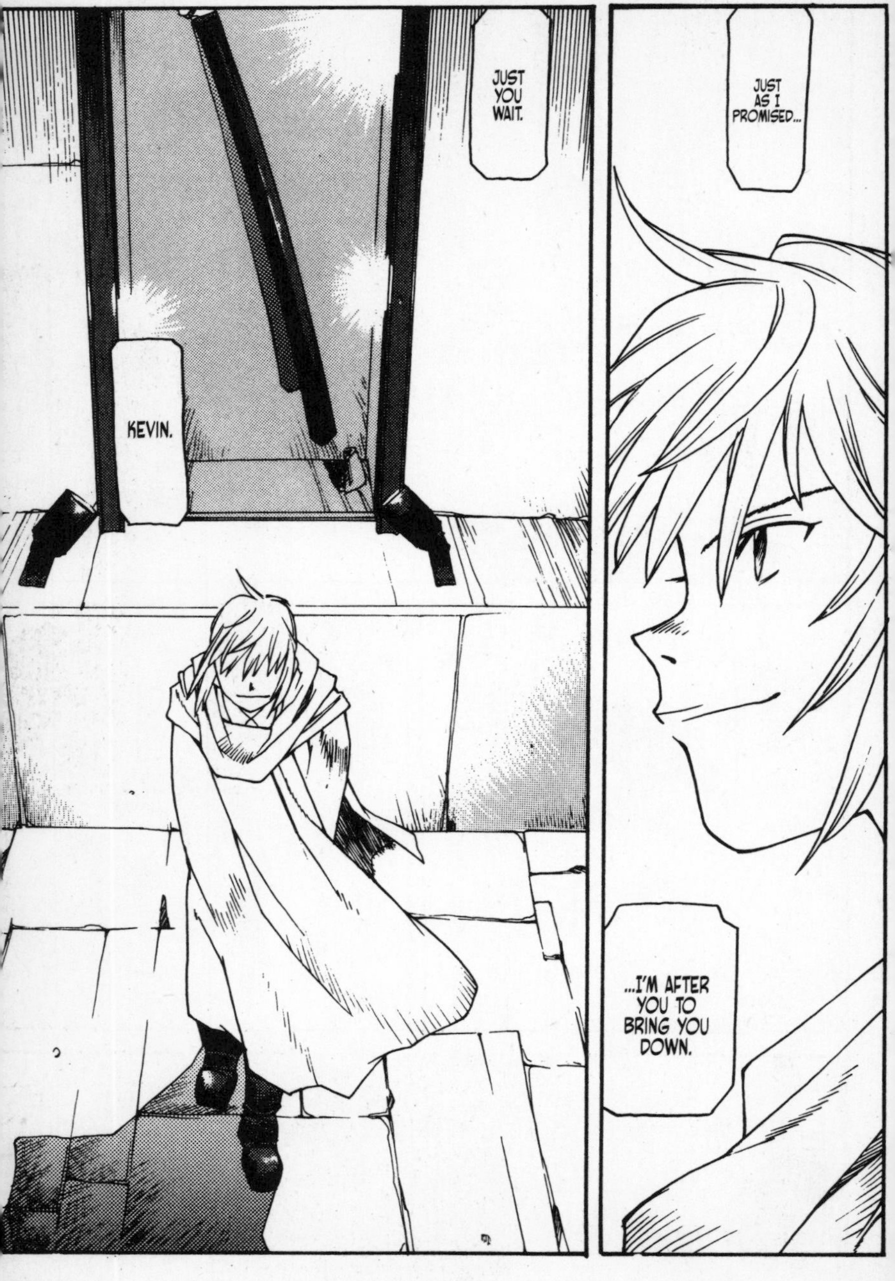
JUST AS I PROMISED...
...I'M AFTER YOU TO BRING YOU DOWN.
JUST YOU WAIT.
KEVIN.

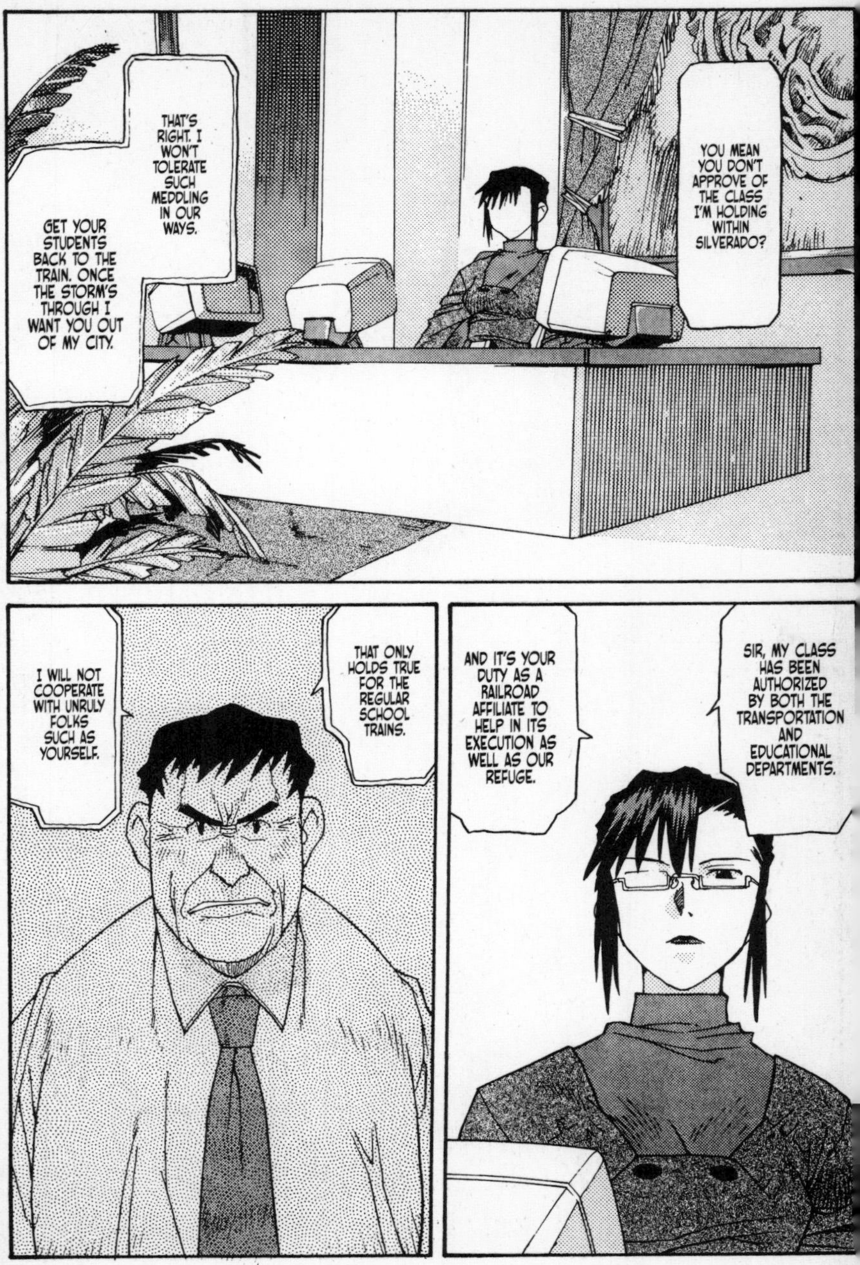
YOU MEAN YOU DON'T APPROVE OF THE CLASS I'M HOLDING WITHIN SILVERADO?
THAT'S RIGHT. I WON'T TOLERATE SUCH MEDDLING IN OUR WAYS.
GET YOUR STUDENTS BACK TO THE TRAIN. ONCE THE STORM'S THROUGH I WANT YOU OUT OF MY CITY.
SIR, MY CLASS HAS BEEN AUTHORIZED BY BOTH THE TRANSPORTATION AND EDUCATIONAL DEPARTMENTS.
AND IT'S YOUR DUTY AS A RAILROAD AFFILIATE TO HELP IN ITS EXECUTION AS WELL AS OUR REFUGE.
THAT ONLY HOLDS TRUE FOR THE REGULAR SCHOOL TRAINS.
I WILL NOT COOPERATE WITH UNRULY FOLKS SUCH AS YOURSELF.

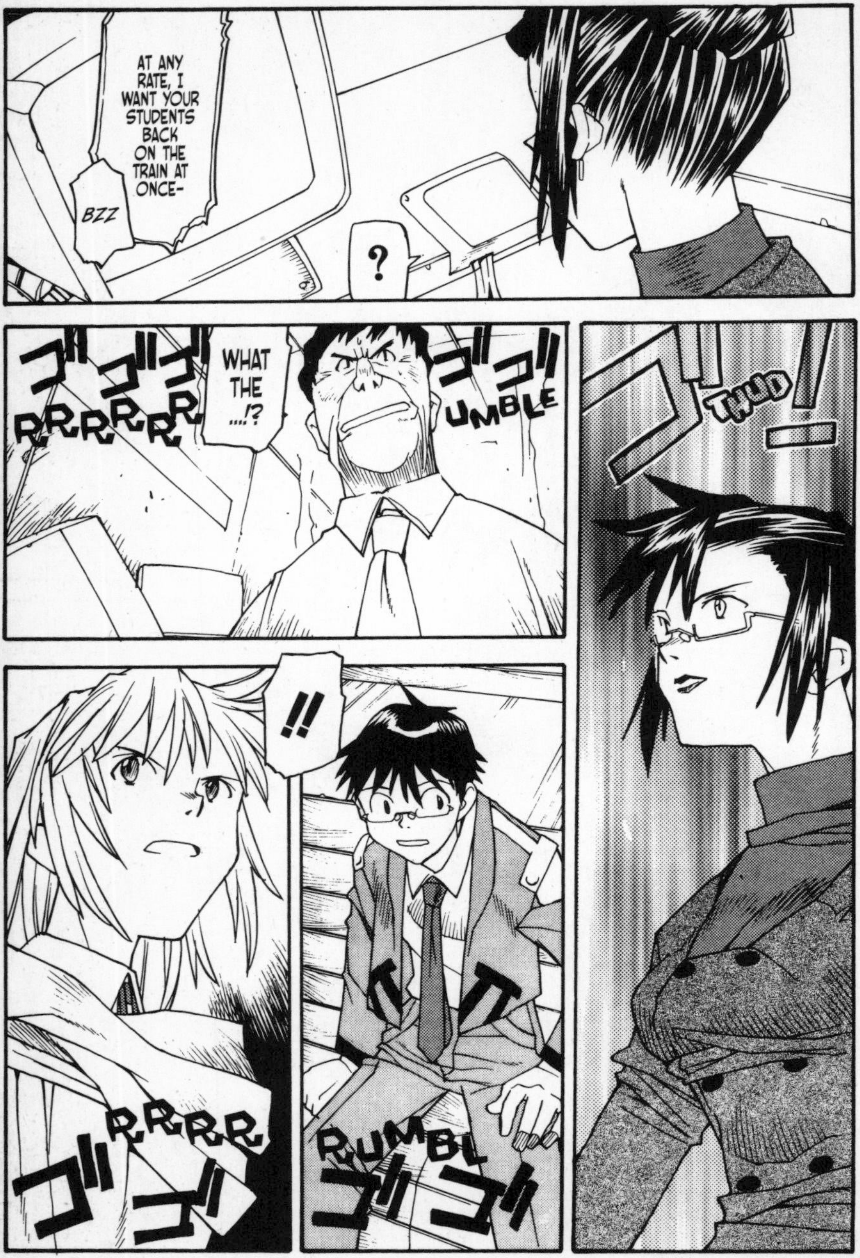
AT ANY RATE, I WANT YOUR STUDENTS BACK ON THE TRAIN AT ONCE-
BZZ
?
THUD
ゴゴ
UMBLE
WHAT THE ...!?
ゴゴゴ
RRRRRRR
!!
RUMBL
ゴゴ
RRRRR
ゴゴ

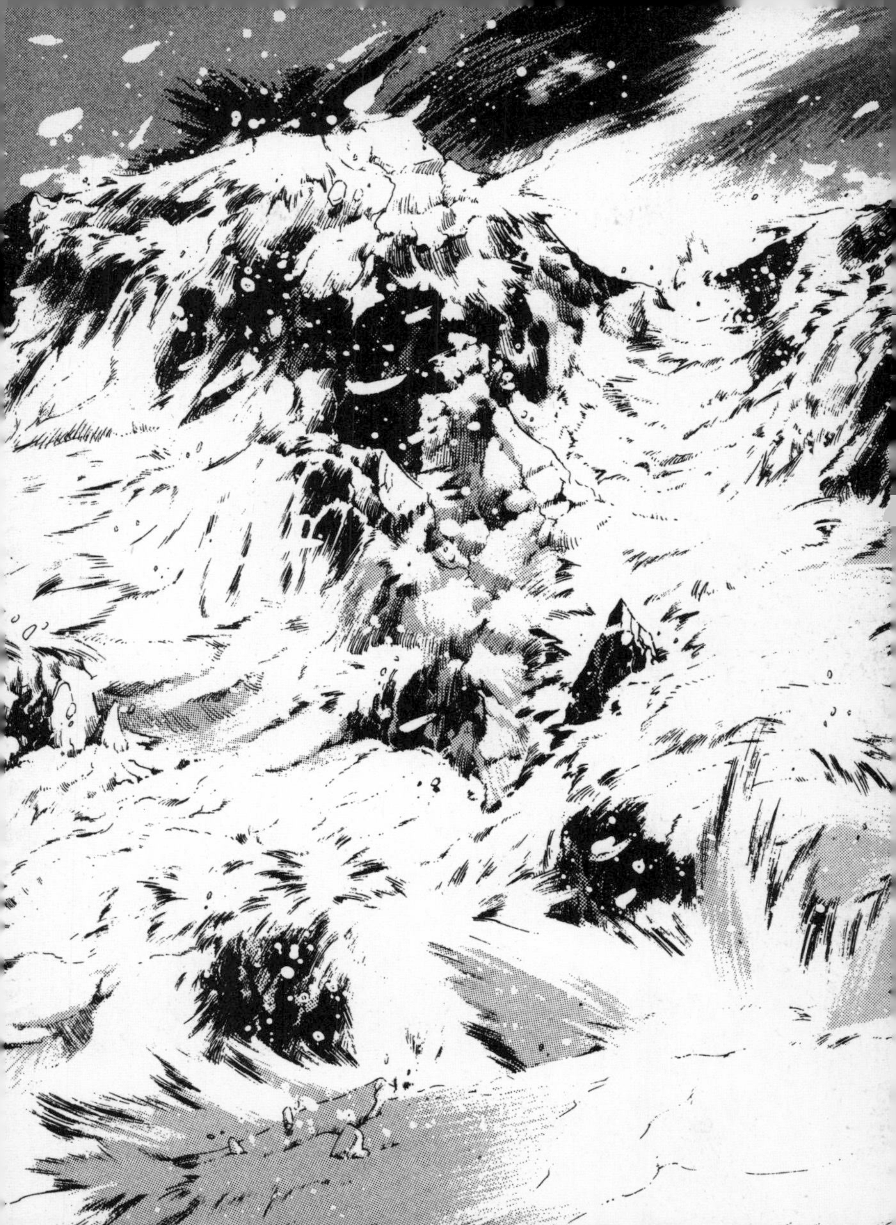

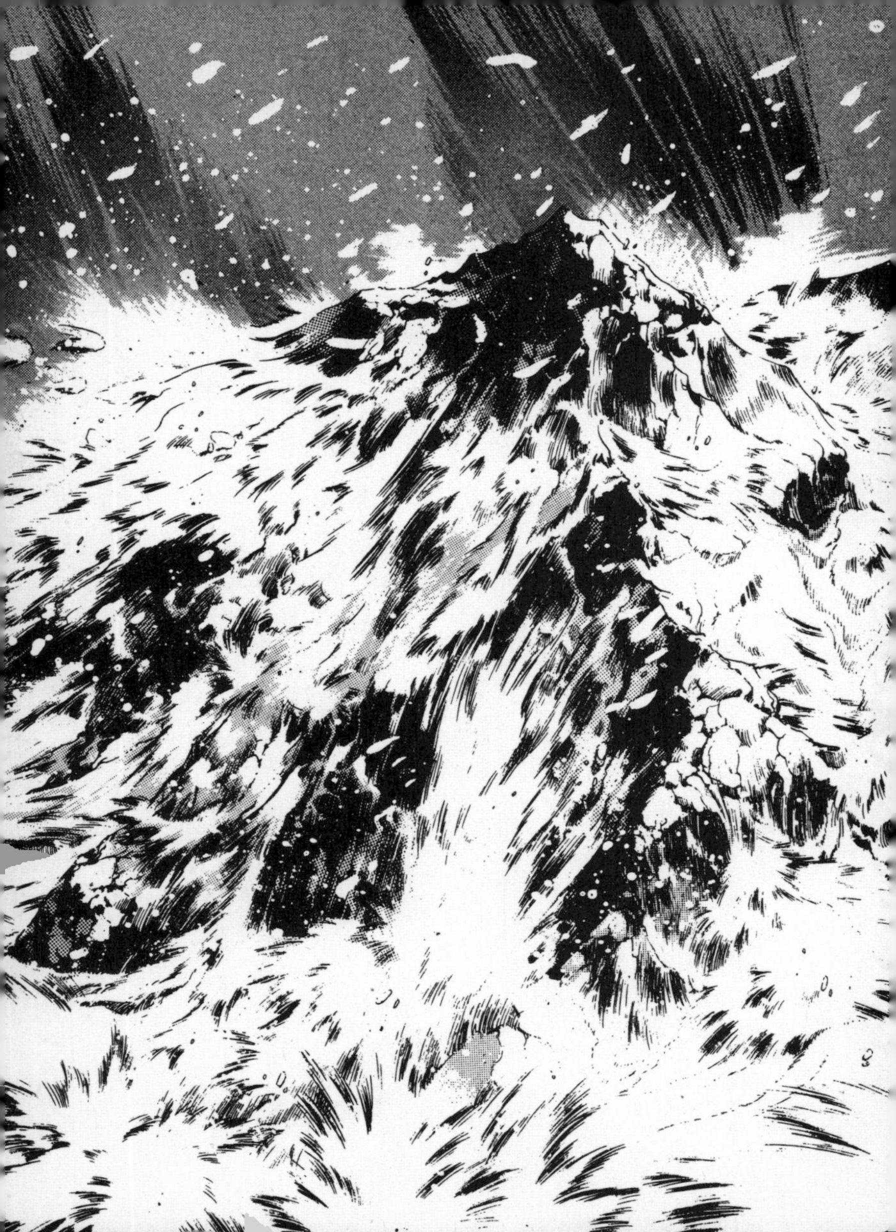

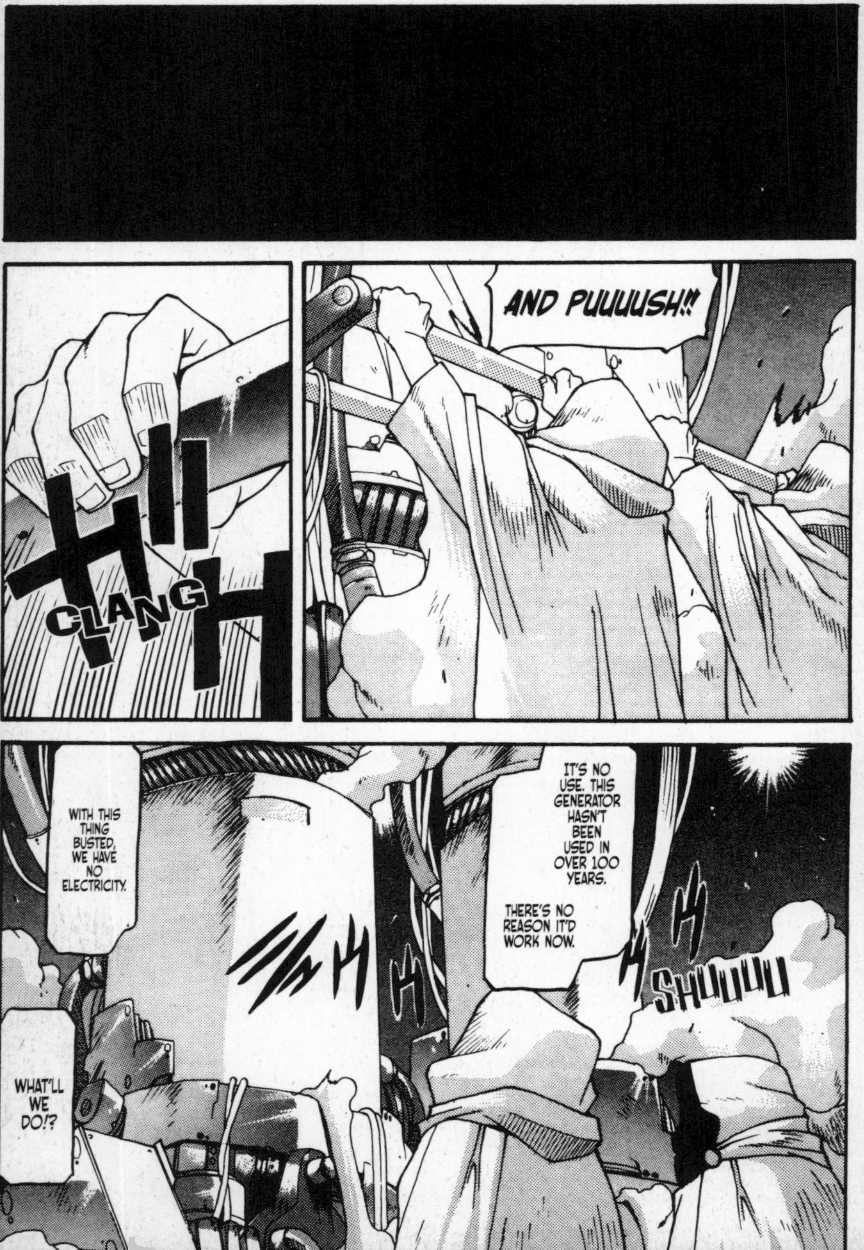
AND PUUUUSH!!
CLANG
IT'S NO USE. THIS GENERATOR HASN'T BEEN USED IN OVER 100 YEARS.
THERE'S NO REASON IT'D WORK NOW.
SHUUUU
WITH THIS THING BUSTED, WE HAVE NO ELECTRICITY.
WHAT'LL WE DO!?

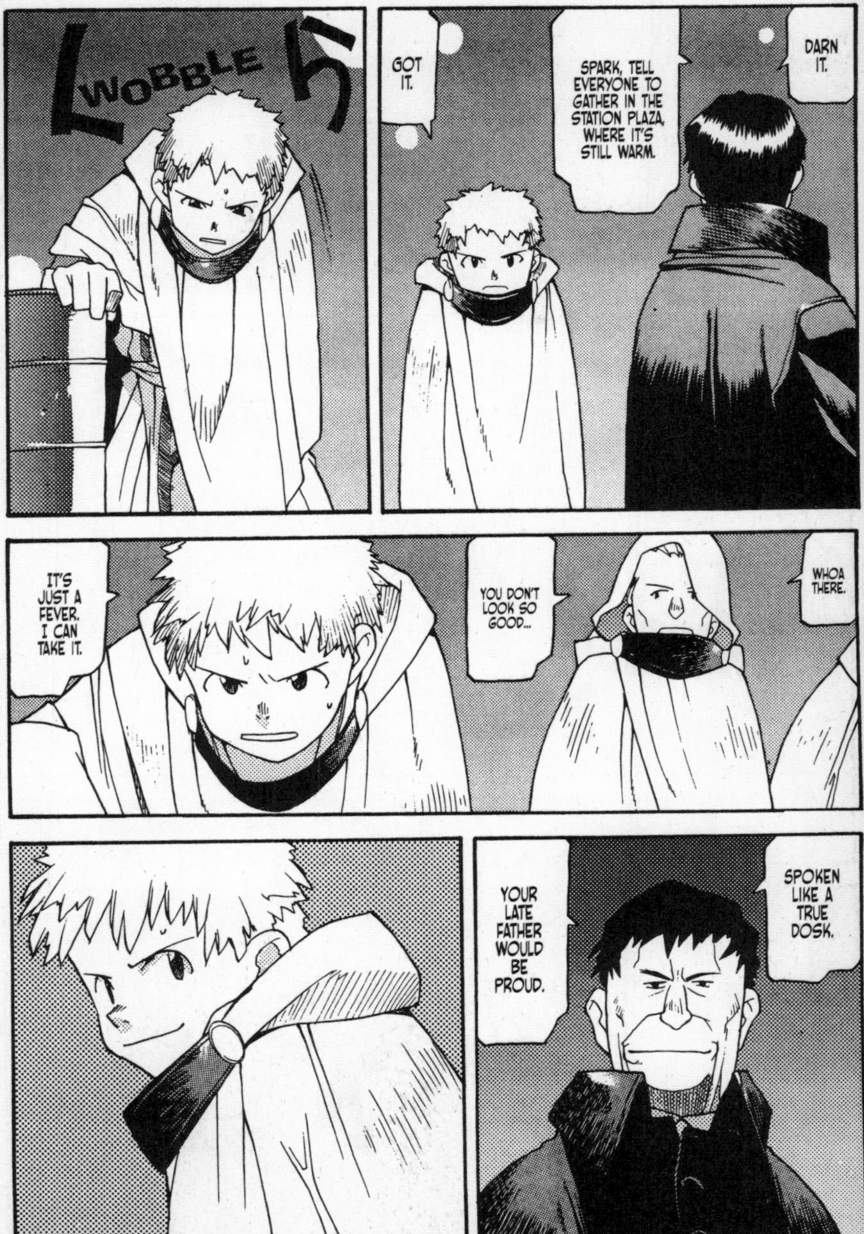
DARN IT.
SPARK, TELL EVERYONE TO GATHER IN THE STATION PLAZA, WHERE IT'S STILL WARM.
GOT IT.
WOBBLE
WHOA THERE.
YOU DON'T LOOK SO GOOD...
IT'S JUST A FEVER. I CAN TAKE IT.
SPOKEN LIKE A TRUE DOSK.
YOUR LATE FATHER WOULD BE PROUD.

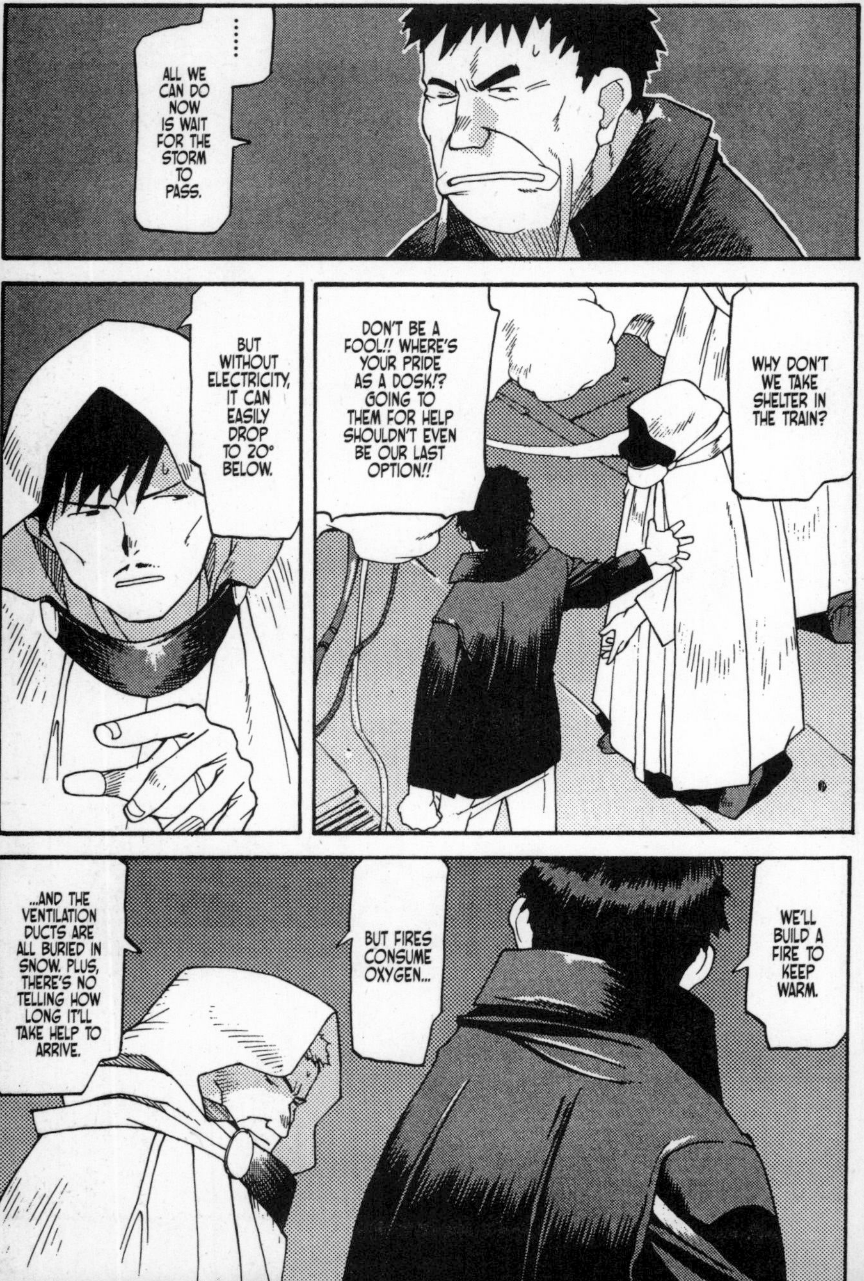
......
ALL WE CAN DO NOW IS WAIT FOR THE STORM TO PASS.
WHY DON'T WE TAKE SHELTER IN THE TRAIN?
DON'T BE A FOOL!! WHERE'S YOUR PRIDE AS A DOSK!? GOING TO THEM FOR HELP SHOULDN'T EVEN BE OUR LAST OPTION!!
BUT WITHOUT ELECTRICITY, IT CAN EASILY DROP TO 20° BELOW.
WE'LL BUILD A FIRE TO KEEP WARM.
BUT FIRES CONSUME OXYGEN...
...AND THE VENTILATION DUCTS ARE ALL BURIED IN SNOW. PLUS, THERE'S NO TELLING HOW LONG IT'LL TAKE HELP TO ARRIVE.

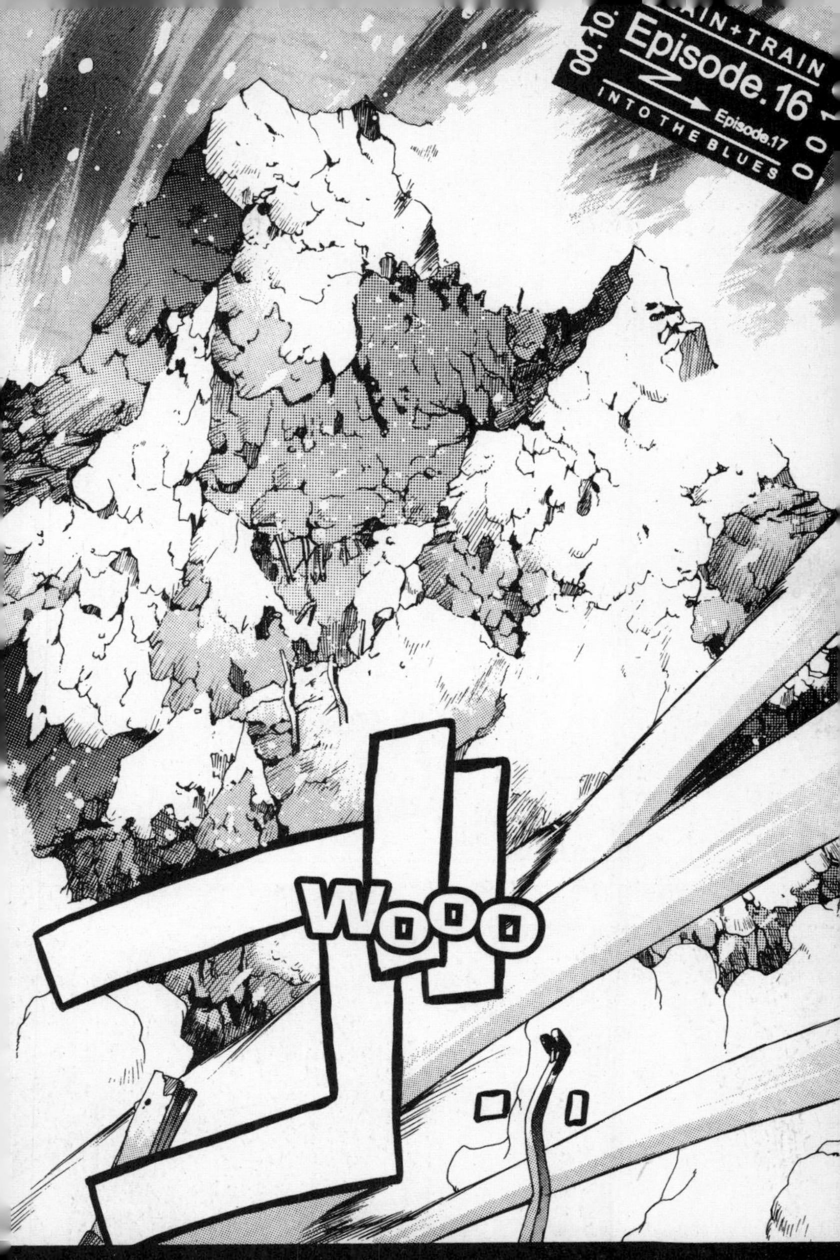
AIN+TRAIN
00:10:
Episode.16
Episode.17
INTO THE BLUES
001
Wooo

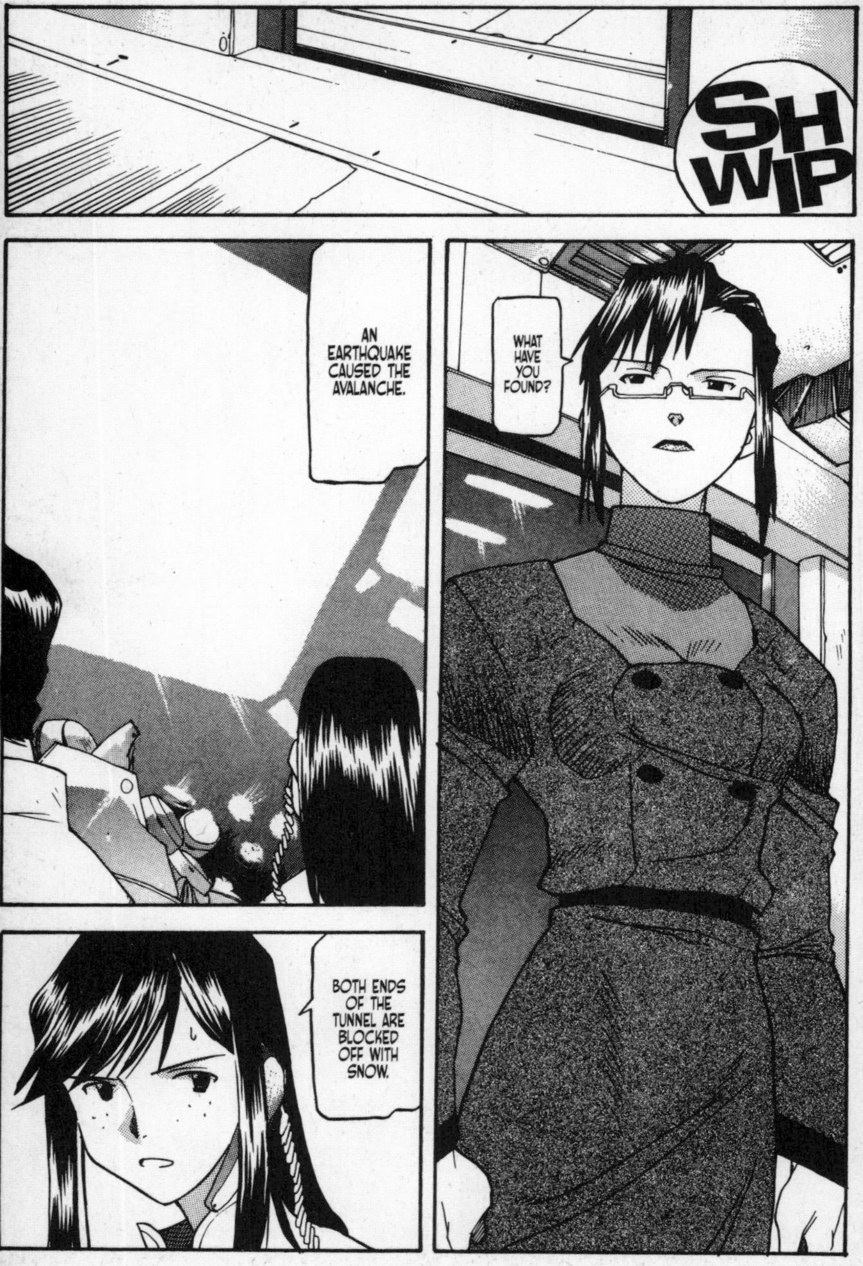
SH WIP
WHAT HAVE YOU FOUND?
AN EARTHQUAKE CAUSED THE AVALANCHE.
BOTH ENDS OF THE TUNNEL ARE BLOCKED OFF WITH SNOW.

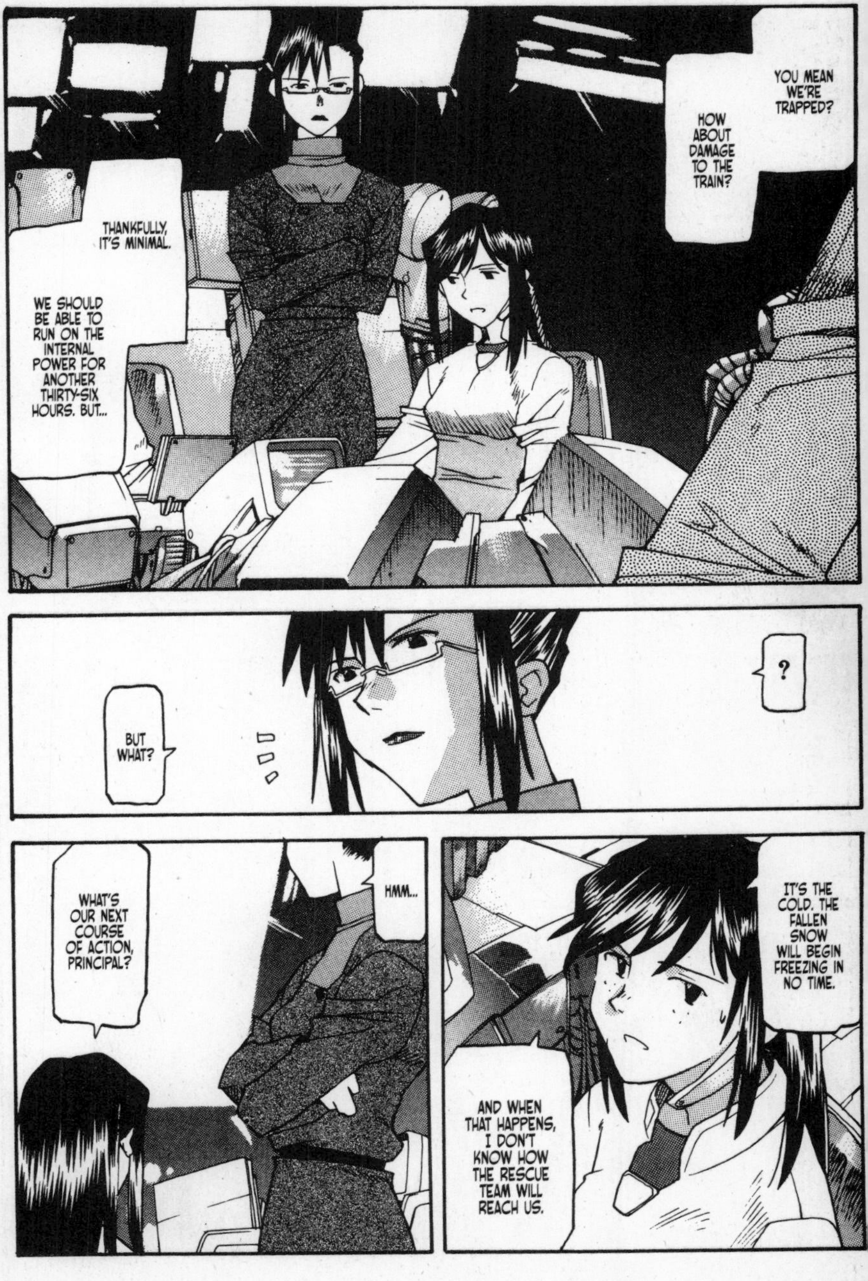
YOU MEAN WE'RE TRAPPED?
HOW ABOUT DAMAGE TO THE TRAIN?
THANKFULLY, IT'S MINIMAL.
WE SHOULD BE ABLE TO RUN ON THE INTERNAL POWER FOR ANOTHER THIRTY-SIX HOURS. BUT...
?
BUT WHAT?
IT'S THE COLD. THE FALLEN SNOW WILL BEGIN FREEZING IN NO TIME.
AND WHEN THAT HAPPENS, I DON'T KNOW HOW THE RESCUE TEAM WILL REACH US.
HMM...
WHAT'S OUR NEXT COURSE OF ACTION, PRINCIPAL?

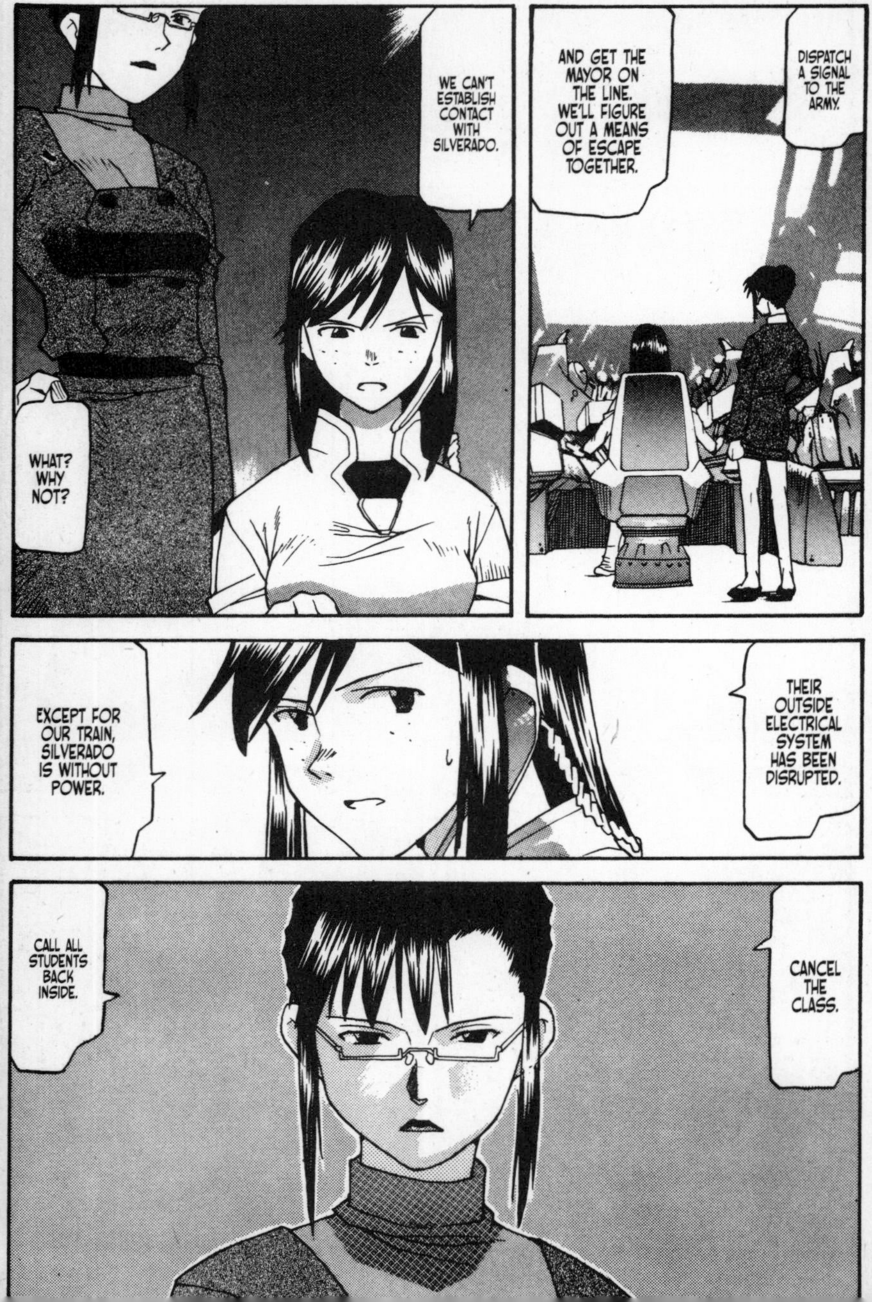
DISPATCH A SIGNAL TO THE ARMY.
AND GET THE MAYOR ON THE LINE. WE'LL FIGURE OUT A MEANS OF ESCAPE TOGETHER.
WE CAN'T ESTABLISH CONTACT WITH SILVERADO.
WHAT? WHY NOT?
THEIR OUTSIDE ELECTRICAL SYSTEM HAS BEEN DISRUPTED.
EXCEPT FOR OUR TRAIN, SILVERADO IS WITHOUT POWER.
CANCEL THE CLASS.
CALL ALL STUDENTS BACK INSIDE.

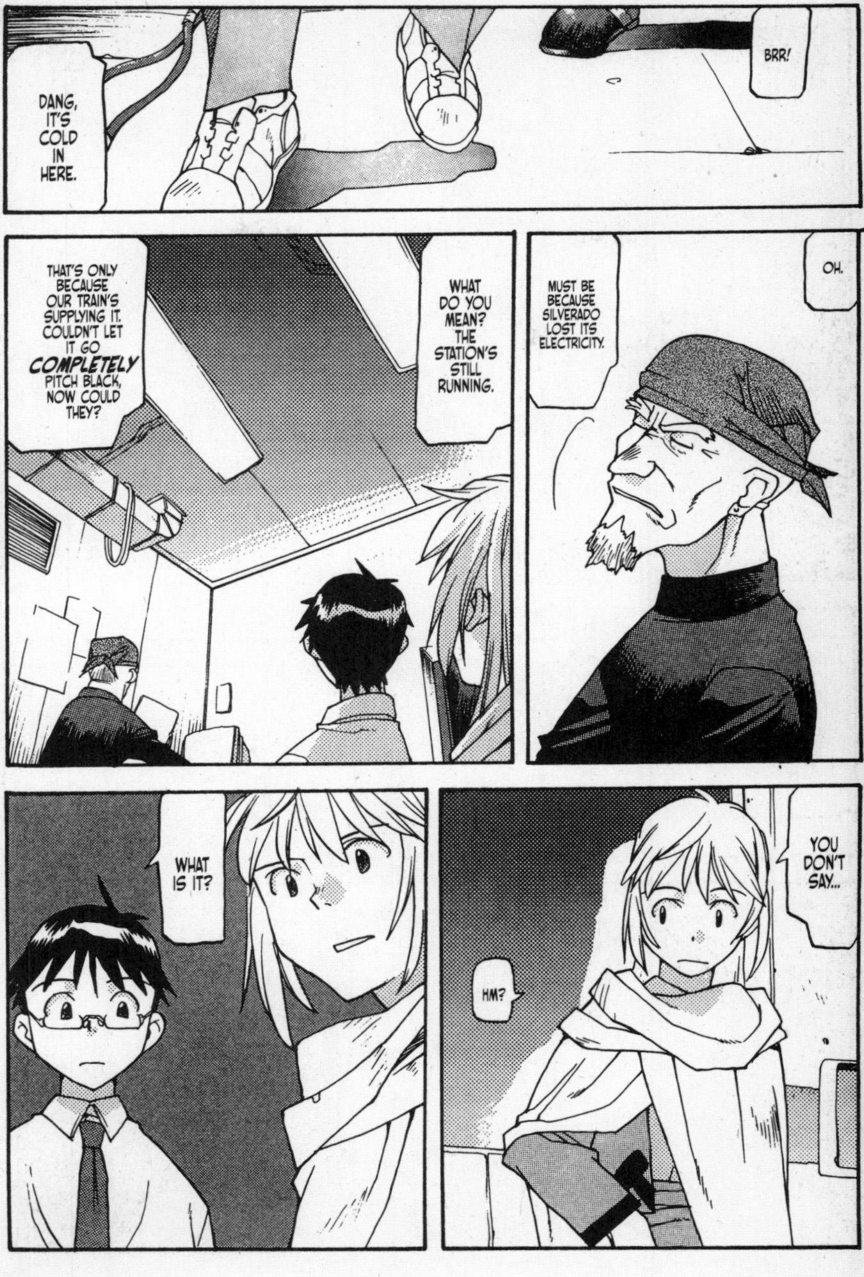
BRR!
DANG, IT'S COLD IN HERE.
OH.
MUST BE BECAUSE SILVERADO LOST ITS ELECTRICITY.
WHAT DO YOU MEAN? THE STATION'S STILL RUNNING.
THAT'S ONLY BECAUSE OUR TRAIN'S SUPPLYING IT. COULDN'T LET IT GO *COMPLETELY* PITCH BLACK, NOW COULD THEY?
YOU DON'T SAY...
HM?
WHAT IS IT?

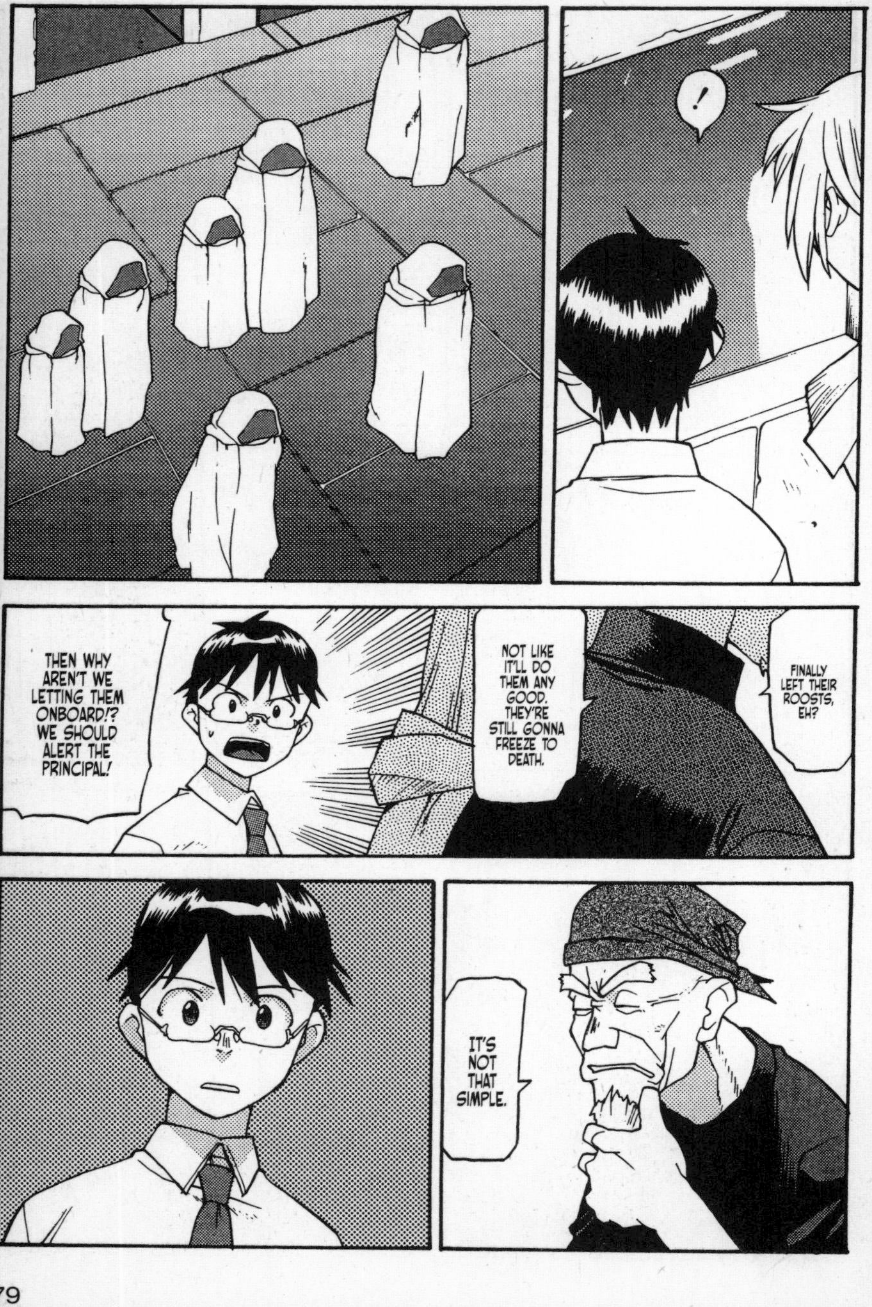
!
FINALLY LEFT THEIR ROOSTS, EH?
NOT LIKE IT'LL DO THEM ANY GOOD. THEY'RE STILL GONNA FREEZE TO DEATH.
THEN WHY AREN'T WE LETTING THEM ONBOARD!? WE SHOULD ALERT THE PRINCIPAL!
IT'S NOT THAT SIMPLE.

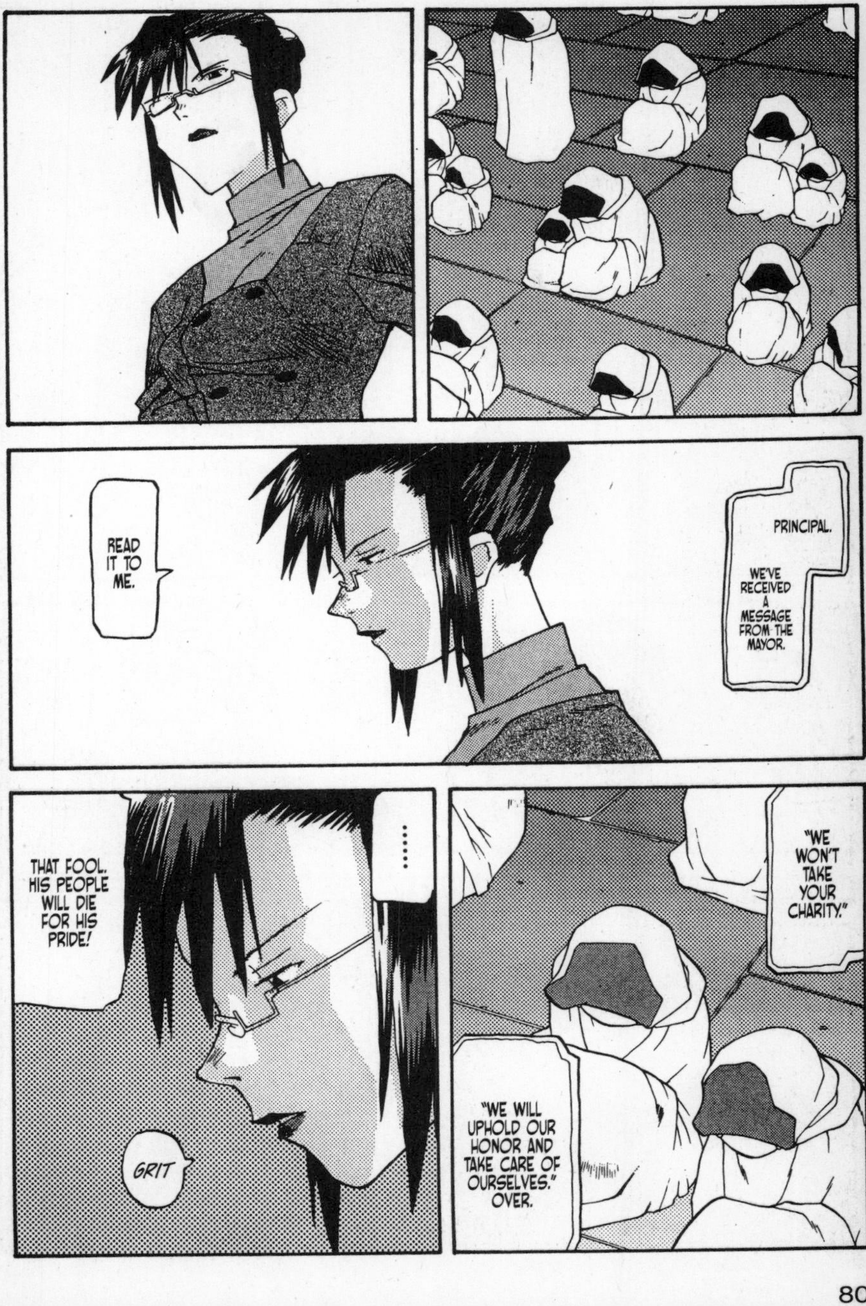
PRINCIPAL.
WE'VE RECEIVED A MESSAGE FROM THE MAYOR.
READ IT TO ME.
"WE WON'T TAKE YOUR CHARITY."
"WE WILL UPHOLD OUR HONOR AND TAKE CARE OF OURSELVES." OVER.
......
THAT FOOL. HIS PEOPLE WILL DIE FOR HIS PRIDE!
GRIT

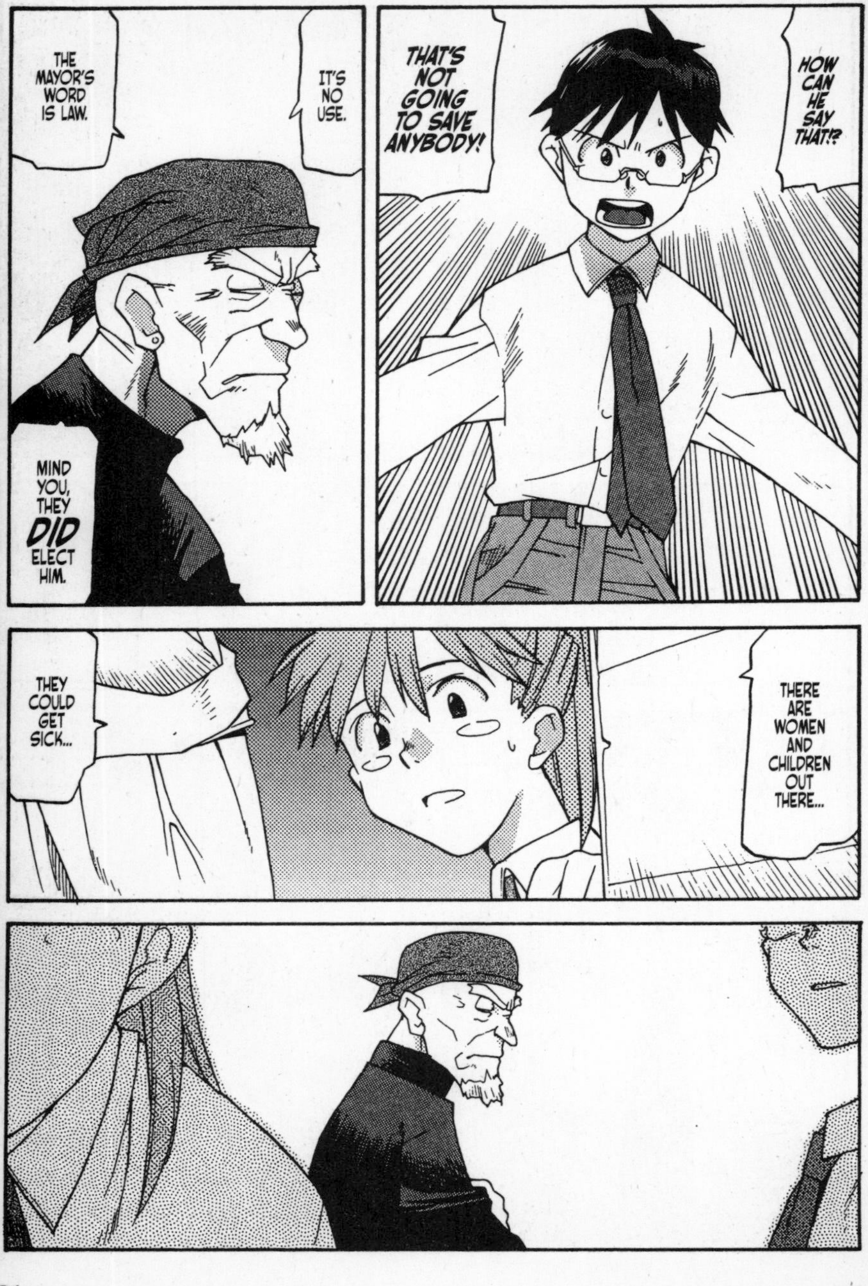
HOW CAN HE SAY THAT!?
THAT'S NOT GOING TO SAVE ANYBODY!
IT'S NO USE.
THE MAYOR'S WORD IS LAW.
MIND YOU, THEY DID ELECT HIM.
THERE ARE WOMEN AND CHILDREN OUT THERE...
THEY COULD GET SICK...

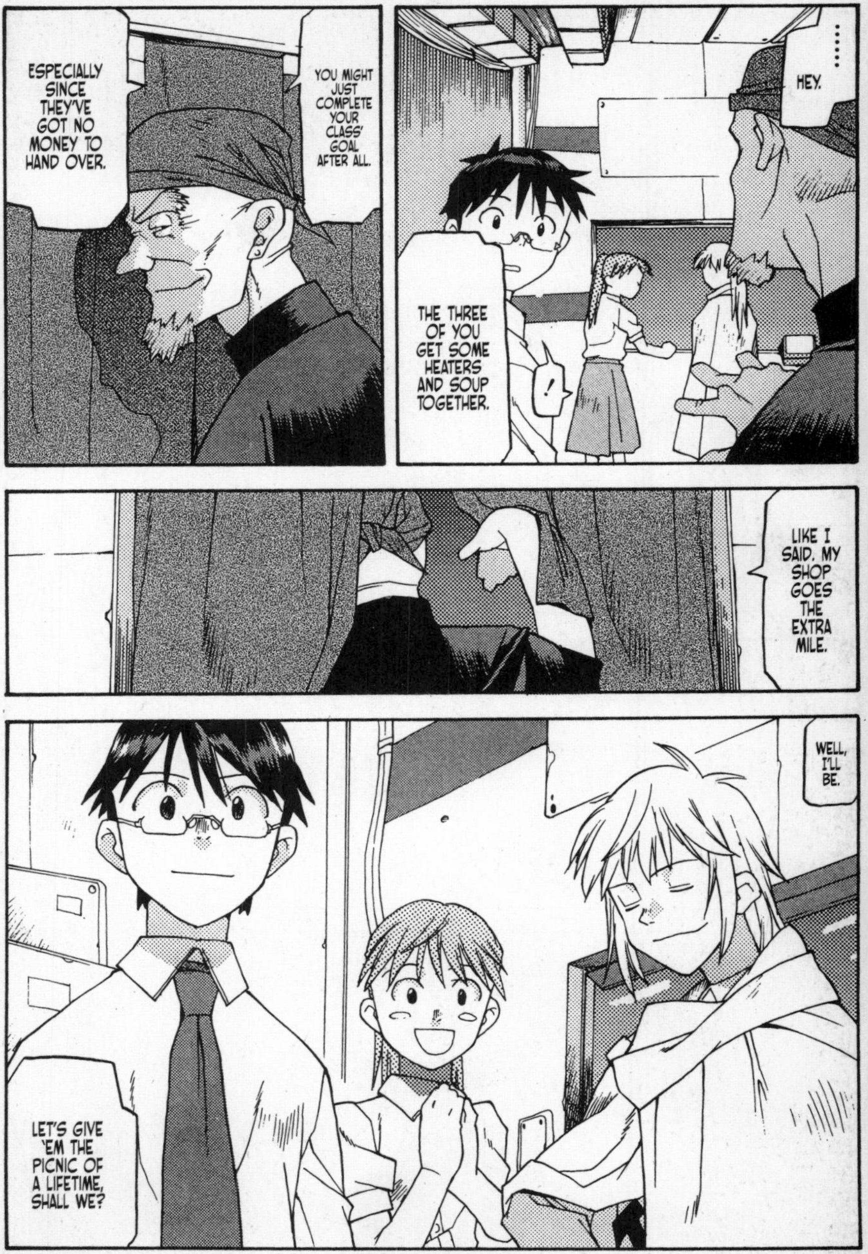
......
HEY.
THE THREE OF YOU GET SOME HEATERS AND SOUP TOGETHER.
!
YOU MIGHT JUST COMPLETE YOUR CLASS' GOAL AFTER ALL.
ESPECIALLY SINCE THEY'VE GOT NO MONEY TO HAND OVER.
LIKE I SAID. MY SHOP GOES THE EXTRA MILE.
WELL, I'LL BE.
LET'S GIVE 'EM THE PICNIC OF A LIFETIME, SHALL WE?

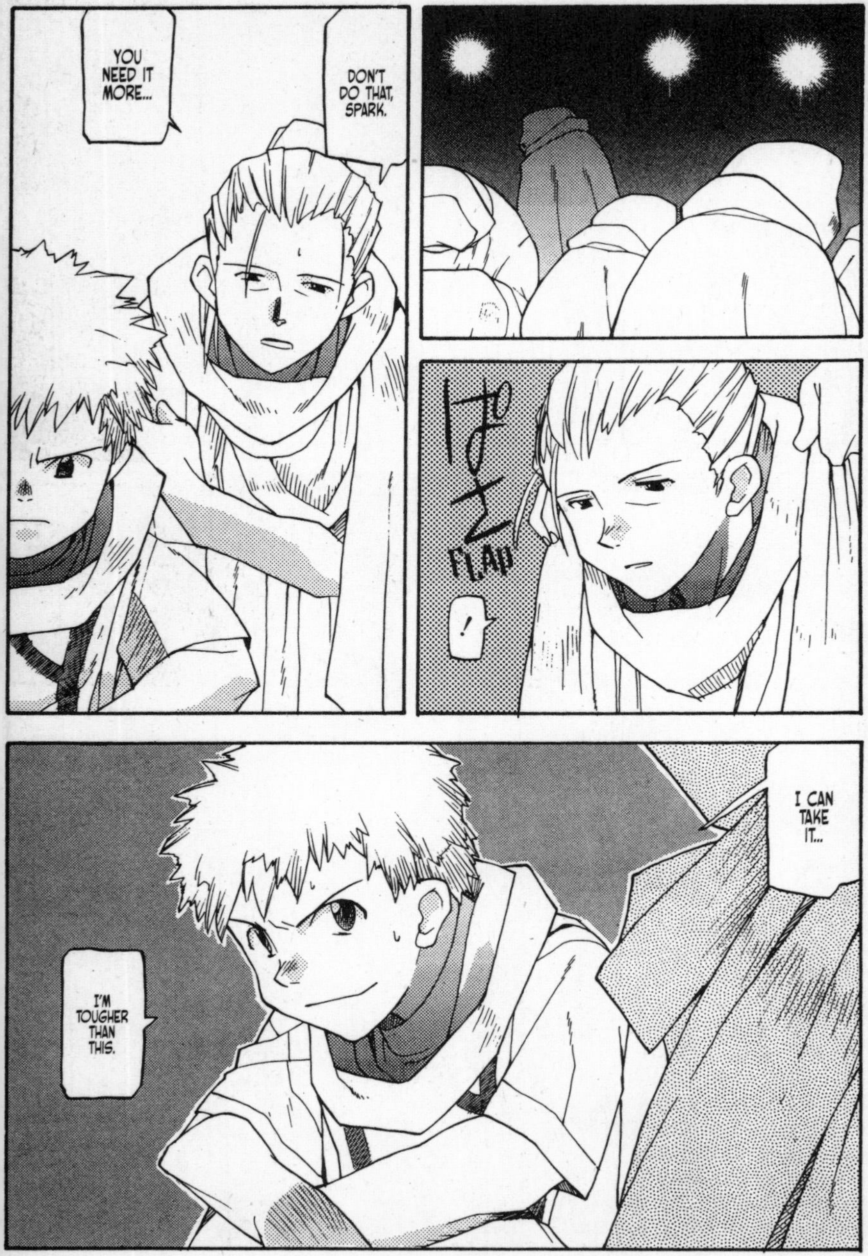
ぱさ
FLAP
!
DON'T DO THAT, SPARK.
YOU NEED IT MORE...
I CAN TAKE IT...
I'M TOUGHER THAN THIS.

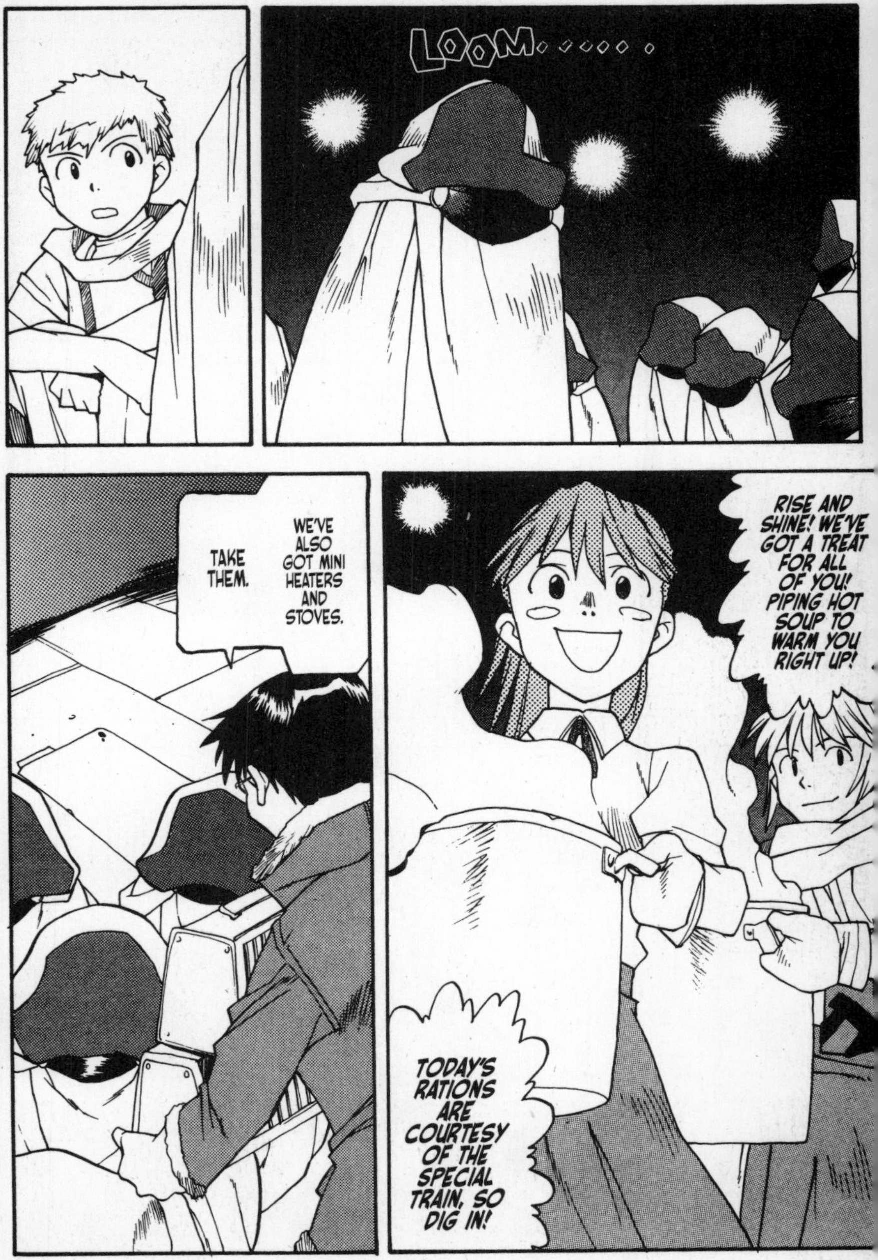
LOOM.......
RISE AND SHINE! WE'VE GOT A TREAT FOR ALL OF YOU! PIPING HOT SOUP TO WARM YOU RIGHT UP!
TODAY'S RATIONS ARE COURTESY OF THE SPECIAL TRAIN, SO DIG IN!
WE'VE ALSO GOT MINI HEATERS AND STOVES.
TAKE THEM.

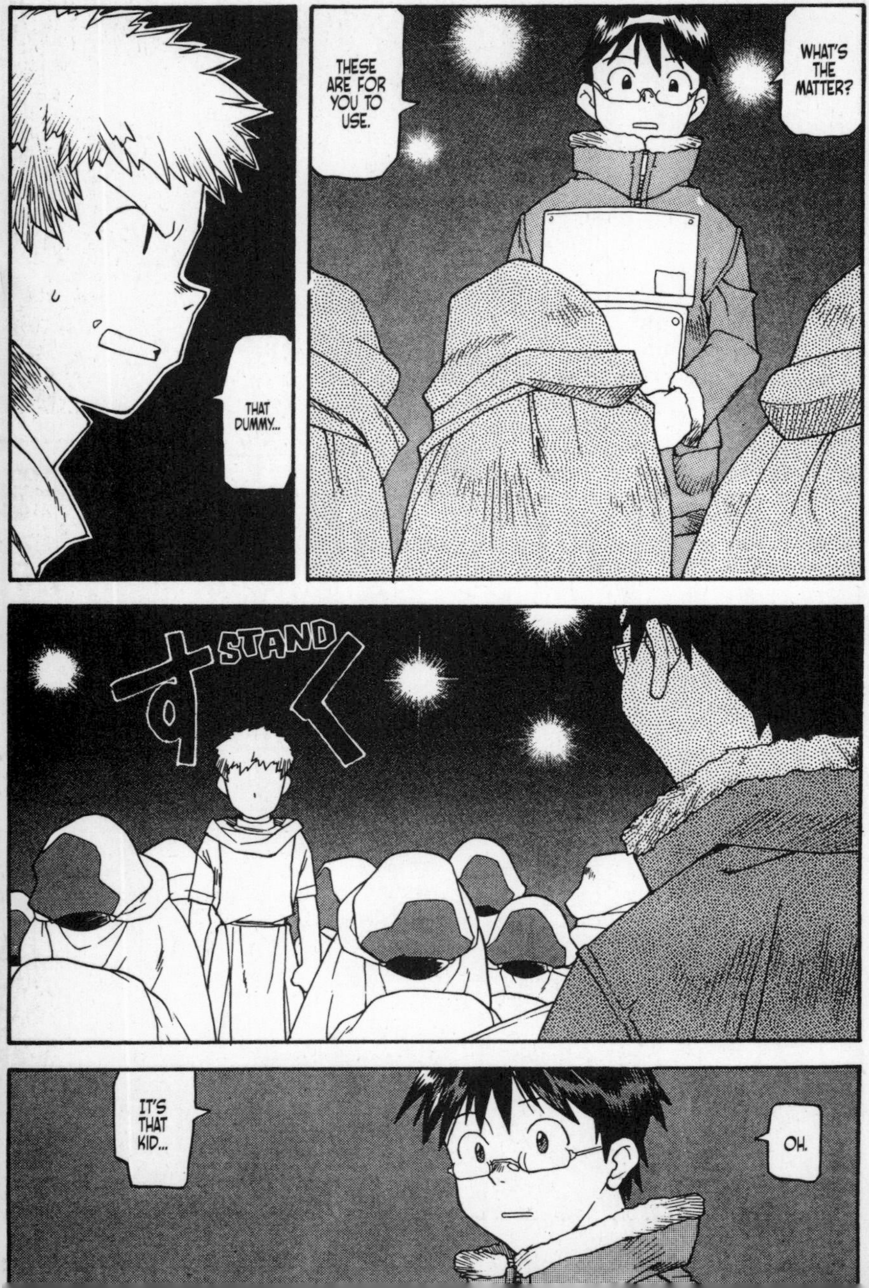

WHAT'S THE MATTER?
THESE ARE FOR YOU TO USE.
THAT DUMMY...
すく
STAND
OH.
IT'S THAT KID...

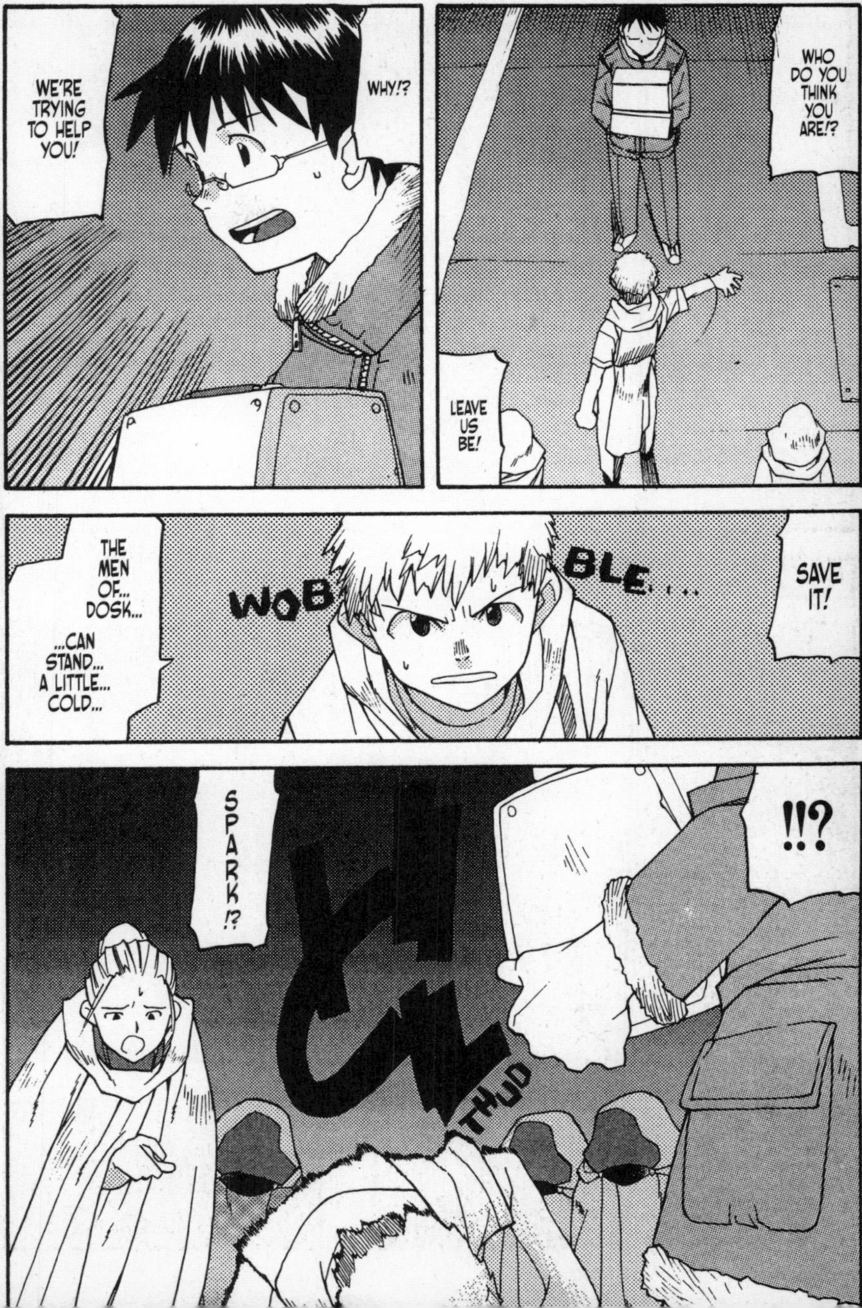
WHO DO YOU THINK YOU ARE!?
LEAVE US BE!
WHY!?
WE'RE TRYING TO HELP YOU!
SAVE IT!
WOBBLE...
THE MEN OF... DOSK...
...CAN STAND... A LITTLE... COLD...
!!?
SPARK!?
THUD

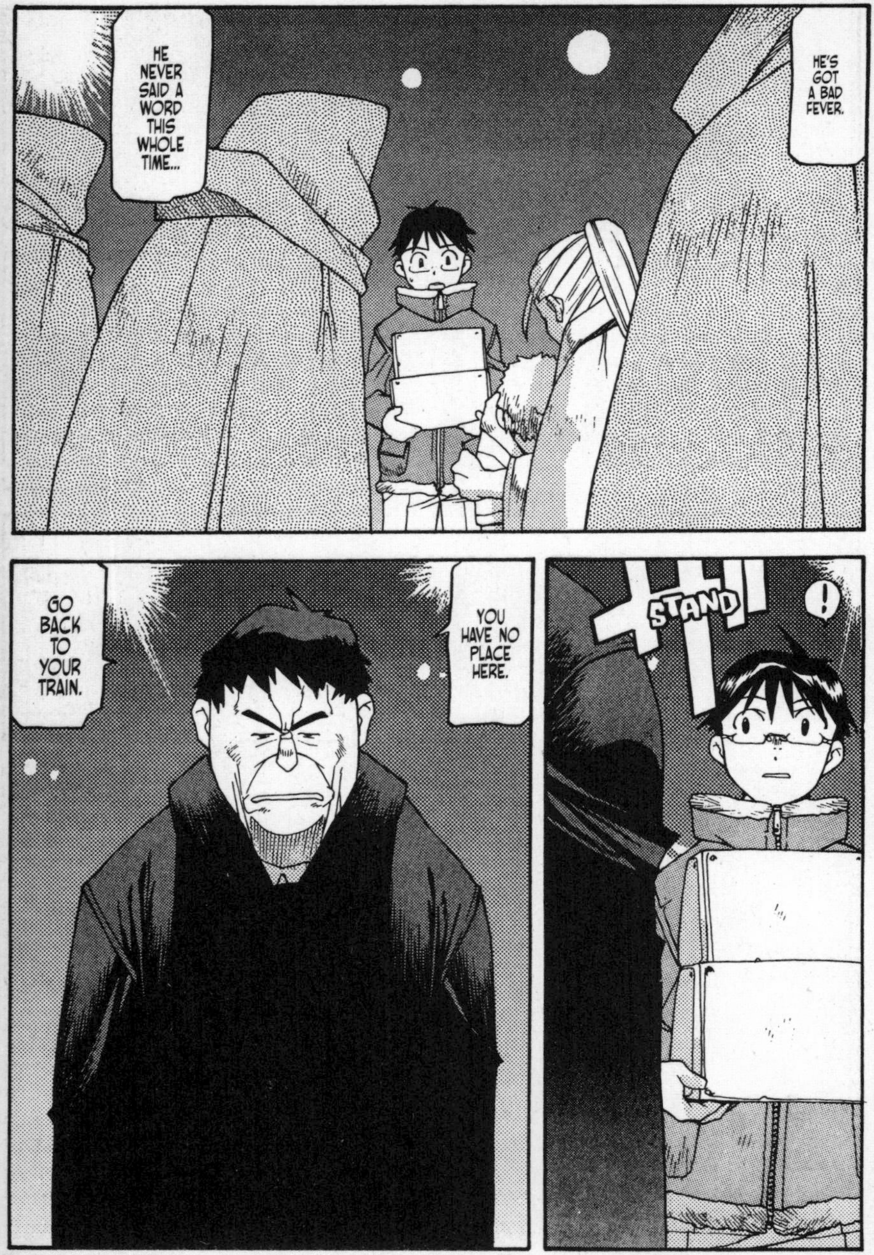
HE'S GOT A BAD FEVER.
HE NEVER SAID A WORD THIS WHOLE TIME...
STAND
!
YOU HAVE NO PLACE HERE.
GO BACK TO YOUR TRAIN.

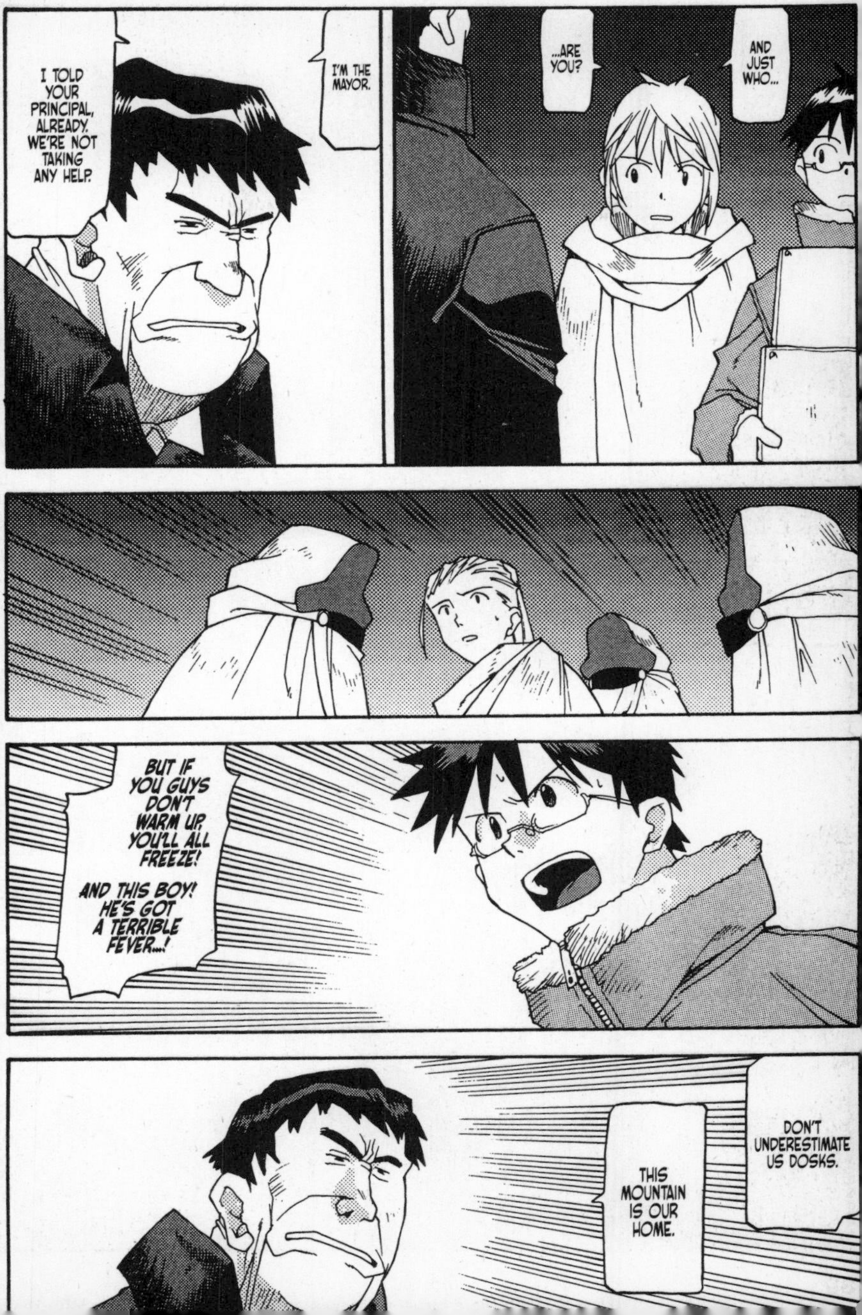
AND JUST WHO...
...ARE YOU?
I'M THE MAYOR.
I TOLD YOUR PRINCIPAL, ALREADY. WE'RE NOT TAKING ANY HELP.
BUT IF YOU GUYS DON'T WARM UP, YOU'LL ALL FREEZE!
AND THIS BOY! HE'S GOT A TERRIBLE FEVER...!
DON'T UNDERESTIMATE US DOSKS.
THIS MOUNTAIN IS OUR HOME.

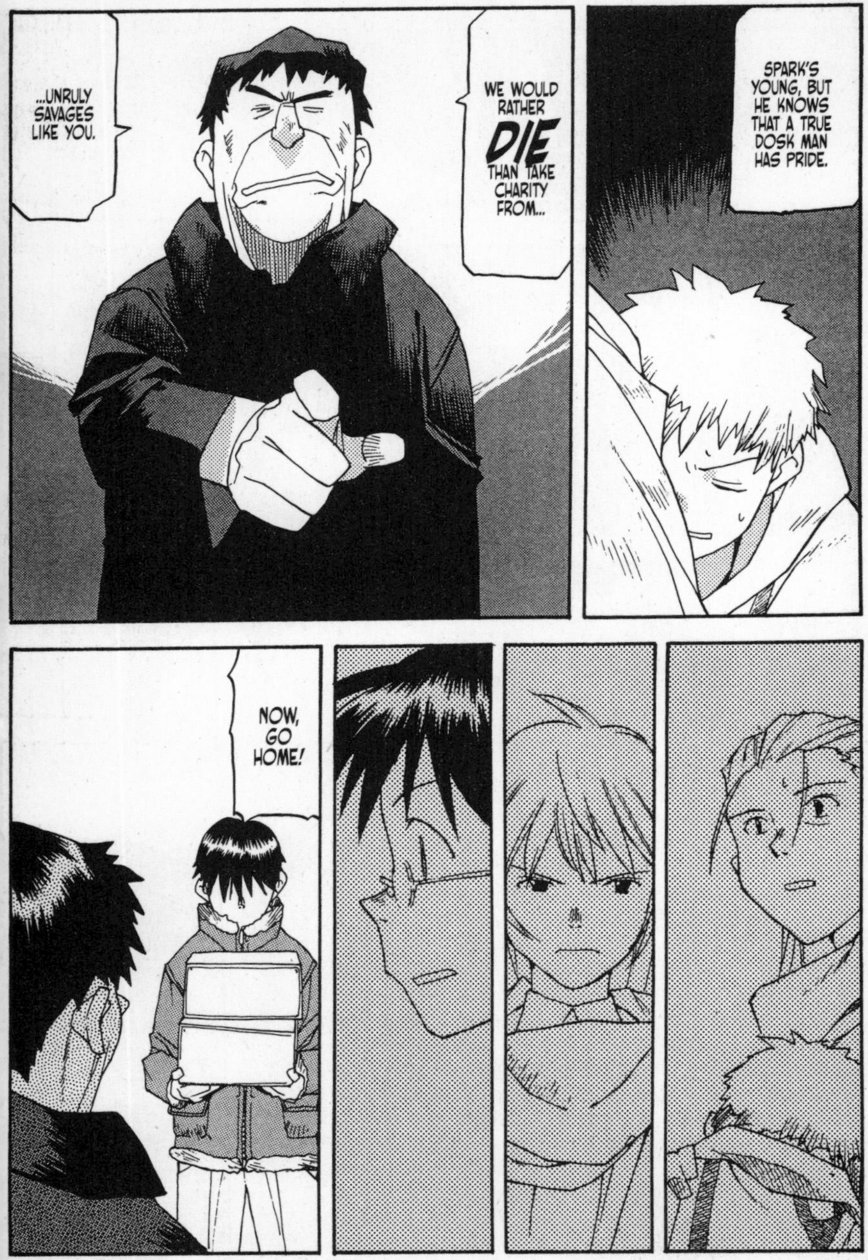
SPARK'S YOUNG, BUT HE KNOWS THAT A TRUE DOSK MAN HAS PRIDE.
WE WOULD RATHER DIE THAN TAKE CHARITY FROM...
...UNRULY SAVAGES LIKE YOU.
NOW, GO HOME!

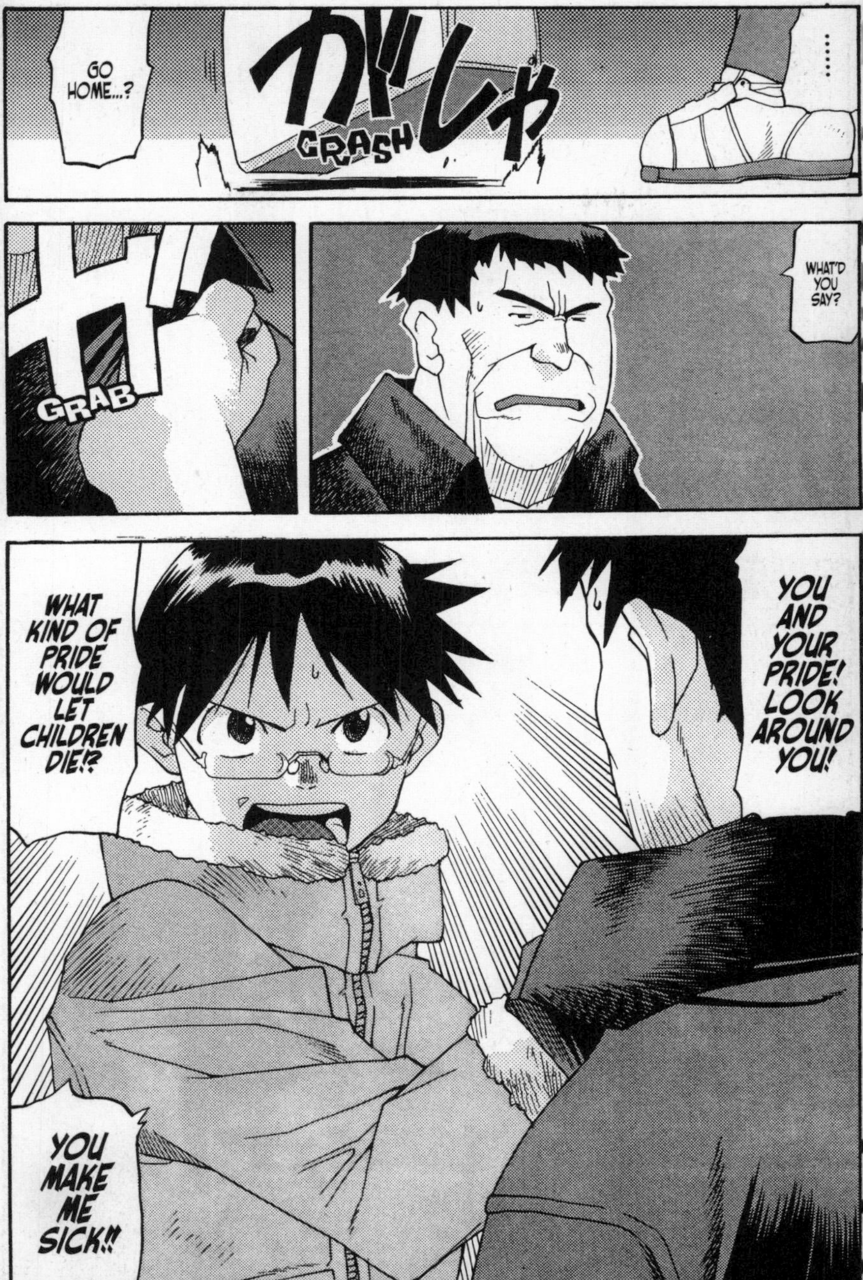
……
CRASH
GO HOME...?
WHAT'D YOU SAY?
GRAB
YOU AND YOUR PRIDE! LOOK AROUND YOU!
WHAT KIND OF PRIDE WOULD LET CHILDREN DIE!?
YOU MAKE ME SICK!!

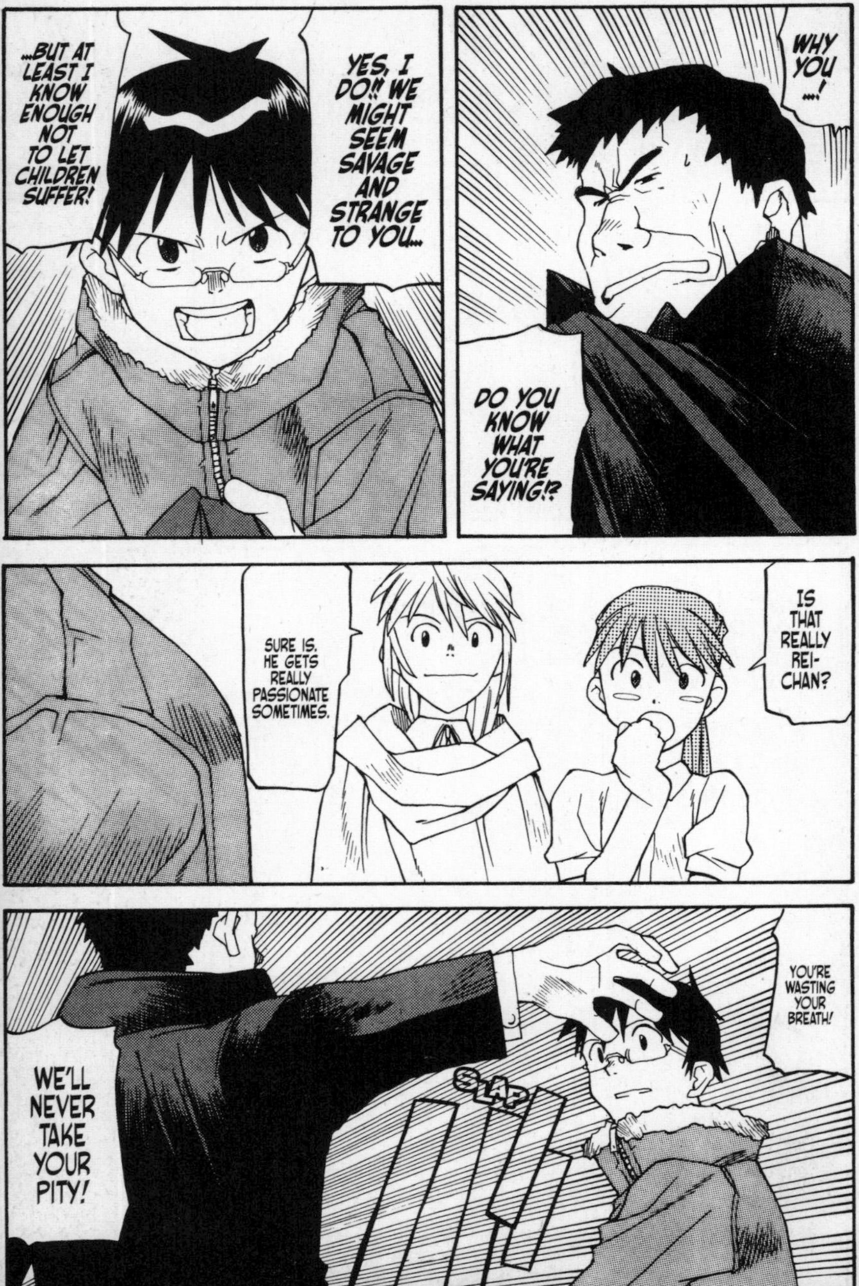
WHY YOU ...!
DO YOU KNOW WHAT YOU'RE SAYING!?
YES, I DO!! WE MIGHT SEEM SAVAGE AND STRANGE TO YOU...
...BUT AT LEAST I KNOW ENOUGH NOT TO LET CHILDREN SUFFER!
IS THAT REALLY REI-CHAN?
SURE IS. HE GETS REALLY PASSIONATE SOMETIMES.
YOU'RE WASTING YOUR BREATH!
SLAP
WE'LL NEVER TAKE YOUR PITY!

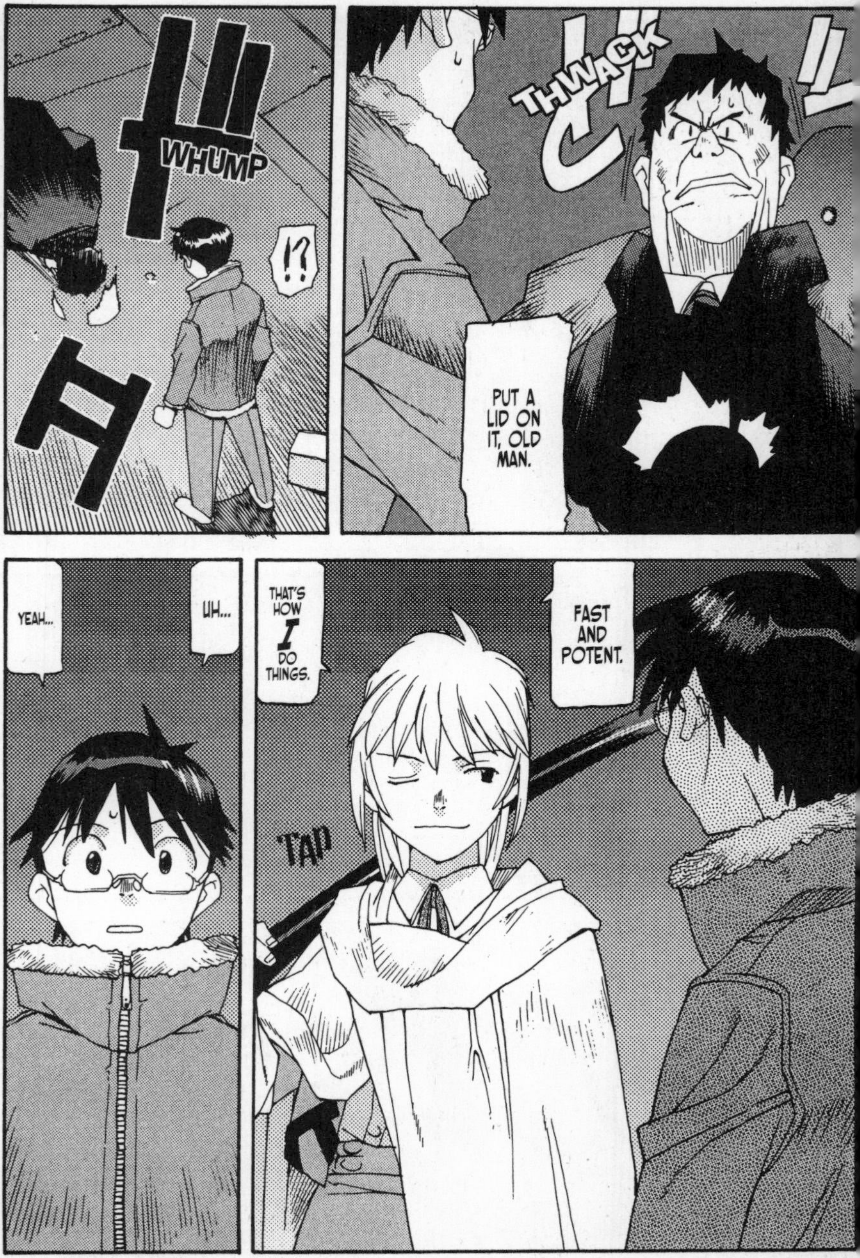
THWACK
PUT A LID ON IT, OLD MAN.
WHUMP
!?
FAST AND POTENT.
THAT'S HOW I DO THINGS.
TAP
UH...
YEAH...

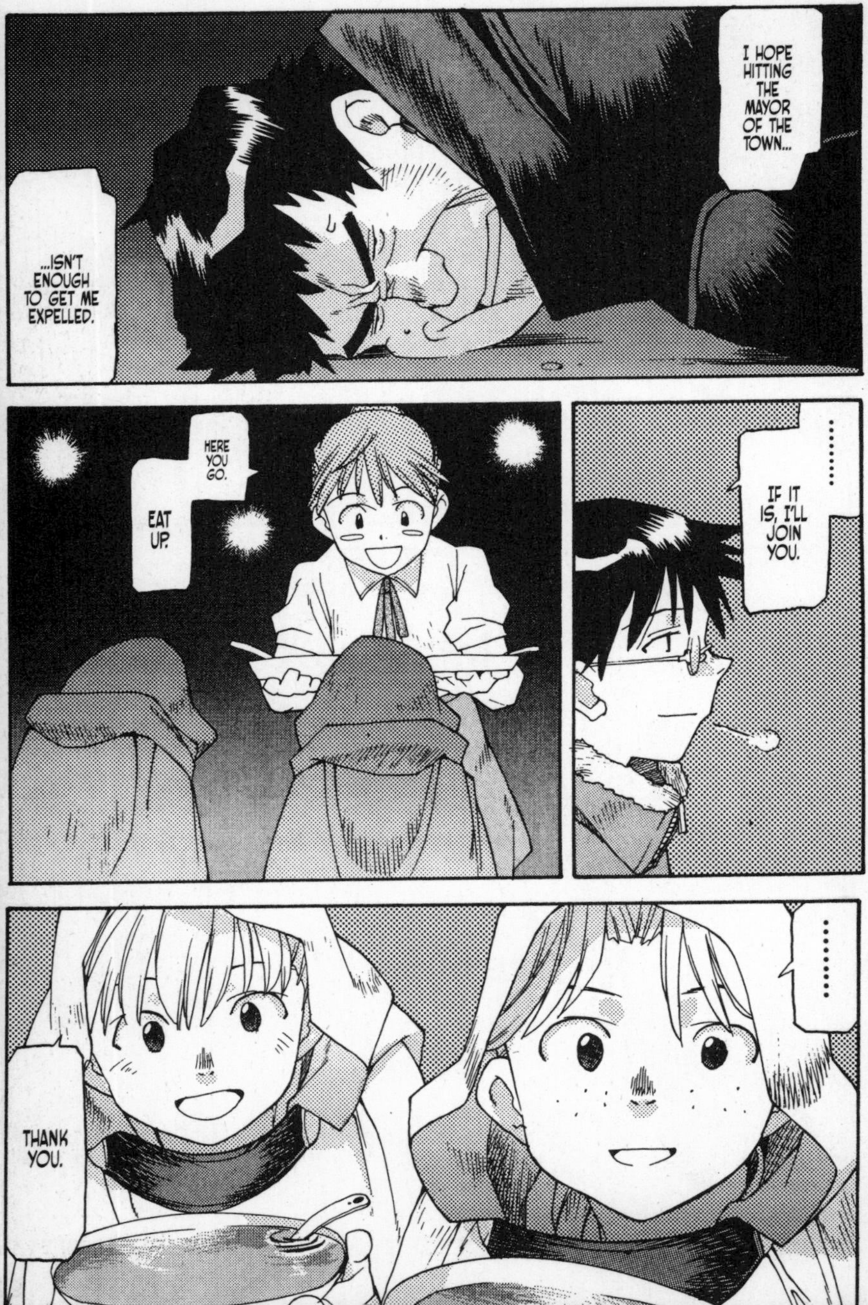

I HOPE HITTING THE MAYOR OF THE TOWN...
...ISN'T ENOUGH TO GET ME EXPELLED.
......
IF IT IS, I'LL JOIN YOU.
HERE YOU GO.
EAT UP.
......
THANK YOU.

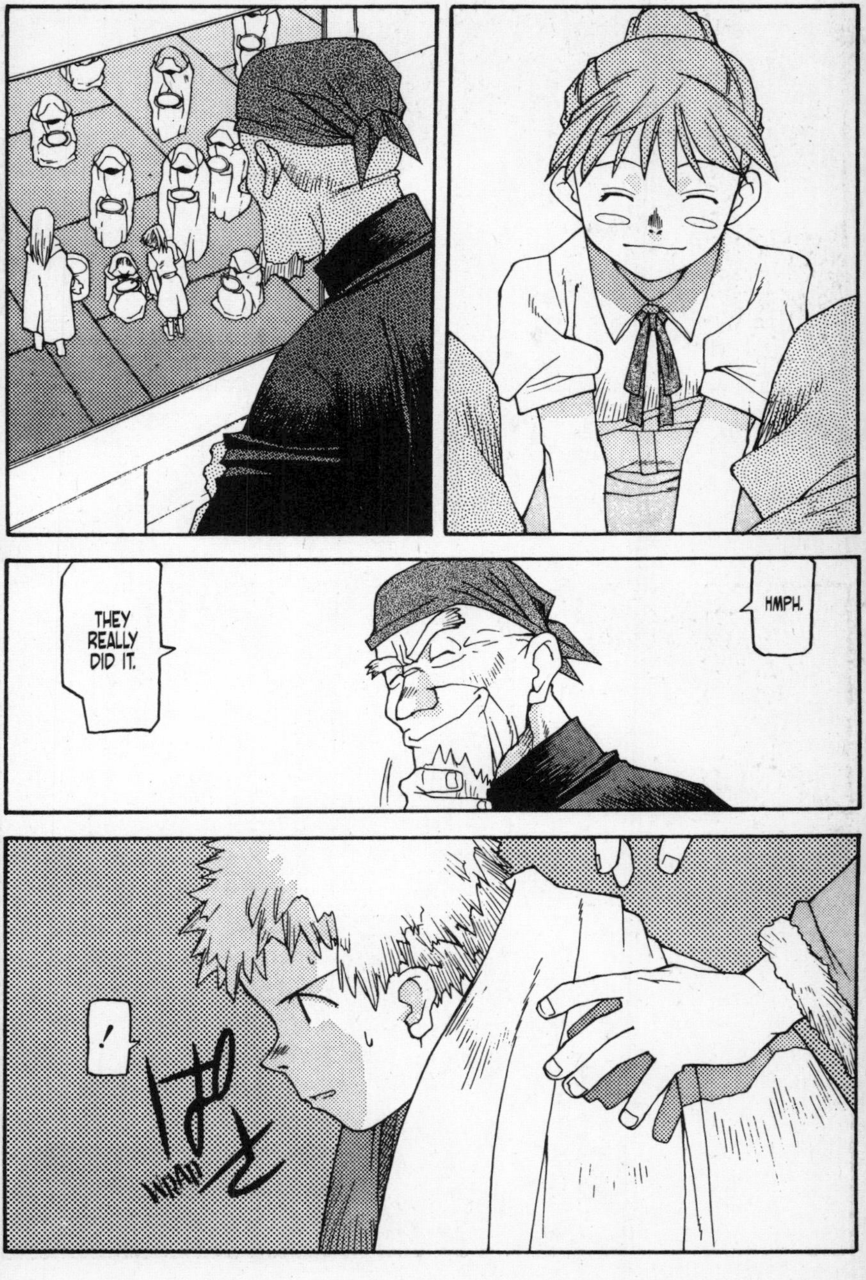
HMPH.
THEY REALLY DID IT.
!
WHAP!

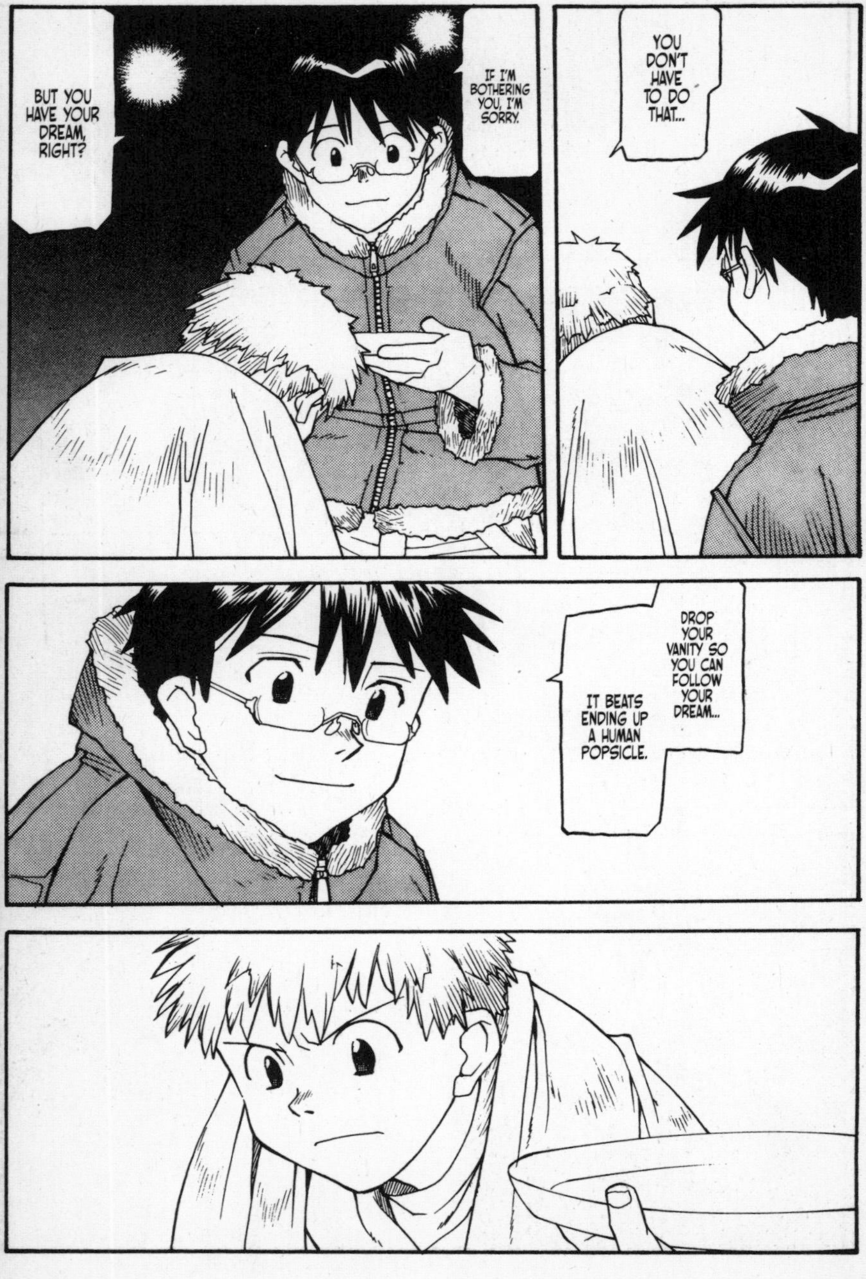
YOU DON'T HAVE TO DO THAT...
IF I'M BOTHERING YOU, I'M SORRY.
BUT YOU HAVE YOUR DREAM, RIGHT?
DROP YOUR VANITY SO YOU CAN FOLLOW YOUR DREAM...
IT BEATS ENDING UP A HUMAN POPSICLE.

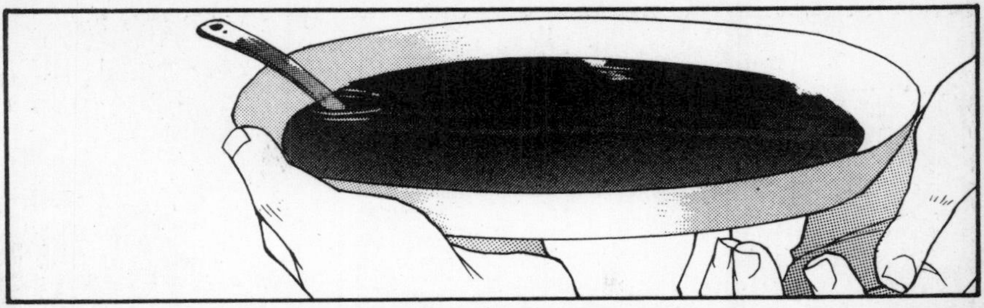

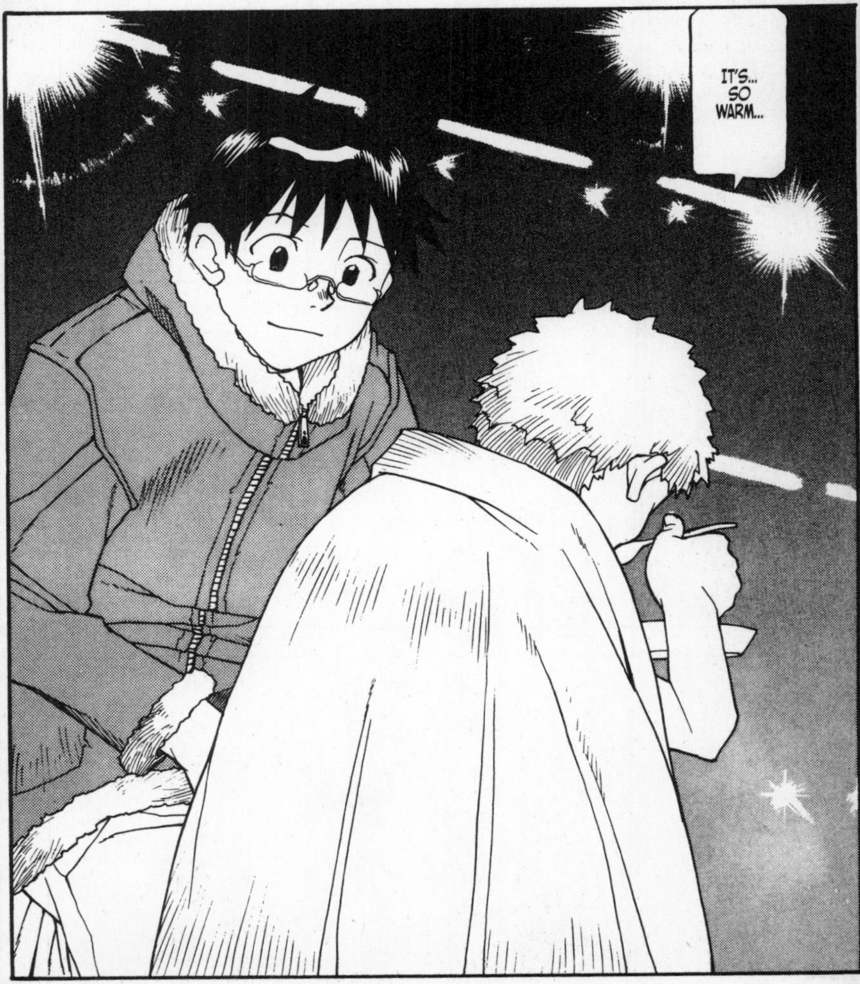
IT'S... SO WARM...

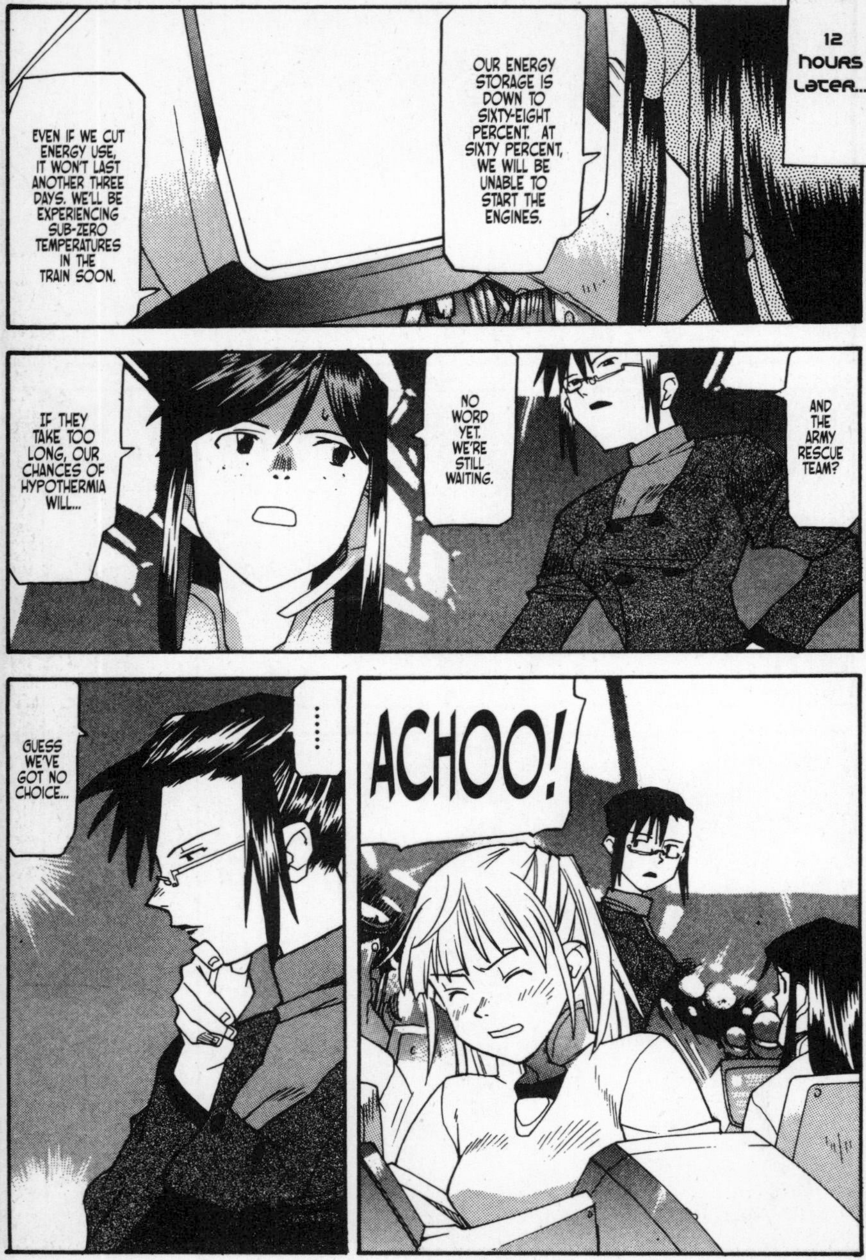
12 HOURS LATER...
OUR ENERGY STORAGE IS DOWN TO SIXTY-EIGHT PERCENT. AT SIXTY PERCENT, WE WILL BE UNABLE TO START THE ENGINES.
EVEN IF WE CUT ENERGY USE, IT WON'T LAST ANOTHER THREE DAYS. WE'LL BE EXPERIENCING SUB-ZERO TEMPERATURES IN THE TRAIN SOON.
AND THE ARMY RESCUE TEAM?
NO WORD YET. WE'RE STILL WAITING.
IF THEY TAKE TOO LONG, OUR CHANCES OF HYPOTHERMIA WILL...
ACHOO!
......
GUESS WE'VE GOT NO CHOICE...

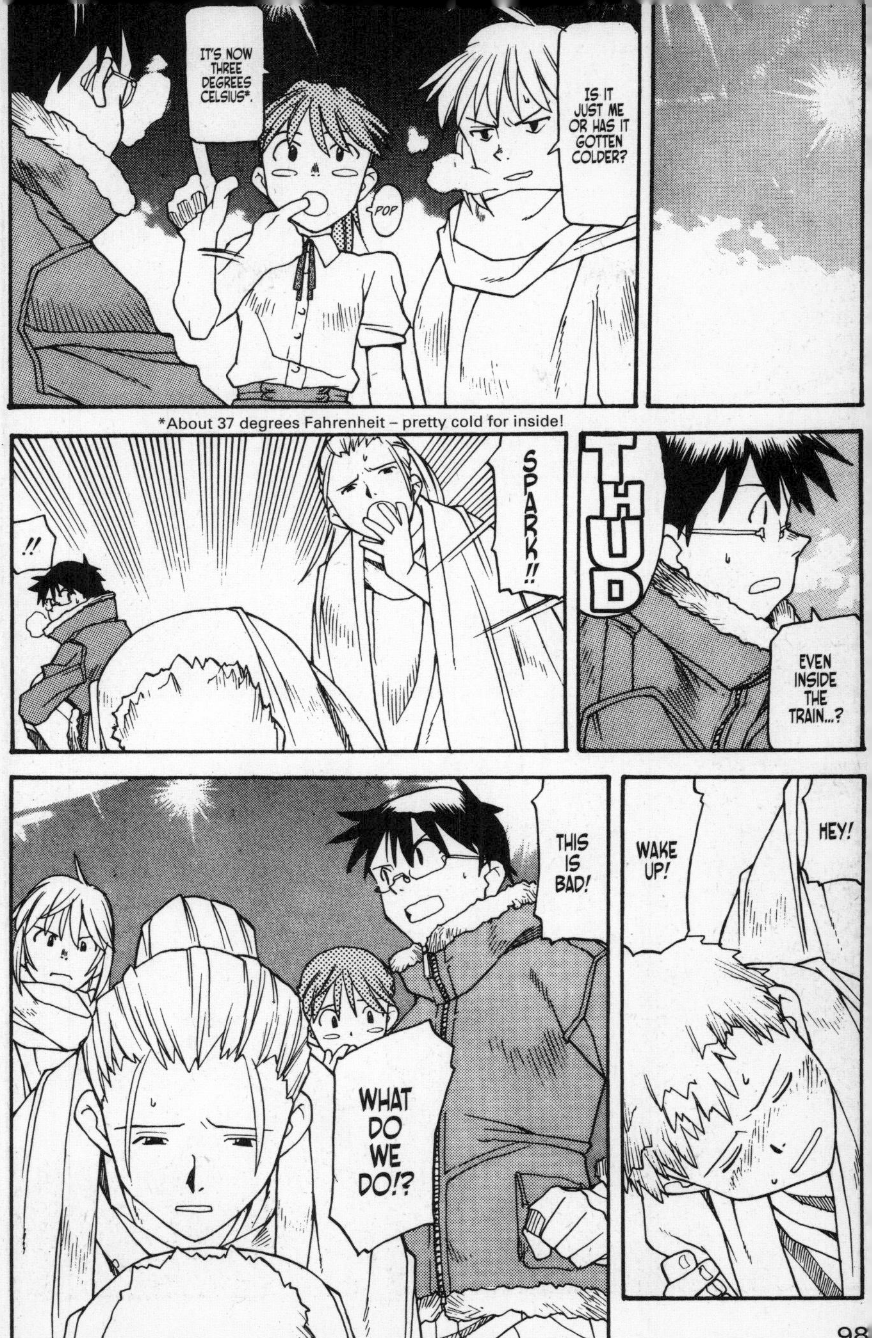
IS IT JUST ME OR HAS IT GOTTEN COLDER?
POP
IT'S NOW THREE DEGREES CELSIUS*.
THUD
EVEN INSIDE THE TRAIN...?
SPARK!!
!!
HEY!
WAKE UP!
THIS IS BAD!
WHAT DO WE DO!?

*About 37 degrees Fahrenheit – pretty cold for inside!

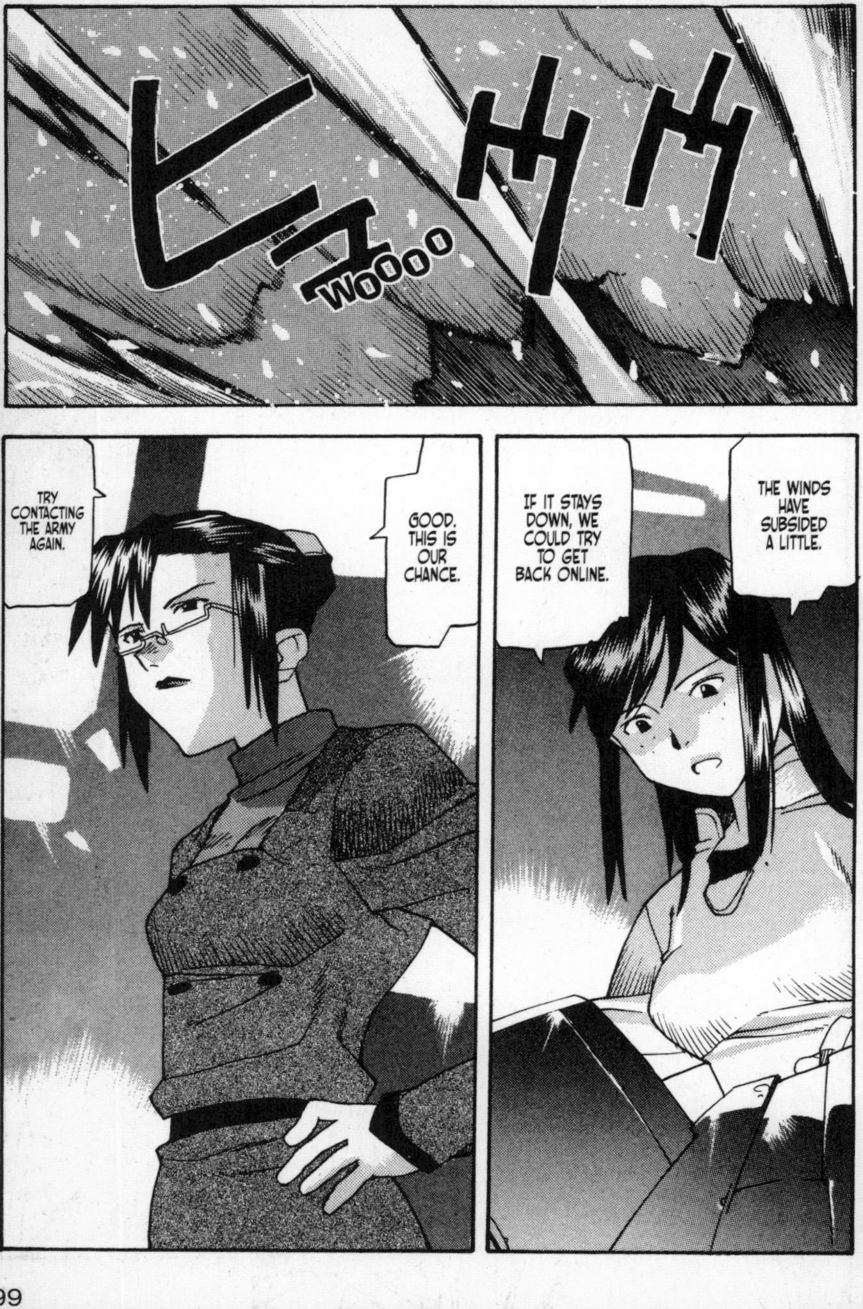
WOOOO
THE WINDS HAVE SUBSIDED A LITTLE.
IF IT STAYS DOWN, WE COULD TRY TO GET BACK ONLINE.
GOOD. THIS IS OUR CHANCE.
TRY CONTACTING THE ARMY AGAIN.

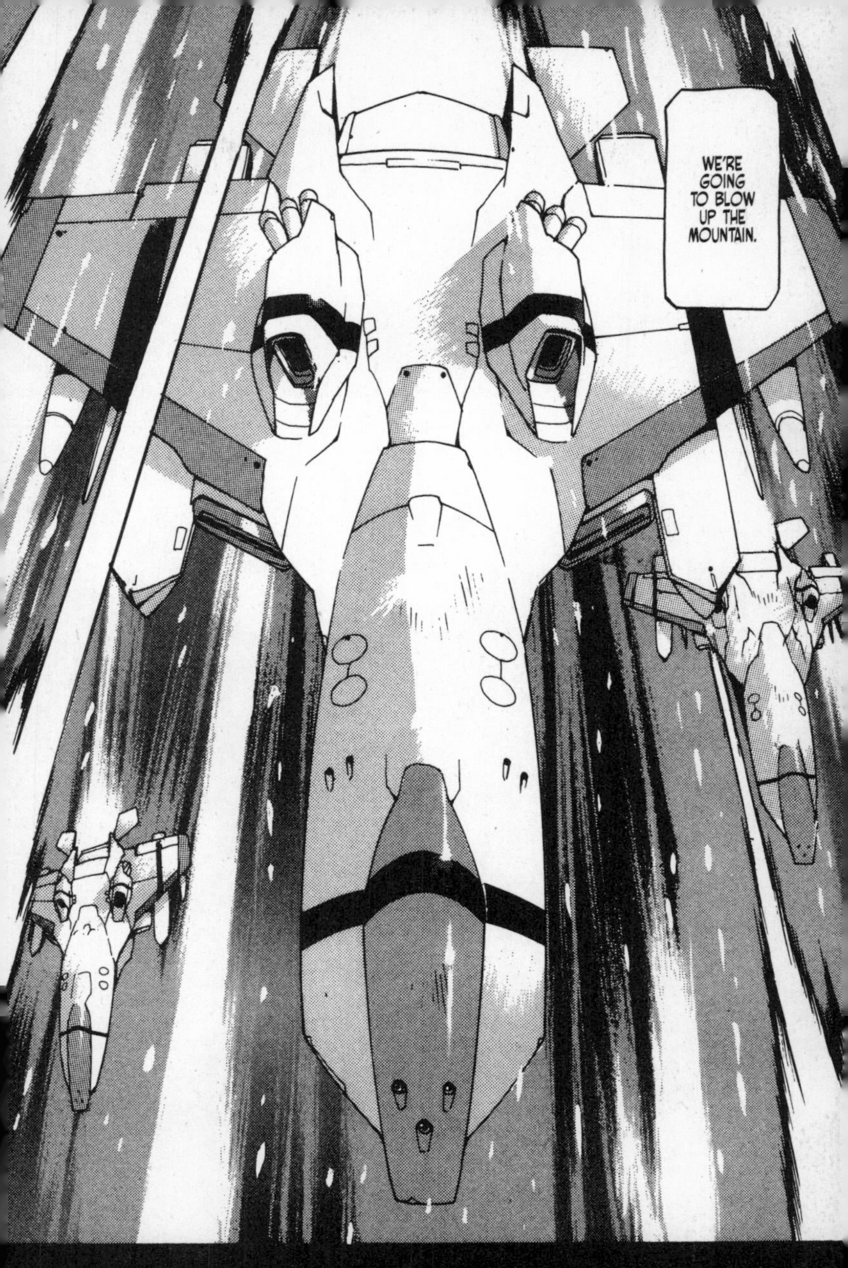
WE'RE GOING TO BLOW UP THE MOUNTAIN.

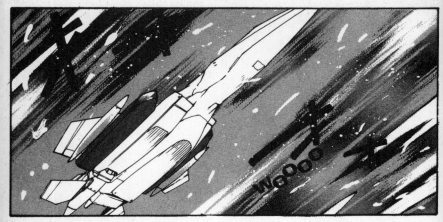

I'D HEARD THE SPECIAL TRAIN STAFF WAS WILD, BUT *THIS!?*

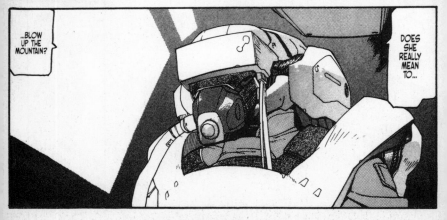

DOES SHE REALLY MEAN TO...

...BLOW UP THE MOUNTAIN?

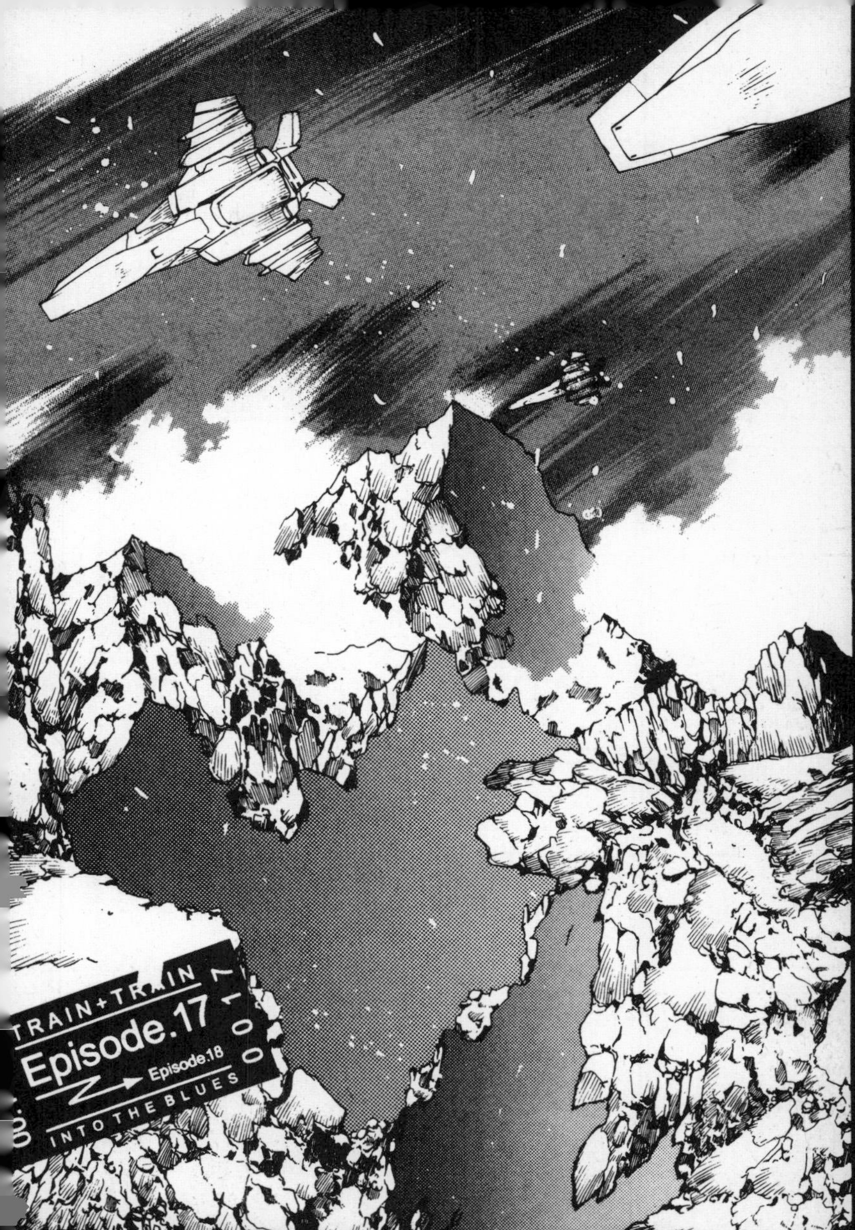
TRAIN+TRAIN
Episode.17
Episode.18
INTO THE BLUES
0017

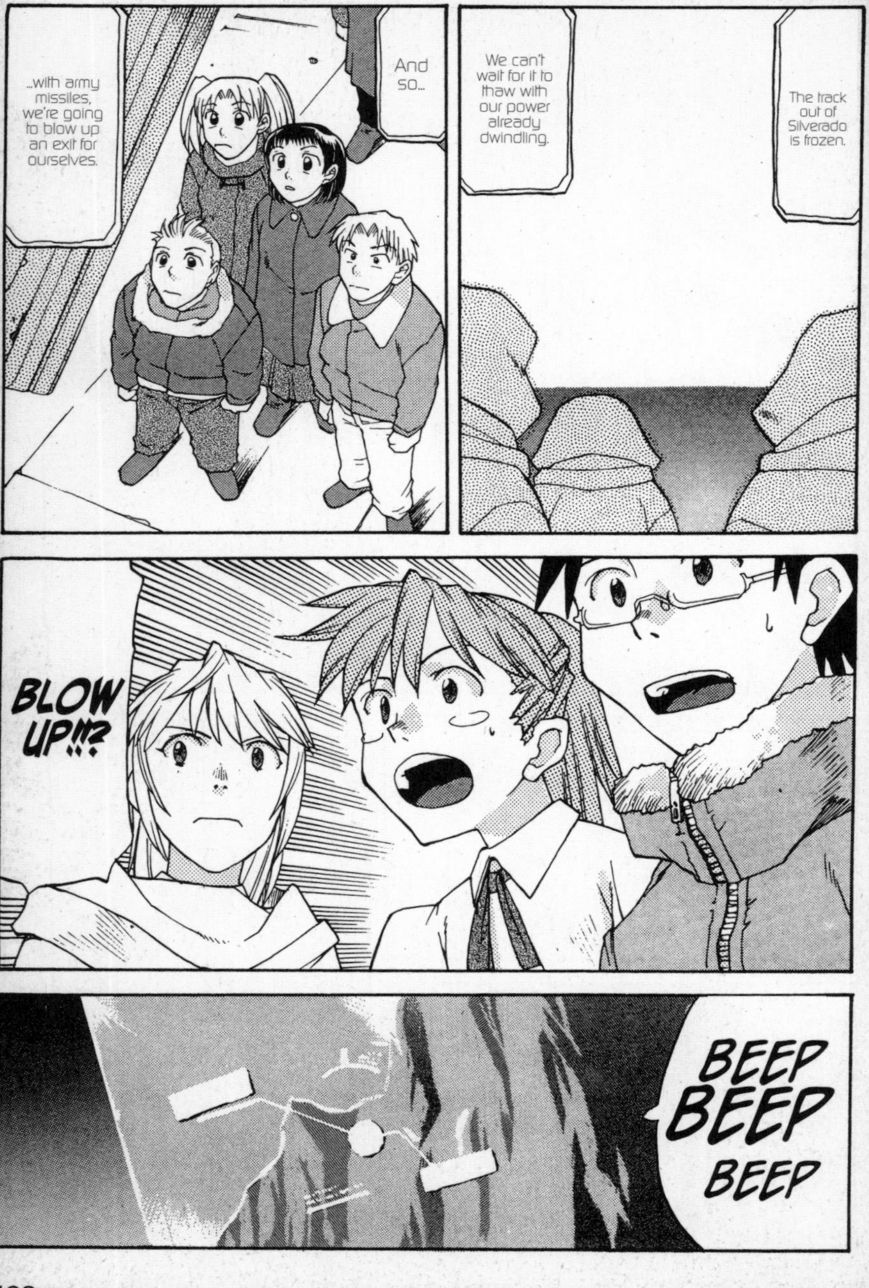
The track out of Silverado is frozen.
We can't wait for it to thaw with our power already dwindling.
And so...
...with army missiles, we're going to blow up an exit for ourselves.
BLOW UP!!?
BEEP BEEP BEEP

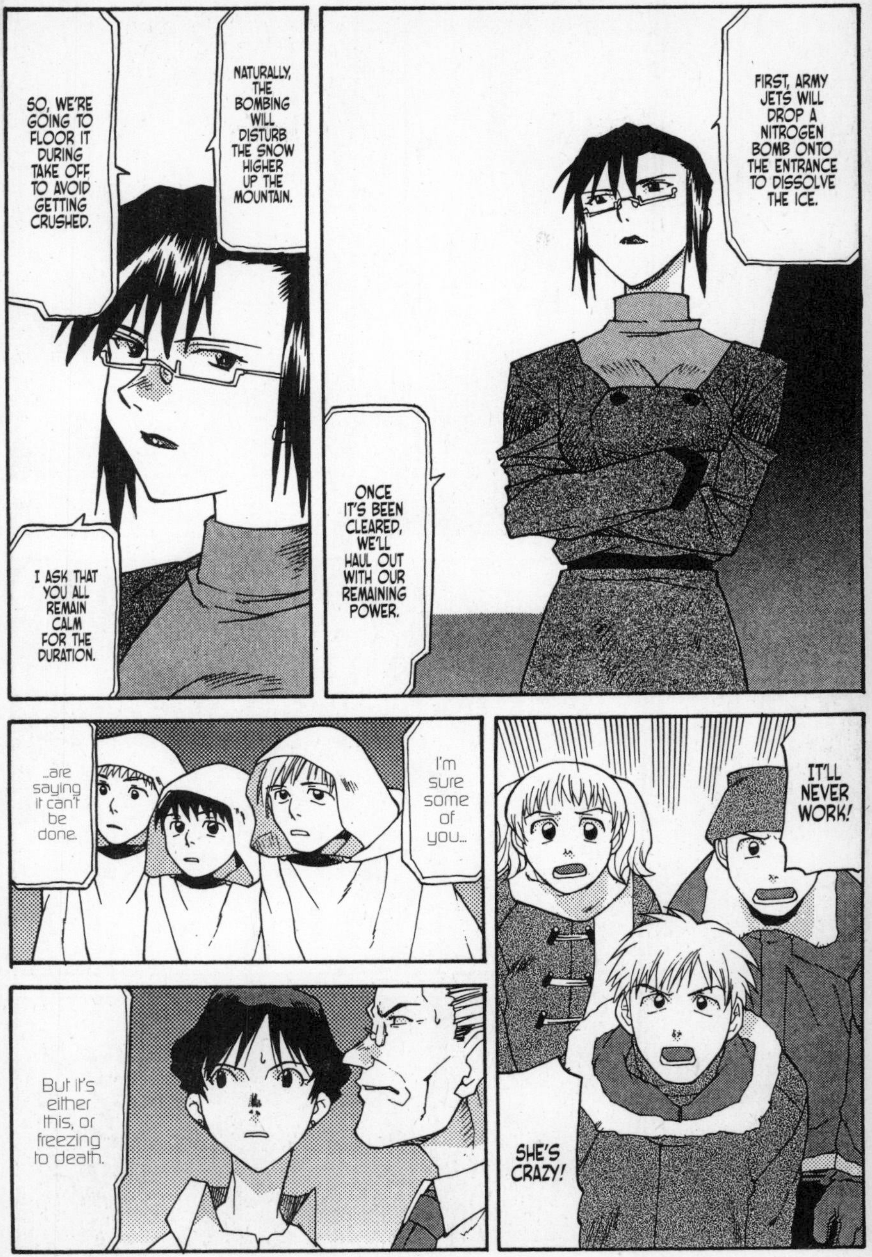

FIRST, ARMY JETS WILL DROP A NITROGEN BOMB ONTO THE ENTRANCE TO DISSOLVE THE ICE.
ONCE IT'S BEEN CLEARED, WE'LL HAUL OUT WITH OUR REMAINING POWER.
NATURALLY, THE BOMBING WILL DISTURB THE SNOW HIGHER UP THE MOUNTAIN.
SO, WE'RE GOING TO FLOOR IT DURING TAKE OFF TO AVOID GETTING CRUSHED.
I ASK THAT YOU ALL REMAIN CALM FOR THE DURATION.
IT'LL NEVER WORK!
SHE'S CRAZY!
I'm sure some of you...
...are saying it can't be done.
But it's either this, or freezing to death.

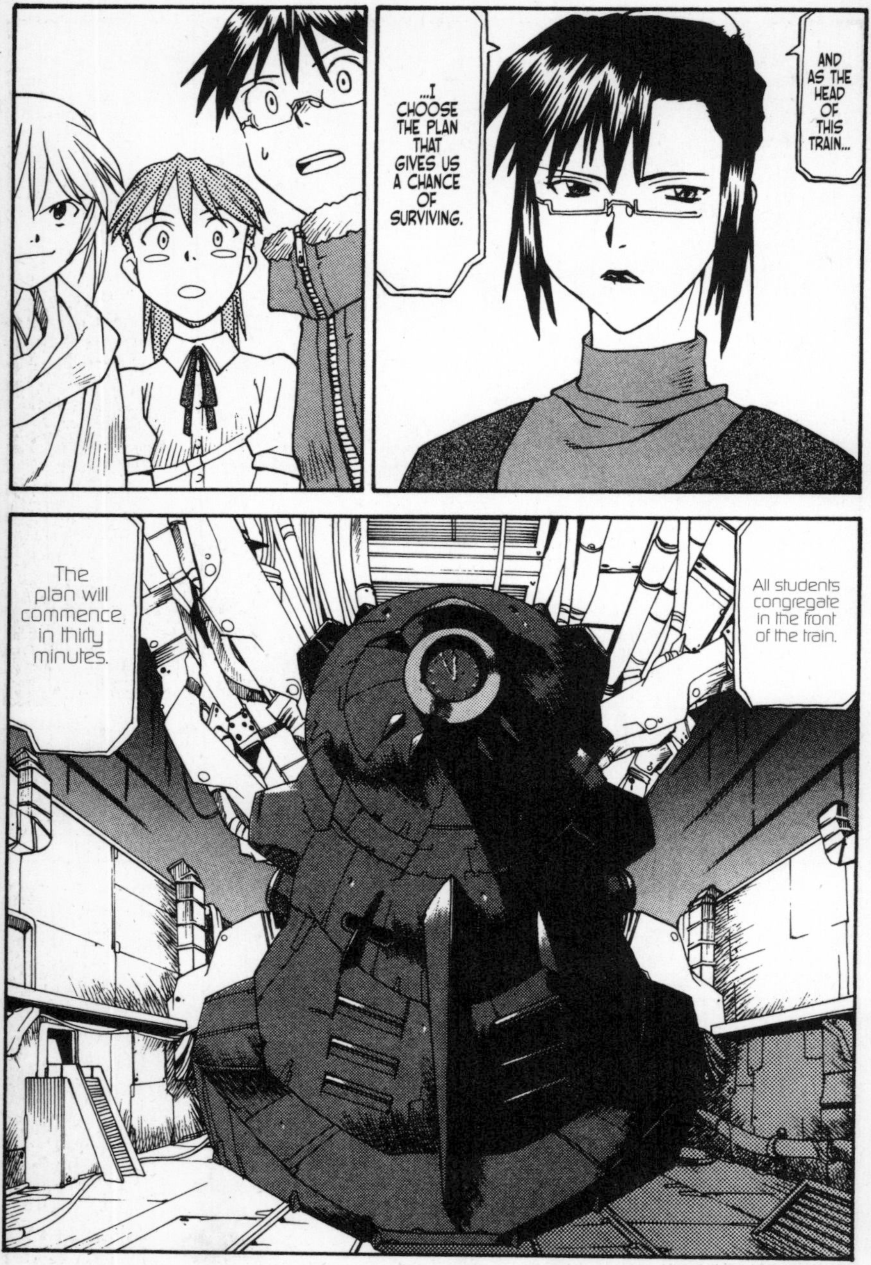
AND AS THE HEAD OF THIS TRAIN...
...I CHOOSE THE PLAN THAT GIVES US A CHANCE OF SURVIVING.
All students congregate in the front of the train.
The plan will commence in thirty minutes.

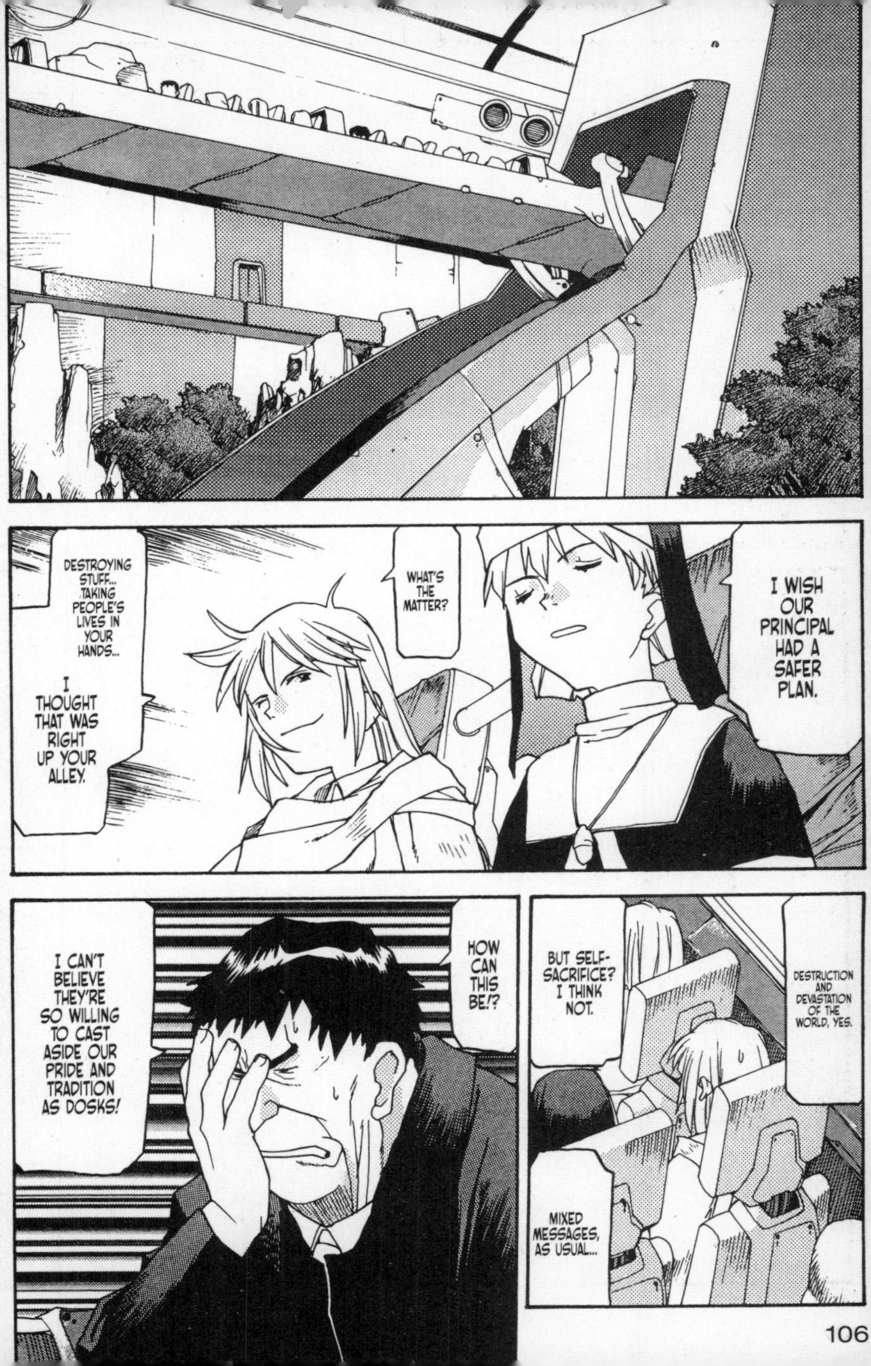
I WISH OUR PRINCIPAL HAD A SAFER PLAN.
WHAT'S THE MATTER?
DESTROYING STUFF... TAKING PEOPLE'S LIVES IN YOUR HANDS...
I THOUGHT THAT WAS RIGHT UP YOUR ALLEY.
DESTRUCTION AND DEVASTATION OF THE WORLD, YES.
BUT SELF-SACRIFICE? I THINK NOT.
MIXED MESSAGES, AS USUAL...
HOW CAN THIS BE!?
I CAN'T BELIEVE THEY'RE SO WILLING TO CAST ASIDE OUR PRIDE AND TRADITION AS DOSKS!

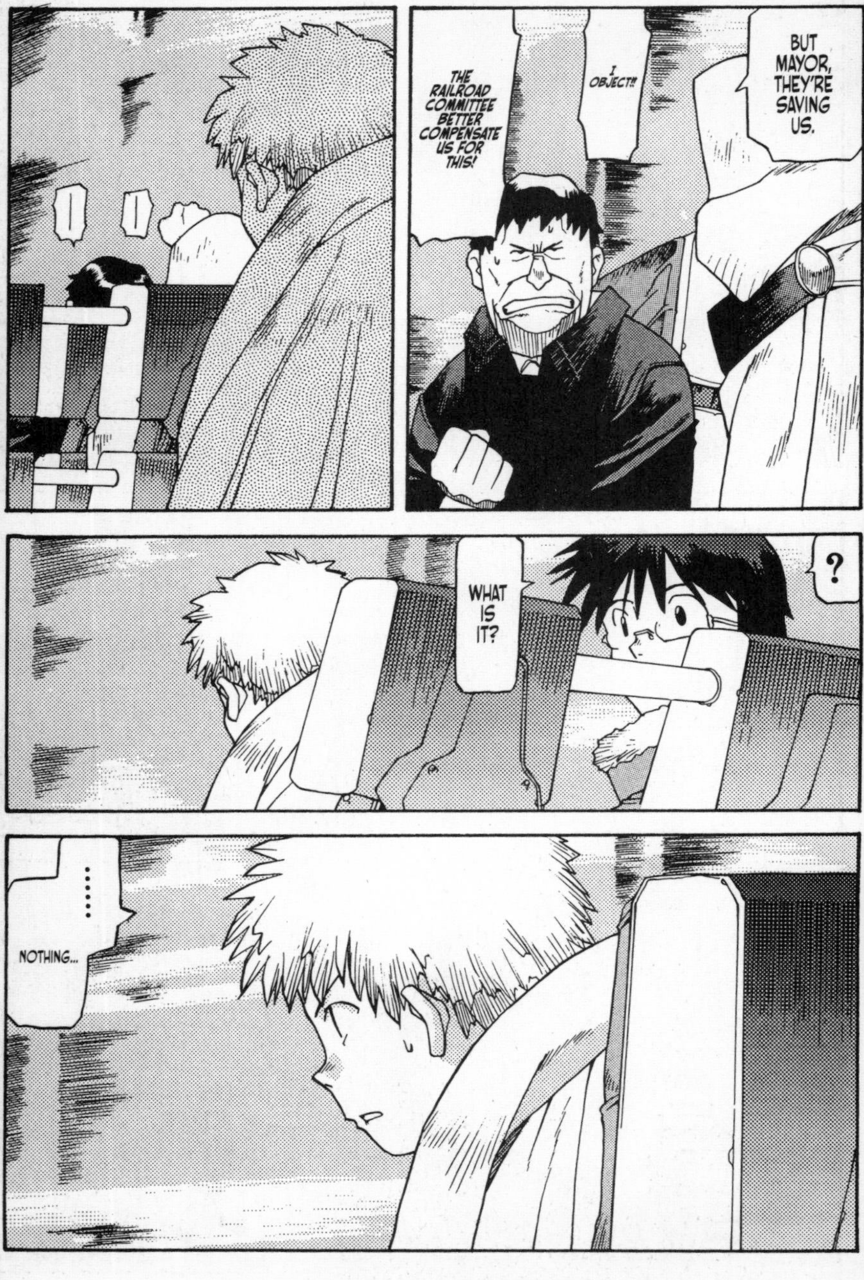
BUT MAYOR, THEY'RE SAVING US.
I OBJECT!!
THE RAILROAD COMMITTEE BETTER COMPENSATE US FOR THIS!
?
WHAT IS IT?
......
NOTHING...

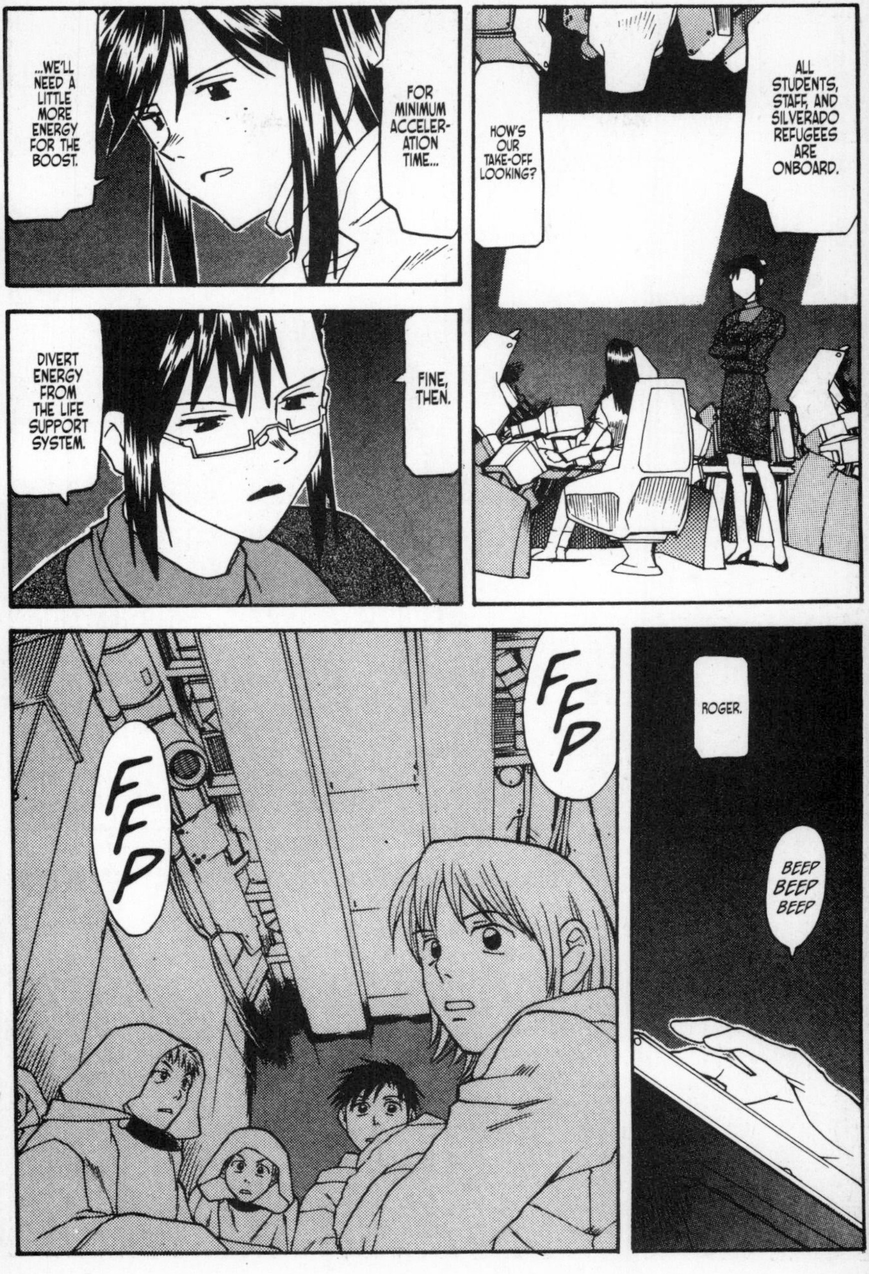
ALL STUDENTS, STAFF, AND SILVERADO REFUGEES ARE ONBOARD.
HOW'S OUR TAKE-OFF LOOKING?
FOR MINIMUM ACCELER-ATION TIME...
...WE'LL NEED A LITTLE MORE ENERGY FOR THE BOOST.
FINE, THEN.
DIVERT ENERGY FROM THE LIFE SUPPORT SYSTEM.
ROGER.
BEEP BEEP BEEP
FFP
FFP

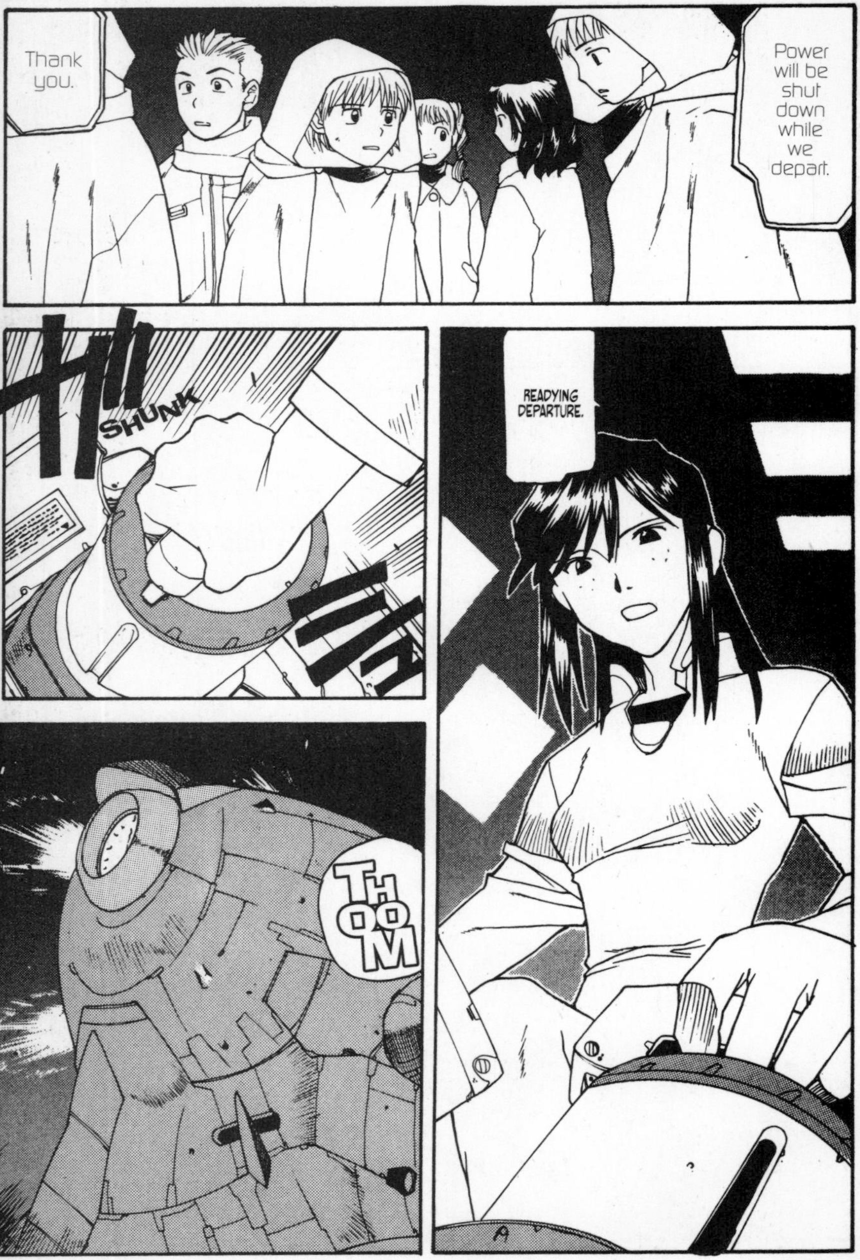
Power will be shut down while we depart.
Thank you.
READYING DEPARTURE.
SHUNK
THOOM

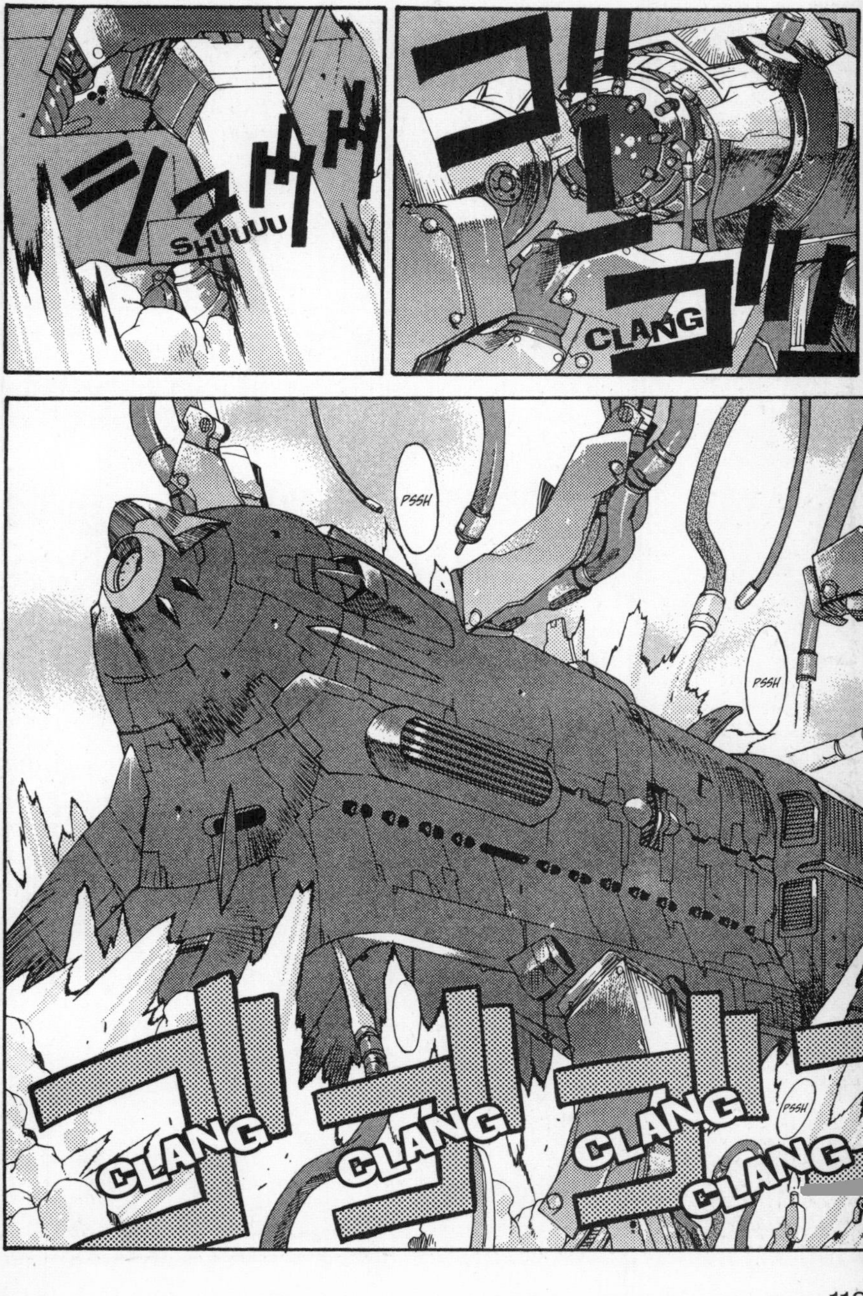
CLANG
SHUUUU
PSSH
PSSH
PSSH
CLANG
CLANG
CLANG
CLANG

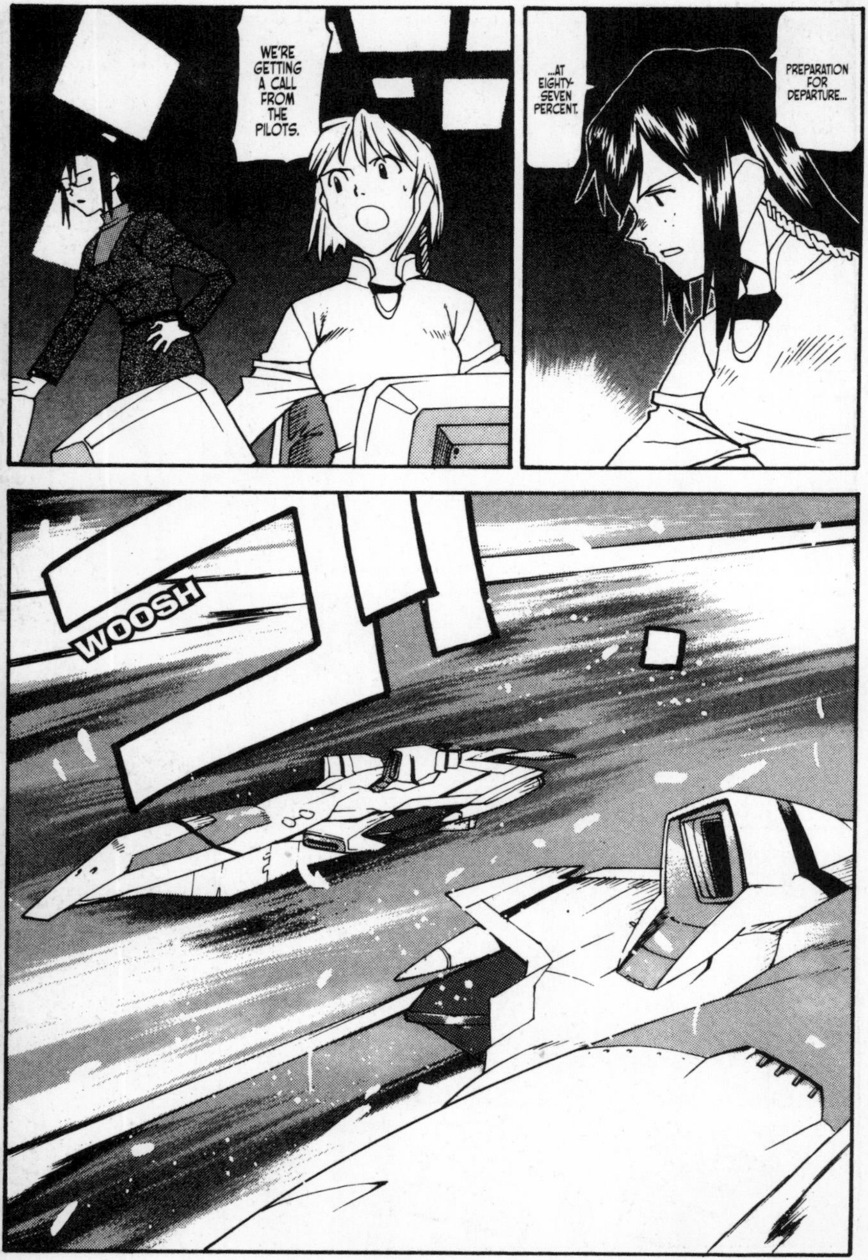
PREPARATION FOR DEPARTURE...
...AT EIGHTY-SEVEN PERCENT.
WE'RE GETTING A CALL FROM THE PILOTS.
WOOSH

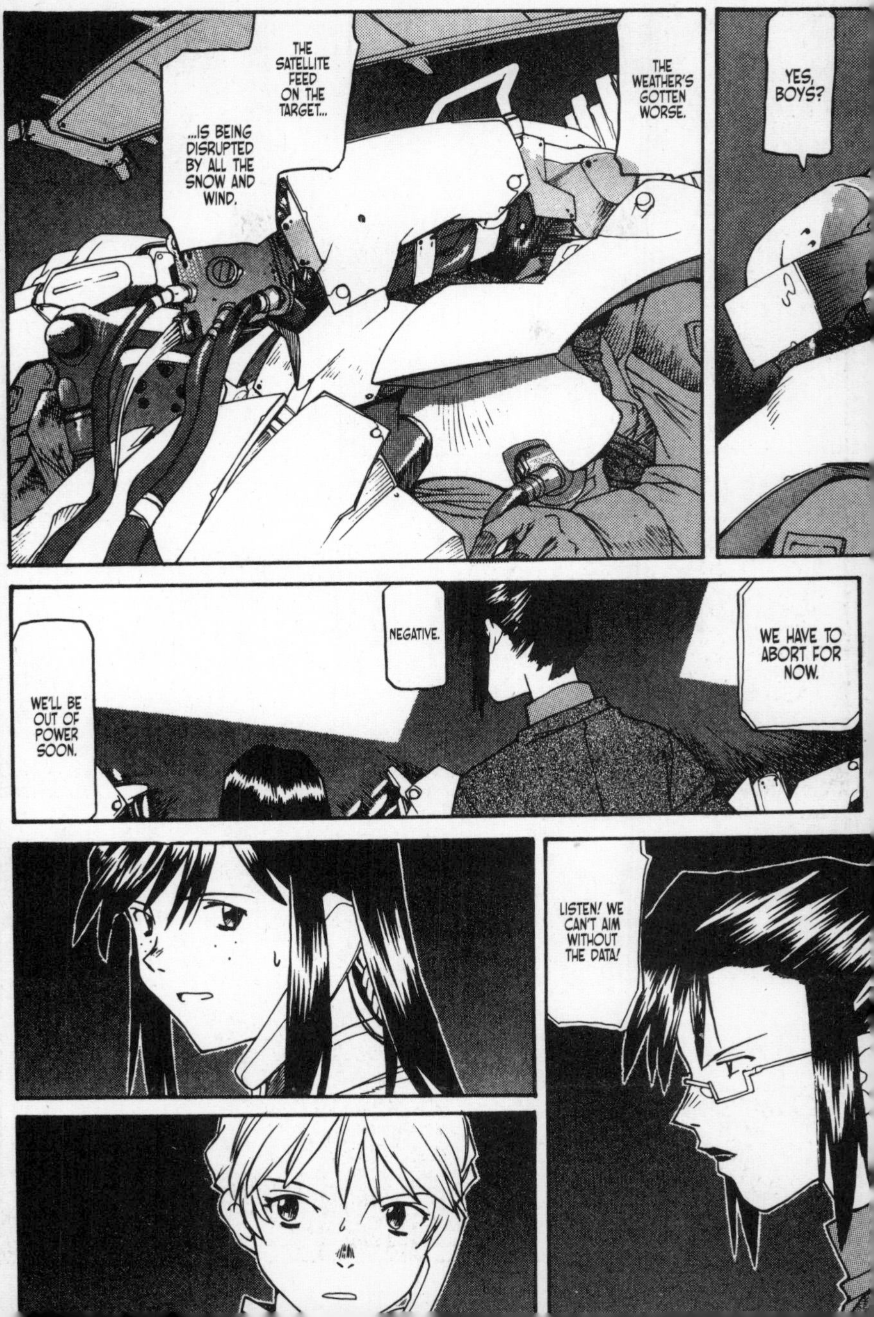
YES, BOYS?
THE WEATHER'S GOTTEN WORSE.
THE SATELLITE FEED ON THE TARGET...
...IS BEING DISRUPTED BY ALL THE SNOW AND WIND.
WE HAVE TO ABORT FOR NOW.
NEGATIVE.
WE'LL BE OUT OF POWER SOON.
LISTEN! WE CAN'T AIM WITHOUT THE DATA!

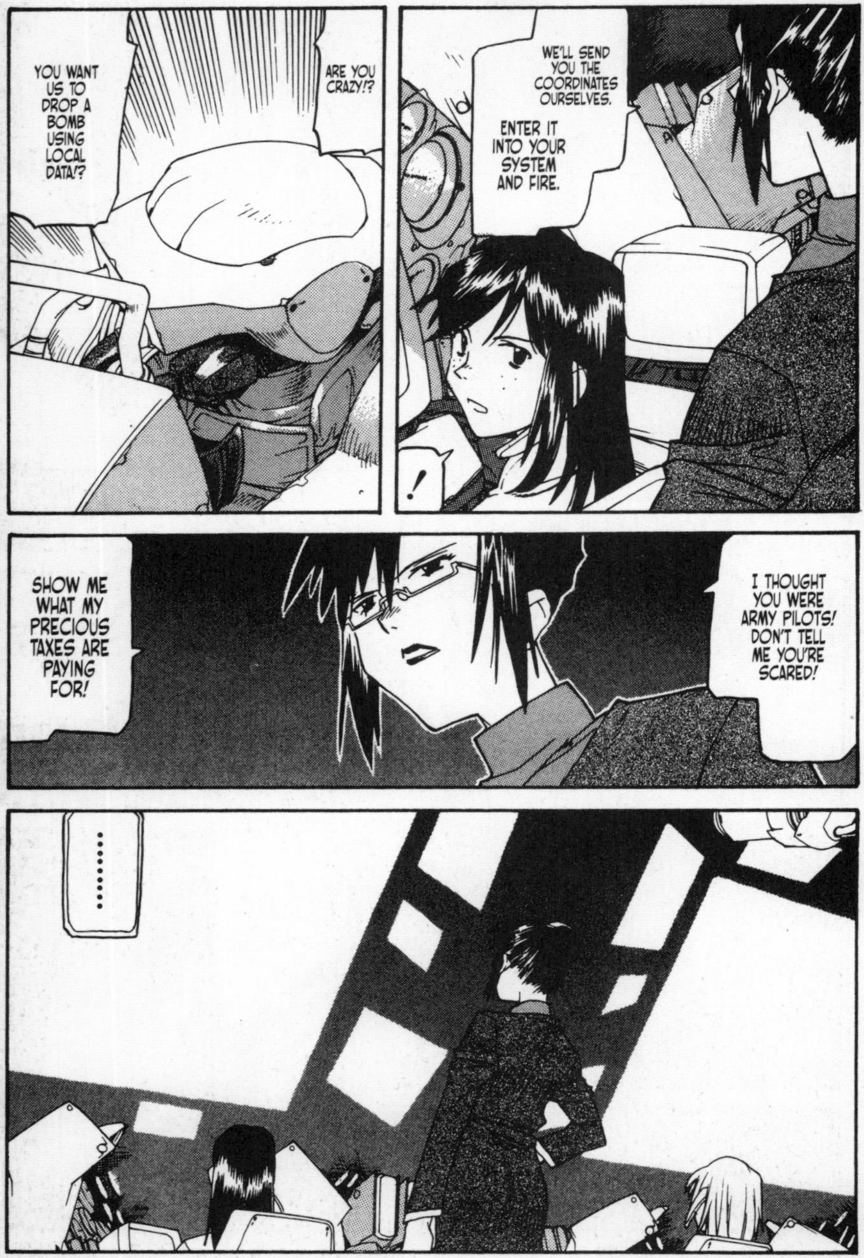
WE'LL SEND YOU THE COORDINATES OURSELVES.
ENTER IT INTO YOUR SYSTEM AND FIRE.
!
ARE YOU CRAZY!?
YOU WANT US TO DROP A BOMB USING LOCAL DATA!?
I THOUGHT YOU WERE ARMY PILOTS! DON'T TELL ME YOU'RE SCARED!
SHOW ME WHAT MY PRECIOUS TAXES ARE PAYING FOR!
....

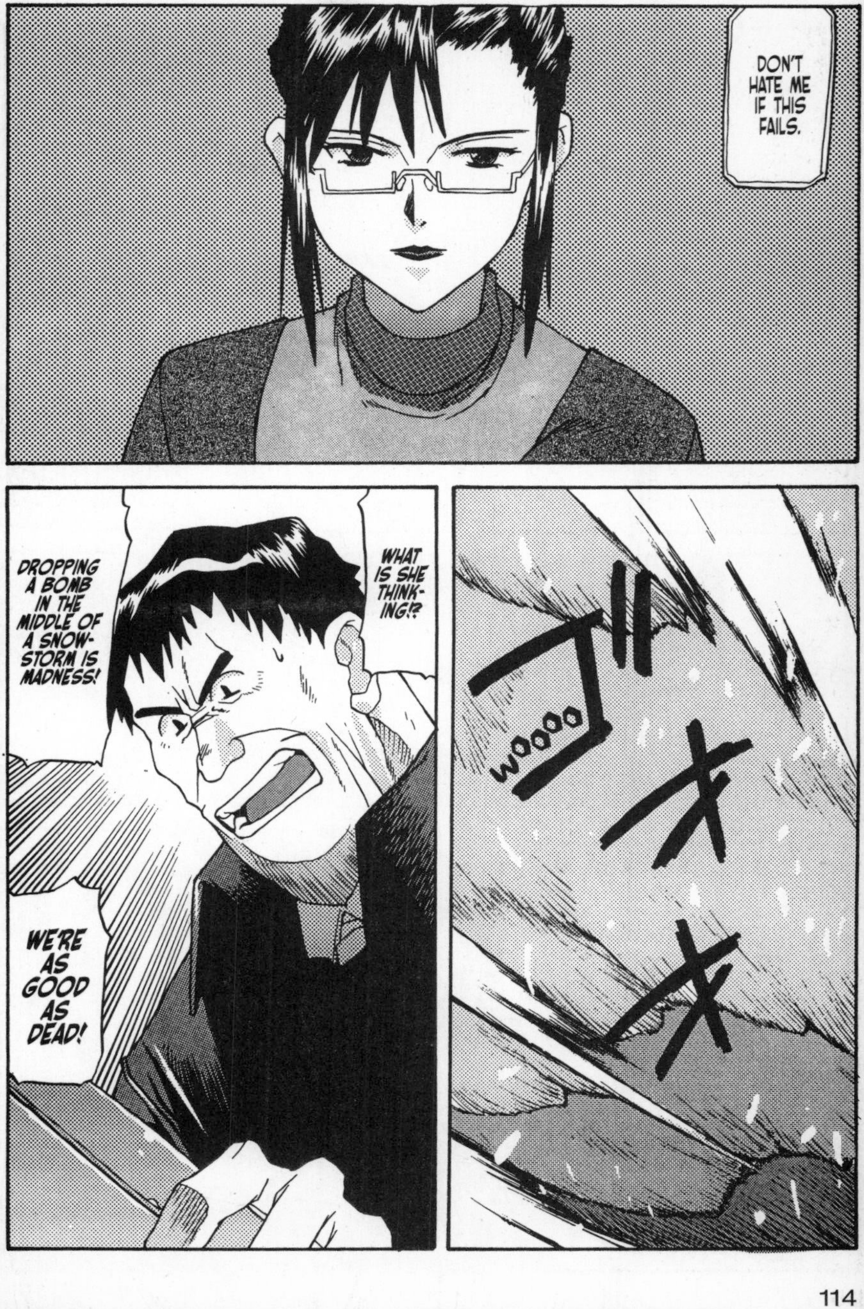
DON'T HATE ME IF THIS FAILS.
WOOOO
WHAT IS SHE THINKING!?
DROPPING A BOMB IN THE MIDDLE OF A SNOW-STORM IS MADNESS!
WE'RE AS GOOD AS DEAD!

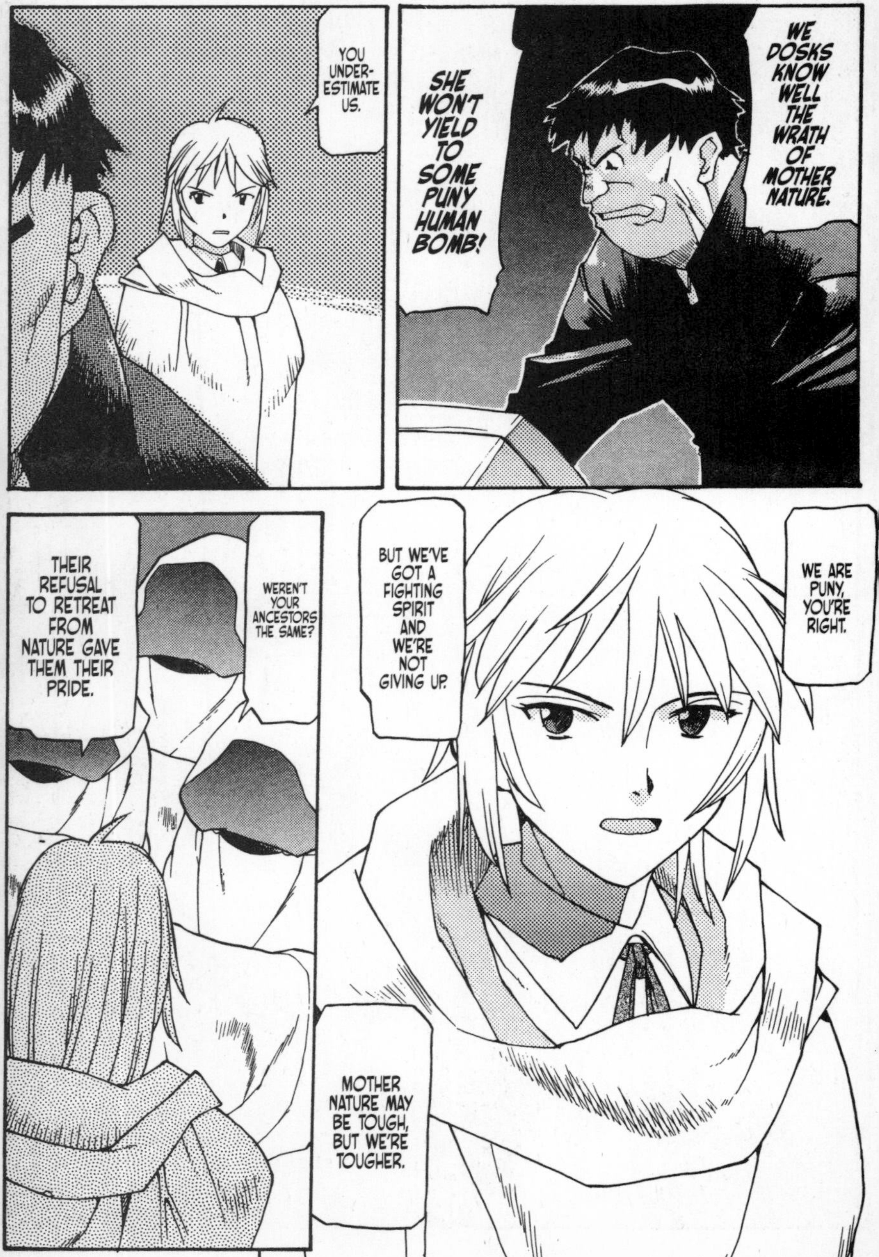
WE DOSKS KNOW WELL THE WRATH OF MOTHER NATURE.
SHE WON'T YIELD TO SOME PUNY HUMAN BOMB!
YOU UNDER-ESTIMATE US.
WE ARE PUNY, YOU'RE RIGHT.
BUT WE'VE GOT A FIGHTING SPIRIT AND WE'RE NOT GIVING UP.
MOTHER NATURE MAY BE TOUGH, BUT WE'RE TOUGHER.
WEREN'T YOUR ANCESTORS THE SAME?
THEIR REFUSAL TO RETREAT FROM NATURE GAVE THEM THEIR PRIDE.

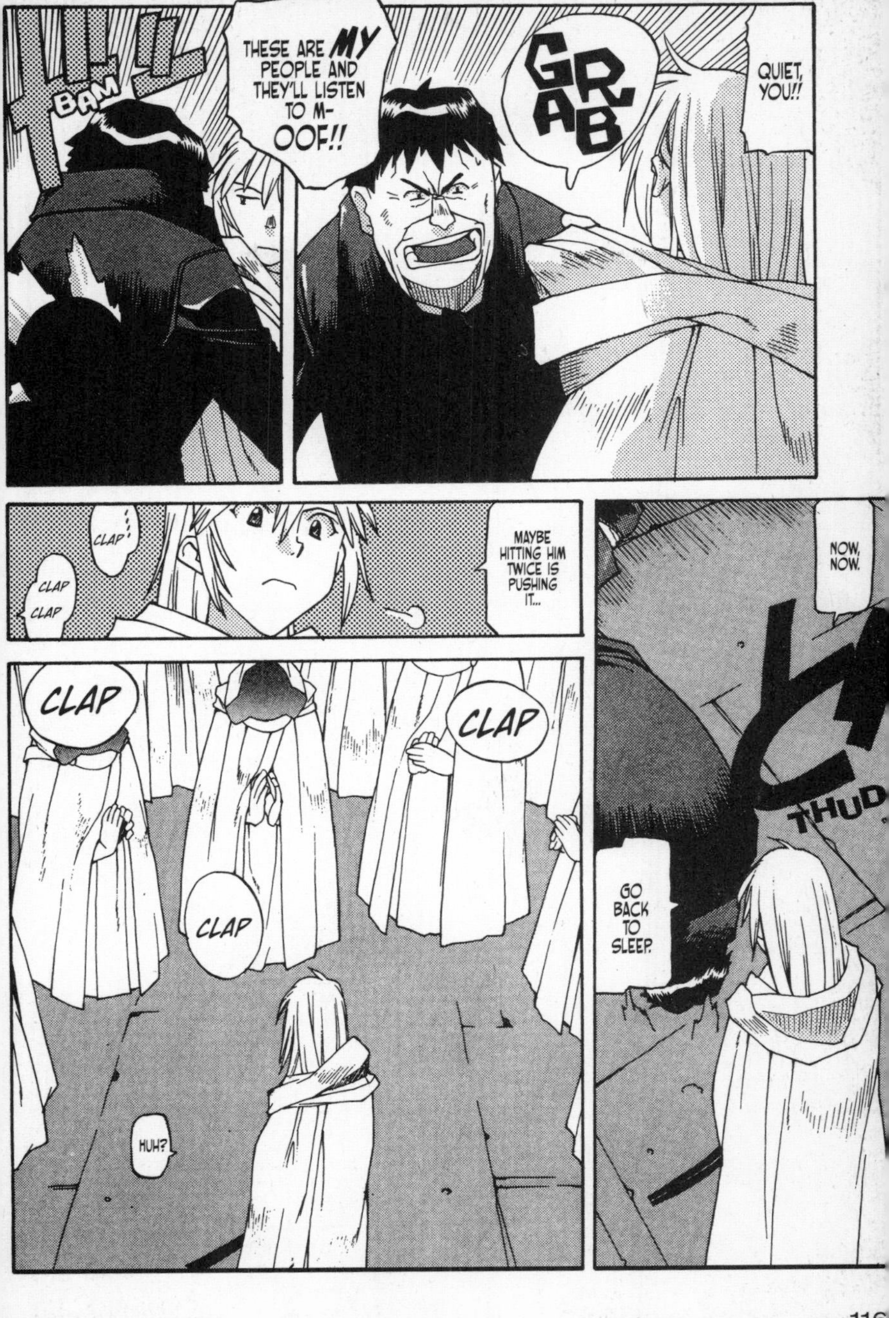
THESE ARE MY PEOPLE AND THEY'LL LISTEN TO M-OOF!!
GRAB
QUIET, YOU!!
BAM
NOW, NOW.
THUD
GO BACK TO SLEEP.
MAYBE HITTING HIM TWICE IS PUSHING IT...
CLAP
CLAP
CLAP
CLAP
CLAP
CLAP
HUH?

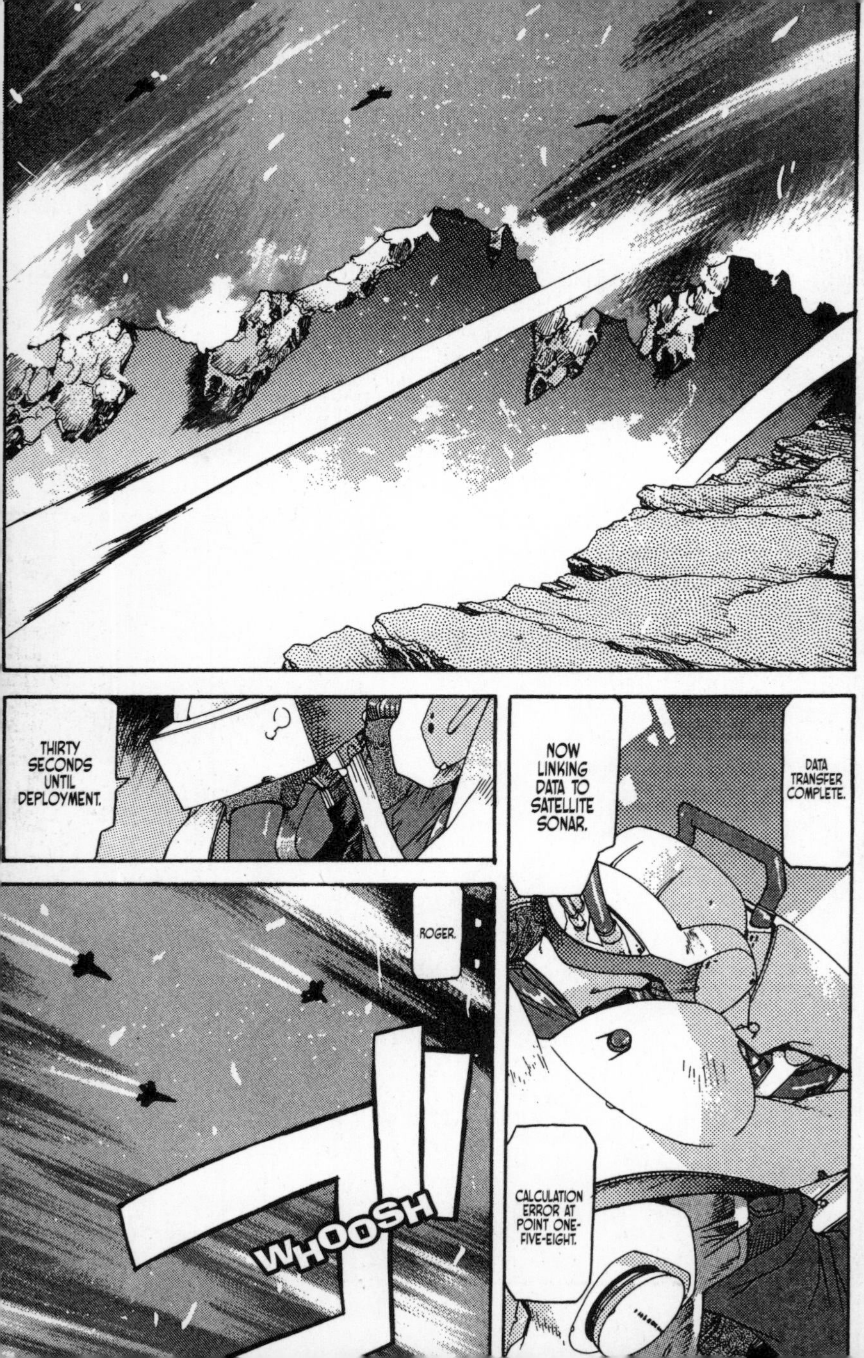
DATA TRANSFER COMPLETE.
NOW LINKING DATA TO SATELLITE SONAR.
CALCULATION ERROR AT POINT ONE-FIVE-EIGHT.
THIRTY SECONDS UNTIL DEPLOYMENT.
ROGER.
WHOOSH

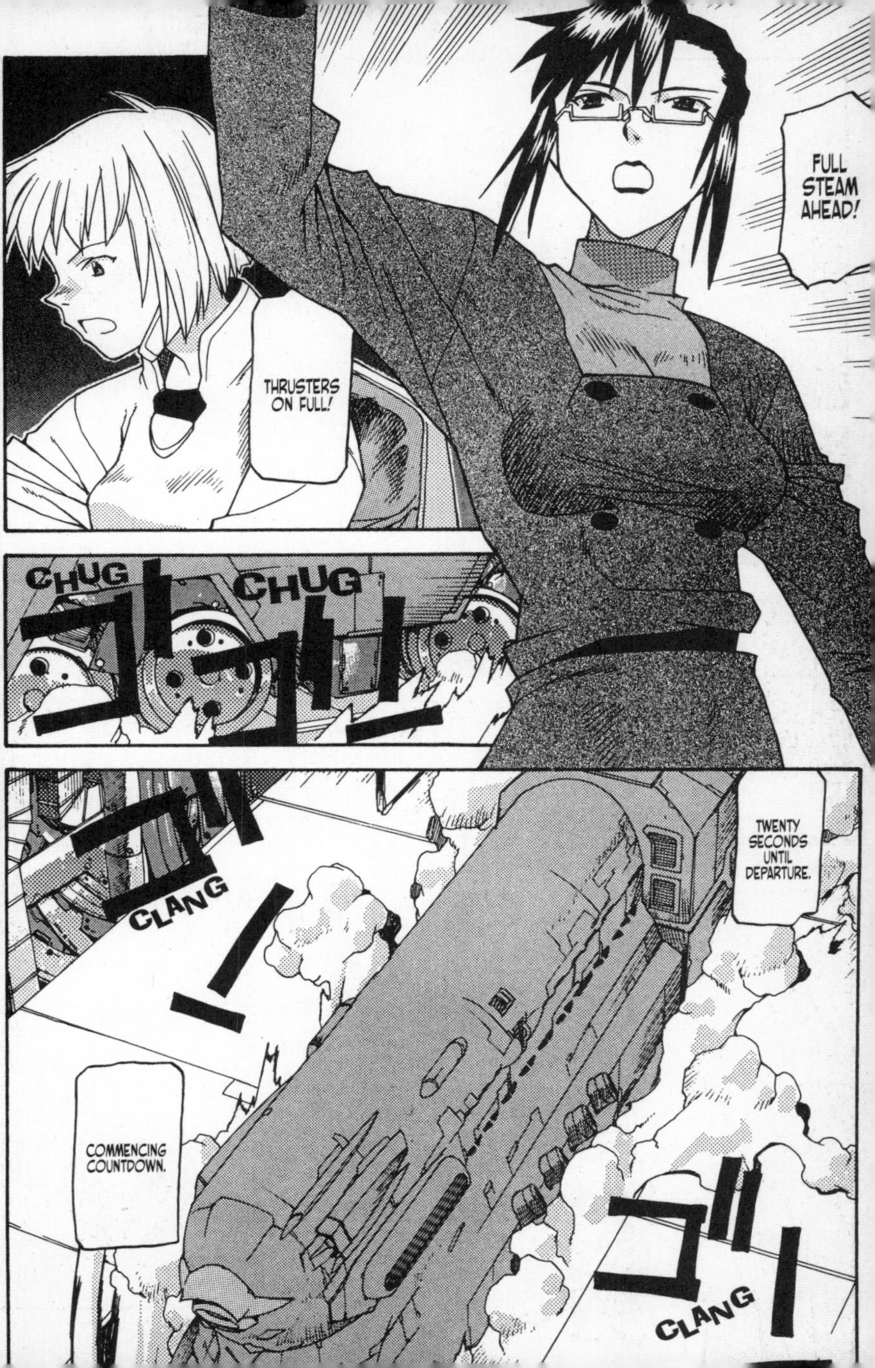
FULL STEAM AHEAD!
THRUSTERS ON FULL!
CHUG CHUG
TWENTY SECONDS UNTIL DEPARTURE.
CLANG
COMMENCING COUNTDOWN.
CLANG

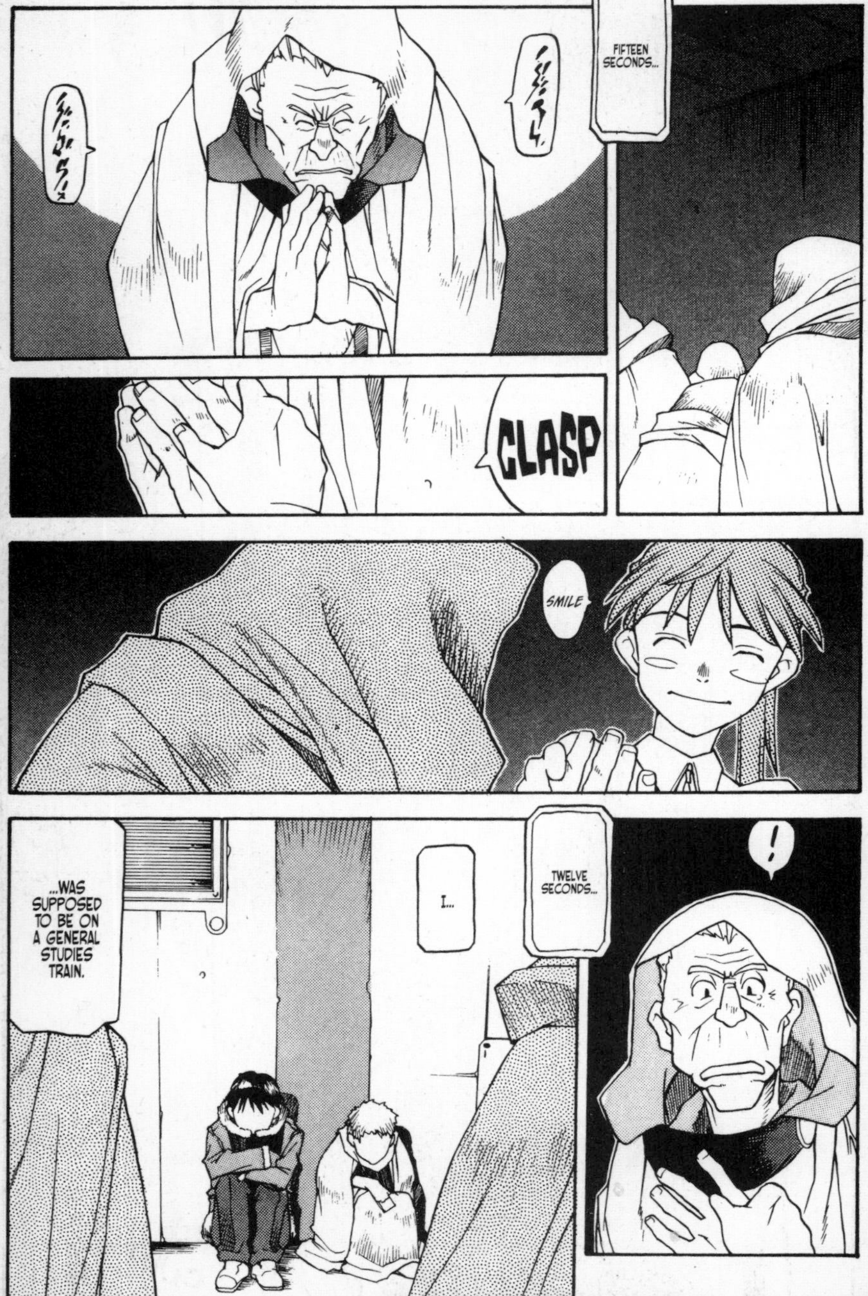

FIFTEEN SECONDS...
CLASP
SMILE
TWELVE SECONDS...
!
I...
...WAS SUPPOSED TO BE ON A GENERAL STUDIES TRAIN.

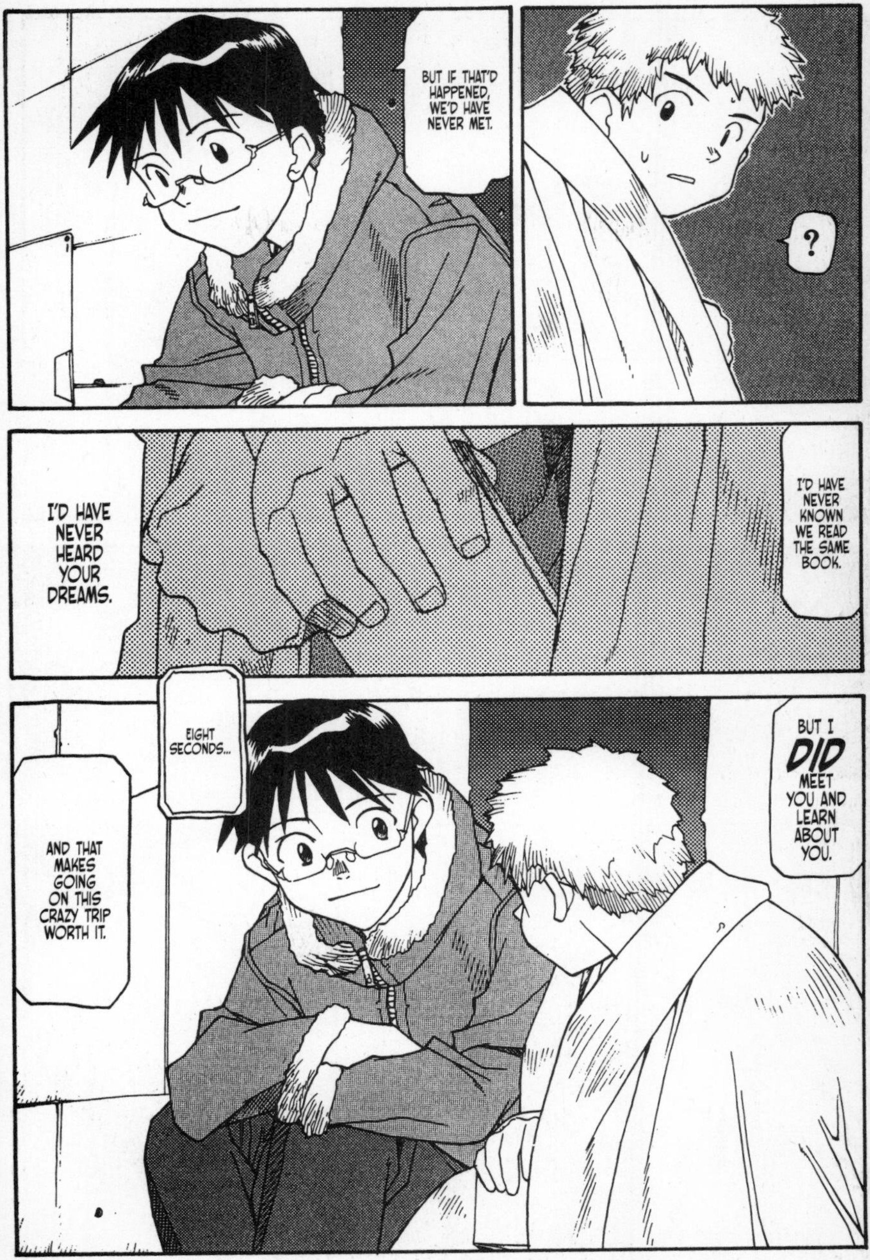
?
BUT IF THAT'D HAPPENED, WE'D HAVE NEVER MET.
I'D HAVE NEVER KNOWN WE READ THE SAME BOOK.
I'D HAVE NEVER HEARD YOUR DREAMS.
BUT I DID MEET YOU AND LEARN ABOUT YOU.
EIGHT SECONDS...
AND THAT MAKES GOING ON THIS CRAZY TRIP WORTH IT.

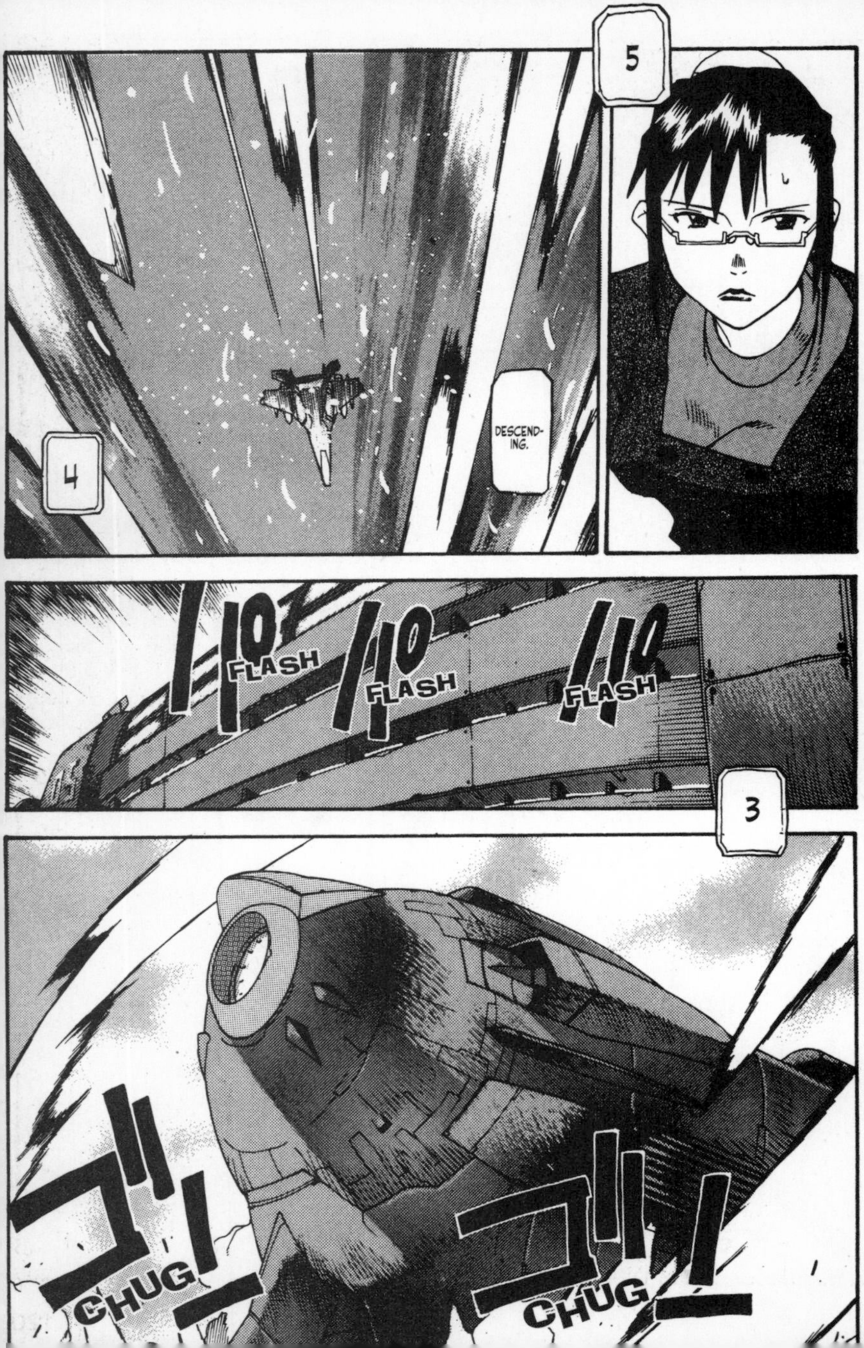
5
DESCEND-ING.
4
FLASH
FLASH
FLASH
3
CHUG
CHUG

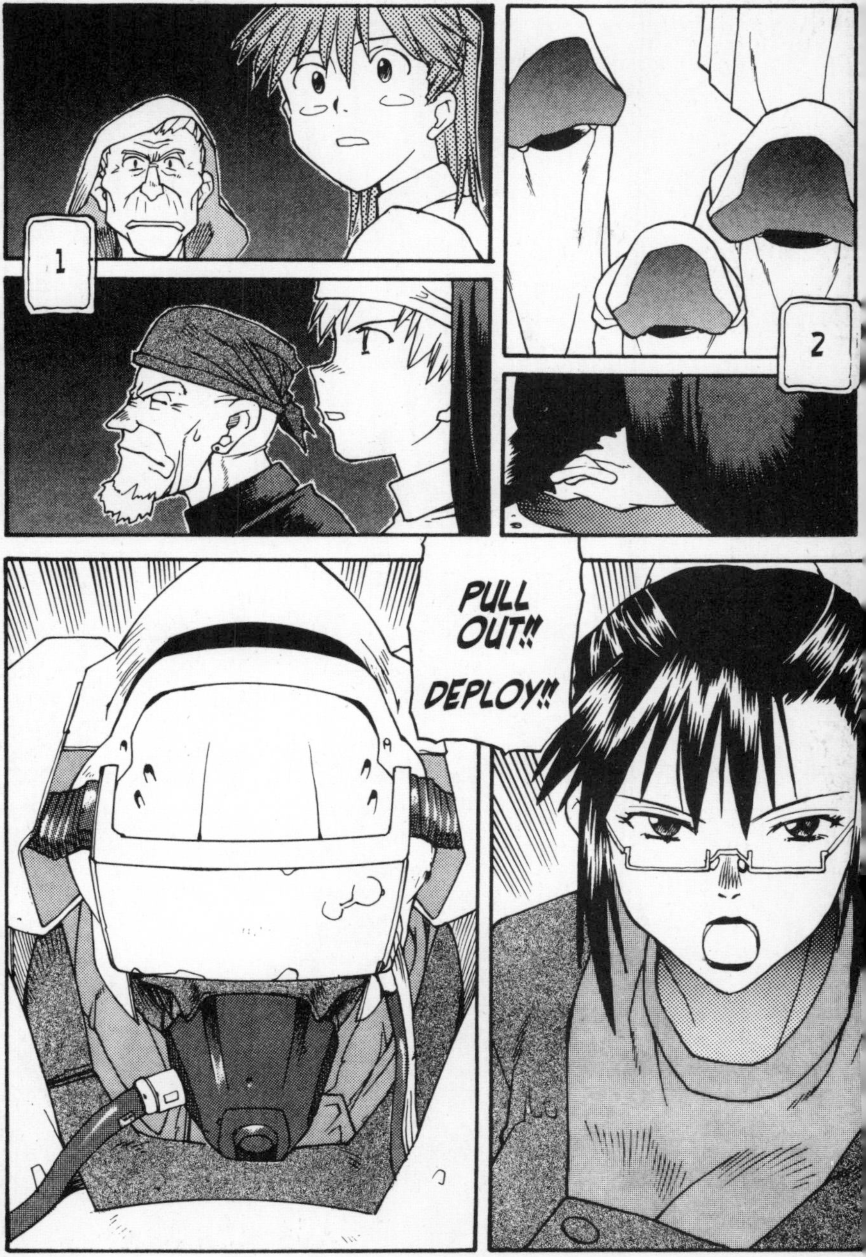
PULL OUT!!
DEPLOY!!

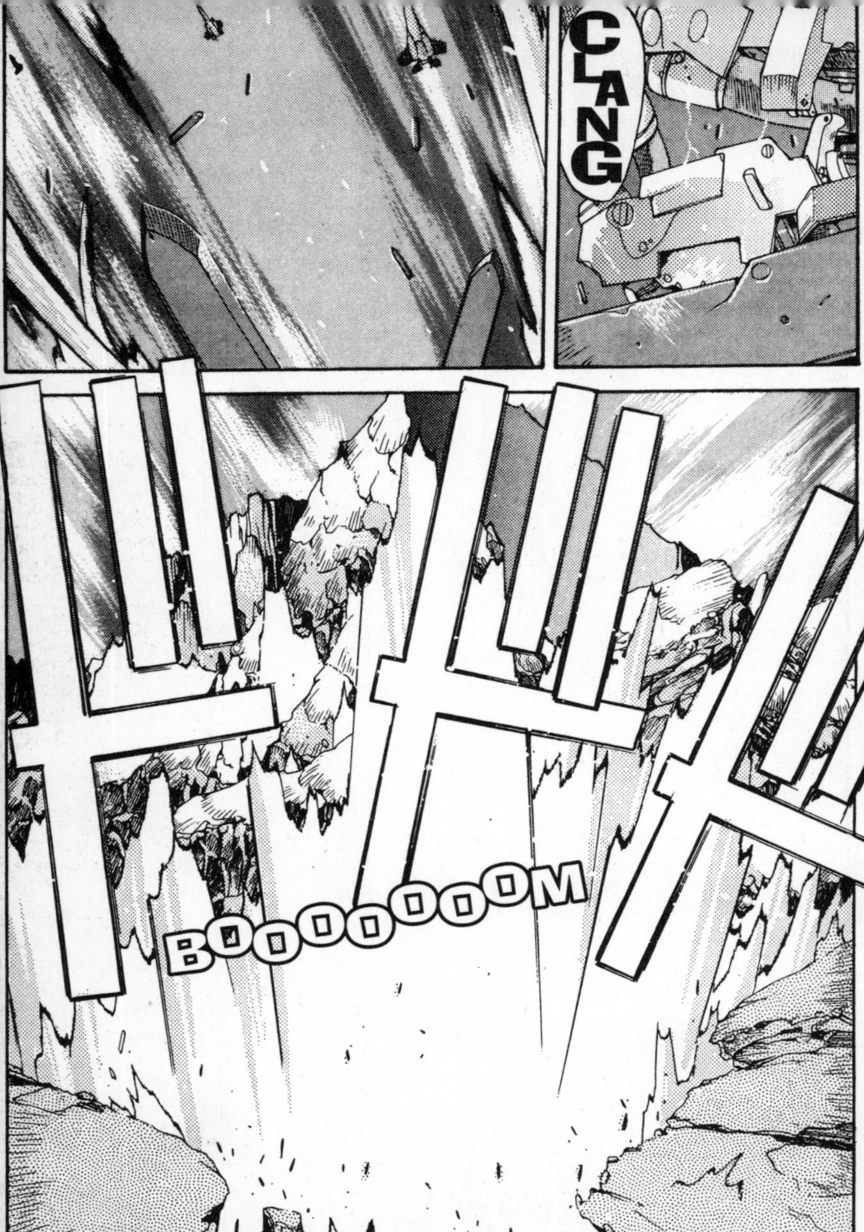
CLANG
BOOOOOOOM

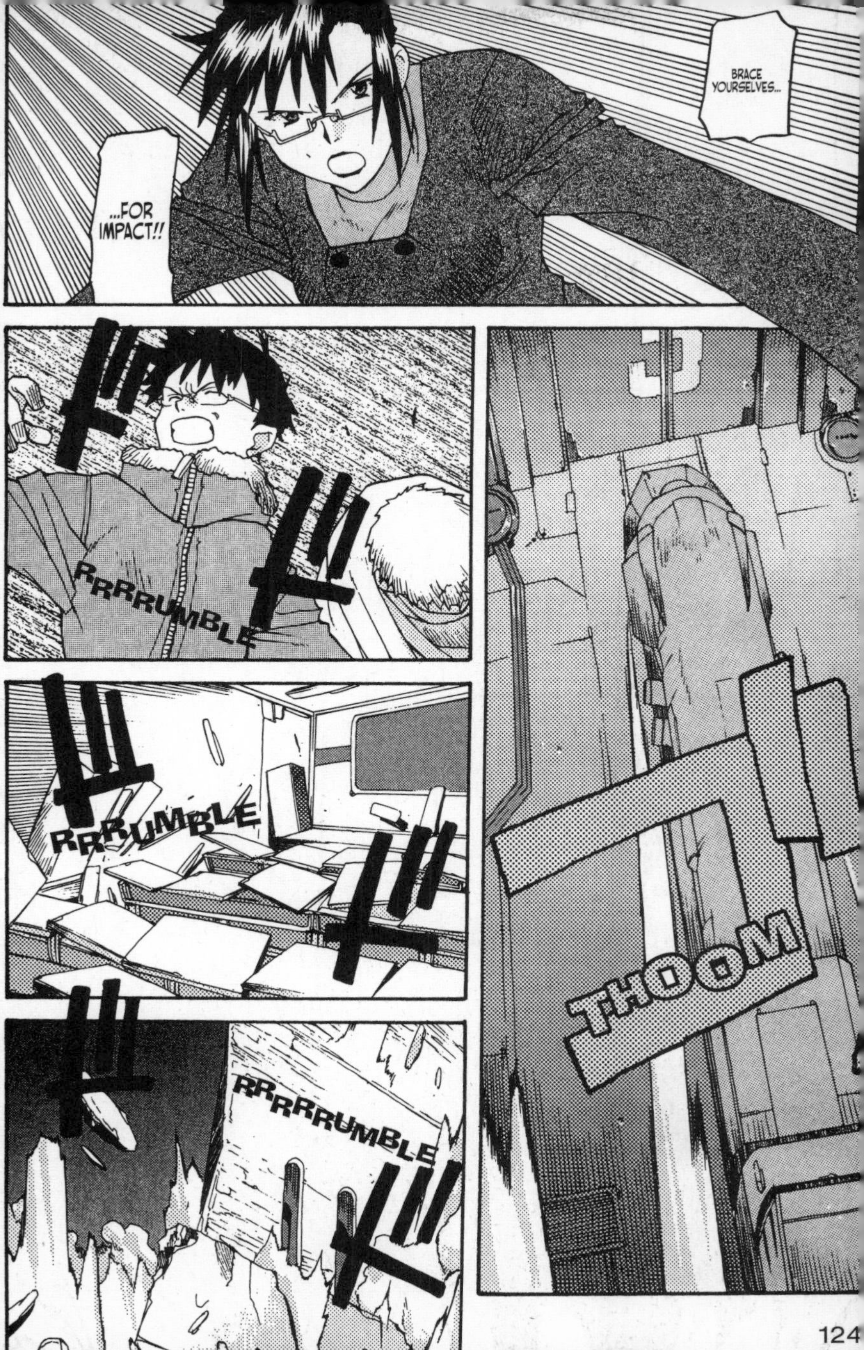
BRACE YOURSELVES...
...FOR IMPACT!!
THOOM
RRRRUMBLE
RRRUMBLE
RRRRRUMBLE

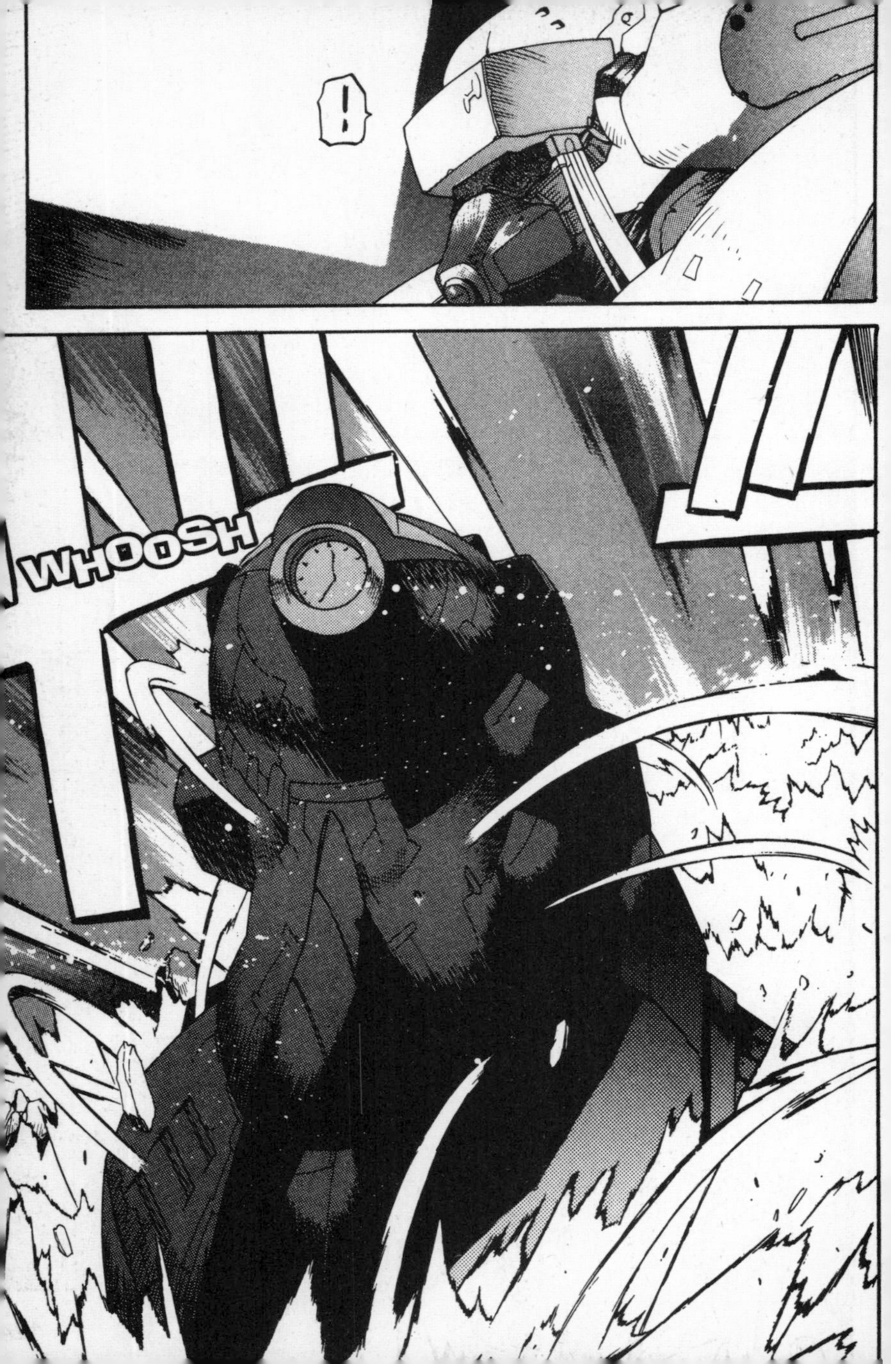
!
WHOOSH

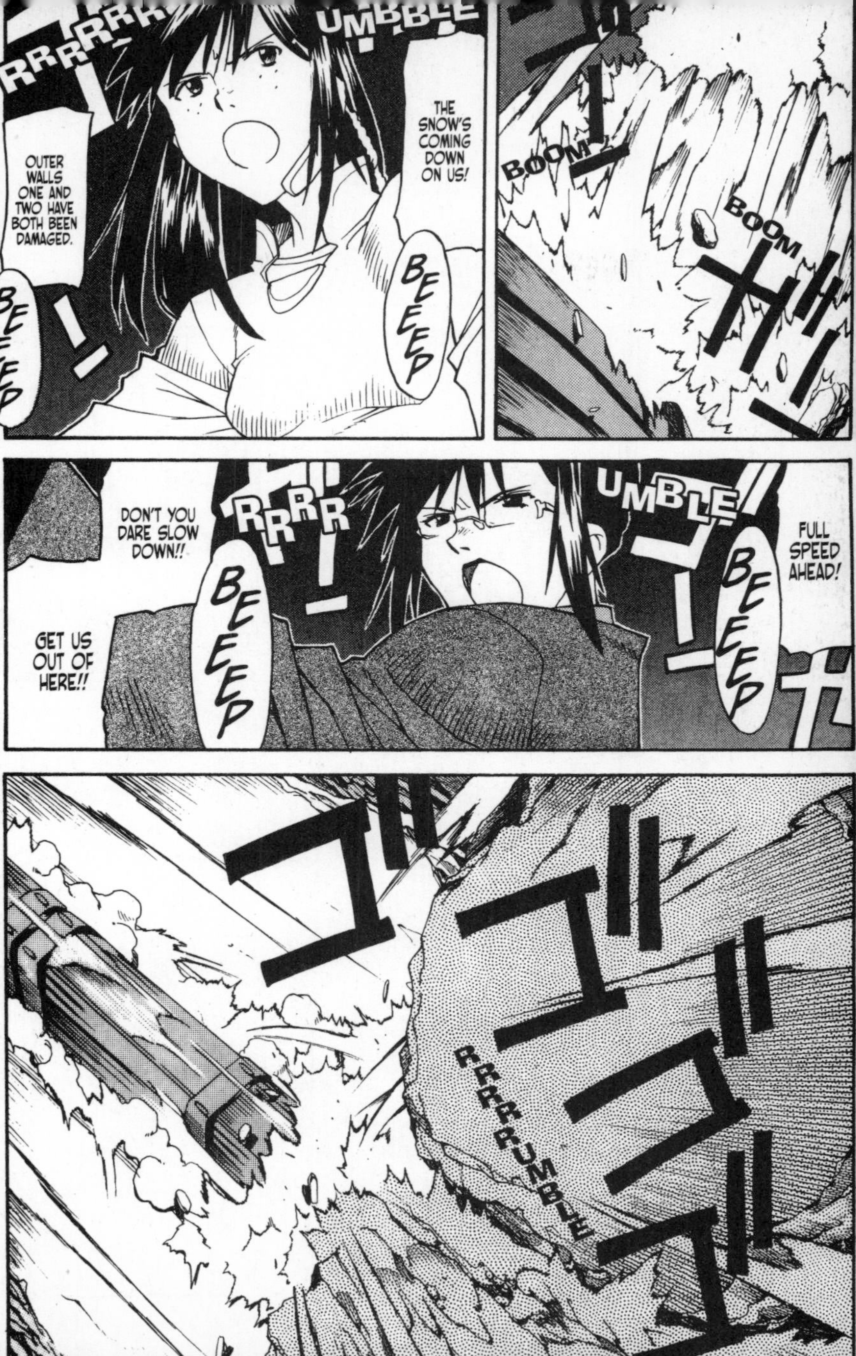

BOOM
BOOM
UMBBLE
THE SNOW'S COMING DOWN ON US!
RRRRRRRR
OUTER WALLS ONE AND TWO HAVE BOTH BEEN DAMAGED.
BEEEP
BEEEP
FULL SPEED AHEAD!
UMBLE
BEEEP
RRRR
DON'T YOU DARE SLOW DOWN!!
BEEEP
GET US OUT OF HERE!!
RRRRRUMBLE

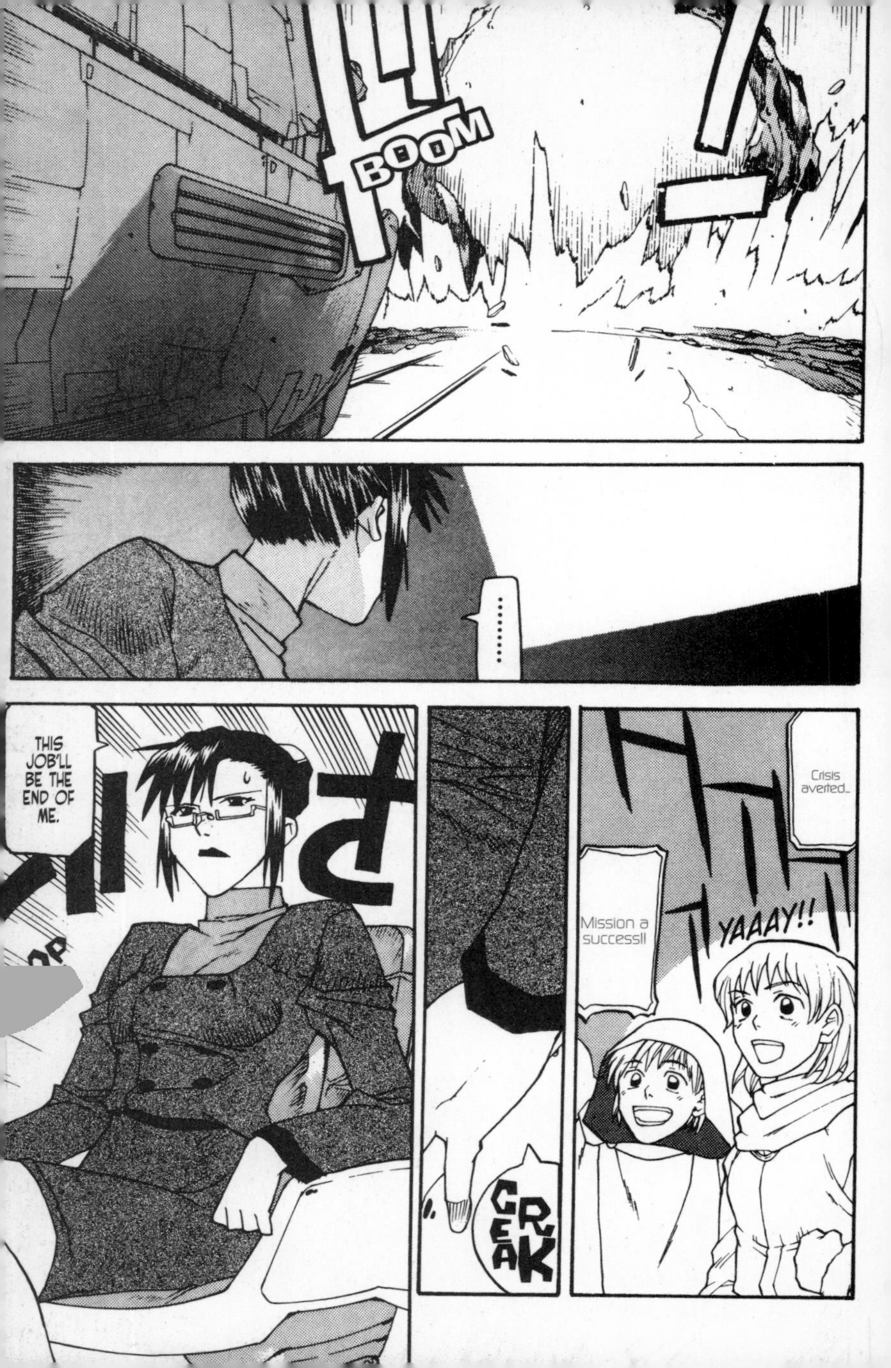
BOOM
....
Crisis averted...
Mission a success!!
YAAAY!!
CREAK
THIS JOB'LL BE THE END OF ME.

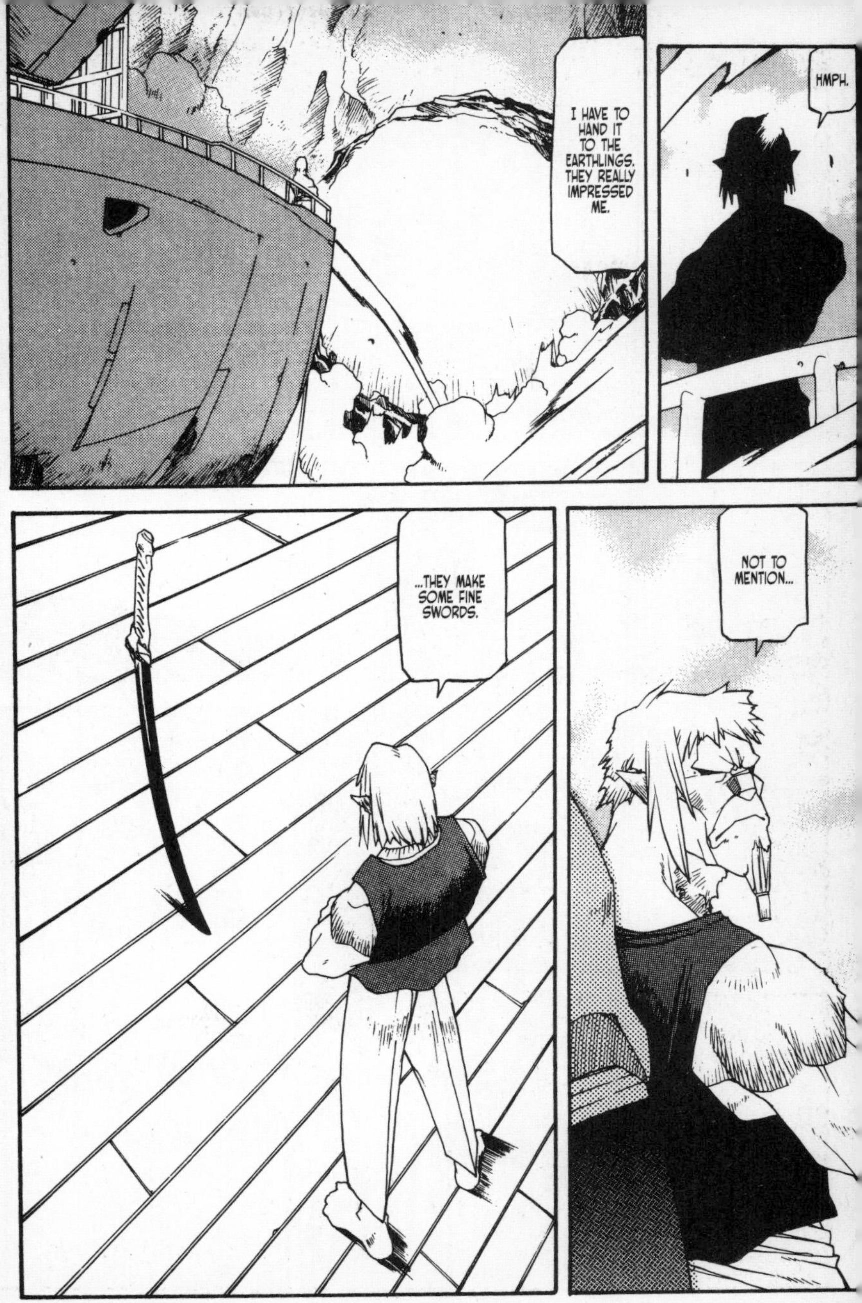
HMPH.
I HAVE TO HAND IT TO THE EARTHLINGS. THEY REALLY IMPRESSED ME.
NOT TO MENTION...
...THEY MAKE SOME FINE SWORDS.

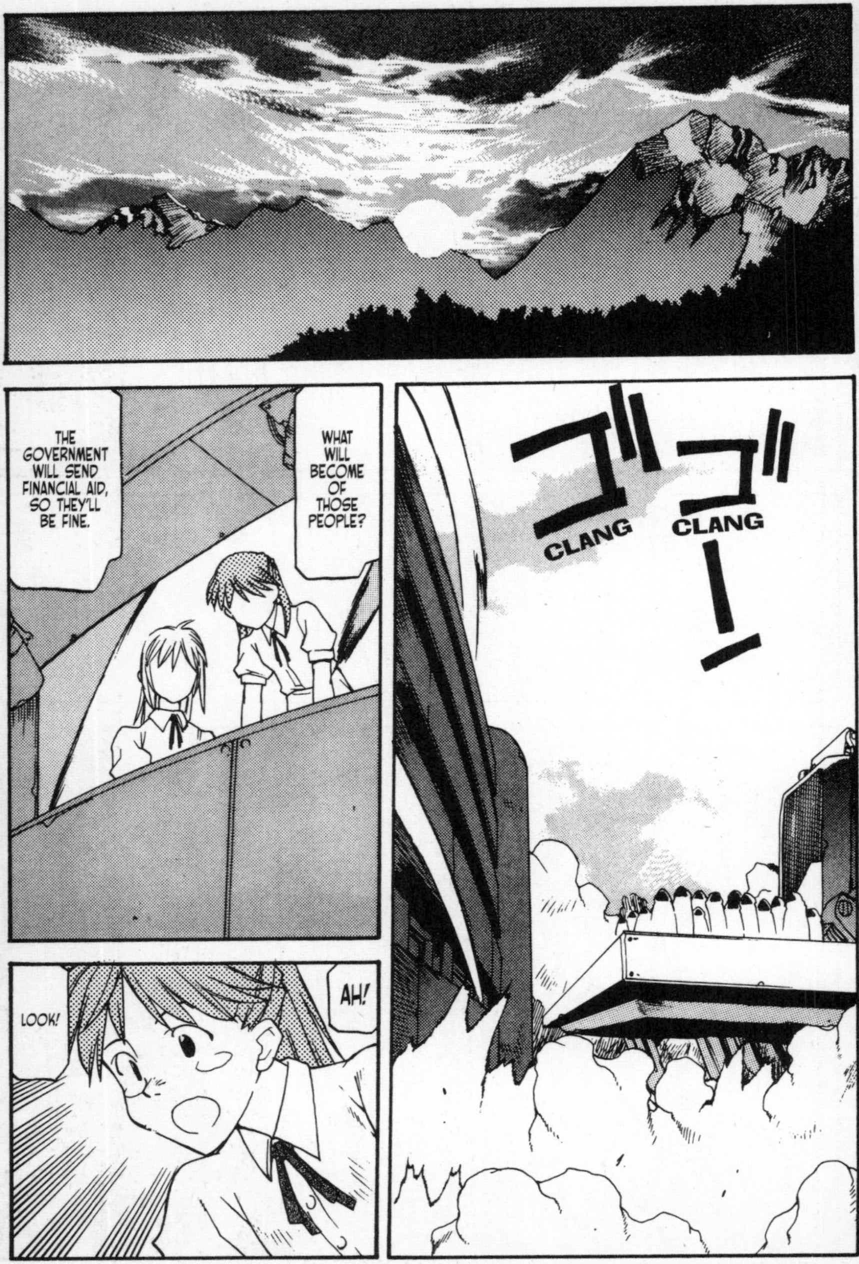
ゴゴー
CLANG
CLANG
WHAT WILL BECOME OF THOSE PEOPLE?
THE GOVERNMENT WILL SEND FINANCIAL AID, SO THEY'LL BE FINE.
AH!
LOOK!

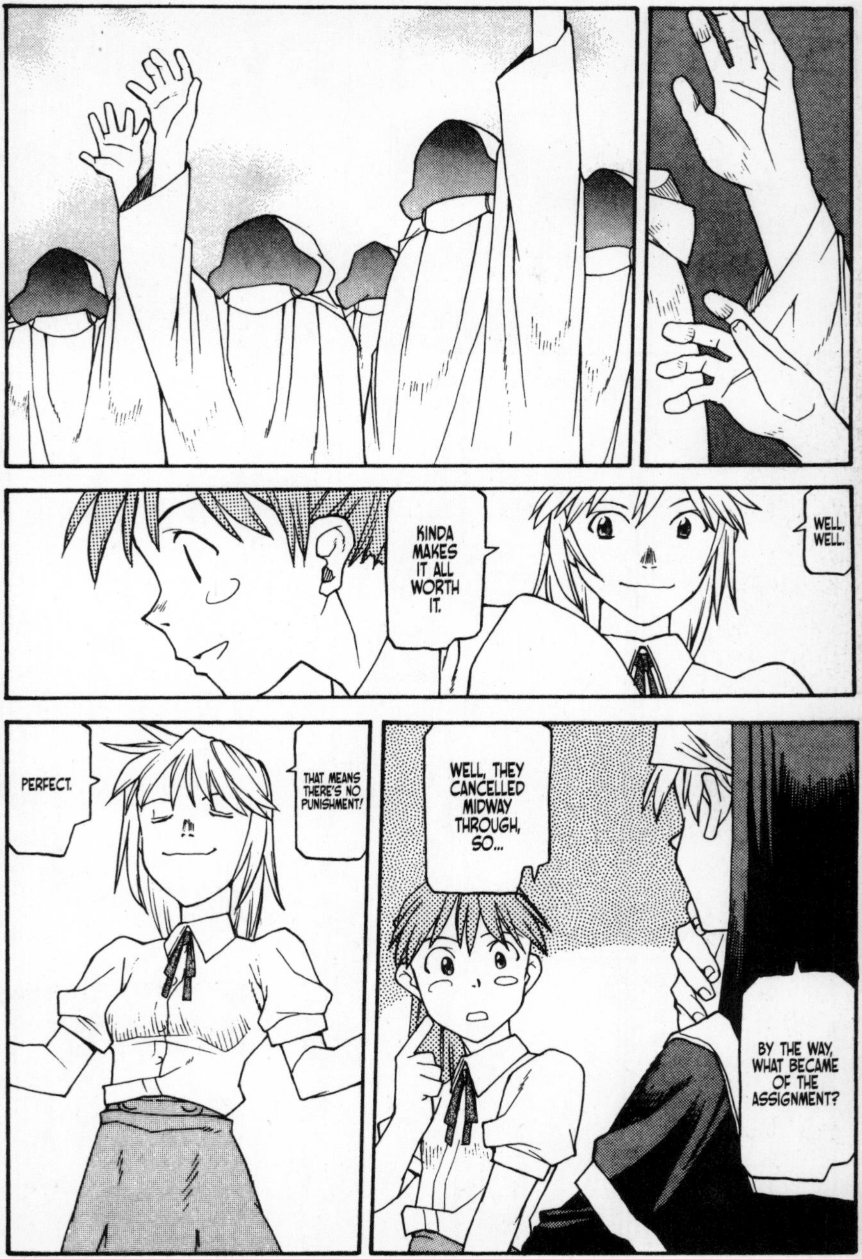
WELL, WELL.
KINDA MAKES IT ALL WORTH IT.
BY THE WAY, WHAT BECAME OF THE ASSIGNMENT?
WELL, THEY CANCELLED MIDWAY THROUGH, SO...
THAT MEANS THERE'S NO PUNISHMENT!
PERFECT.

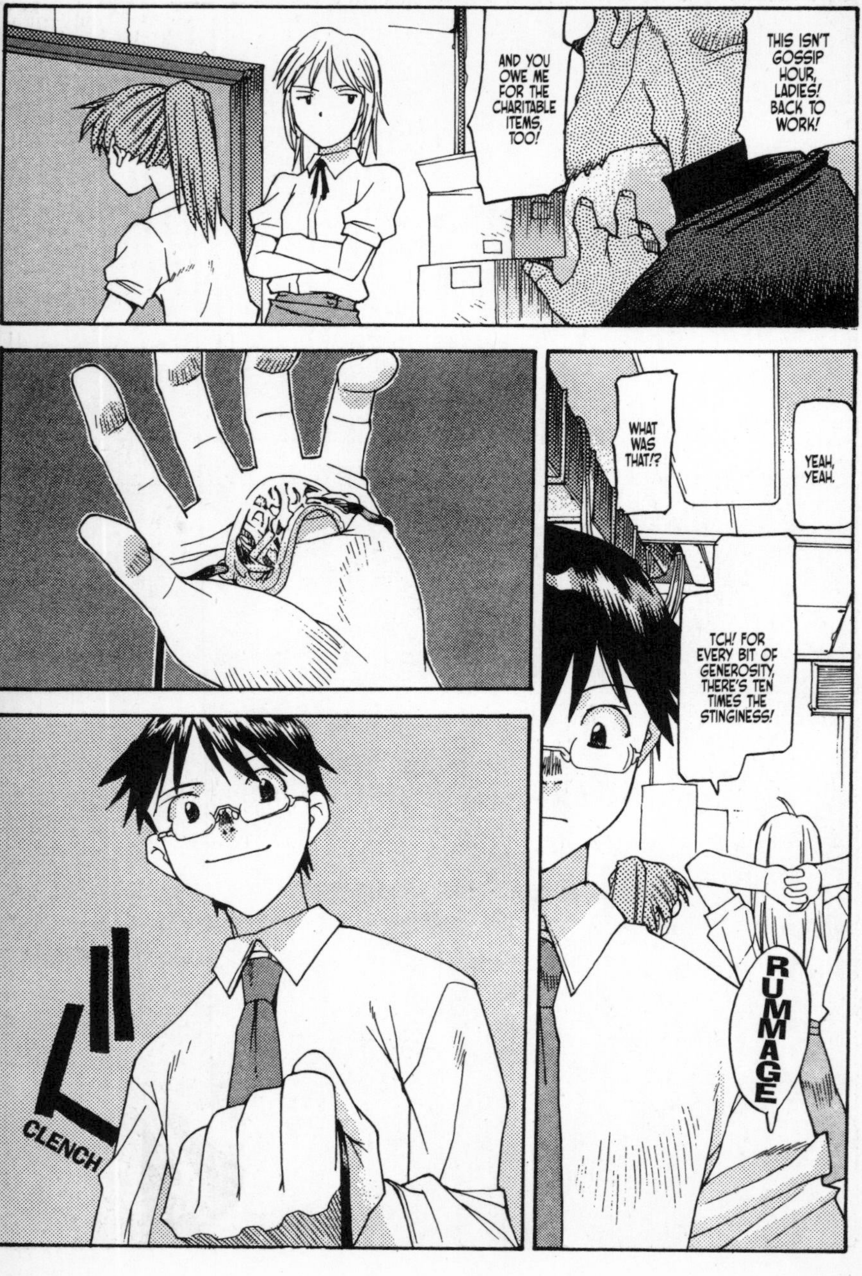
THIS ISN'T GOSSIP HOUR, LADIES! BACK TO WORK!
AND YOU OWE ME FOR THE CHARITABLE ITEMS, TOO!
YEAH, YEAH.
WHAT WAS THAT!?
TCH! FOR EVERY BIT OF GENEROSITY, THERE'S TEN TIMES THE STINGINESS!
RUMMAGE
CLENCH

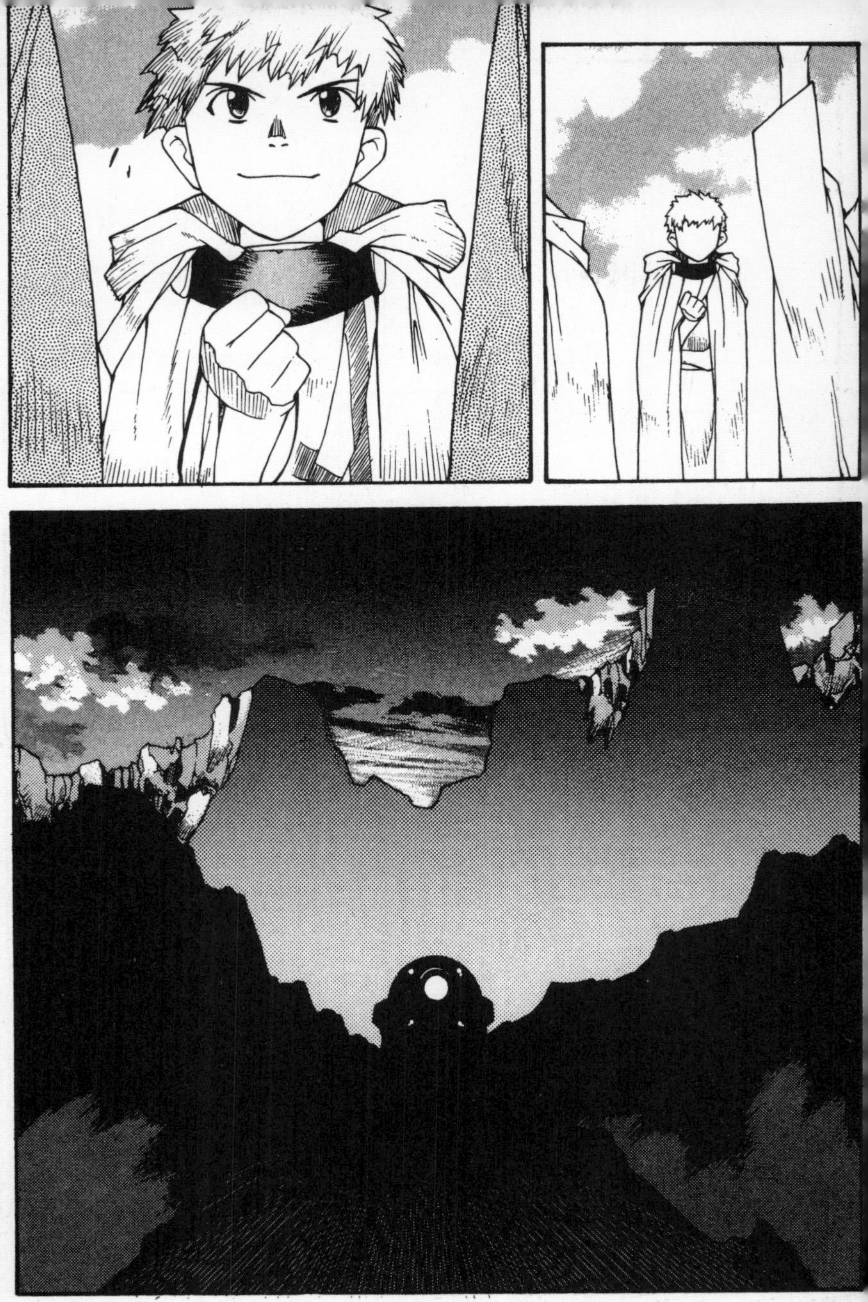

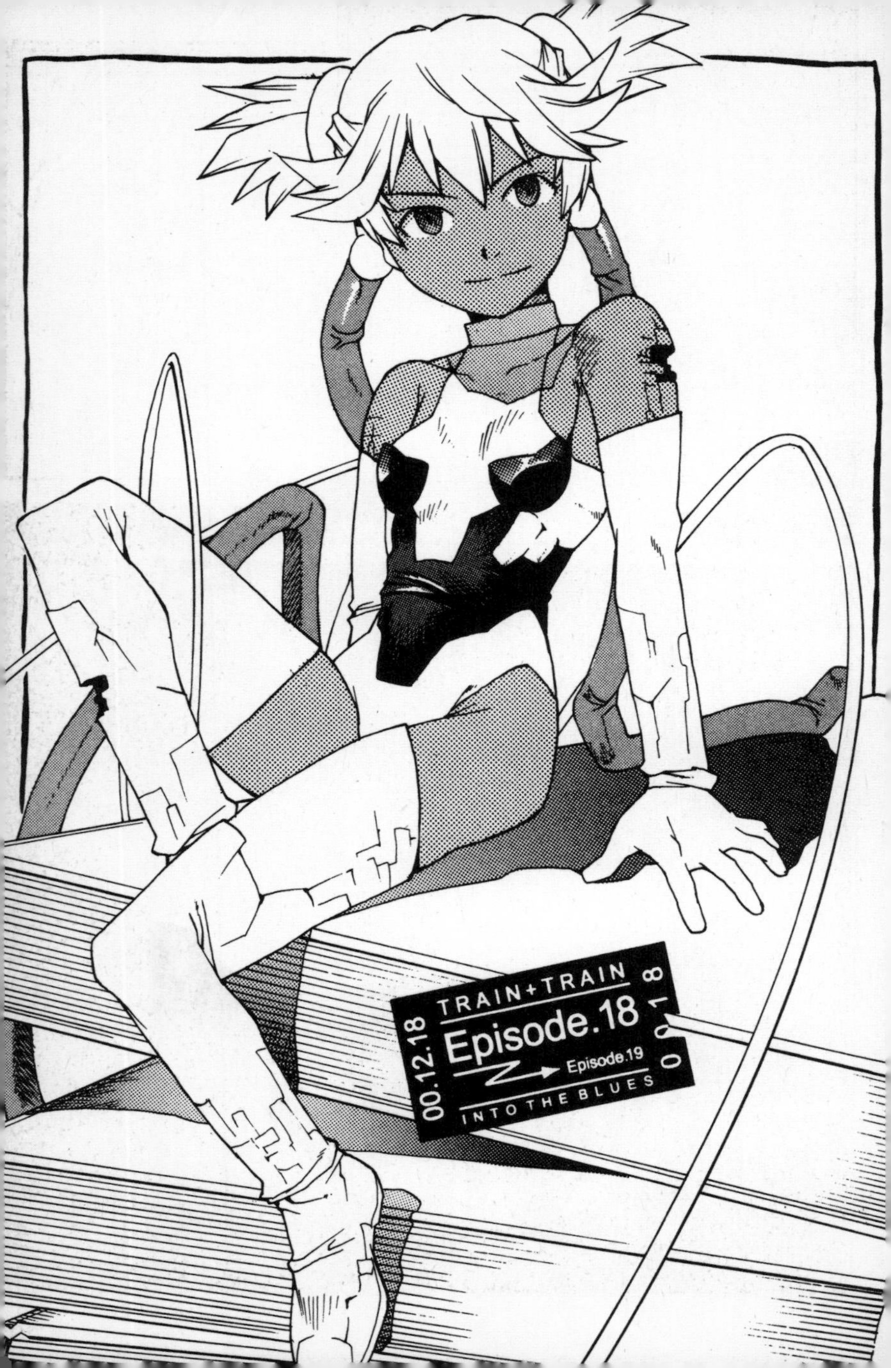
TRAIN+TRAIN
Episode.18
Episode.19
INTO THE BLUES
00.12.18

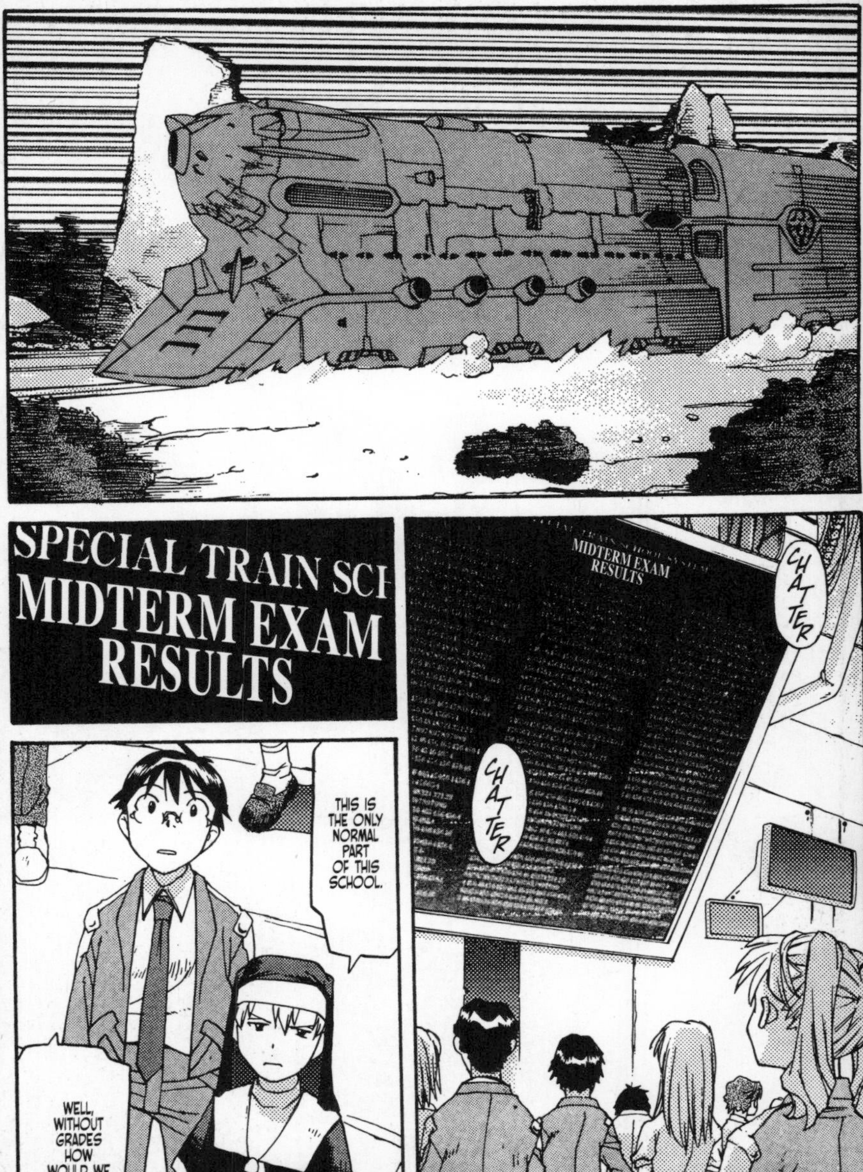
MIDTERM EXAM RESULTS
CHATTER
CHATTER
SPECIAL TRAIN SCH
MIDTERM EXAM RESULTS
THIS IS THE ONLY NORMAL PART OF THIS SCHOOL.
WELL, WITHOUT GRADES HOW WOULD WE GRADUATE?

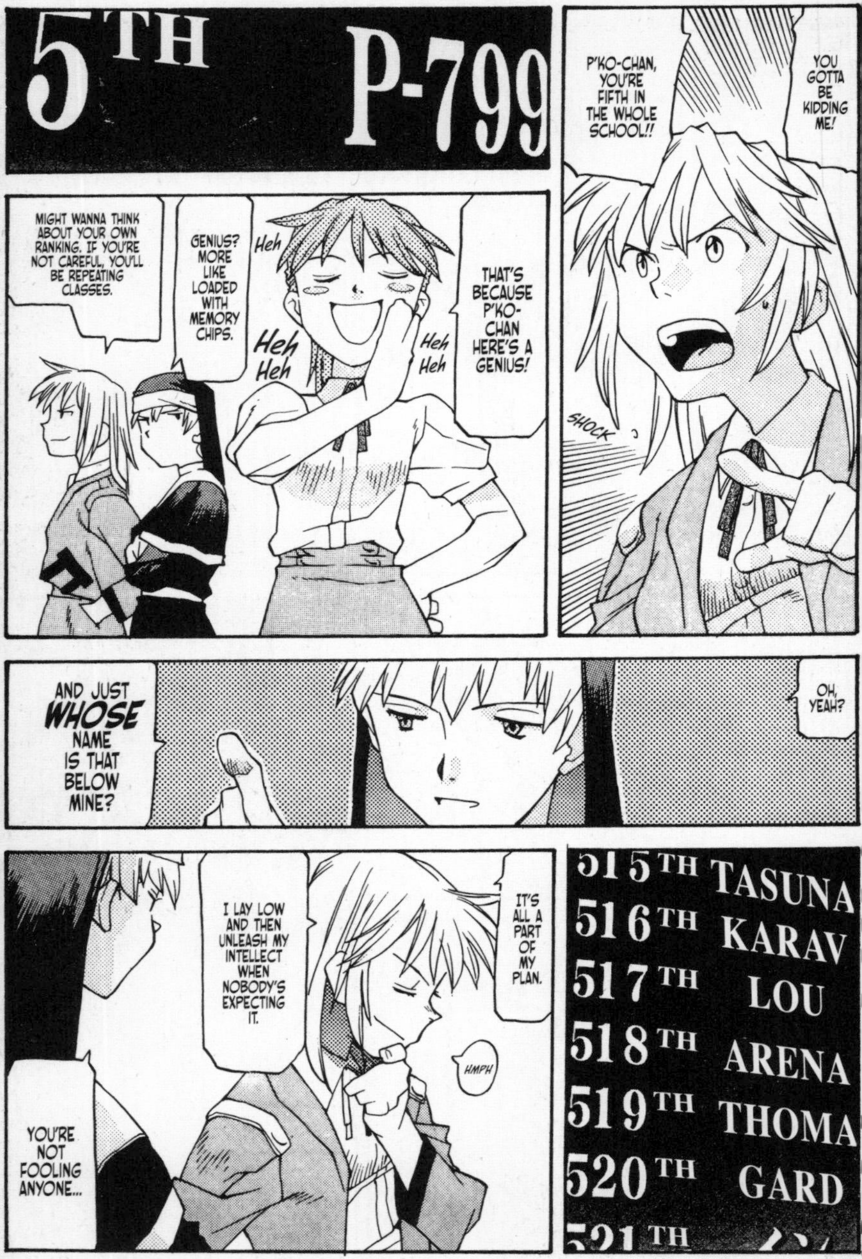
YOU GOTTA BE KIDDING ME!
P'KO-CHAN, YOU'RE FIFTH IN THE WHOLE SCHOOL!!
SHOCK
5TH P-799
THAT'S BECAUSE P'KO-CHAN HERE'S A GENIUS!
Heh Heh
Heh
Heh Heh
GENIUS? MORE LIKE LOADED WITH MEMORY CHIPS.
MIGHT WANNA THINK ABOUT YOUR OWN RANKING. IF YOU'RE NOT CAREFUL, YOU'LL BE REPEATING CLASSES.
OH, YEAH?
AND JUST WHOSE NAME IS THAT BELOW MINE?
515TH TASUNA
516TH KARAV
517TH LOU
518TH ARENA
519TH THOMA
520TH GARD
IT'S ALL A PART OF MY PLAN.
I LAY LOW AND THEN UNLEASH MY INTELLECT WHEN NOBODY'S EXPECTING IT.
HMPH
YOU'RE NOT FOOLING ANYONE...

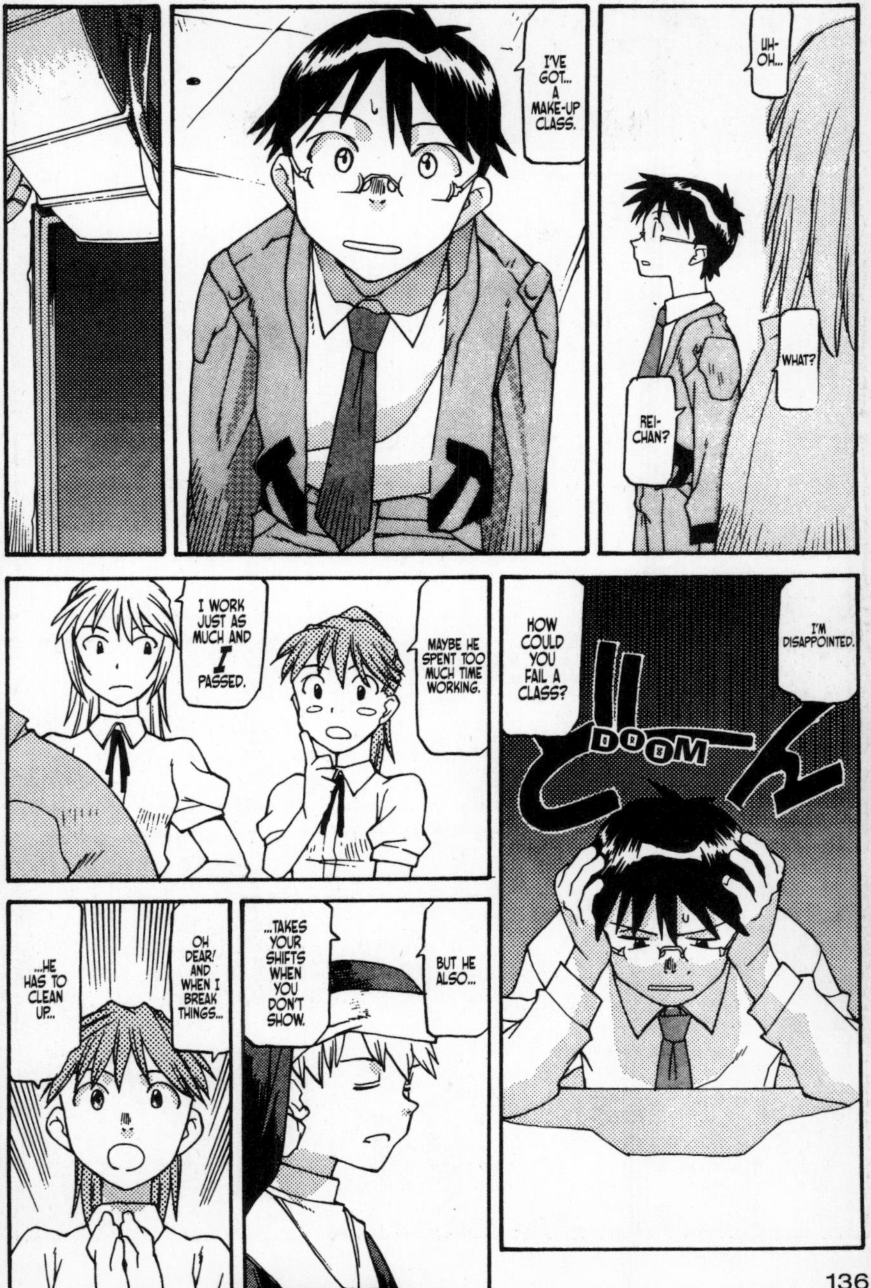
UH-OH...
WHAT?
REI-CHAN?
I'VE GOT... A MAKE-UP CLASS.
I'M DISAPPOINTED.
HOW COULD YOU FAIL A CLASS?
DOOM
MAYBE HE SPENT TOO MUCH TIME WORKING.
I WORK JUST AS MUCH AND I PASSED.
BUT HE ALSO...
...TAKES YOUR SHIFTS WHEN YOU DON'T SHOW.
OH DEAR! AND WHEN I BREAK THINGS...
...HE HAS TO CLEAN UP...

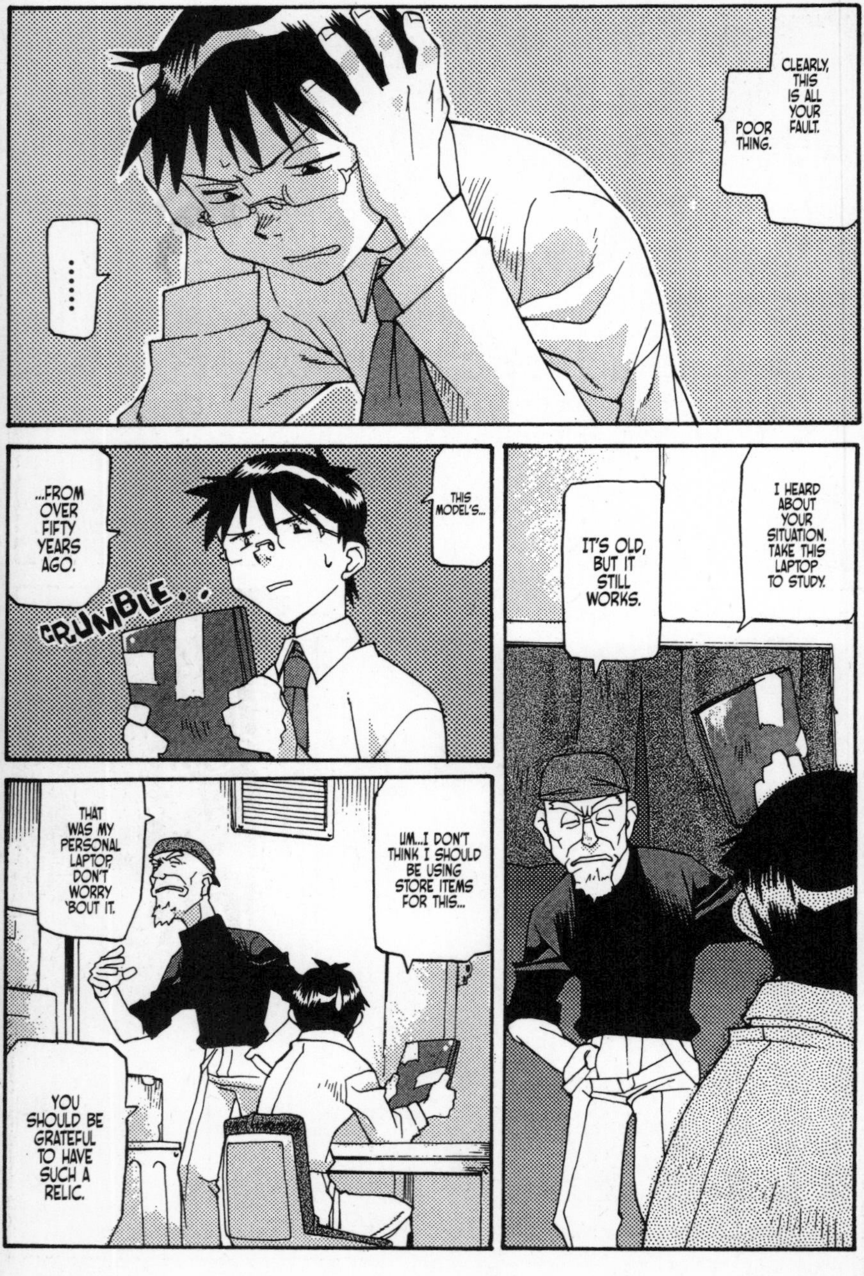
CLEARLY, THIS IS ALL YOUR FAULT.
POOR THING.
......
I HEARD ABOUT YOUR SITUATION. TAKE THIS LAPTOP TO STUDY.
IT'S OLD, BUT IT STILL WORKS.
THIS MODEL'S...
...FROM OVER FIFTY YEARS AGO.
GRUMBLE..
UM...I DON'T THINK I SHOULD BE USING STORE ITEMS FOR THIS...
THAT WAS MY PERSONAL LAPTOP, DON'T WORRY 'BOUT IT.
YOU SHOULD BE GRATEFUL TO HAVE SUCH A RELIC.

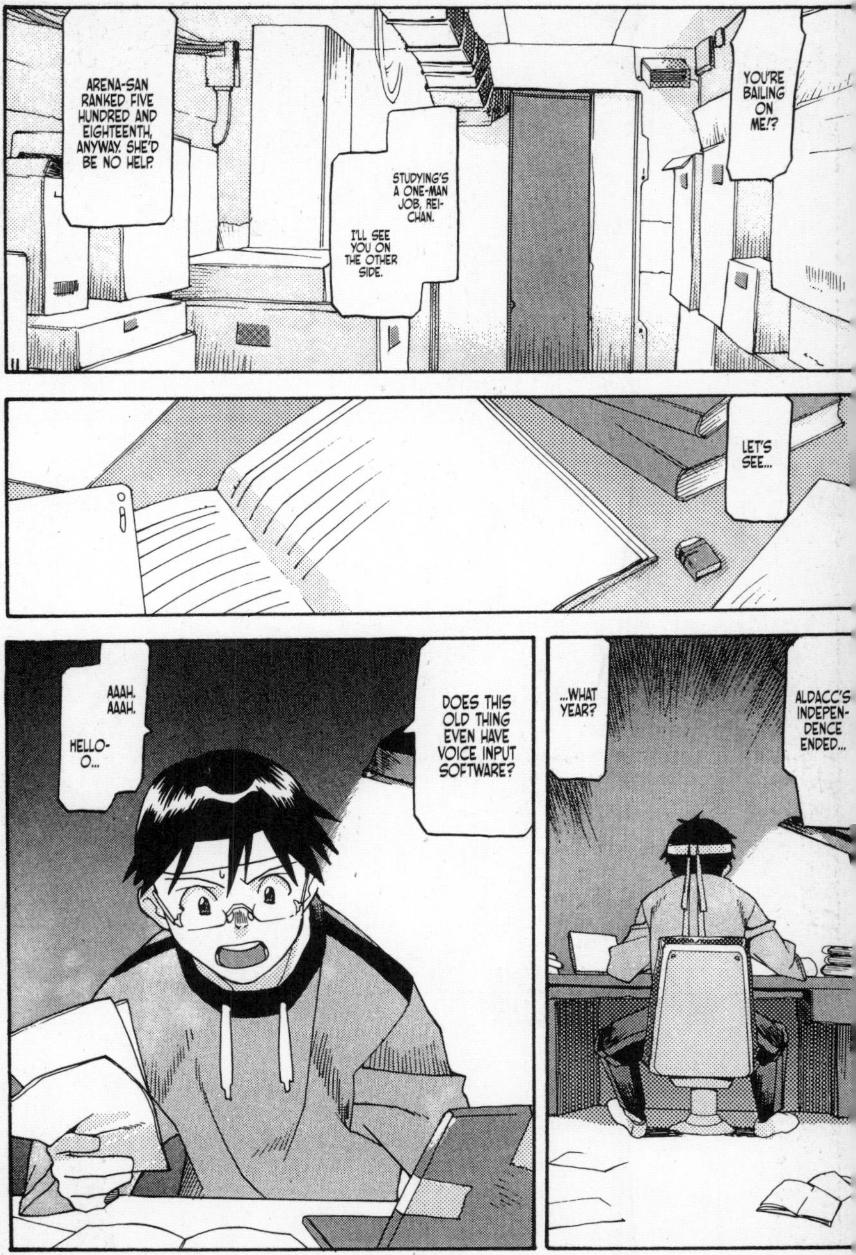
YOU'RE BAILING ON ME!?
STUDYING'S A ONE-MAN JOB, REI-CHAN.
I'LL SEE YOU ON THE OTHER SIDE.
ARENA-SAN RANKED FIVE HUNDRED AND EIGHTEENTH, ANYWAY. SHE'D BE NO HELP.
LET'S SEE...
ALDACC'S INDEPENDENCE ENDED...
...WHAT YEAR?
DOES THIS OLD THING EVEN HAVE VOICE INPUT SOFTWARE?
AAAH. AAAH.
HELLO-O...

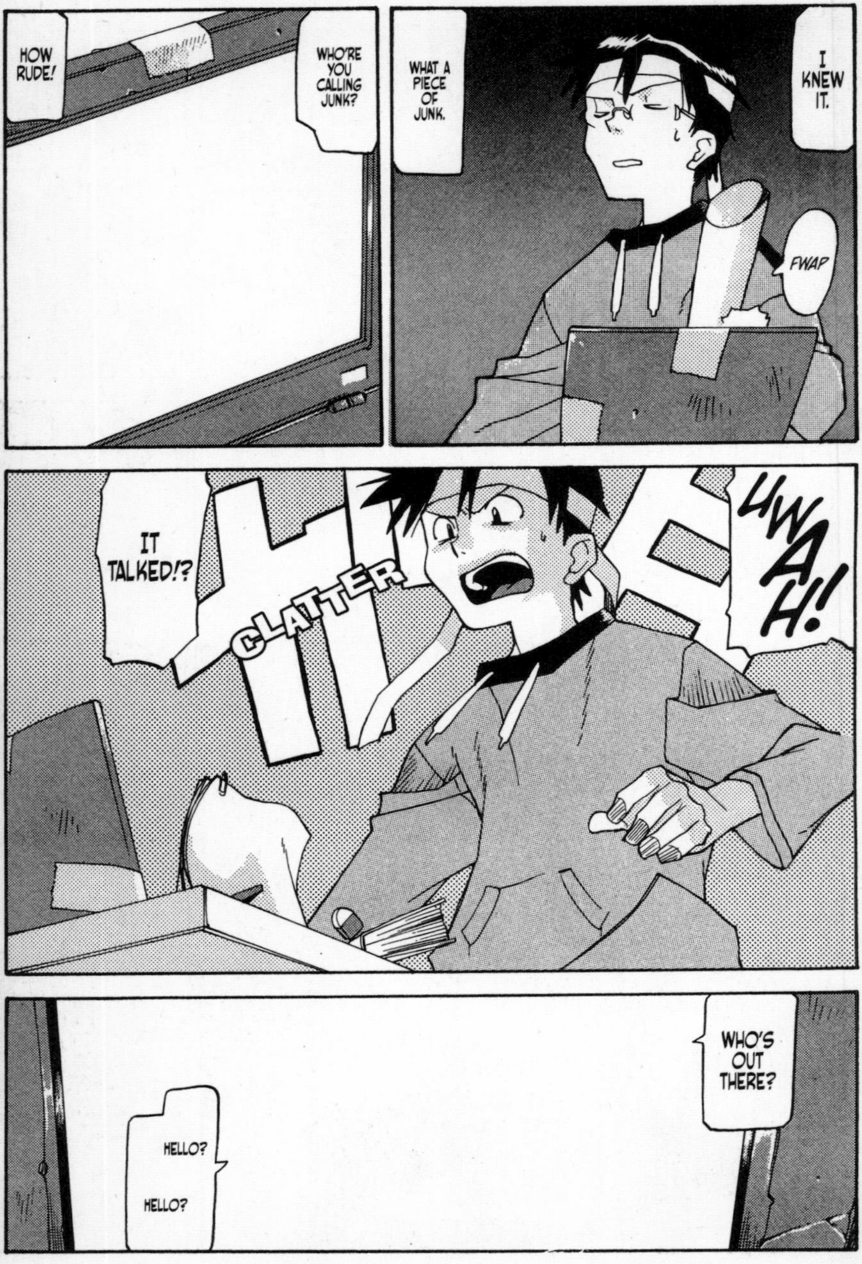
I KNEW IT.
WHAT A PIECE OF JUNK.
FWAP
WHO'RE YOU CALLING JUNK?
HOW RUDE!
UWAH!
CLATTER
IT TALKED!?
WHO'S OUT THERE?
HELLO?
HELLO?

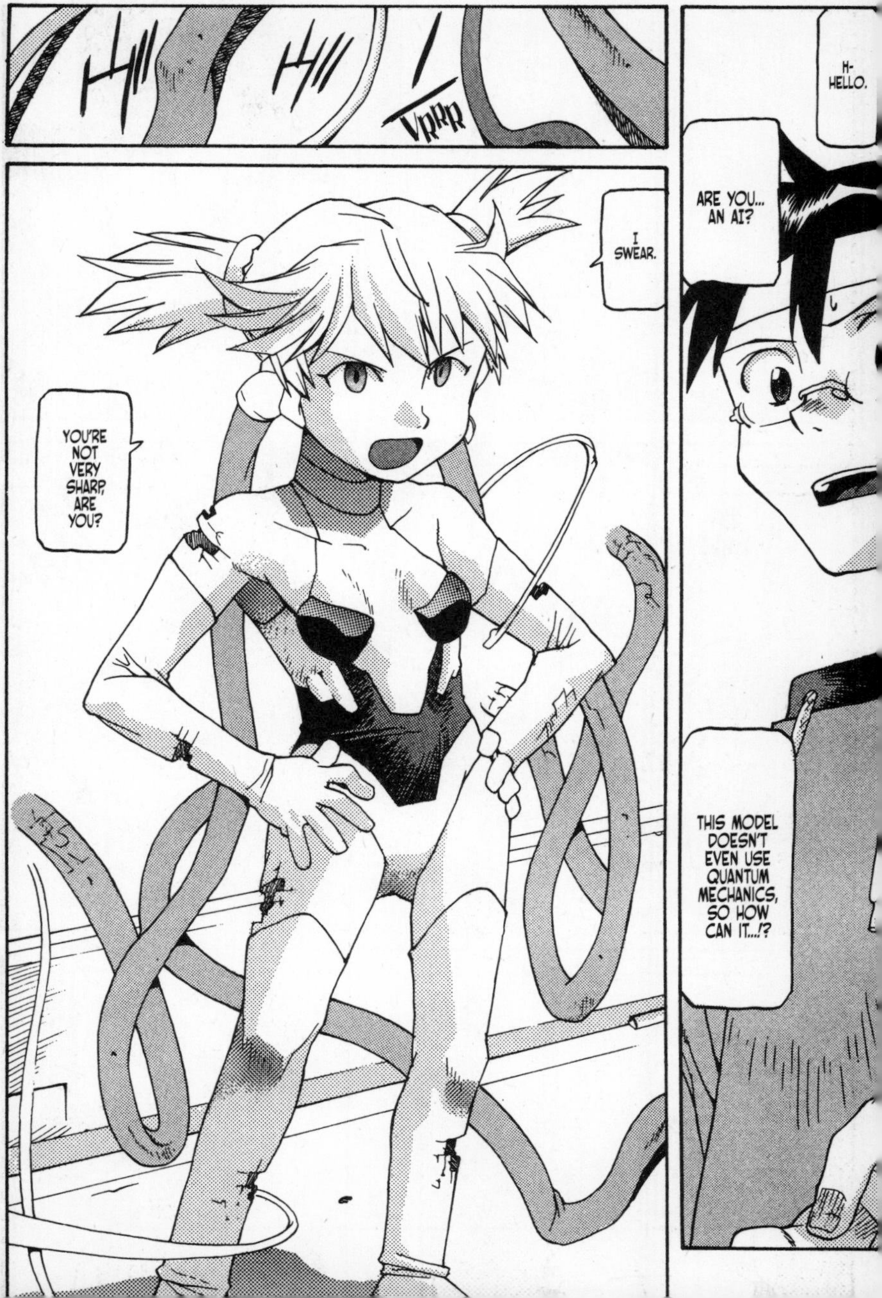
H-HELLO.
ARE YOU... AN AI?
THIS MODEL DOESN'T EVEN USE QUANTUM MECHANICS, SO HOW CAN IT...!?
VRRR
I SWEAR.
YOU'RE NOT VERY SHARP, ARE YOU?

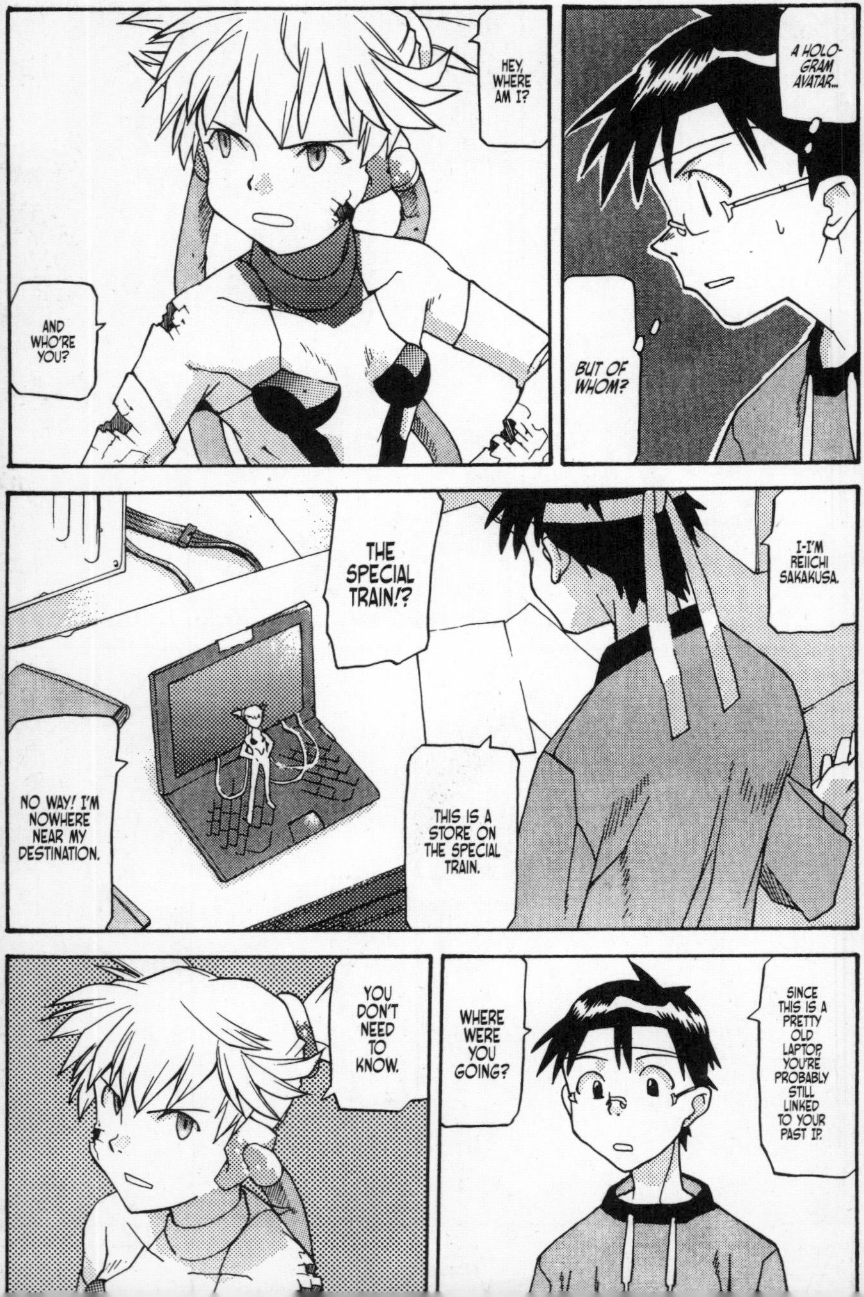
A HOLO-GRAM AVATAR...
BUT OF WHOM?
HEY, WHERE AM I?
AND WHO'RE YOU?
I-I'M REIICHI SAKAKUSA.
THIS IS A STORE ON THE SPECIAL TRAIN.
THE SPECIAL TRAIN!?
NO WAY! I'M NOWHERE NEAR MY DESTINATION.
SINCE THIS IS A PRETTY OLD LAPTOP, YOU'RE PROBABLY STILL LINKED TO YOUR PAST IP.
WHERE WERE YOU GOING?
YOU DON'T NEED TO KNOW.

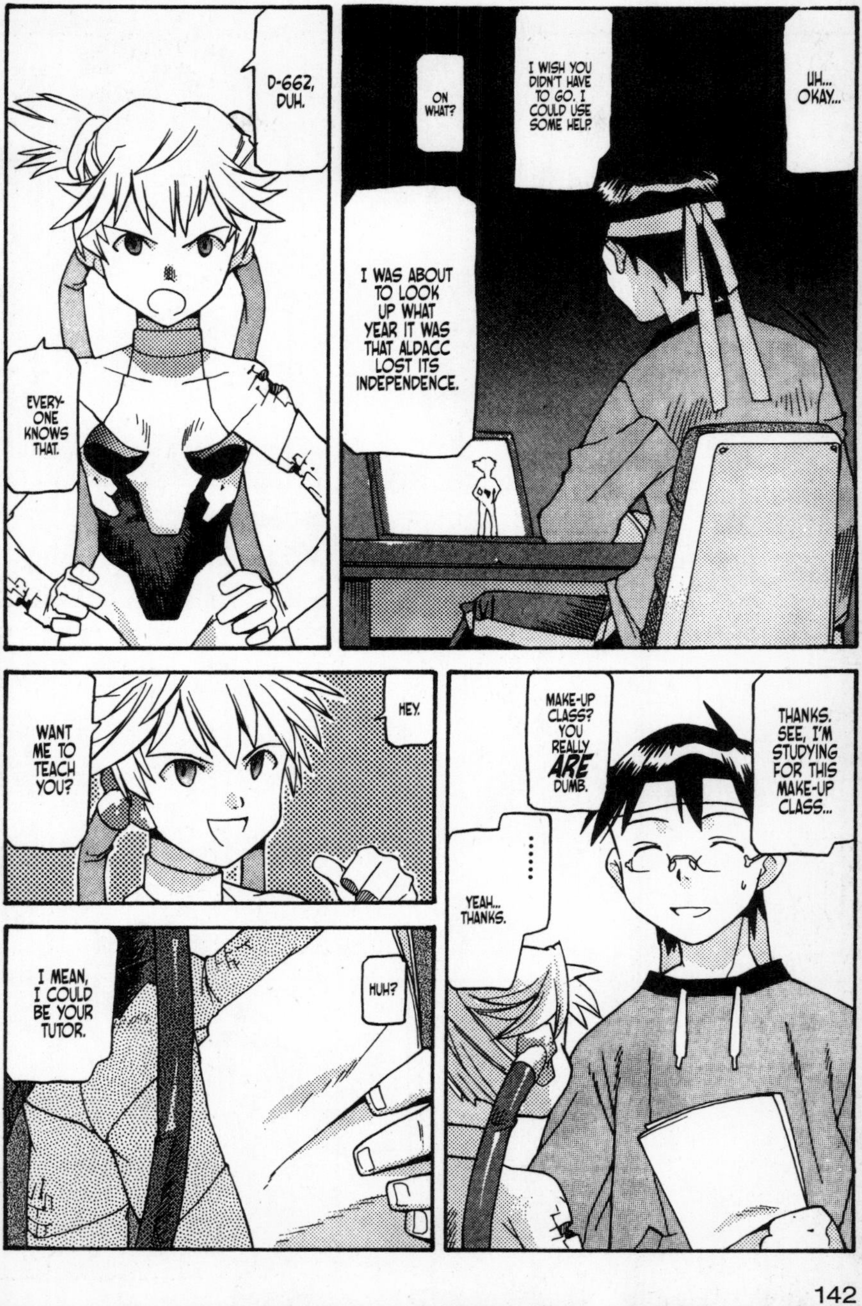
UH... OKAY...
I WISH YOU DIDN'T HAVE TO GO. I COULD USE SOME HELP.
ON WHAT?
I WAS ABOUT TO LOOK UP WHAT YEAR IT WAS THAT ALDACC LOST ITS INDEPENDENCE.
D-662, DUH.
EVERY-ONE KNOWS THAT.
THANKS. SEE, I'M STUDYING FOR THIS MAKE-UP CLASS...
MAKE-UP CLASS? YOU REALLY ARE DUMB.
......
YEAH... THANKS.
HEY.
WANT ME TO TEACH YOU?
HUH?
I MEAN, I COULD BE YOUR TUTOR.

※ Ice = moving firewall   Fire = sedentary firewall

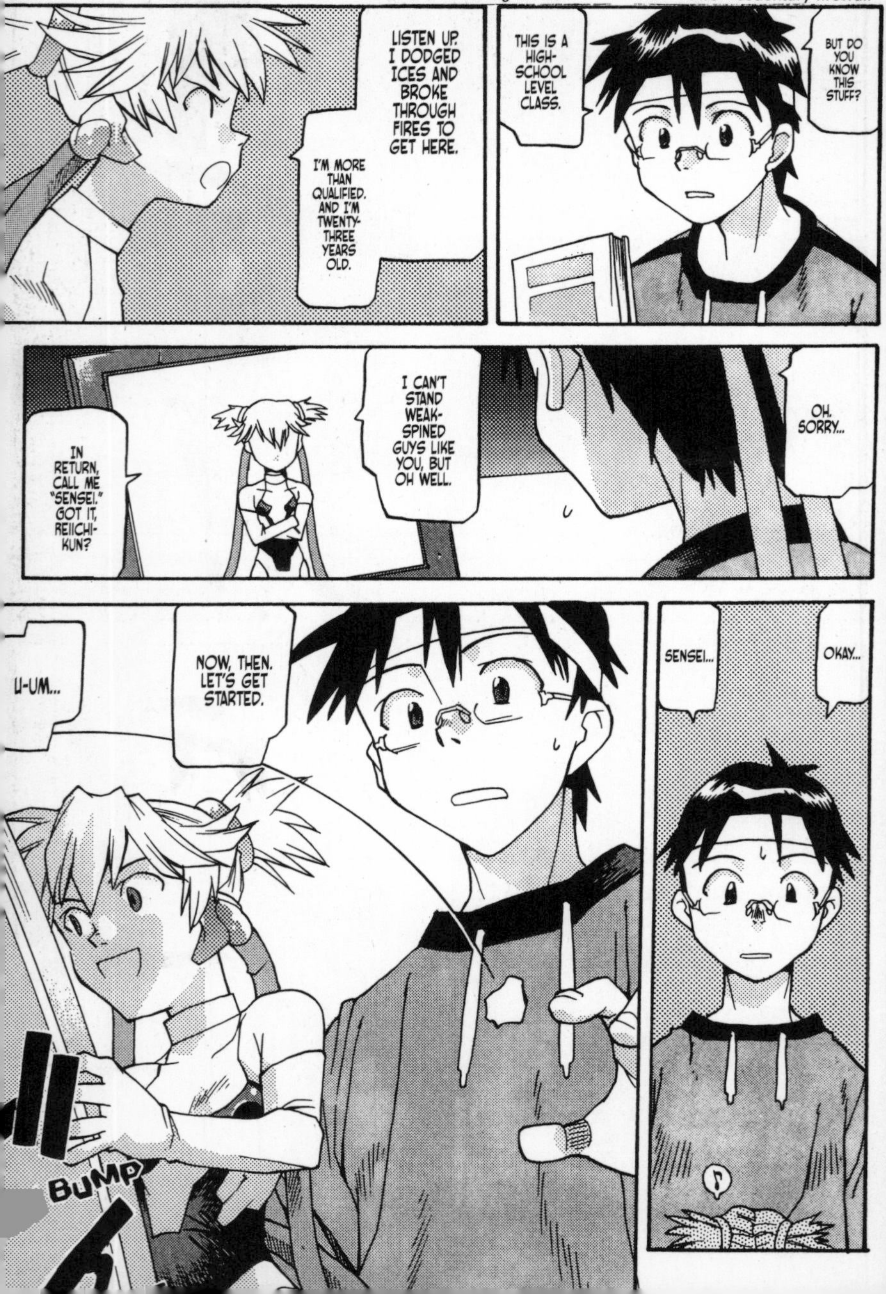
BUT DO YOU KNOW THIS STUFF?
THIS IS A HIGH-SCHOOL LEVEL CLASS.
LISTEN UP. I DODGED ICES AND BROKE THROUGH FIRES TO GET HERE.
I'M MORE THAN QUALIFIED. AND I'M TWENTY-THREE YEARS OLD.
OH. SORRY...
I CAN'T STAND WEAK-SPINED GUYS LIKE YOU, BUT OH WELL.
IN RETURN, CALL ME "SENSEI." GOT IT, REIICHI-KUN?
OKAY...
SENSEI...
NOW, THEN. LET'S GET STARTED.
U-UM...
BUMP

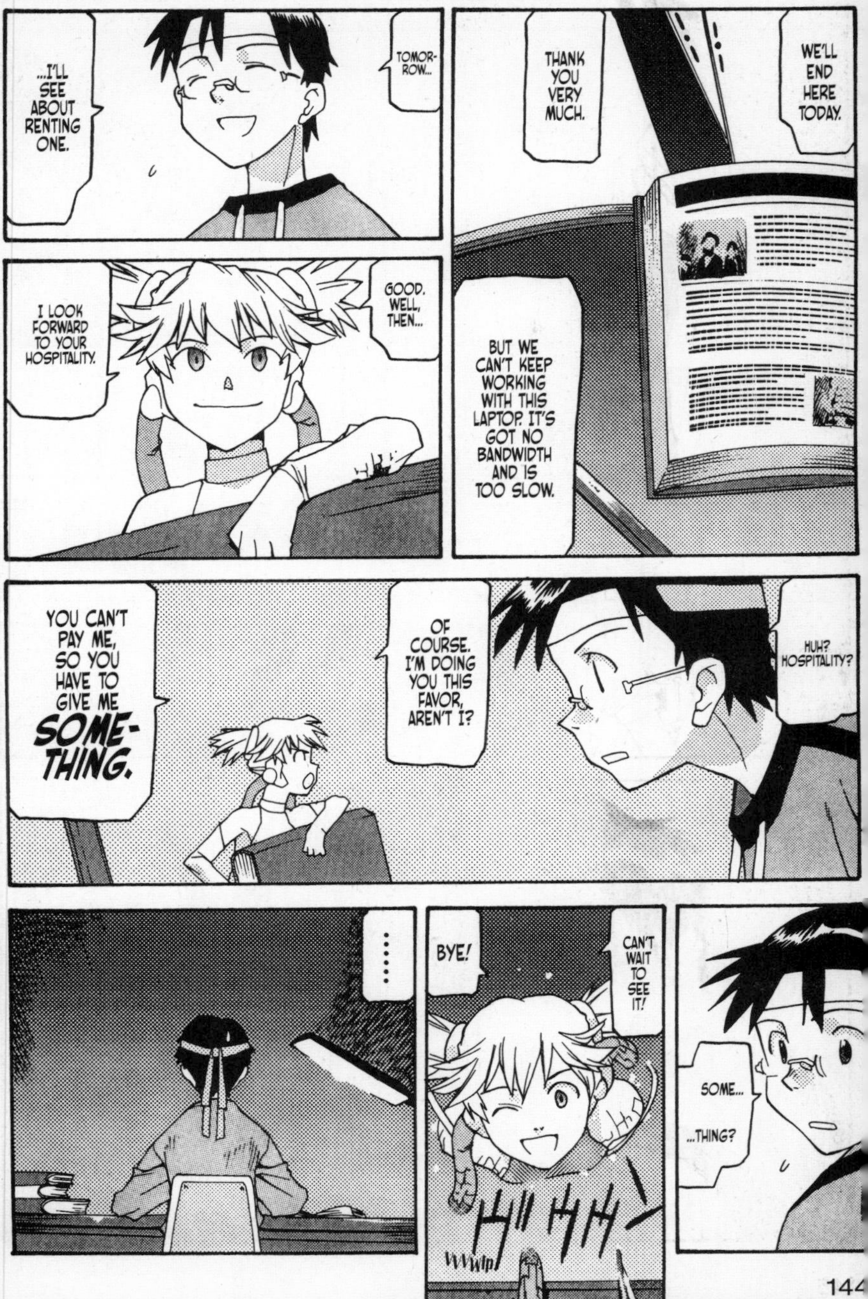
WE'LL END HERE TODAY.
THANK YOU VERY MUCH.
BUT WE CAN'T KEEP WORKING WITH THIS LAPTOP. IT'S GOT NO BANDWIDTH AND IS TOO SLOW.
TOMORROW...
...I'LL SEE ABOUT RENTING ONE.
GOOD. WELL, THEN...
I LOOK FORWARD TO YOUR HOSPITALITY.
HUH? HOSPITALITY?
OF COURSE. I'M DOING YOU THIS FAVOR, AREN'T I?
YOU CAN'T PAY ME, SO YOU HAVE TO GIVE ME **SOMETHING.**
SOME...
...THING?
CAN'T WAIT TO SEE IT!
BYE!
......

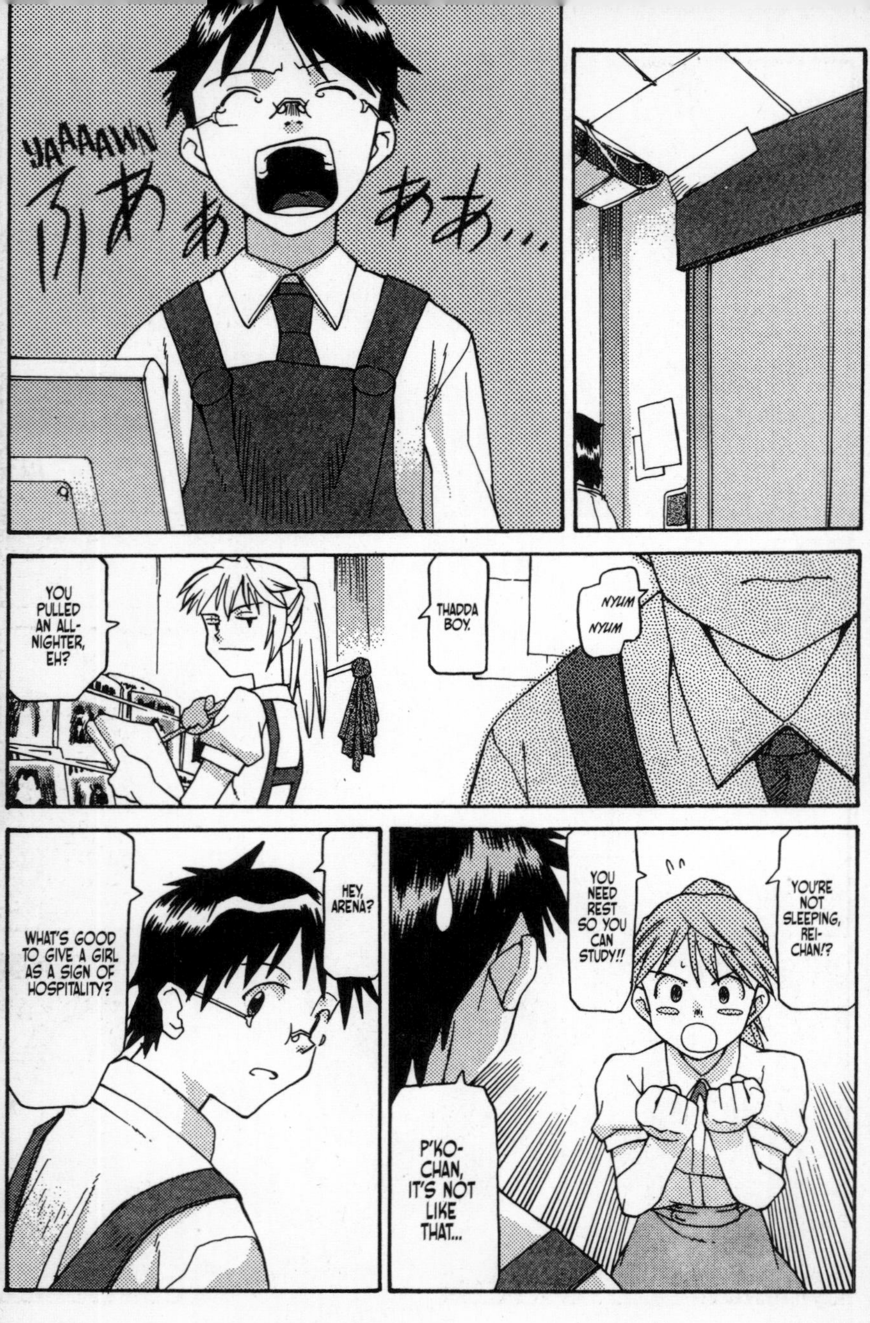
YAAAAWN
ふあぁああ...
NYUM NYUM
THADDA BOY.
YOU PULLED AN ALL-NIGHTER, EH?
YOU'RE NOT SLEEPING, REI-CHAN!?
YOU NEED REST SO YOU CAN STUDY!!
P'KO-CHAN, IT'S NOT LIKE THAT...
HEY, ARENA?
WHAT'S GOOD TO GIVE A GIRL AS A SIGN OF HOSPITALITY?

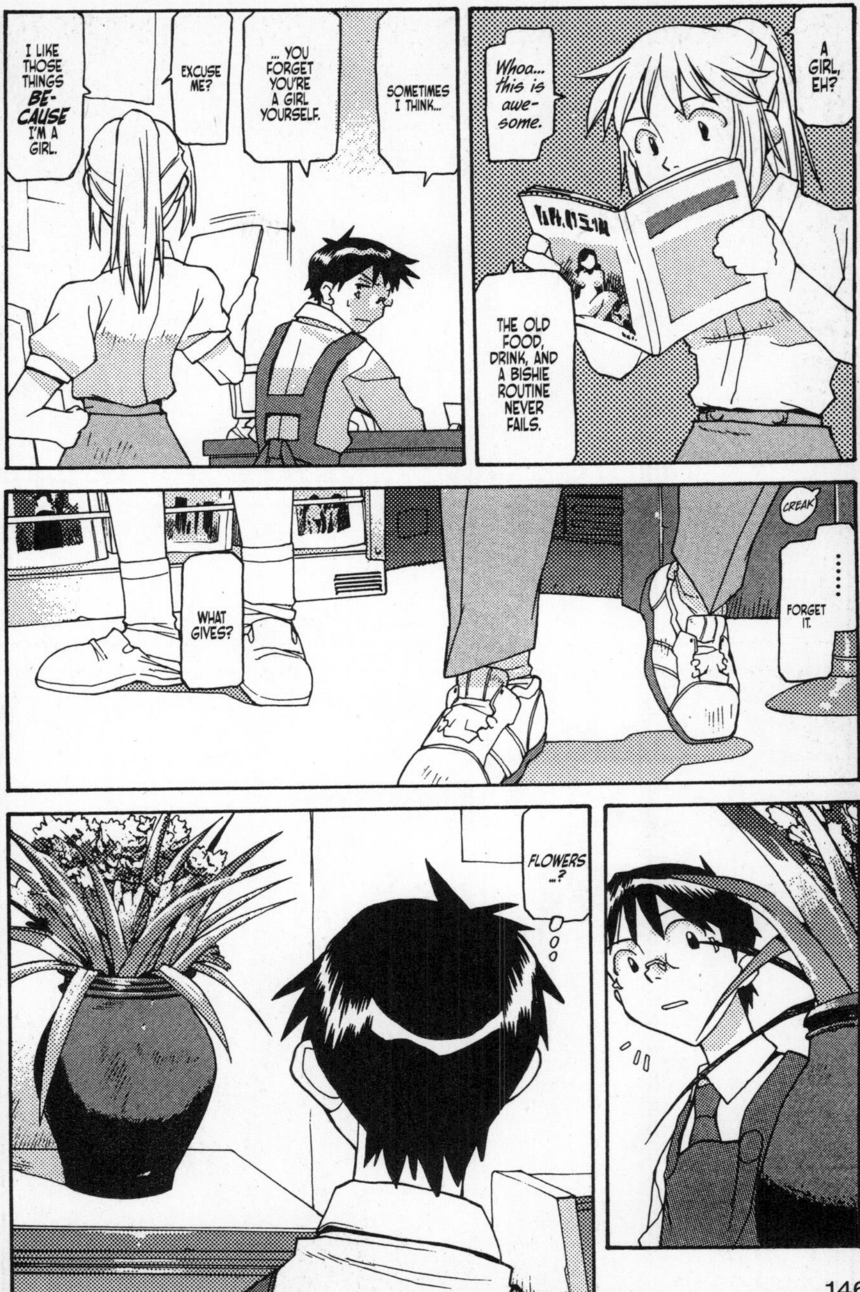
A GIRL, EH?
Whoa... this is awe-some.
THE OLD FOOD, DRINK, AND A BISHIE ROUTINE NEVER FAILS.
SOMETIMES I THINK...
... YOU FORGET YOU'RE A GIRL YOURSELF.
EXCUSE ME?
I LIKE THOSE THINGS **BE-CAUSE** I'M A GIRL.
CREAK
...... FORGET IT.
WHAT GIVES?
FLOWERS ...?

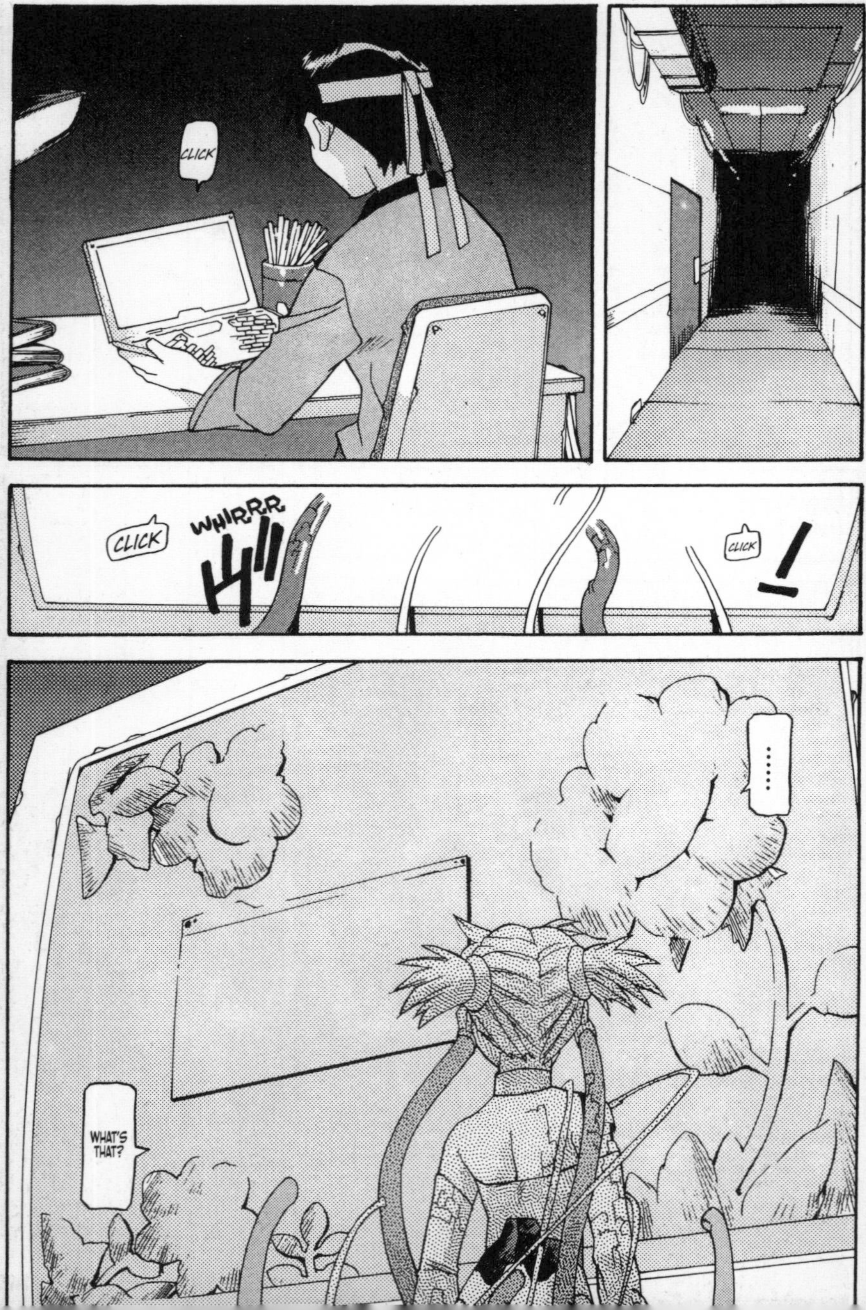
CLICK
CLICK
!
WHIRRR
CLICK
......
WHAT'S THAT?

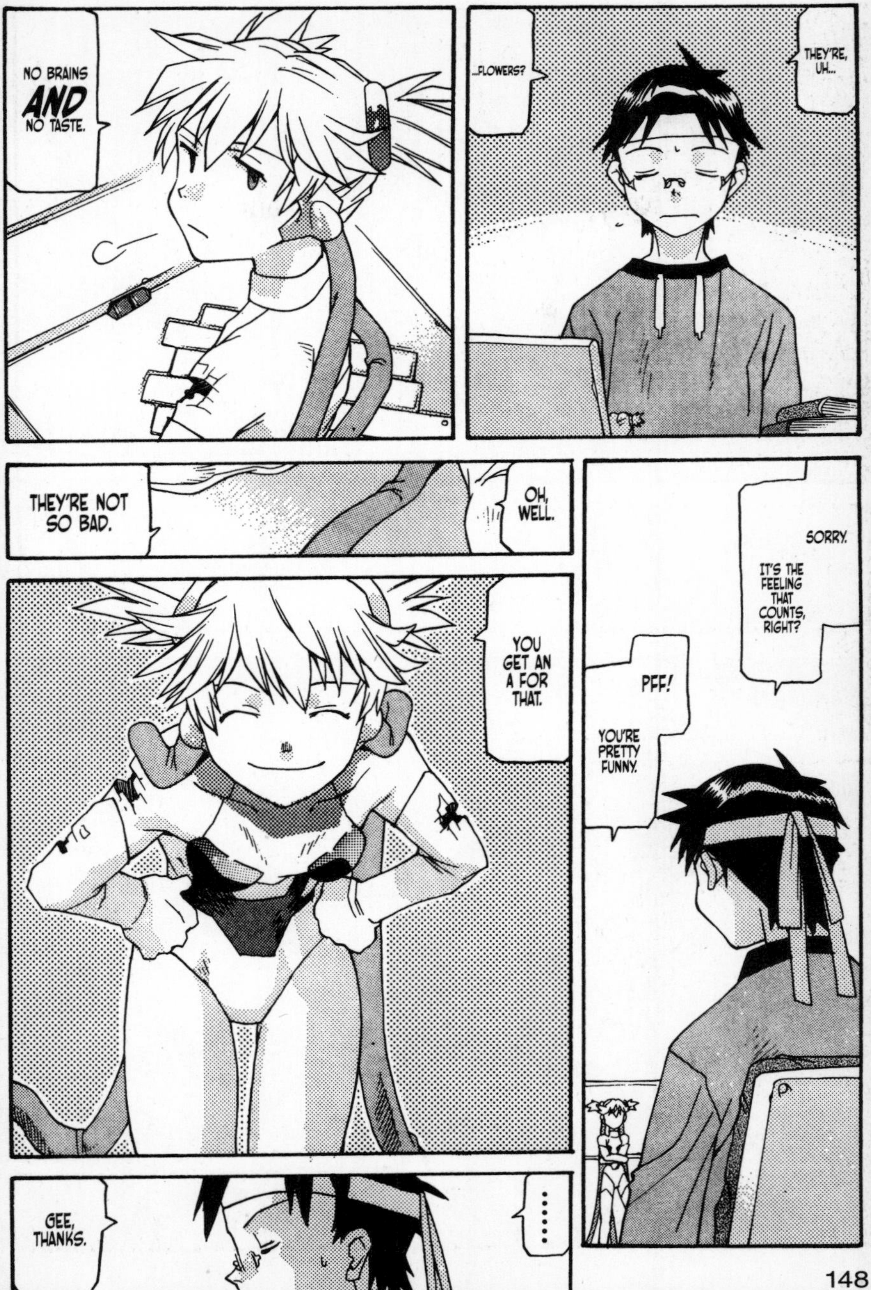
THEY'RE, UH...
...FLOWERS?
NO BRAINS AND NO TASTE.
SORRY.
IT'S THE FEELING THAT COUNTS, RIGHT?
PFF!
YOU'RE PRETTY FUNNY.
OH, WELL.
THEY'RE NOT SO BAD.
YOU GET AN A FOR THAT.
......
GEE, THANKS.

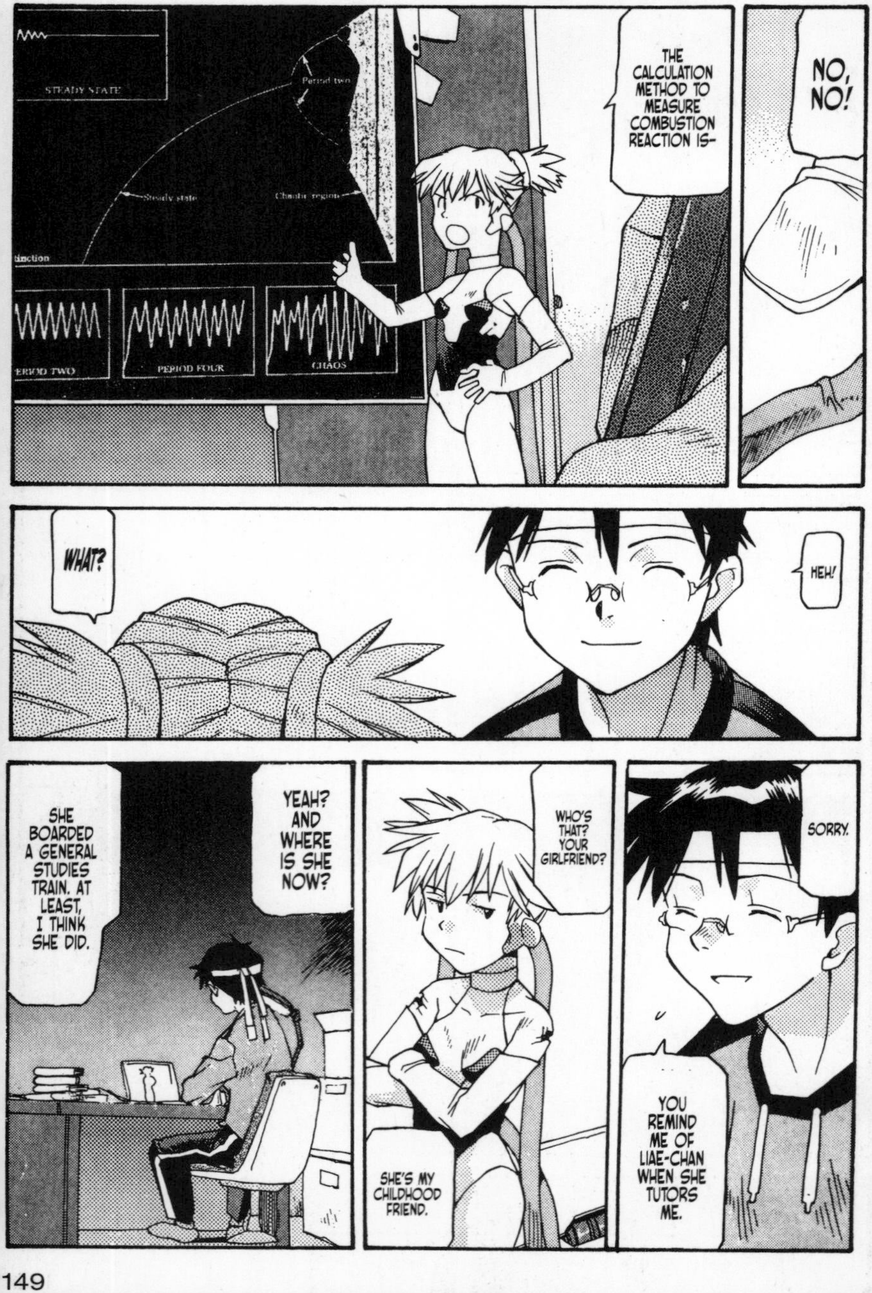
NO, NO!
THE CALCULATION METHOD TO MEASURE COMBUSTION REACTION IS-
STEADY STATE
Period two
Steady state
PERIOD FOUR
CHAOS
HEH!
WHAT?
SORRY.
. . .
YOU REMIND ME OF LIAE-CHAN WHEN SHE TUTORS ME.
WHO'S THAT? YOUR GIRLFRIEND?
SHE'S MY CHILDHOOD FRIEND.
YEAH? AND WHERE IS SHE NOW?
SHE BOARDED A GENERAL STUDIES TRAIN. AT LEAST, I THINK SHE DID.

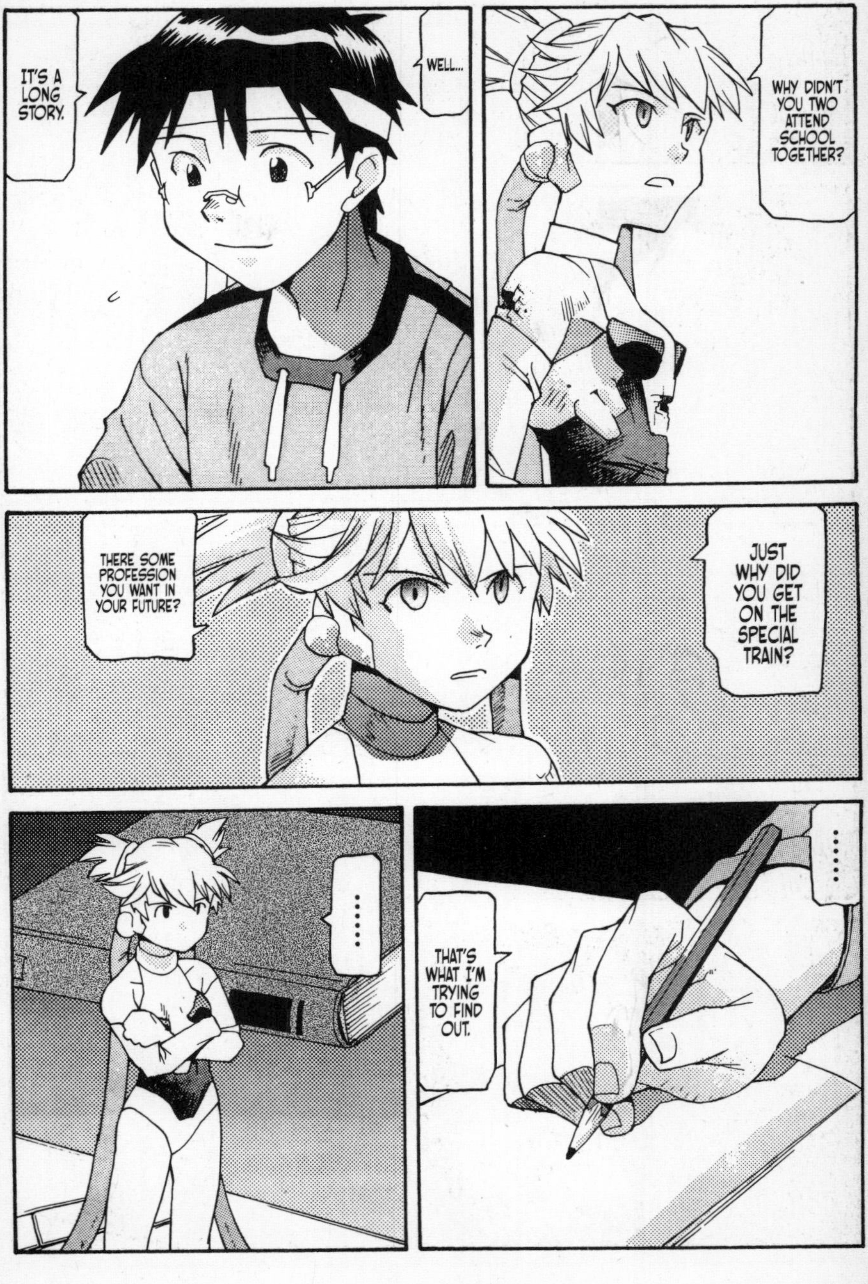
WHY DIDN'T YOU TWO ATTEND SCHOOL TOGETHER?
WELL...
IT'S A LONG STORY.
JUST WHY DID YOU GET ON THE SPECIAL TRAIN?
THERE SOME PROFESSION YOU WANT IN YOUR FUTURE?
......
THAT'S WHAT I'M TRYING TO FIND OUT.
......

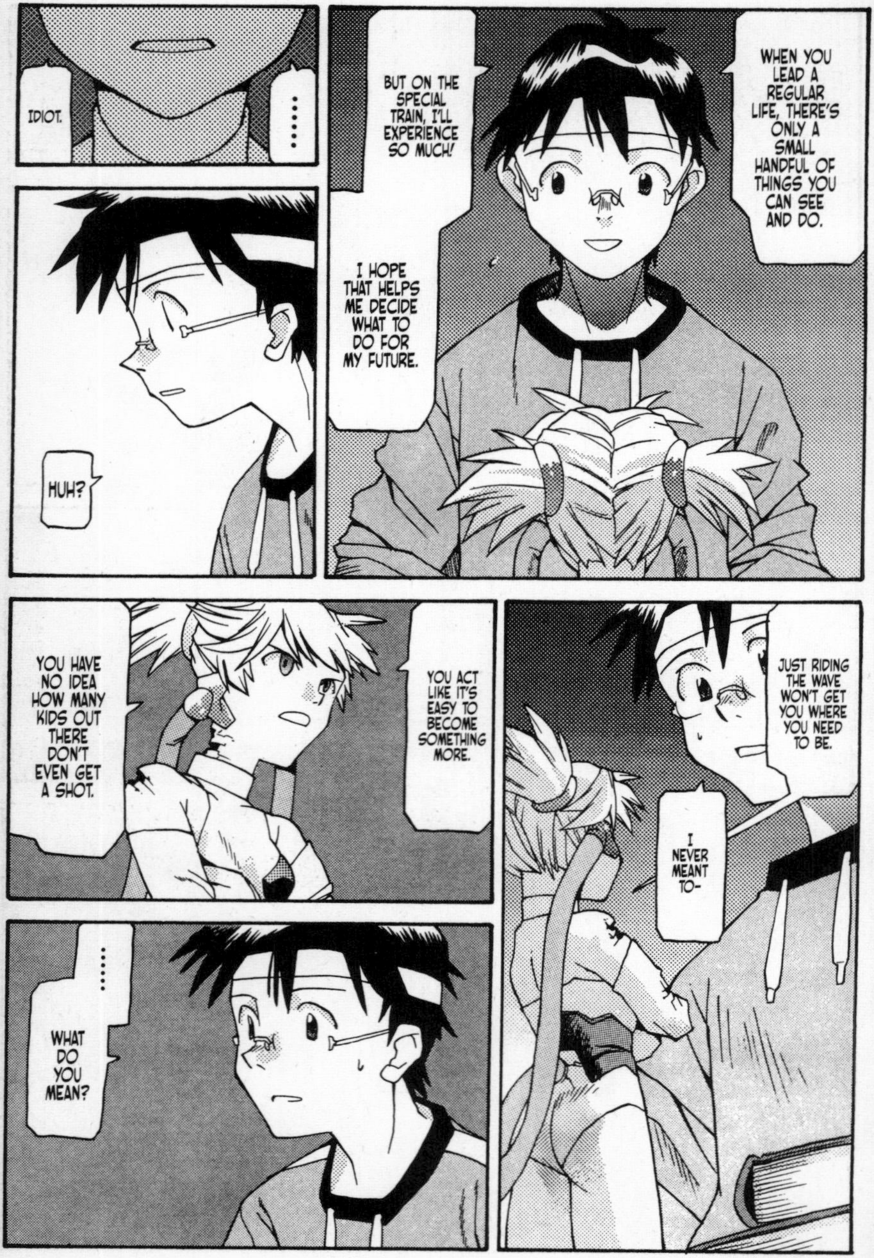
WHEN YOU LEAD A REGULAR LIFE, THERE'S ONLY A SMALL HANDFUL OF THINGS YOU CAN SEE AND DO.
BUT ON THE SPECIAL TRAIN, I'LL EXPERIENCE SO MUCH!
I HOPE THAT HELPS ME DECIDE WHAT TO DO FOR MY FUTURE.
......
IDIOT.
HUH?
JUST RIDING THE WAVE WON'T GET YOU WHERE YOU NEED TO BE.
I NEVER MEANT TO-
YOU ACT LIKE IT'S EASY TO BECOME SOMETHING MORE.
YOU HAVE NO IDEA HOW MANY KIDS OUT THERE DON'T EVEN GET A SHOT.
......
WHAT DO YOU MEAN?

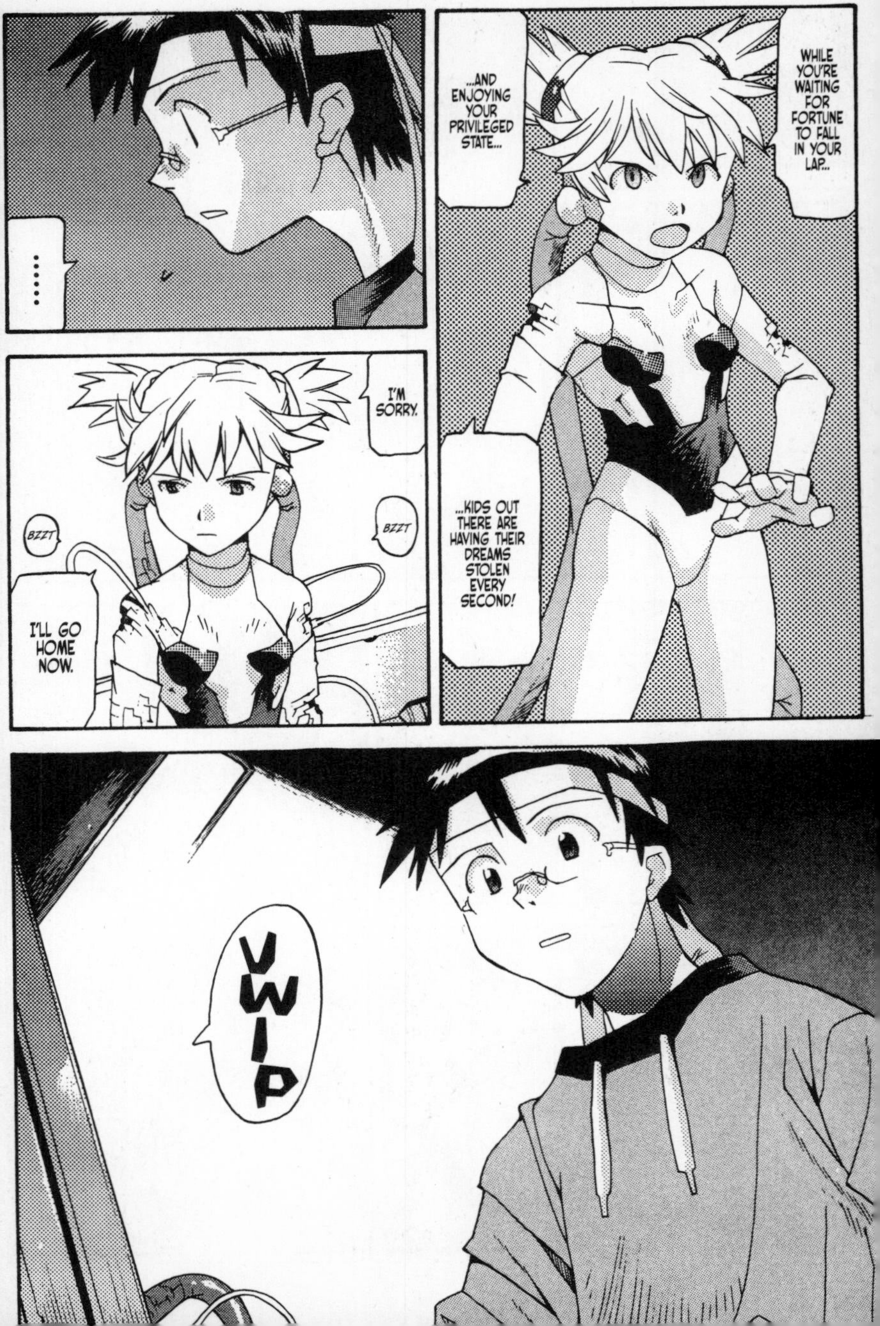
WHILE YOU'RE WAITING FOR FORTUNE TO FALL IN YOUR LAP...
...AND ENJOYING YOUR PRIVILEGED STATE...
...KIDS OUT THERE ARE HAVING THEIR DREAMS STOLEN EVERY SECOND!
......
I'M SORRY.
BZZT
BZZT
I'LL GO HOME NOW.
VWIP

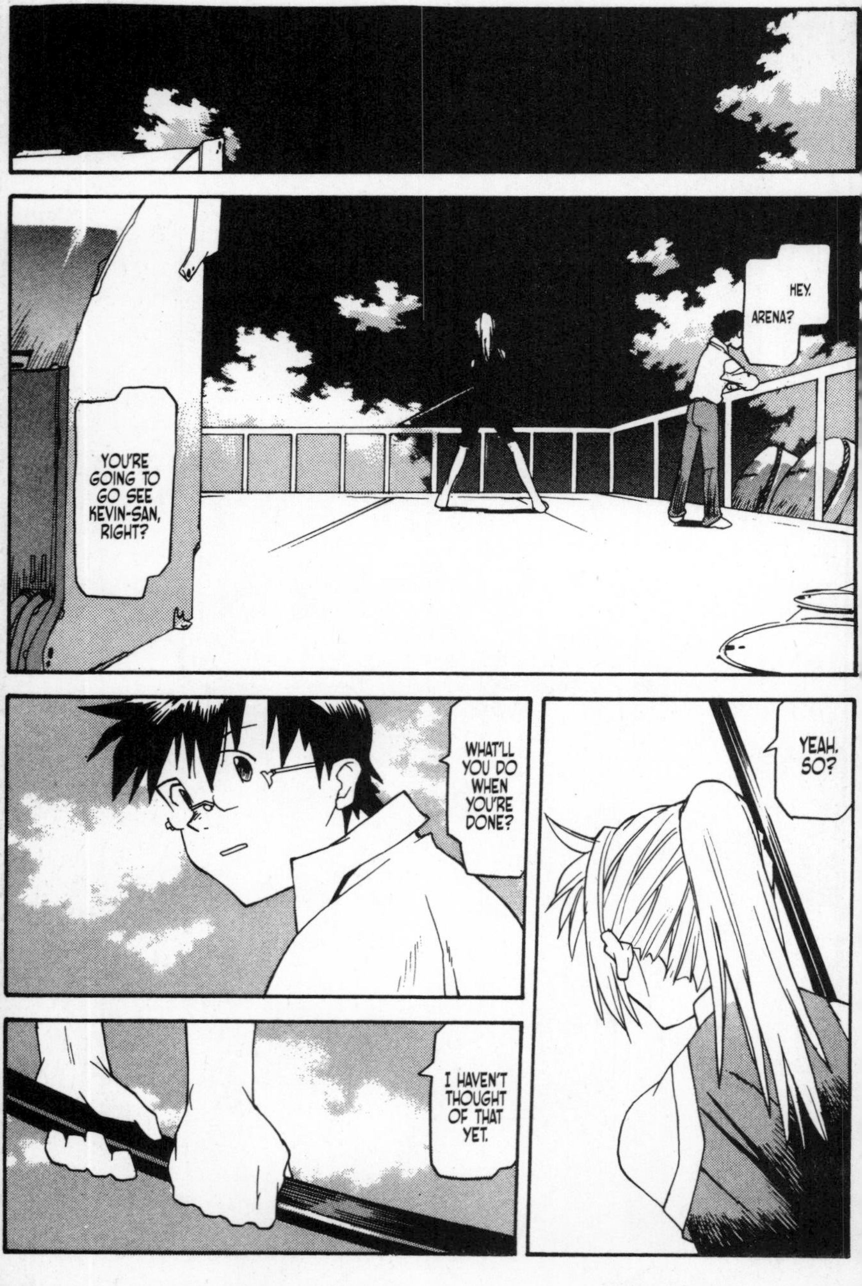
HEY. ARENA?
YOU'RE GOING TO GO SEE KEVIN-SAN, RIGHT?
YEAH. SO?
WHAT'LL YOU DO WHEN YOU'RE DONE?
I HAVEN'T THOUGHT OF THAT YET.

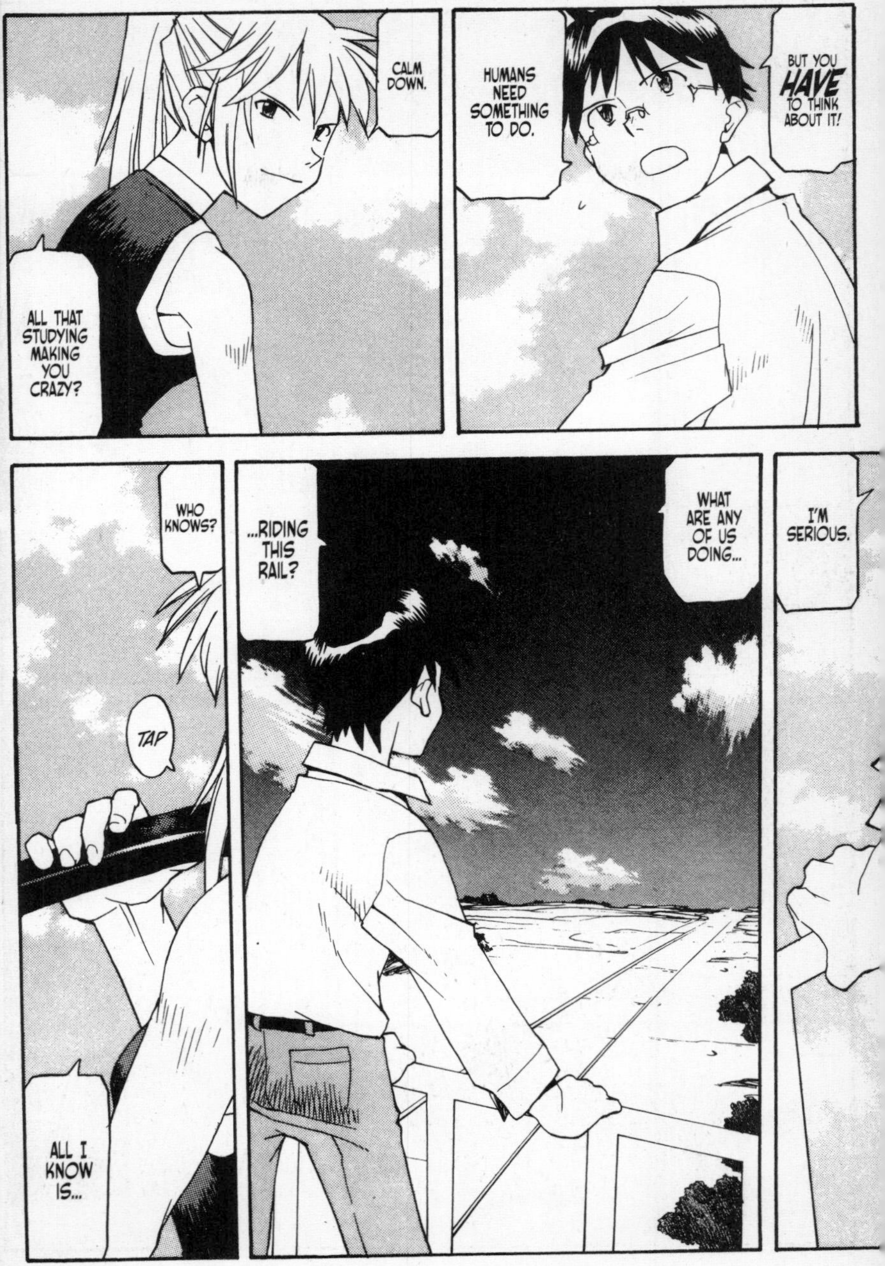
BUT YOU HAVE TO THINK ABOUT IT!
HUMANS NEED SOMETHING TO DO.
CALM DOWN.
ALL THAT STUDYING MAKING YOU CRAZY?
I'M SERIOUS.
WHAT ARE ANY OF US DOING...
...RIDING THIS RAIL?
WHO KNOWS?
TAP
ALL I KNOW IS...

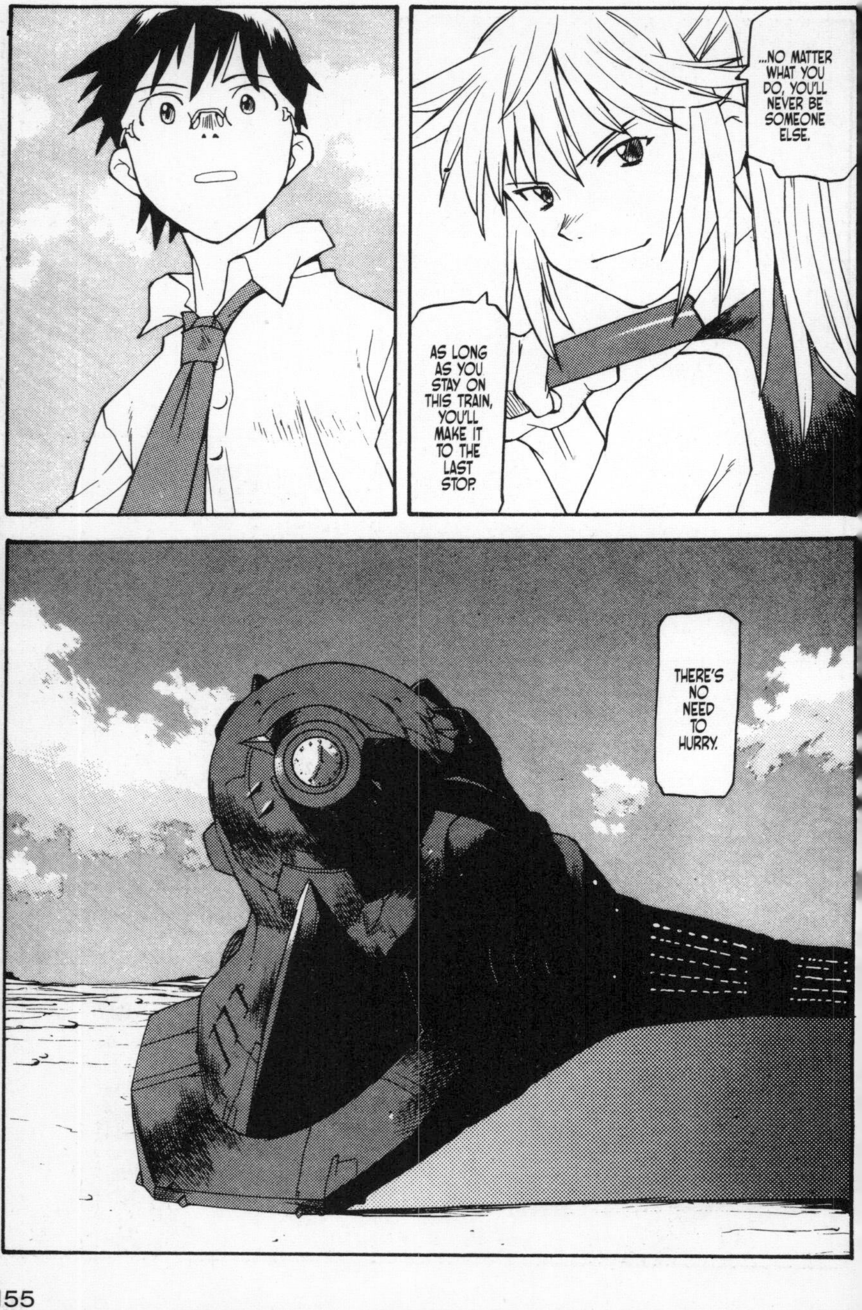
...NO MATTER WHAT YOU DO, YOU'LL NEVER BE SOMEONE ELSE.
AS LONG AS YOU STAY ON THIS TRAIN, YOU'LL MAKE IT TO THE LAST STOP.
THERE'S NO NEED TO HURRY.

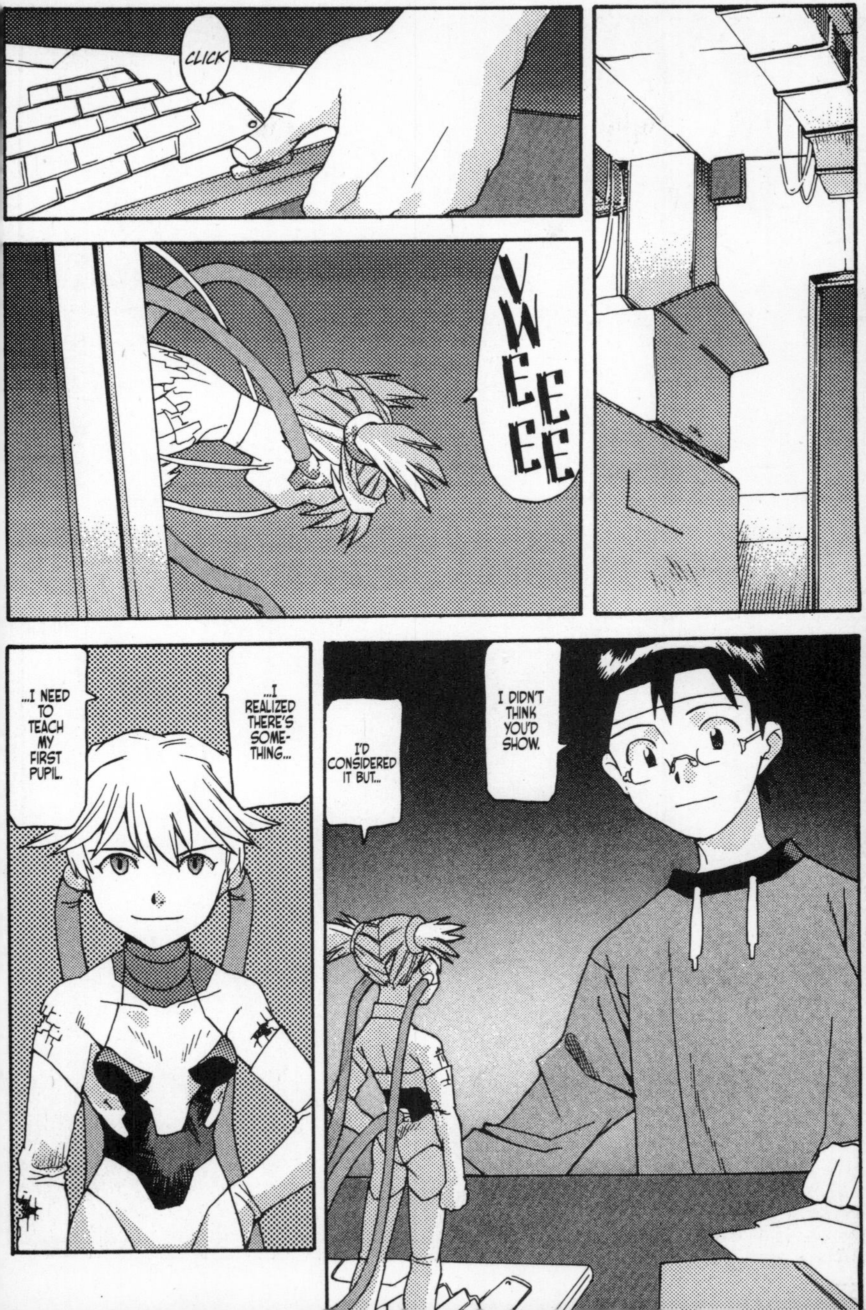
CLICK
WEEEEE
I DIDN'T THINK YOU'D SHOW.
I'D CONSIDERED IT BUT...
...I REALIZED THERE'S SOMETHING...
...I NEED TO TEACH MY FIRST PUPIL.

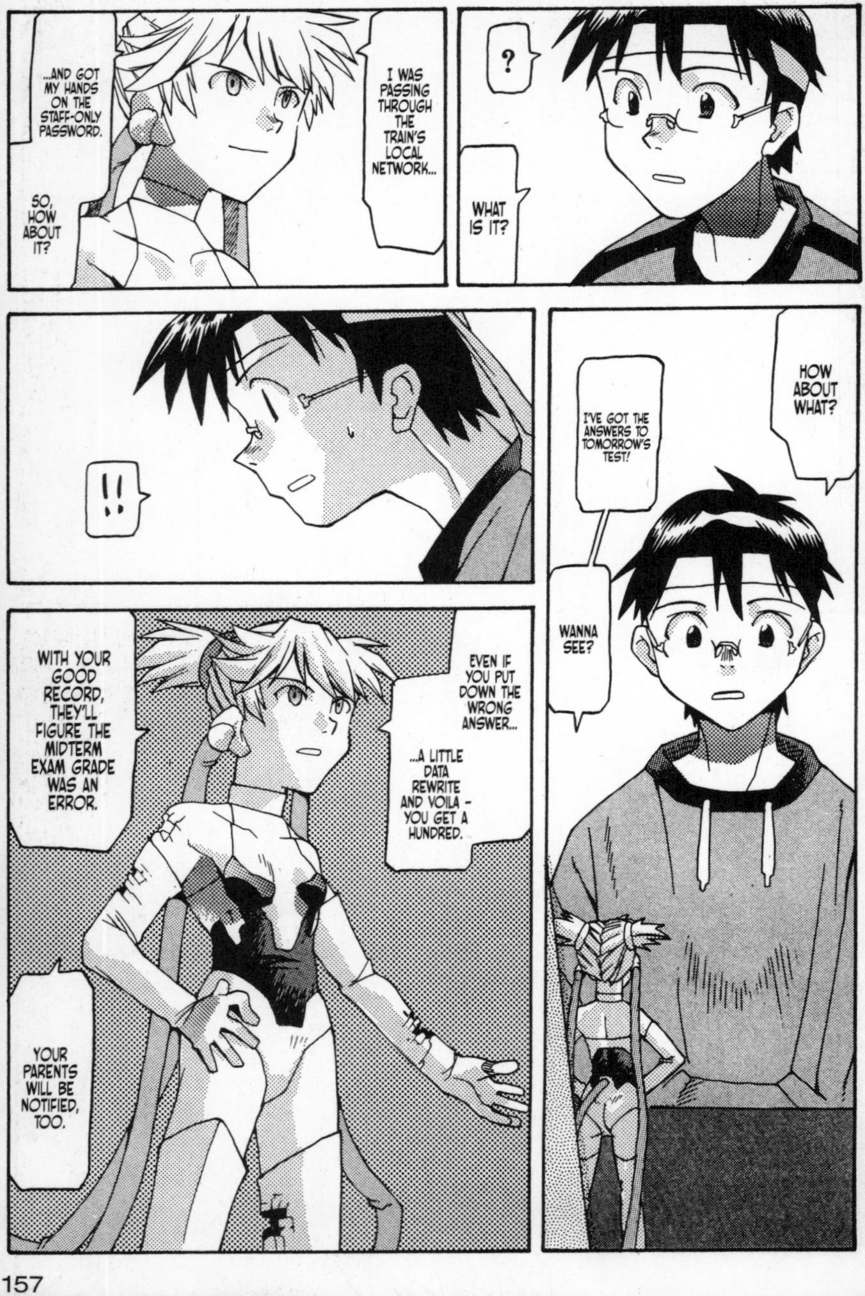

?
WHAT IS IT?
I WAS PASSING THROUGH THE TRAIN'S LOCAL NETWORK...
...AND GOT MY HANDS ON THE STAFF-ONLY PASSWORD.
SO, HOW ABOUT IT?
HOW ABOUT WHAT?
I'VE GOT THE ANSWERS TO TOMORROW'S TEST!
WANNA SEE?
!!
EVEN IF YOU PUT DOWN THE WRONG ANSWER...
...A LITTLE DATA REWRITE AND VOILA - YOU GET A HUNDRED.
WITH YOUR GOOD RECORD, THEY'LL FIGURE THE MIDTERM EXAM GRADE WAS AN ERROR.
YOUR PARENTS WILL BE NOTIFIED, TOO.

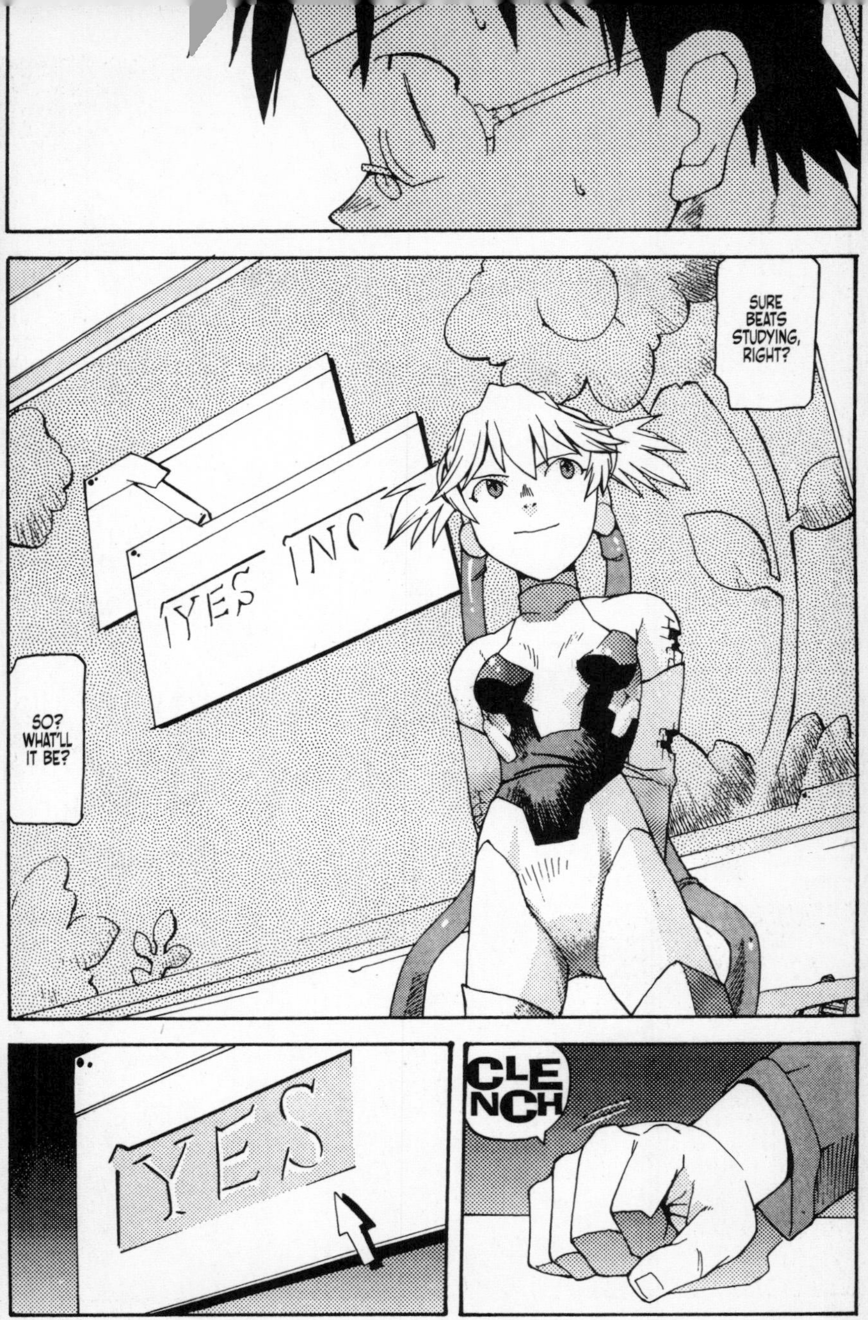
SURE BEATS STUDYING, RIGHT?
YES INC
SO? WHAT'LL IT BE?
CLENCH
YES

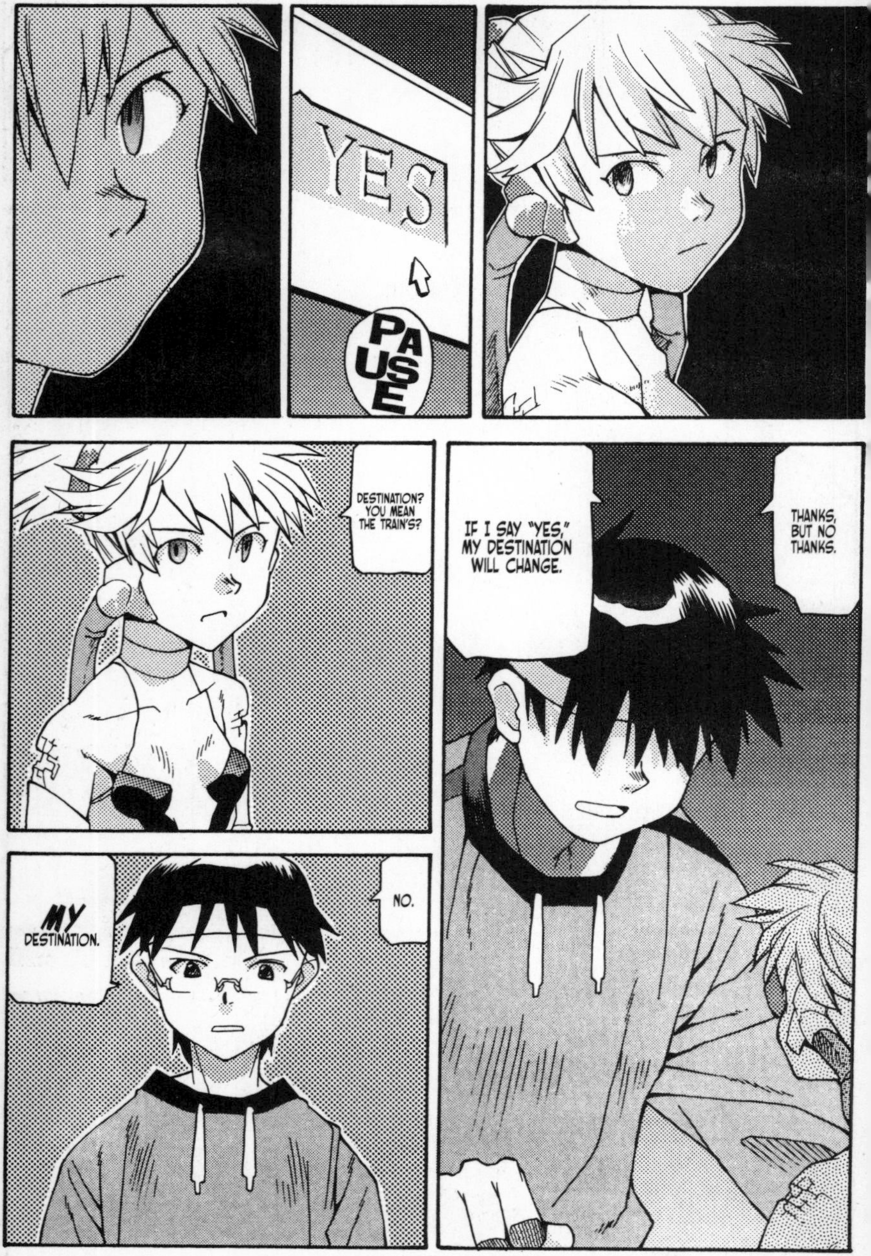
YES
PAUSE
THANKS, BUT NO THANKS.
IF I SAY "YES," MY DESTINATION WILL CHANGE.
DESTINATION? YOU MEAN THE TRAIN'S?
NO.
MY DESTINATION.

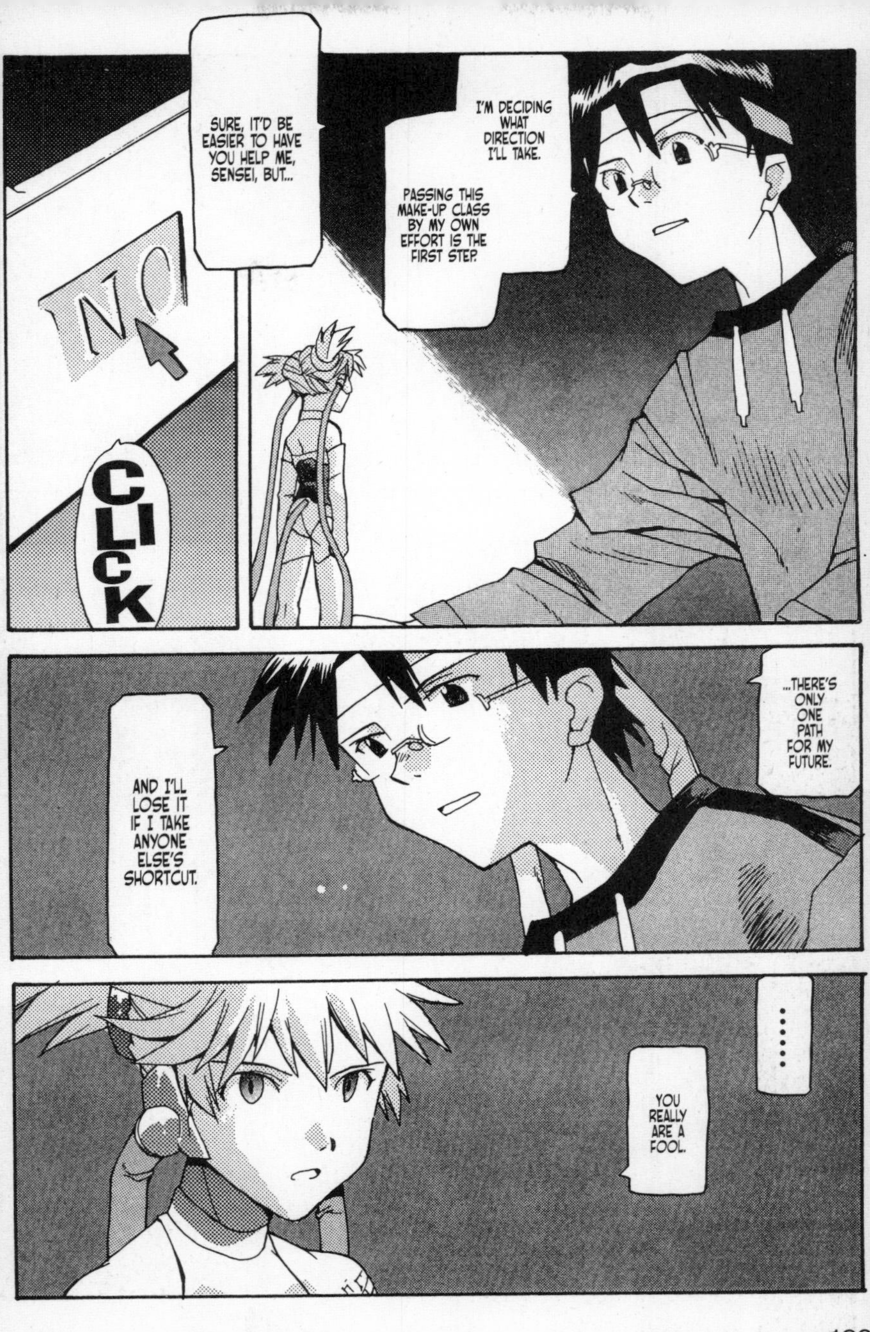
I'M DECIDING WHAT DIRECTION I'LL TAKE.
PASSING THIS MAKE-UP CLASS BY MY OWN EFFORT IS THE FIRST STEP.
SURE, IT'D BE EASIER TO HAVE YOU HELP ME, SENSEI, BUT...
NO
CLICK
...THERE'S ONLY ONE PATH FOR MY FUTURE.
AND I'LL LOSE IT IF I TAKE ANYONE ELSE'S SHORTCUT.
......
YOU REALLY ARE A FOOL.

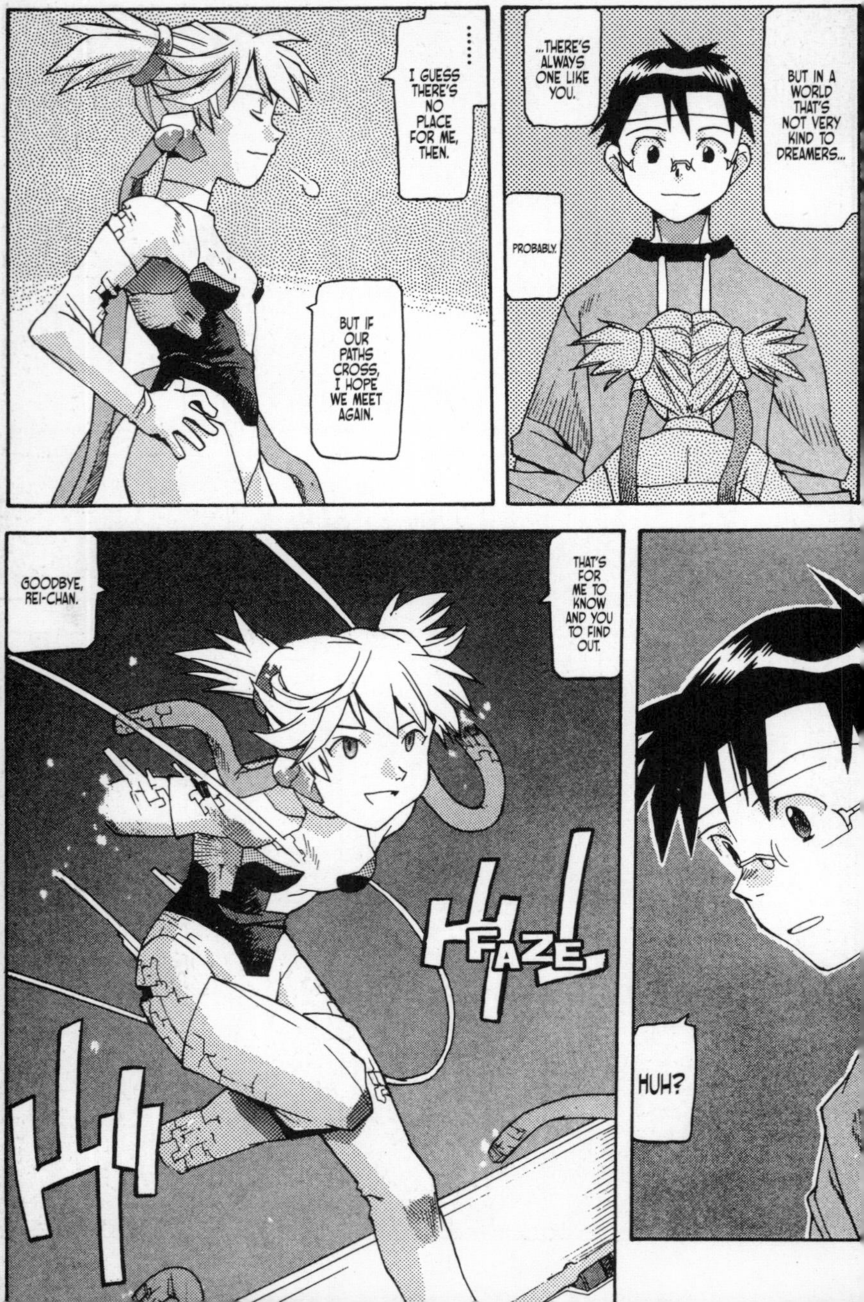
BUT IN A WORLD THAT'S NOT VERY KIND TO DREAMERS...
...THERE'S ALWAYS ONE LIKE YOU.
PROBABLY.
......
I GUESS THERE'S NO PLACE FOR ME, THEN.
BUT IF OUR PATHS CROSS, I HOPE WE MEET AGAIN.
HUH?
THAT'S FOR ME TO KNOW AND YOU TO FIND OUT.
GOODBYE, REI-CHAN.
FAZE

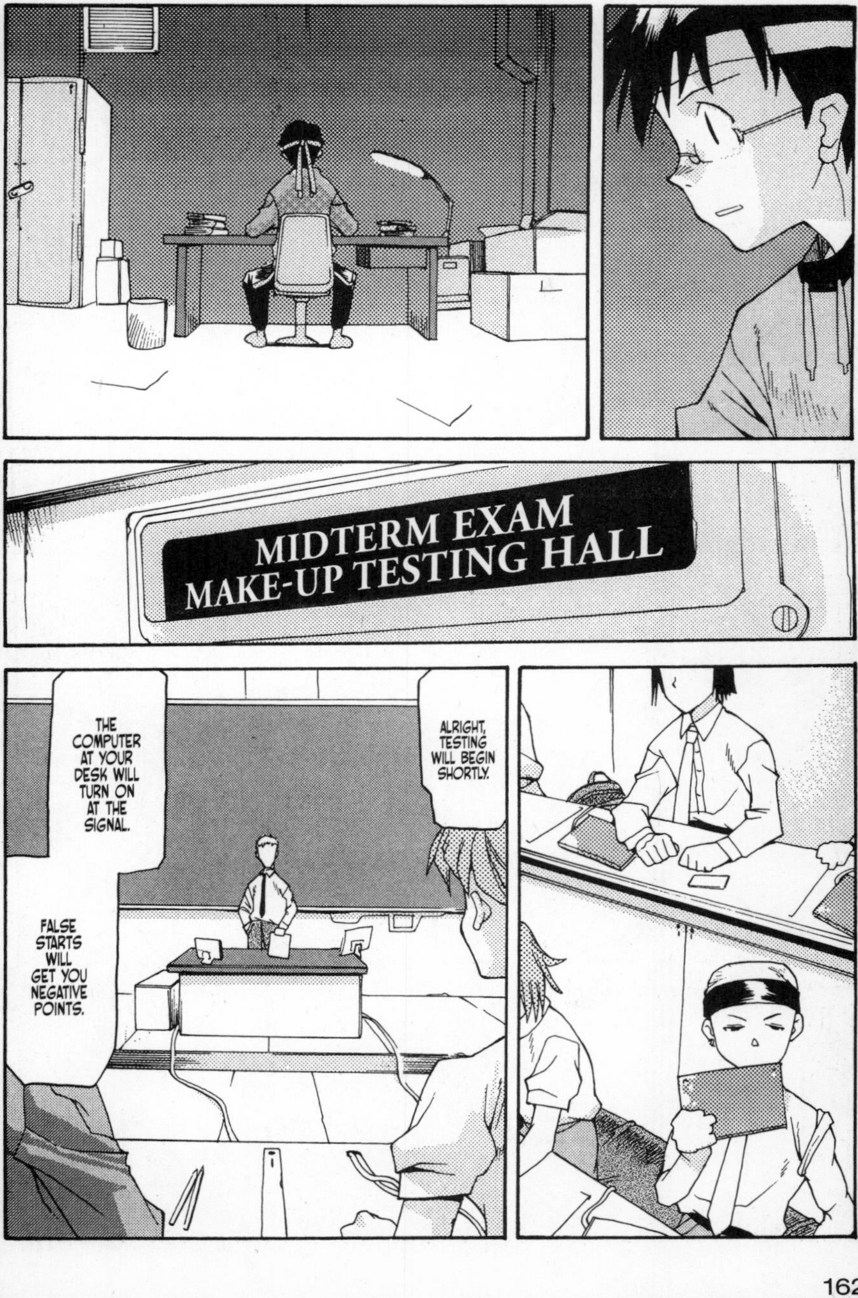
MIDTERM EXAM MAKE-UP TESTING HALL
ALRIGHT, TESTING WILL BEGIN SHORTLY.
THE COMPUTER AT YOUR DESK WILL TURN ON AT THE SIGNAL.
FALSE STARTS WILL GET YOU NEGATIVE POINTS.

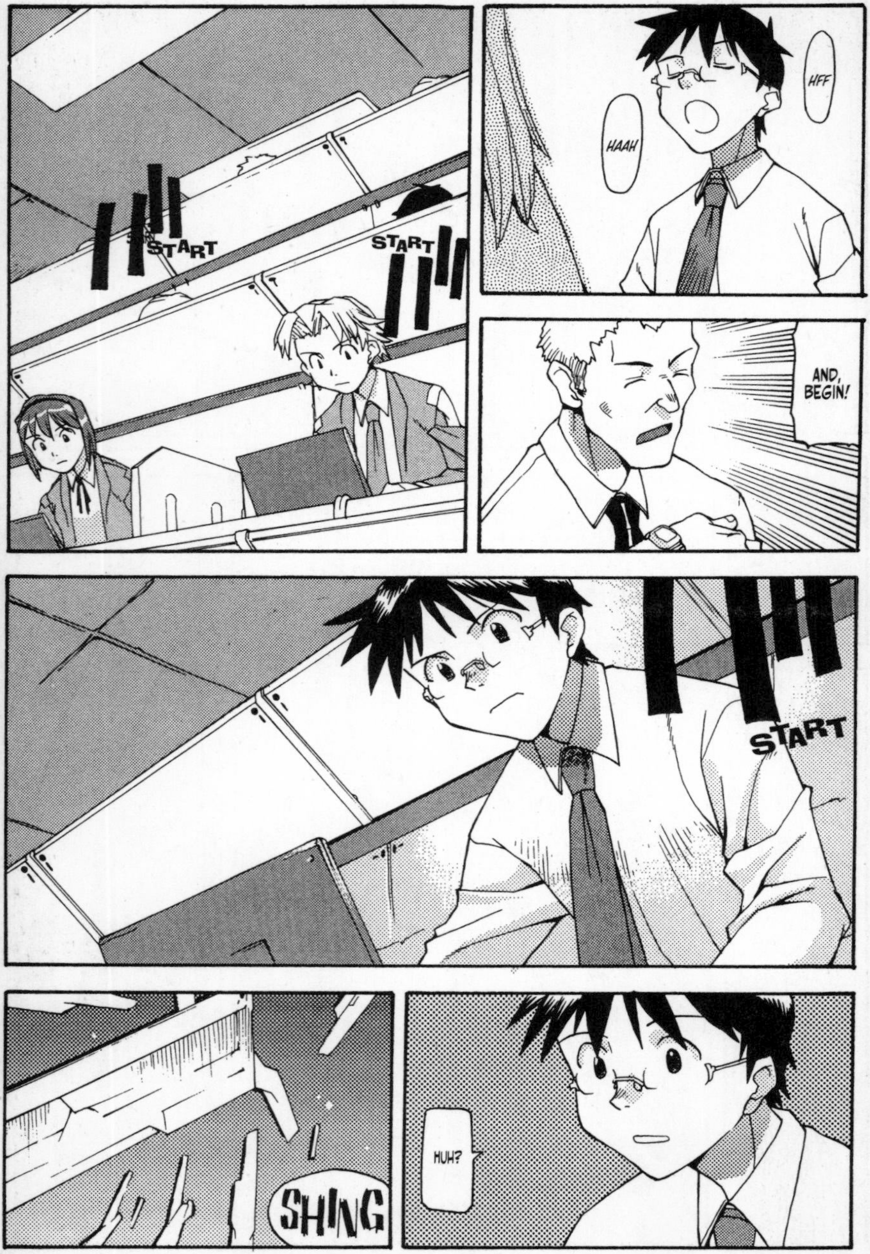
HFF
HAAH
AND, BEGIN!
START
START
START
HUH?
SHING

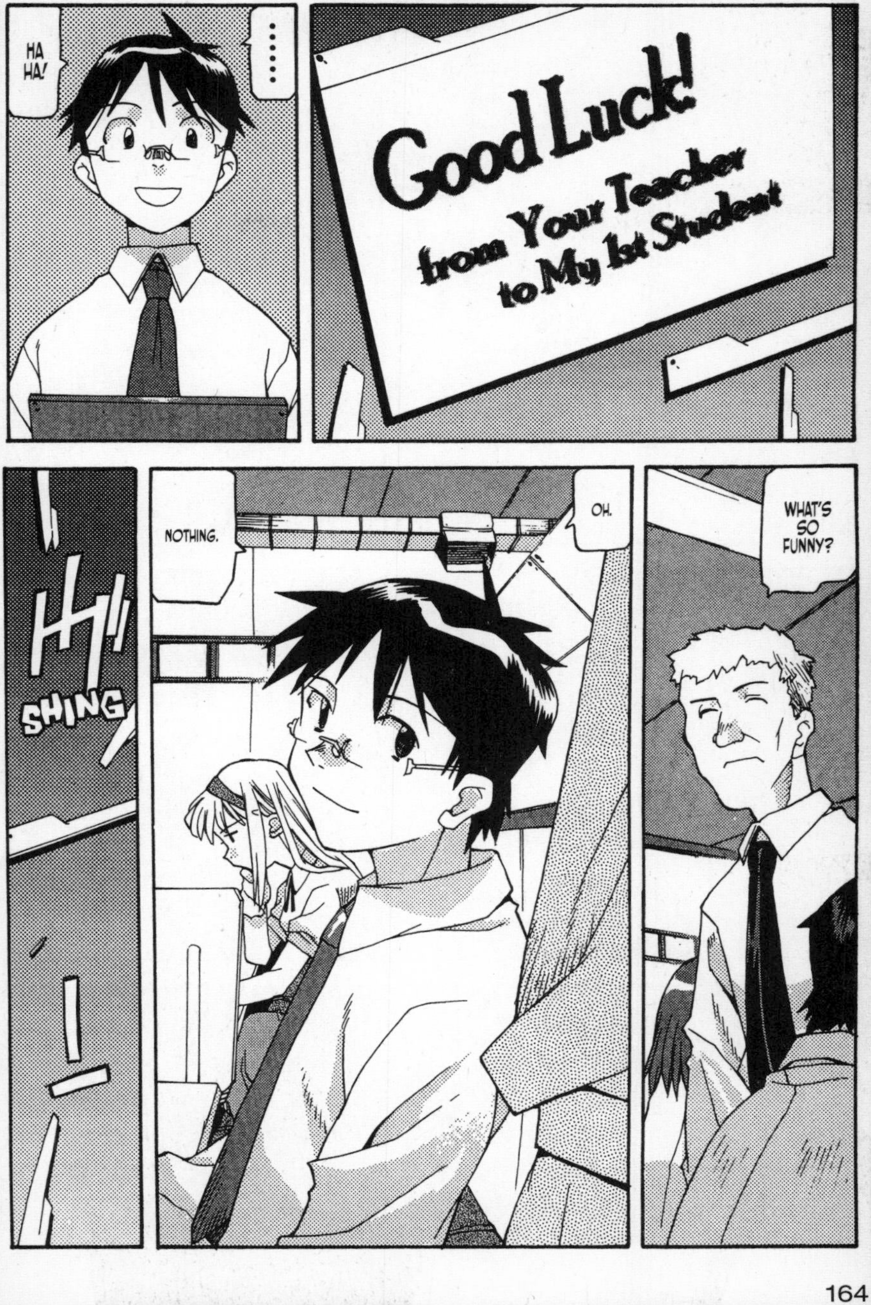
Good Luck!
from Your Teacher
to My 1st Student
......
HA HA!
WHAT'S SO FUNNY?
OH.
NOTHING.
SHING

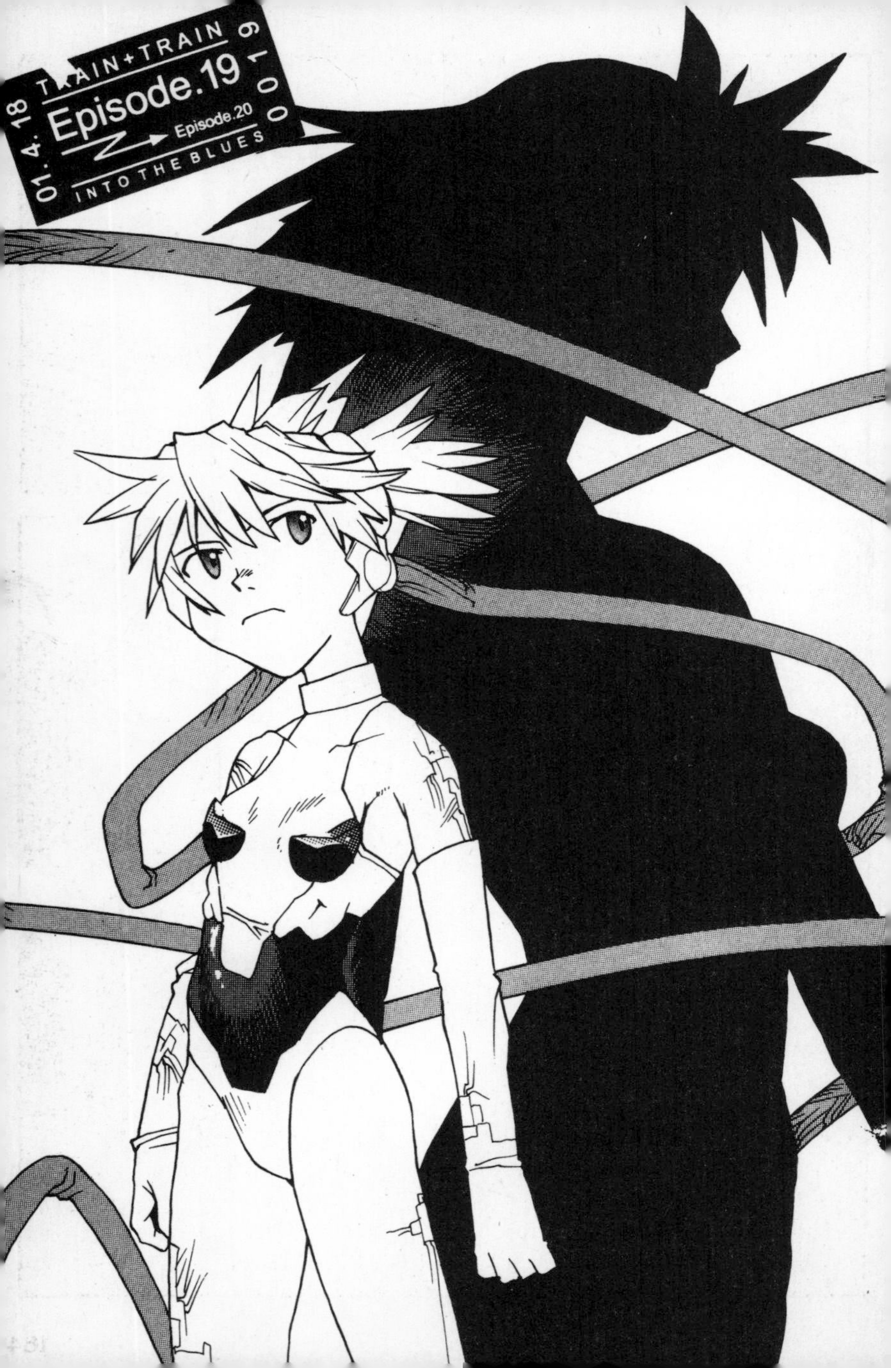
TRAIN+TRAIN
Episode.19
Episode.20
INTO THE BLUES
01. 4. 18
0019

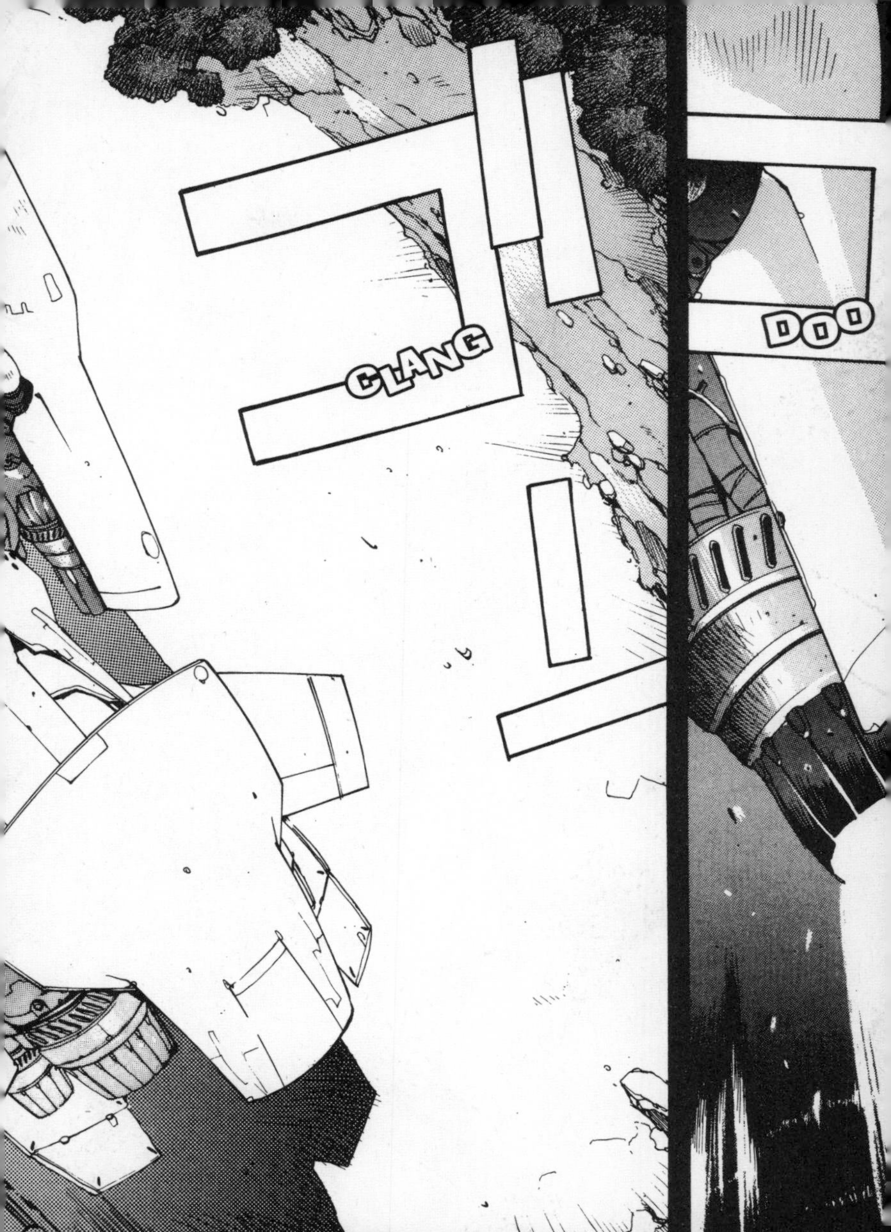
DOO
CLANG

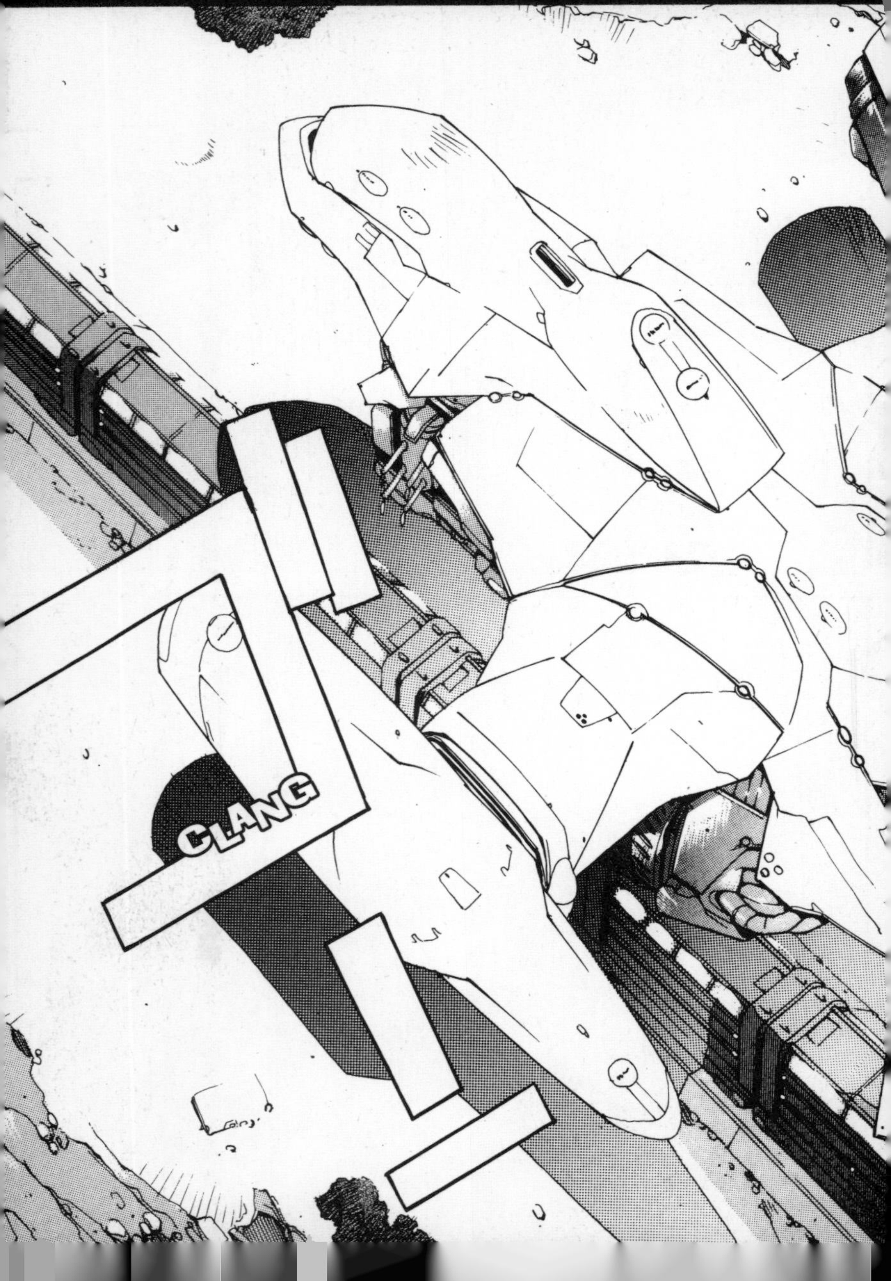
CLANG

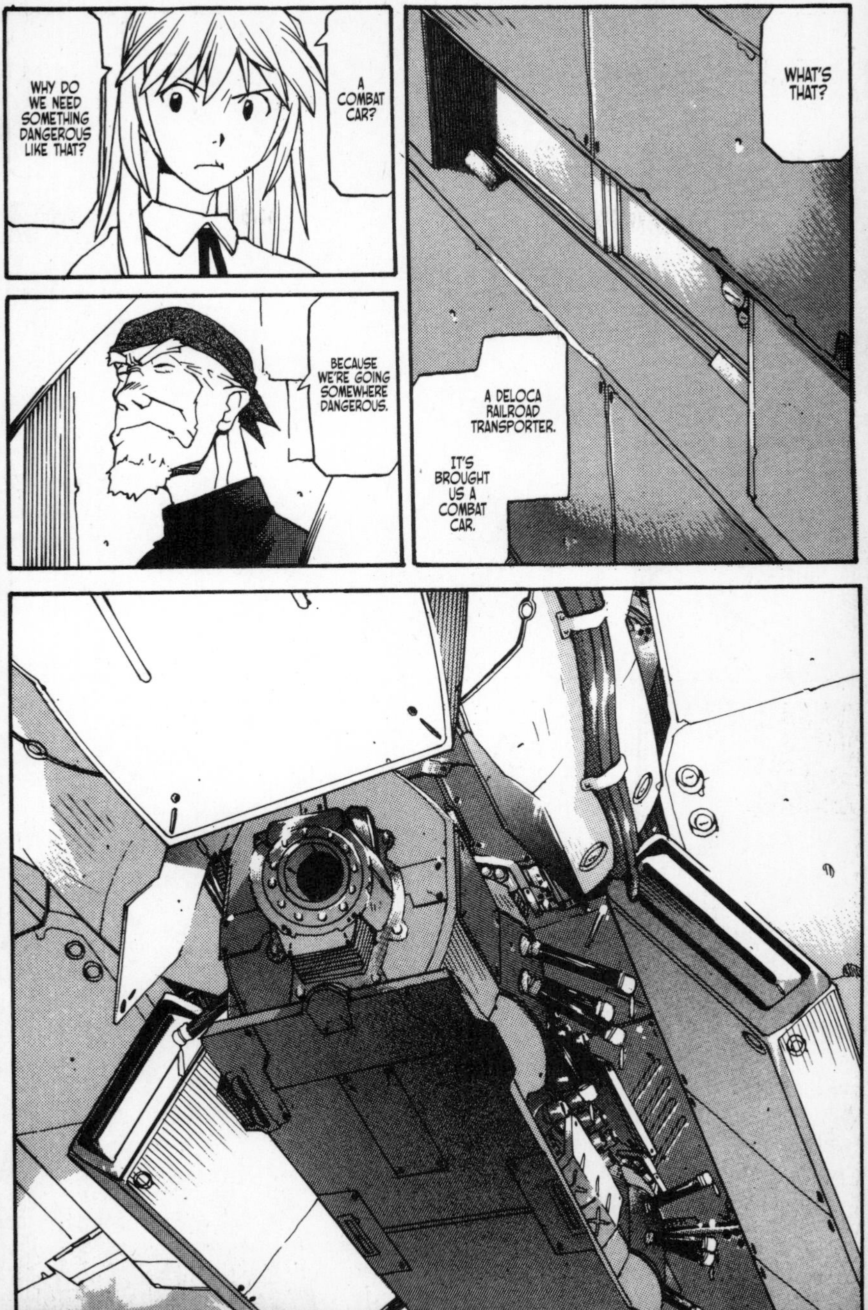
WHAT'S THAT?
A DELOCA RAILROAD TRANSPORTER.
IT'S BROUGHT US A COMBAT CAR.
A COMBAT CAR?
WHY DO WE NEED SOMETHING DANGEROUS LIKE THAT?
BECAUSE WE'RE GOING SOMEWHERE DANGEROUS.

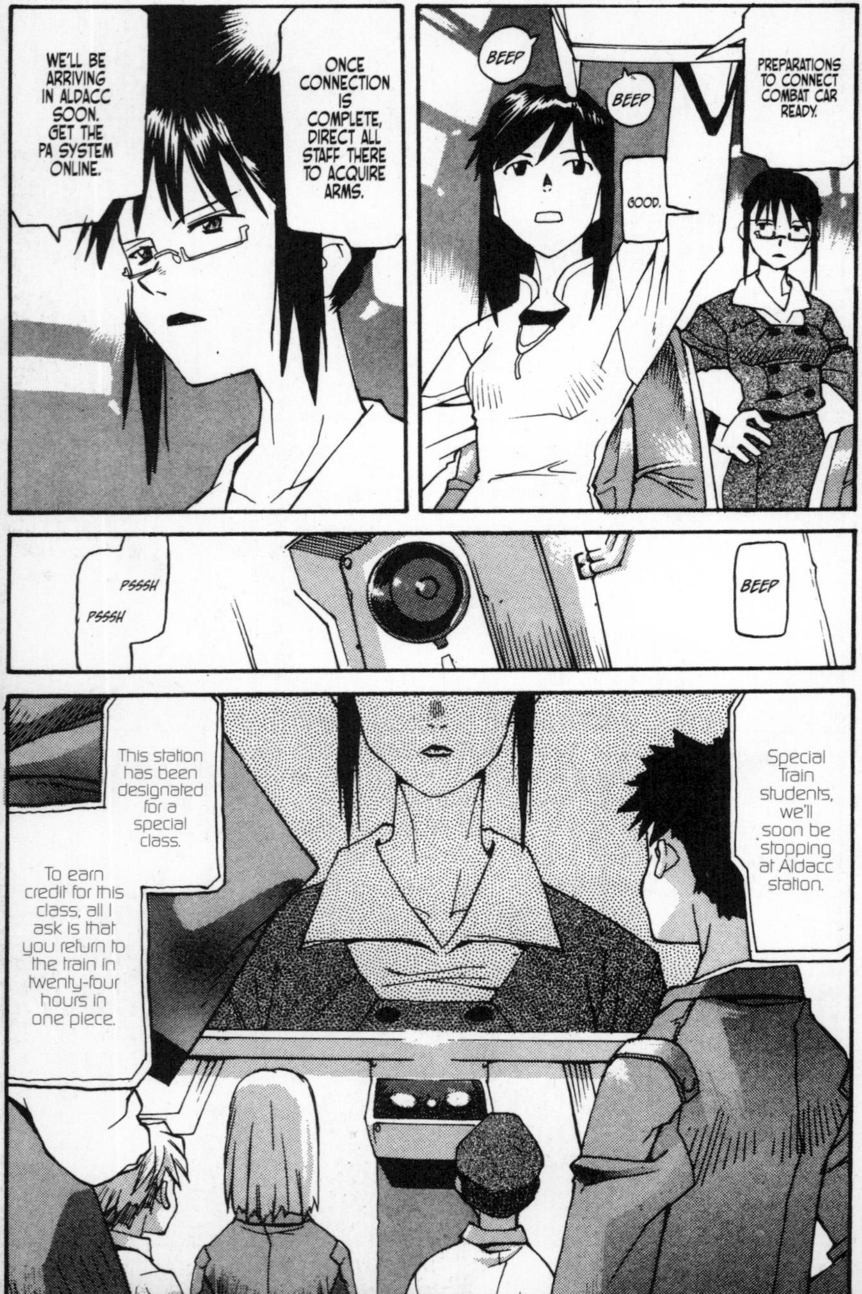
PREPARATIONS TO CONNECT COMBAT CAR READY.
BEEP
BEEP
GOOD.
ONCE CONNECTION IS COMPLETE, DIRECT ALL STAFF THERE TO ACQUIRE ARMS.
WE'LL BE ARRIVING IN ALDACC SOON. GET THE PA SYSTEM ONLINE.
BEEP
PSSSH
PSSSH
Special Train students, we'll soon be stopping at Aldacc station.
This station has been designated for a special class.
To earn credit for this class, all I ask is that you return to the train in twenty-four hours in one piece.

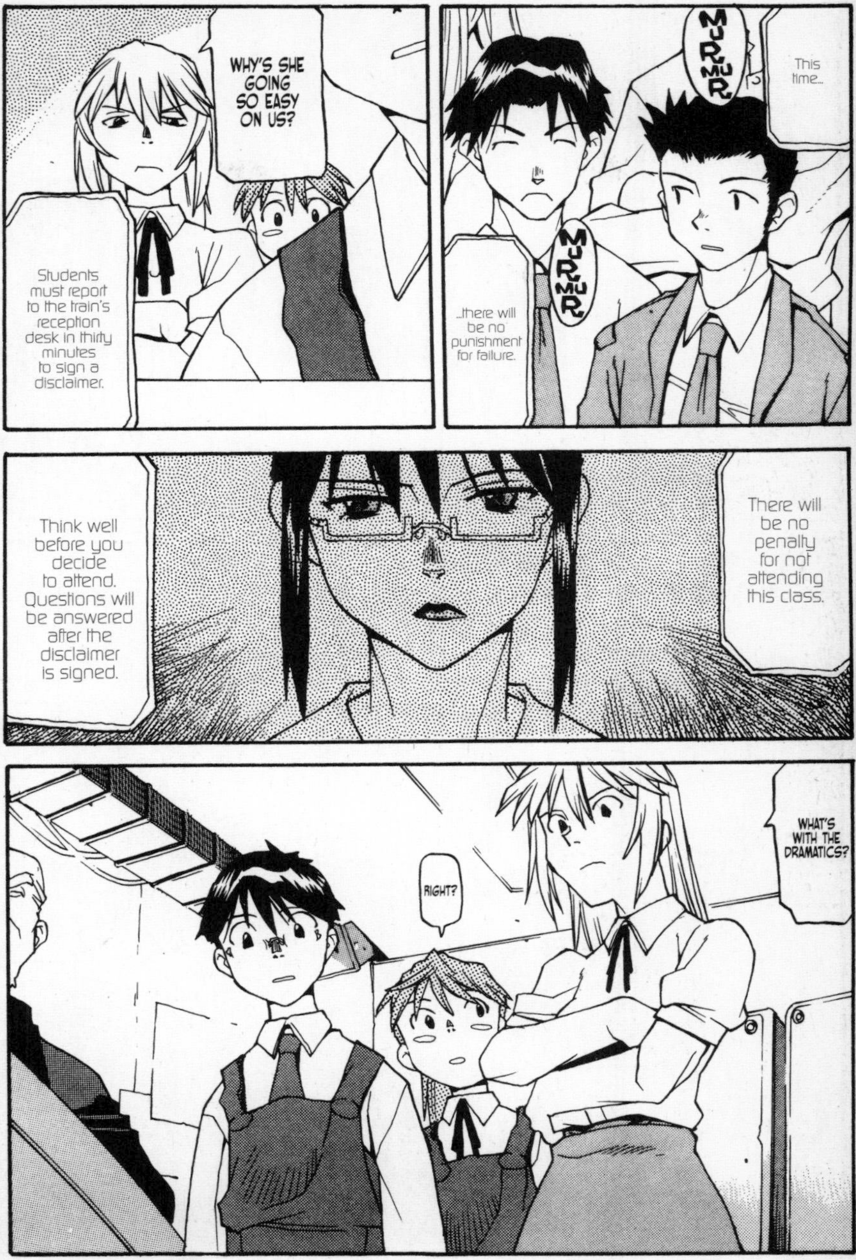
This time...
MURMUR
MURMUR
...there will be no punishment for failure.
WHY'S SHE GOING SO EASY ON US?
Students must report to the train's reception desk in thirty minutes to sign a disclaimer.
There will be no penalty for not attending this class.
Think well before you decide to attend. Questions will be answered after the disclaimer is signed.
WHAT'S WITH THE DRAMATICS?
RIGHT?

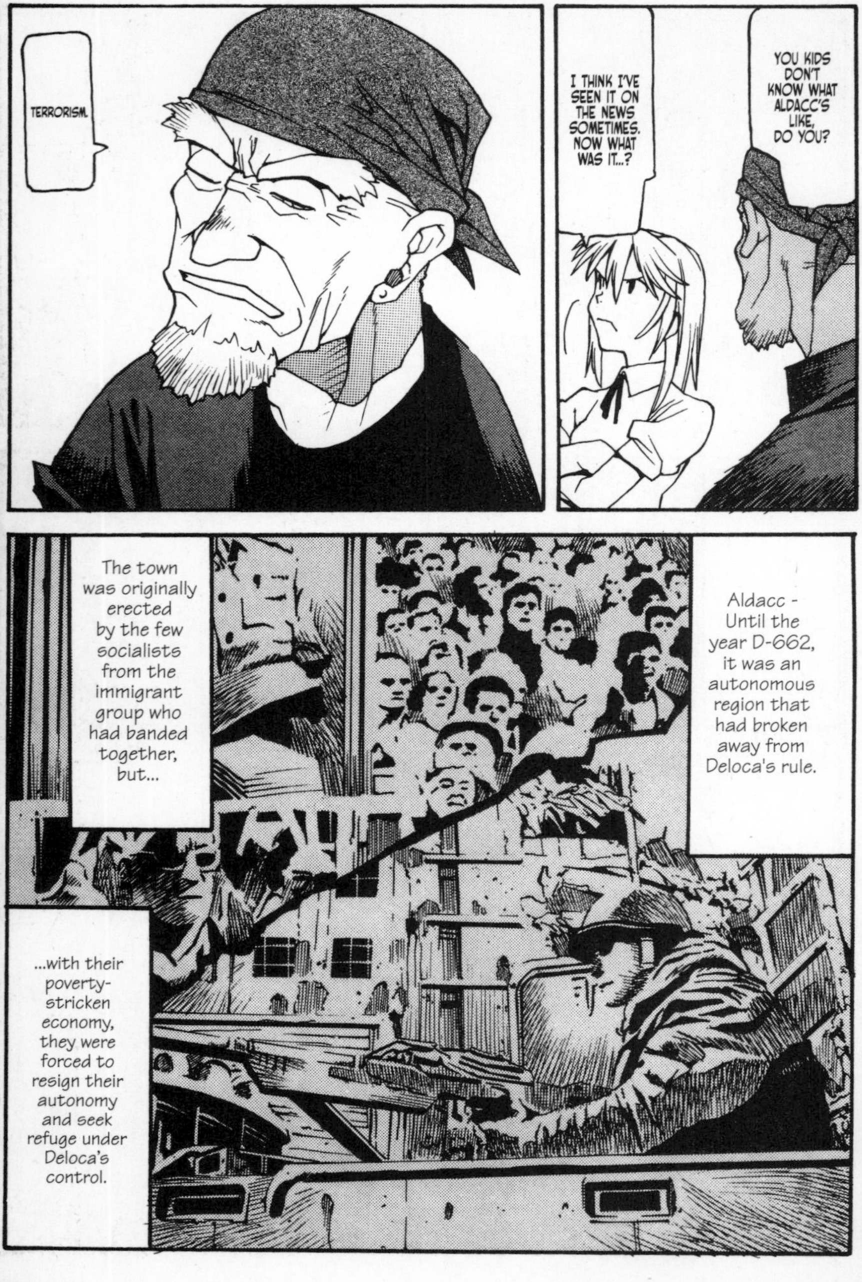
YOU KIDS DON'T KNOW WHAT ALDACC'S LIKE, DO YOU?
I THINK I'VE SEEN IT ON THE NEWS SOMETIMES. NOW WHAT WAS IT...?
TERRORISM.
Aldacc - Until the year D-662, it was an autonomous region that had broken away from Deloca's rule.
The town was originally erected by the few socialists from the immigrant group who had banded together, but...
...with their poverty-stricken economy, they were forced to resign their autonomy and seek refuge under Deloca's control.

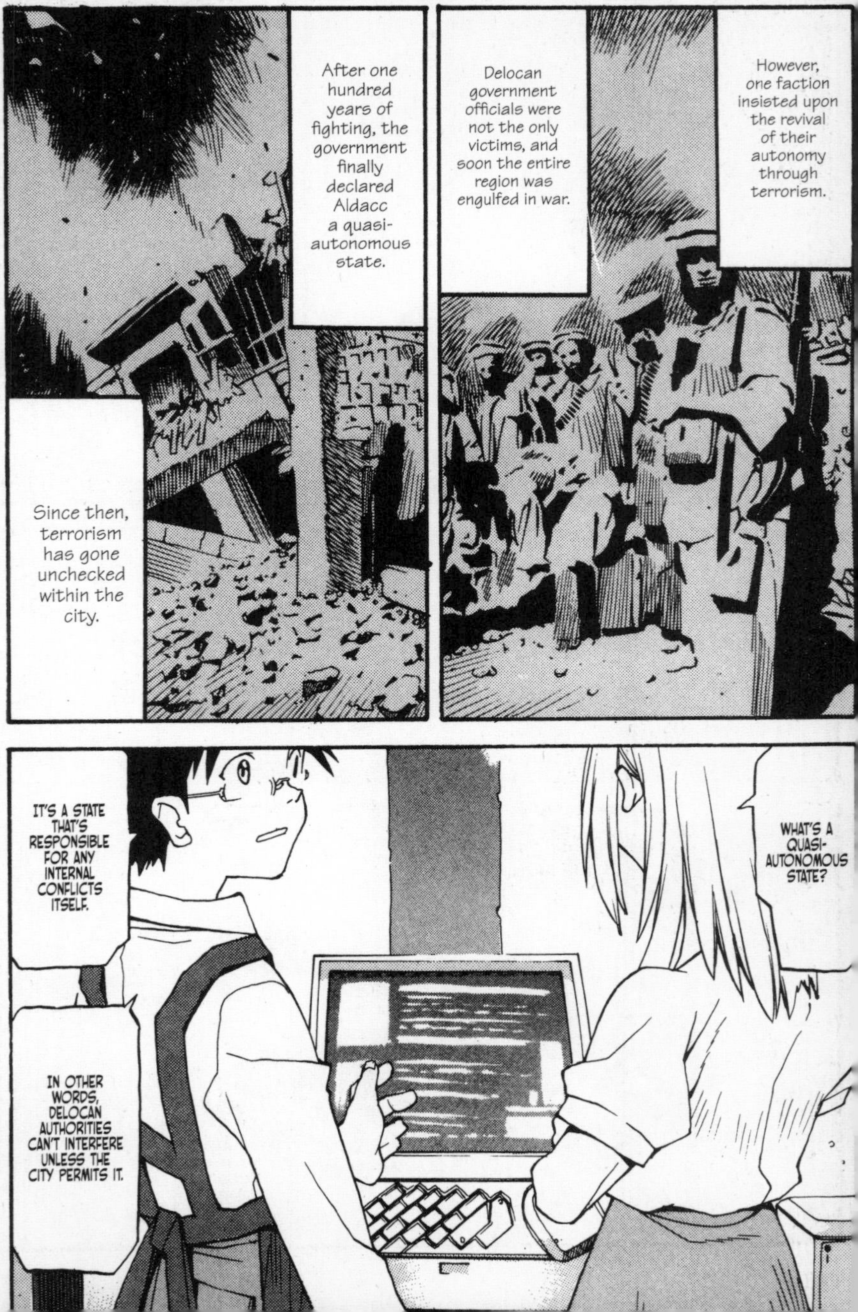

Delocan government officials were not the only victims, and soon the entire region was engulfed in war.
However, one faction insisted upon the revival of their autonomy through terrorism.
After one hundred years of fighting, the government finally declared Aldacc a quasi-autonomous state.
Since then, terrorism has gone unchecked within the city.
WHAT'S A QUASI-AUTONOMOUS STATE?
IT'S A STATE THAT'S RESPONSIBLE FOR ANY INTERNAL CONFLICTS ITSELF.
IN OTHER WORDS, DELOCAN AUTHORITIES CAN'T INTERFERE UNLESS THE CITY PERMITS IT.

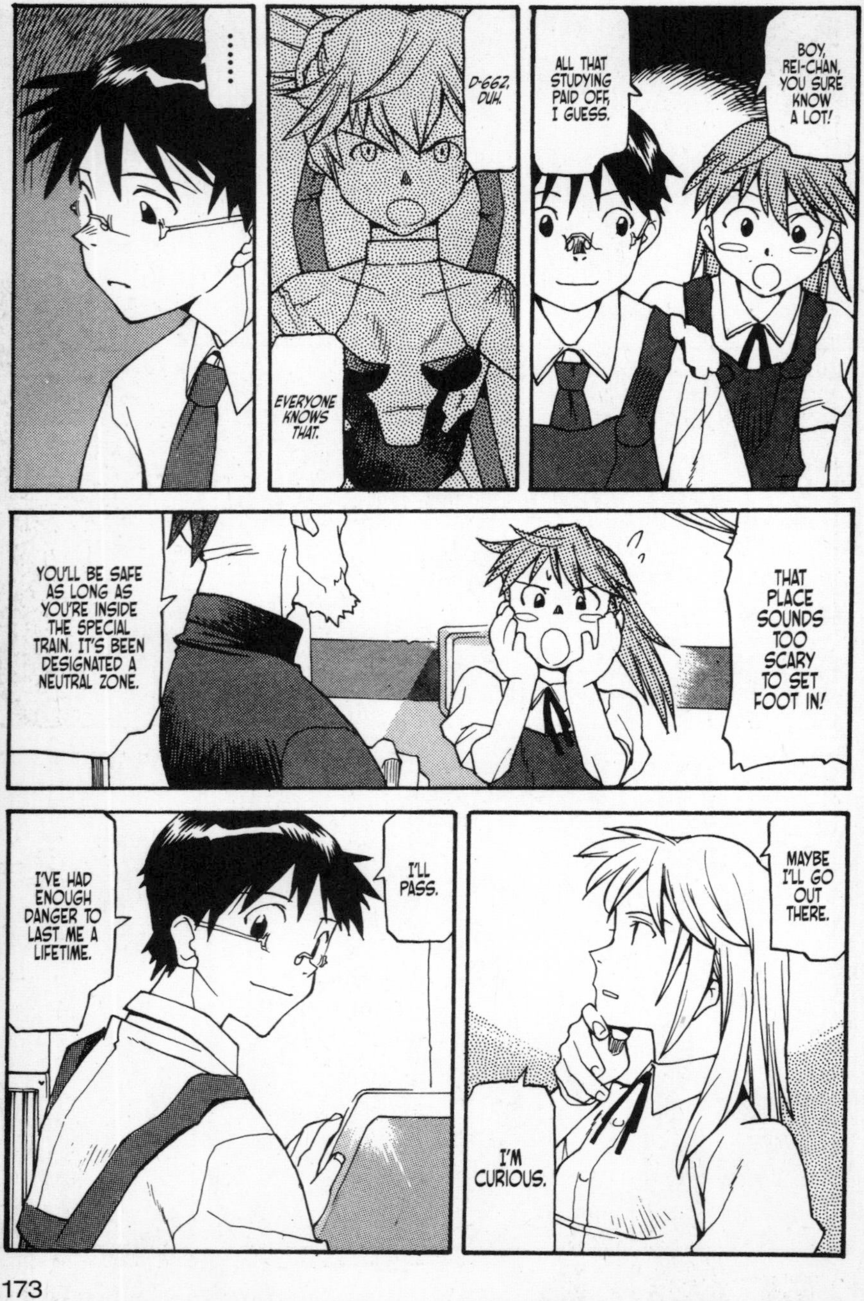
BOY, REI-CHAN, YOU SURE KNOW A LOT!
ALL THAT STUDYING PAID OFF, I GUESS.
D-662, DUH.
EVERYONE KNOWS THAT.
......
THAT PLACE SOUNDS TOO SCARY TO SET FOOT IN!
YOU'LL BE SAFE AS LONG AS YOU'RE INSIDE THE SPECIAL TRAIN. IT'S BEEN DESIGNATED A NEUTRAL ZONE.
MAYBE I'LL GO OUT THERE.
I'M CURIOUS.
I'LL PASS.
I'VE HAD ENOUGH DANGER TO LAST ME A LIFETIME.

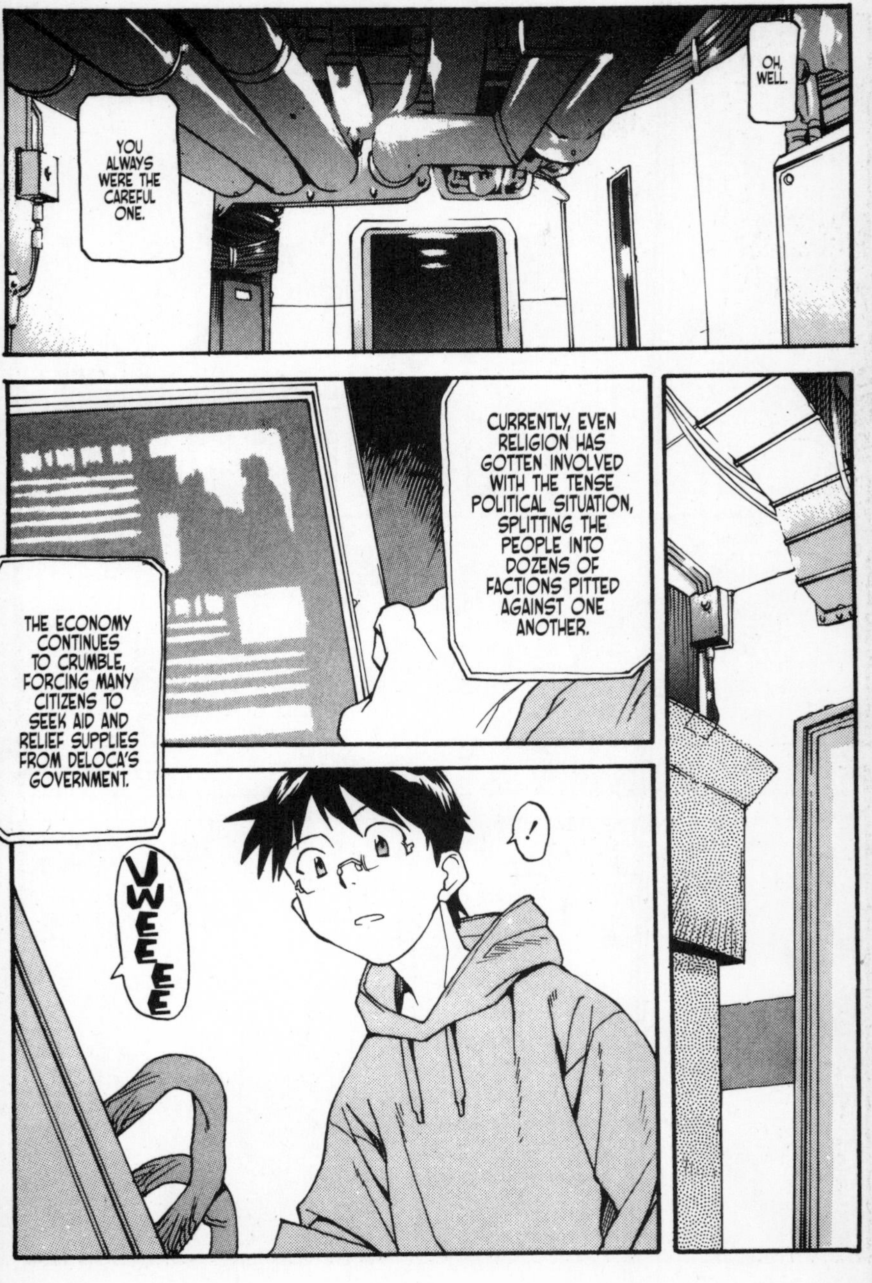
OH, WELL.
YOU ALWAYS WERE THE CAREFUL ONE.
CURRENTLY, EVEN RELIGION HAS GOTTEN INVOLVED WITH THE TENSE POLITICAL SITUATION, SPLITTING THE PEOPLE INTO DOZENS OF FACTIONS PITTED AGAINST ONE ANOTHER.
THE ECONOMY CONTINUES TO CRUMBLE, FORCING MANY CITIZENS TO SEEK AID AND RELIEF SUPPLIES FROM DELOCA'S GOVERNMENT.
!
UWEEEE

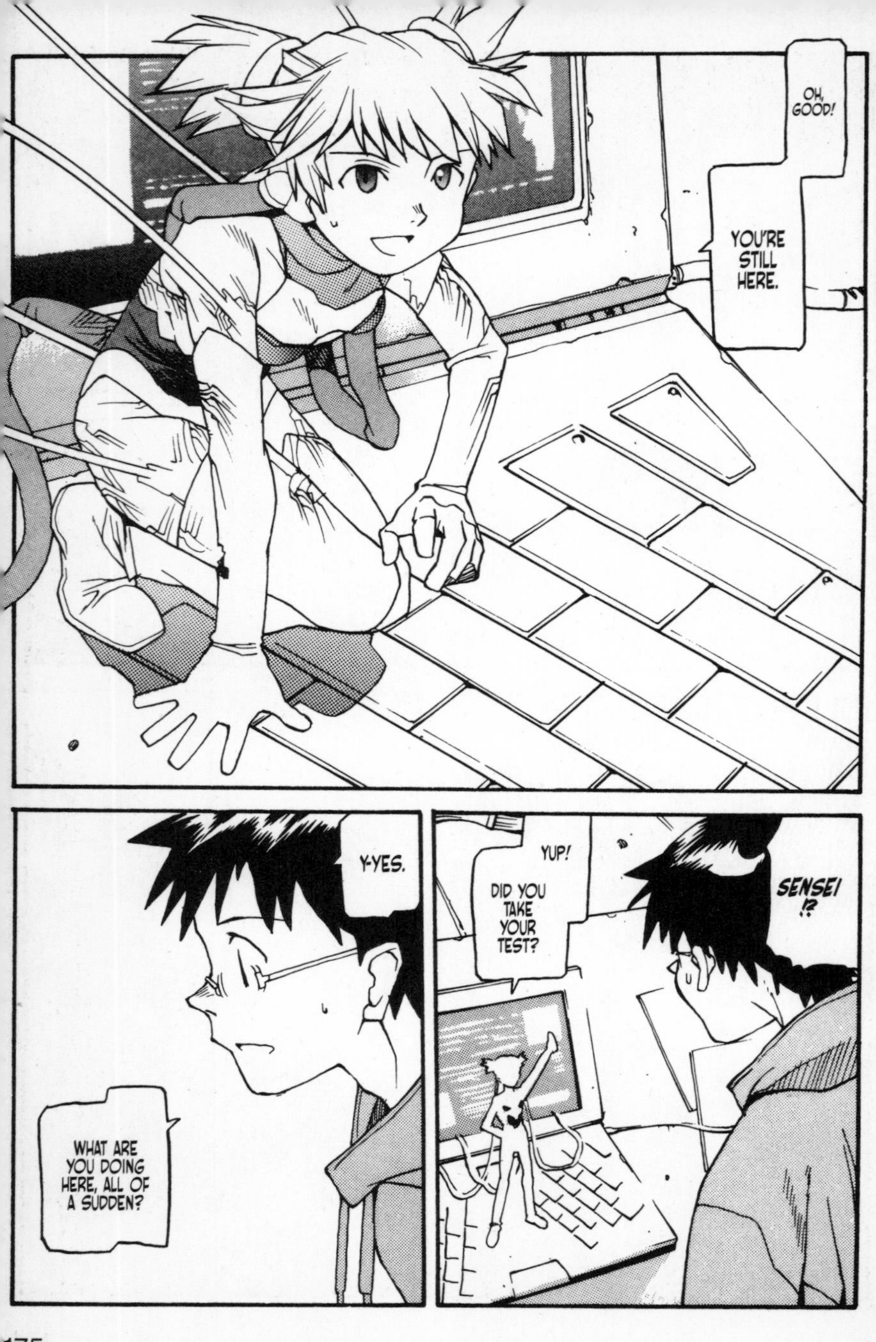
OH, GOOD!
YOU'RE STILL HERE.
SENSEI!?
YUP!
DID YOU TAKE YOUR TEST?
Y-YES.
WHAT ARE YOU DOING HERE, ALL OF A SUDDEN?

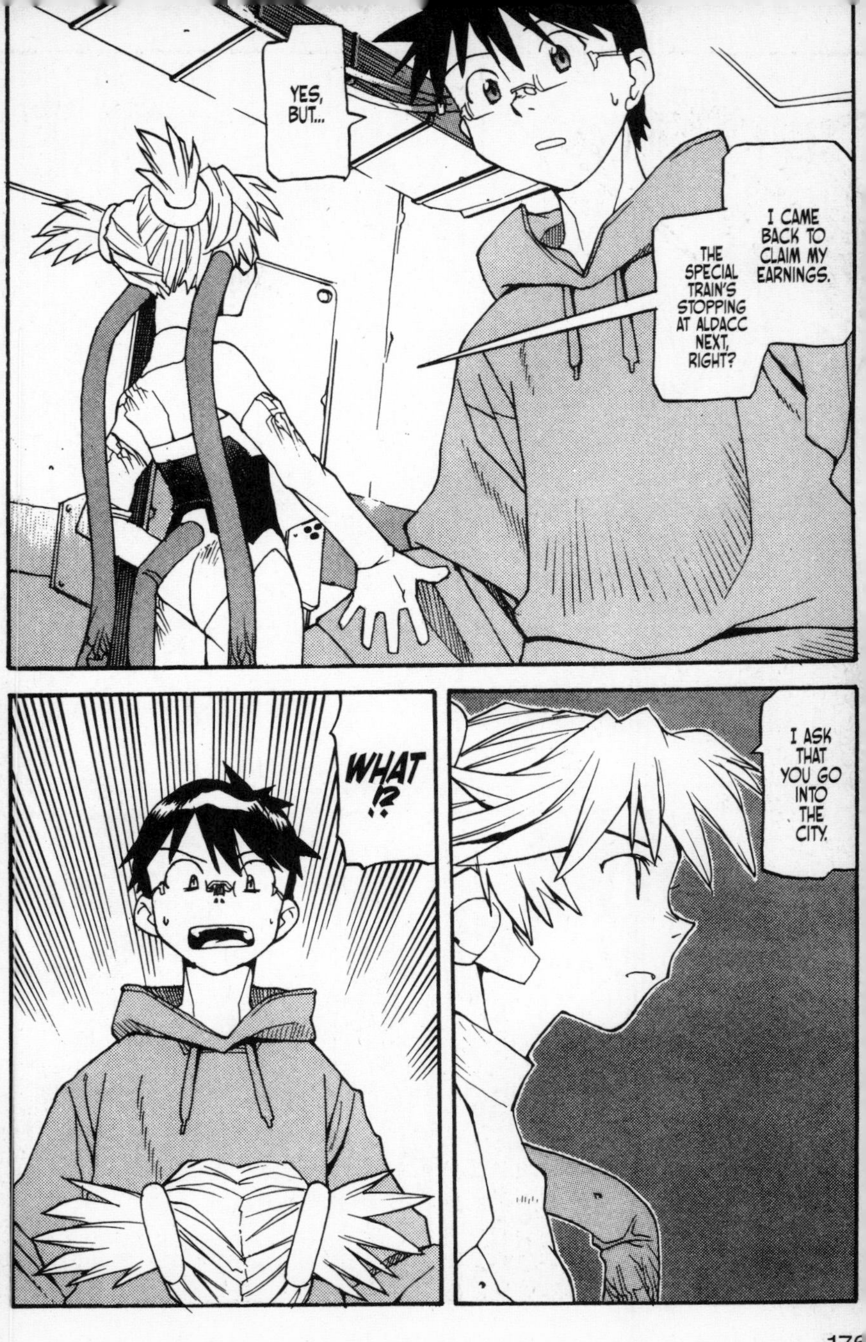
I CAME BACK TO CLAIM MY EARNINGS.
THE SPECIAL TRAIN'S STOPPING AT ALDACC NEXT, RIGHT?
YES, BUT...
I ASK THAT YOU GO INTO THE CITY.
WHAT!?

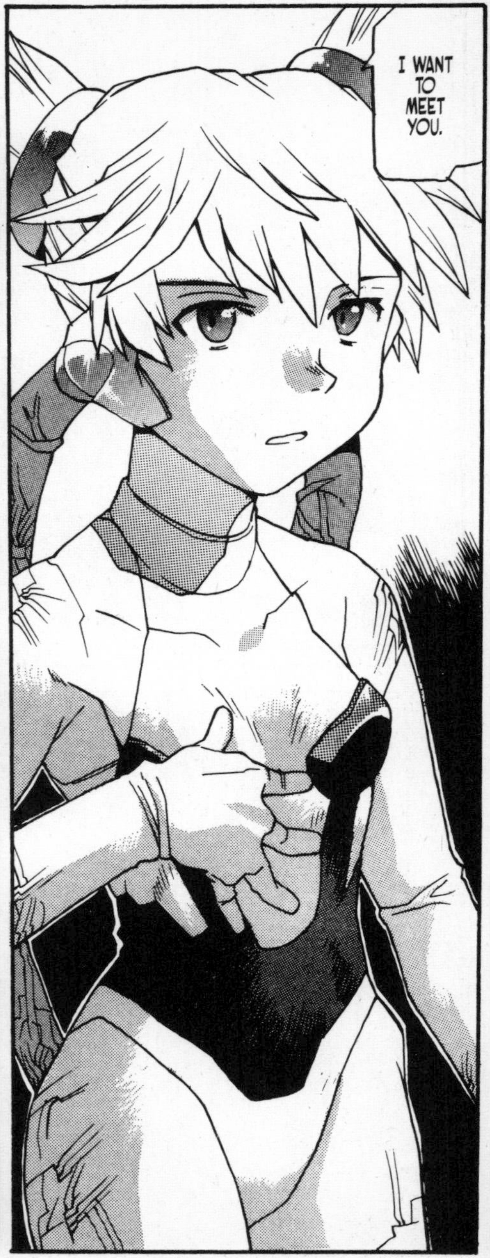
I WANT TO MEET YOU.

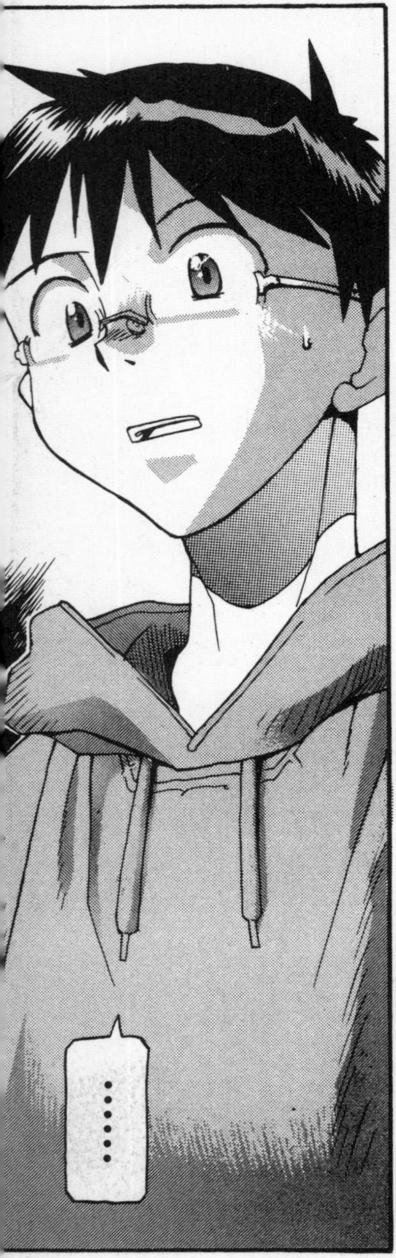
……

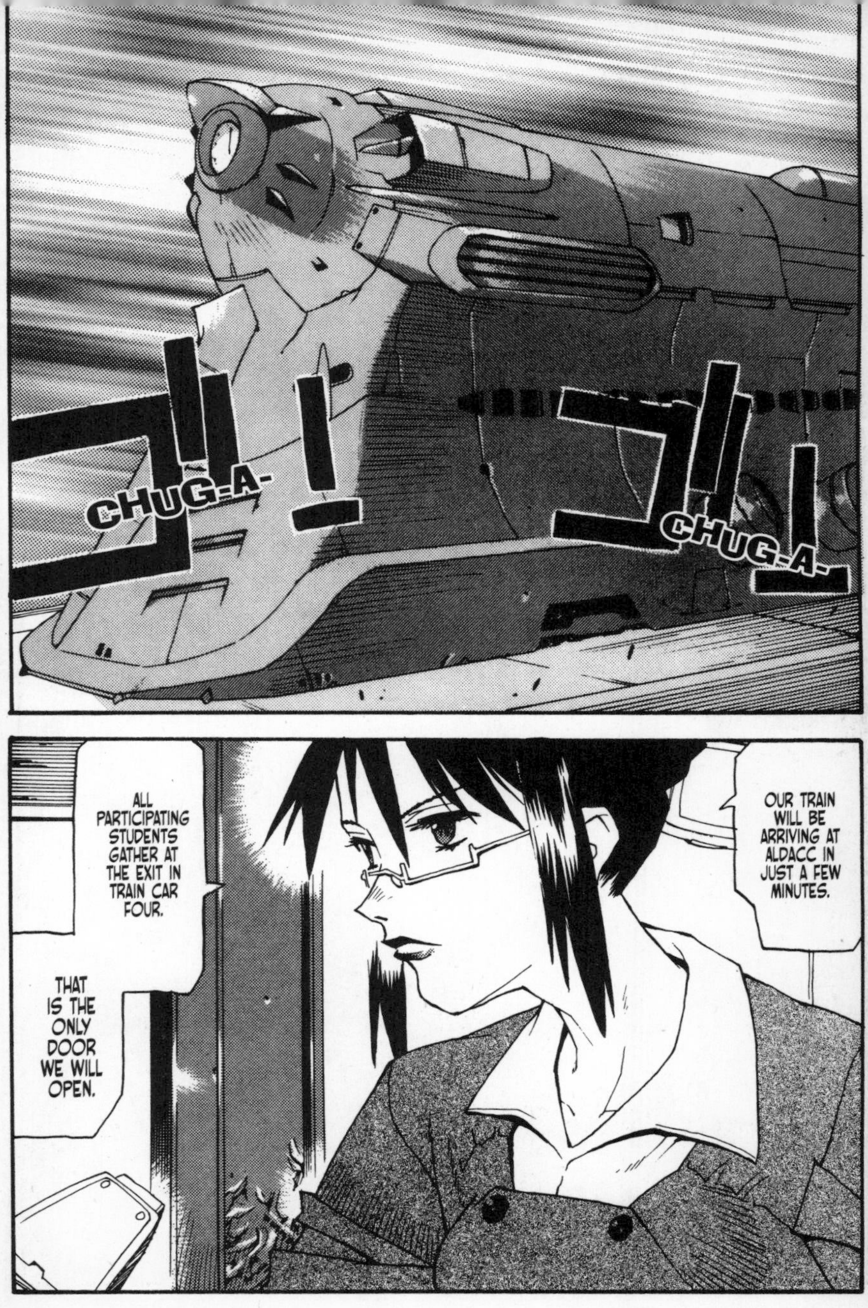
CHUG-A-
CHUG-A-
OUR TRAIN WILL BE ARRIVING AT ALDACC IN JUST A FEW MINUTES.
ALL PARTICIPATING STUDENTS GATHER AT THE EXIT IN TRAIN CAR FOUR.
THAT IS THE ONLY DOOR WE WILL OPEN.

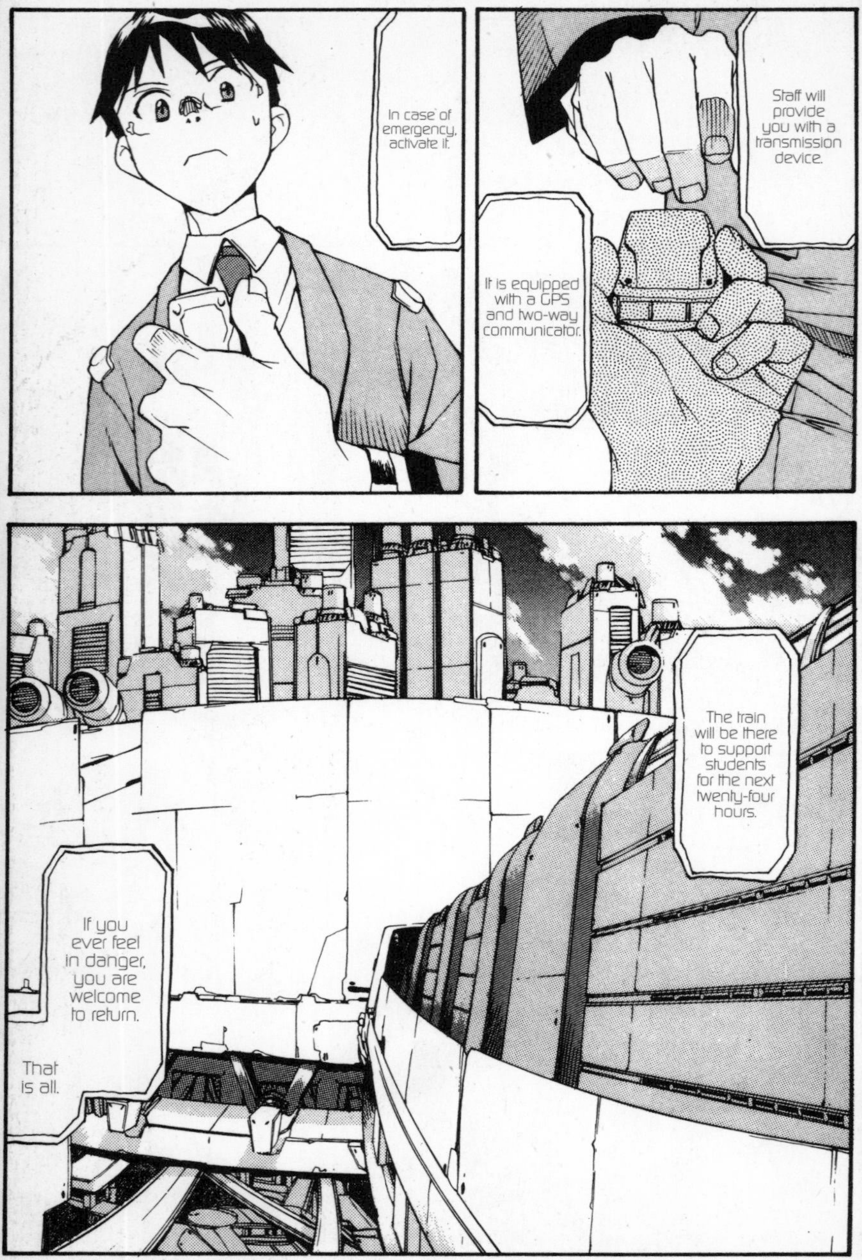
Staff will provide you with a transmission device.
It is equipped with a GPS and two-way communicator.
In case of emergency, activate it.
The train will be there to support students for the next twenty-four hours.
If you ever feel in danger, you are welcome to return.
That is all.

SHUUUU

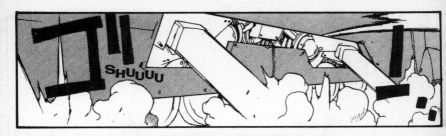

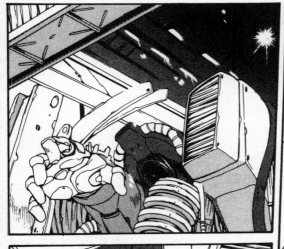

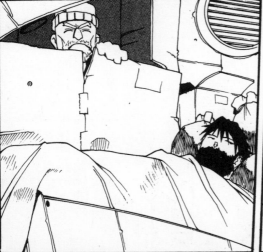

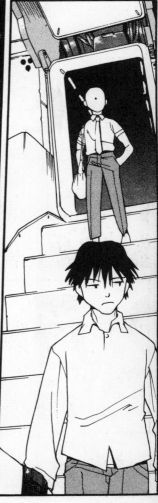

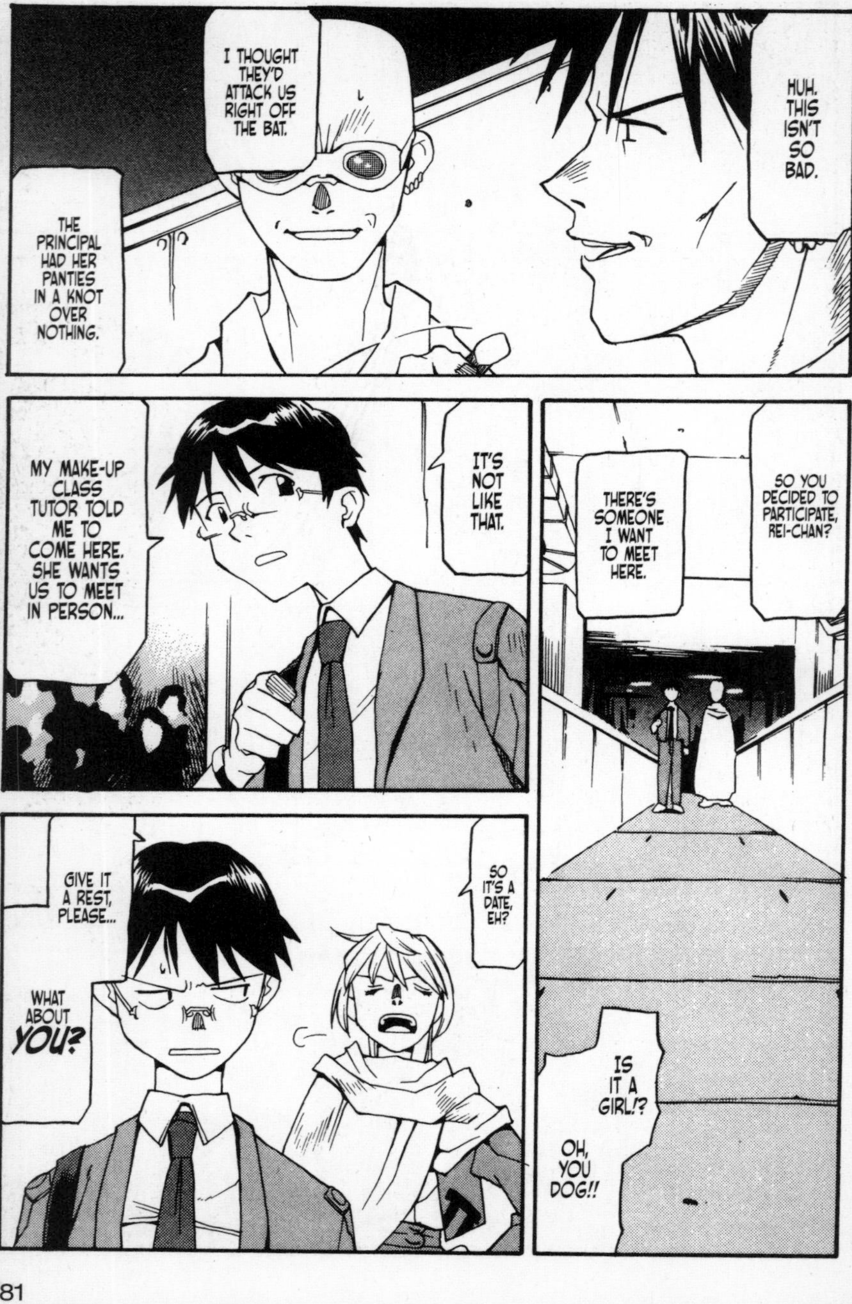
HUH. THIS ISN'T SO BAD.
I THOUGHT THEY'D ATTACK US RIGHT OFF THE BAT.
THE PRINCIPAL HAD HER PANTIES IN A KNOT OVER NOTHING.
SO YOU DECIDED TO PARTICIPATE, REI-CHAN?
THERE'S SOMEONE I WANT TO MEET HERE.
IS IT A GIRL!?
OH, YOU DOG!!
IT'S NOT LIKE THAT.
MY MAKE-UP CLASS TUTOR TOLD ME TO COME HERE. SHE WANTS US TO MEET IN PERSON...
SO IT'S A DATE, EH?
GIVE IT A REST, PLEASE...
WHAT ABOUT *YOU?*

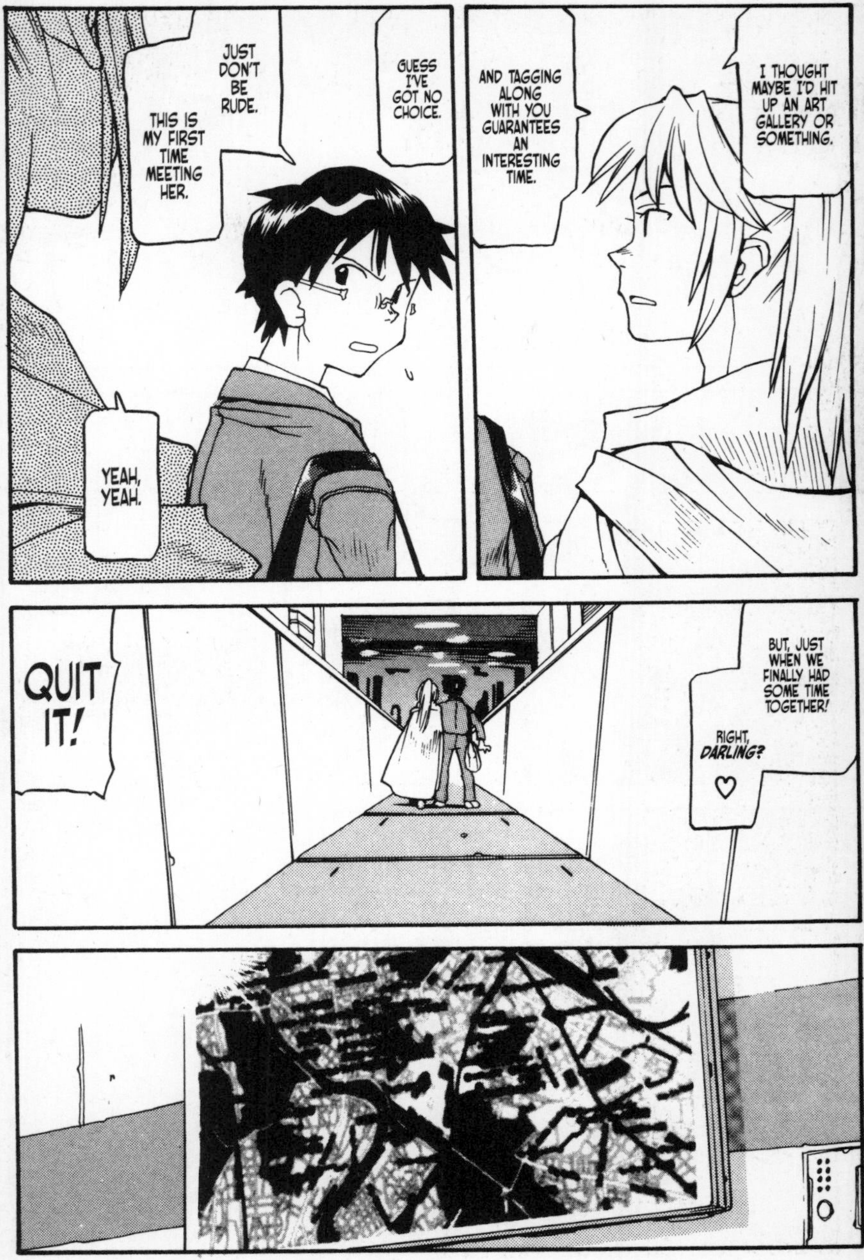
I THOUGHT MAYBE I'D HIT UP AN ART GALLERY OR SOMETHING.
AND TAGGING ALONG WITH YOU GUARANTEES AN INTERESTING TIME.
GUESS I'VE GOT NO CHOICE.
JUST DON'T BE RUDE.
THIS IS MY FIRST TIME MEETING HER.
YEAH, YEAH.
BUT, JUST WHEN WE FINALLY HAD SOME TIME TOGETHER!
RIGHT, *DARLING?* ♡
QUIT IT!

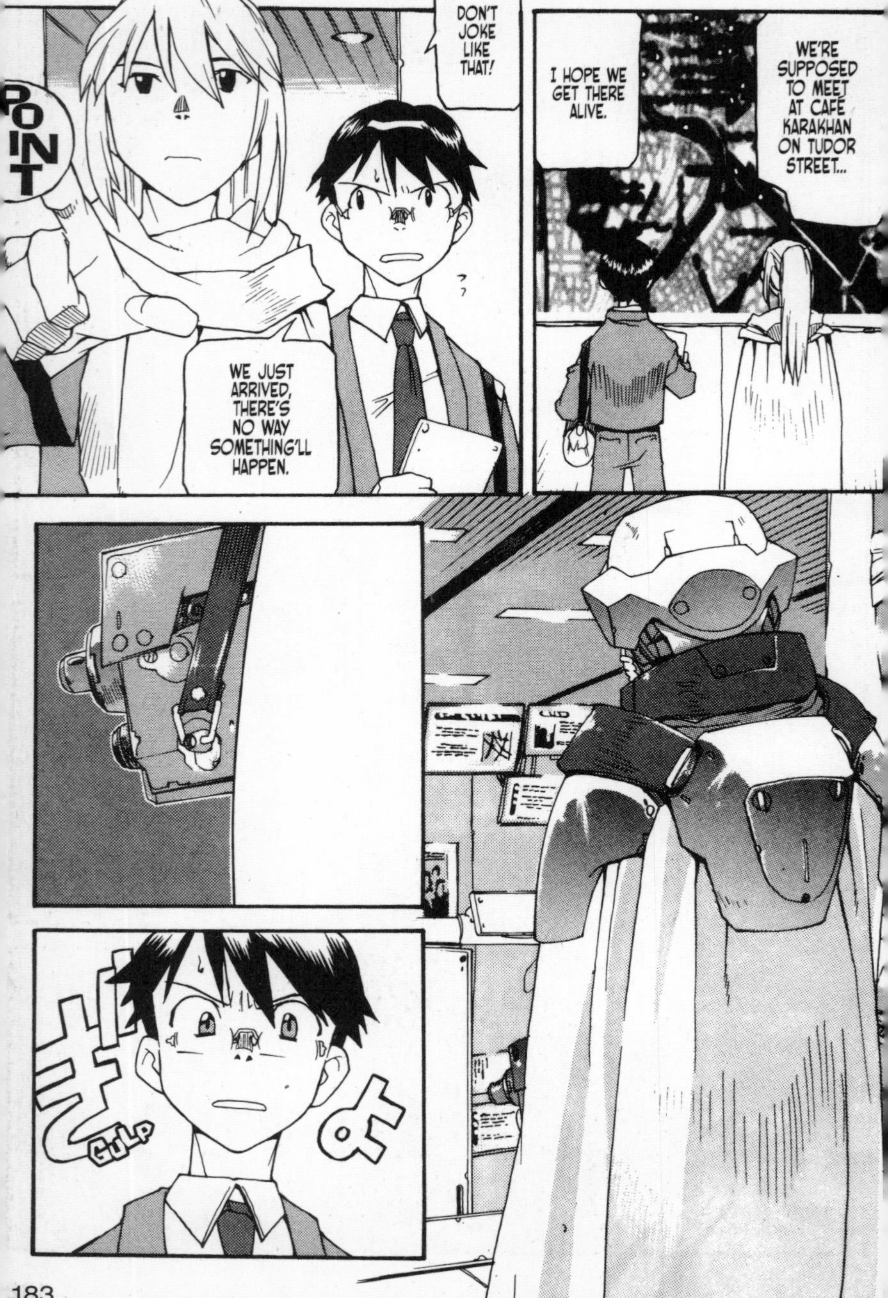
WE'RE SUPPOSED TO MEET AT CAFÉ KARAKHAN ON TUDOR STREET...
I HOPE WE GET THERE ALIVE.
DON'T JOKE LIKE THAT!
POINT
WE JUST ARRIVED, THERE'S NO WAY SOMETHING'LL HAPPEN.
GULP

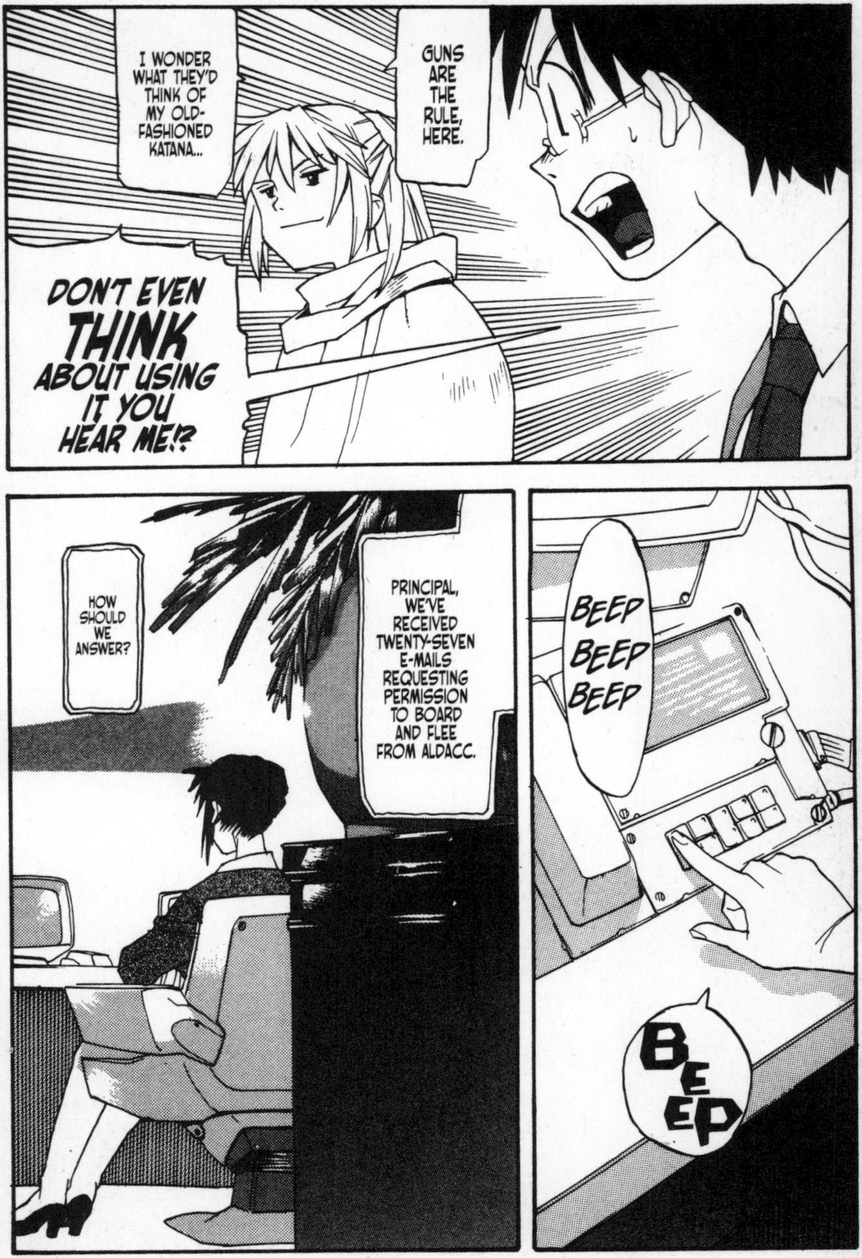
GUNS ARE THE RULE, HERE.
I WONDER WHAT THEY'D THINK OF MY OLD-FASHIONED KATANA...
DON'T EVEN THINK ABOUT USING IT YOU HEAR ME!?
BEEP BEEP BEEP
BEEP
PRINCIPAL, WE'VE RECEIVED TWENTY-SEVEN E-MAILS REQUESTING PERMISSION TO BOARD AND FLEE FROM ALDACC.
HOW SHOULD WE ANSWER?

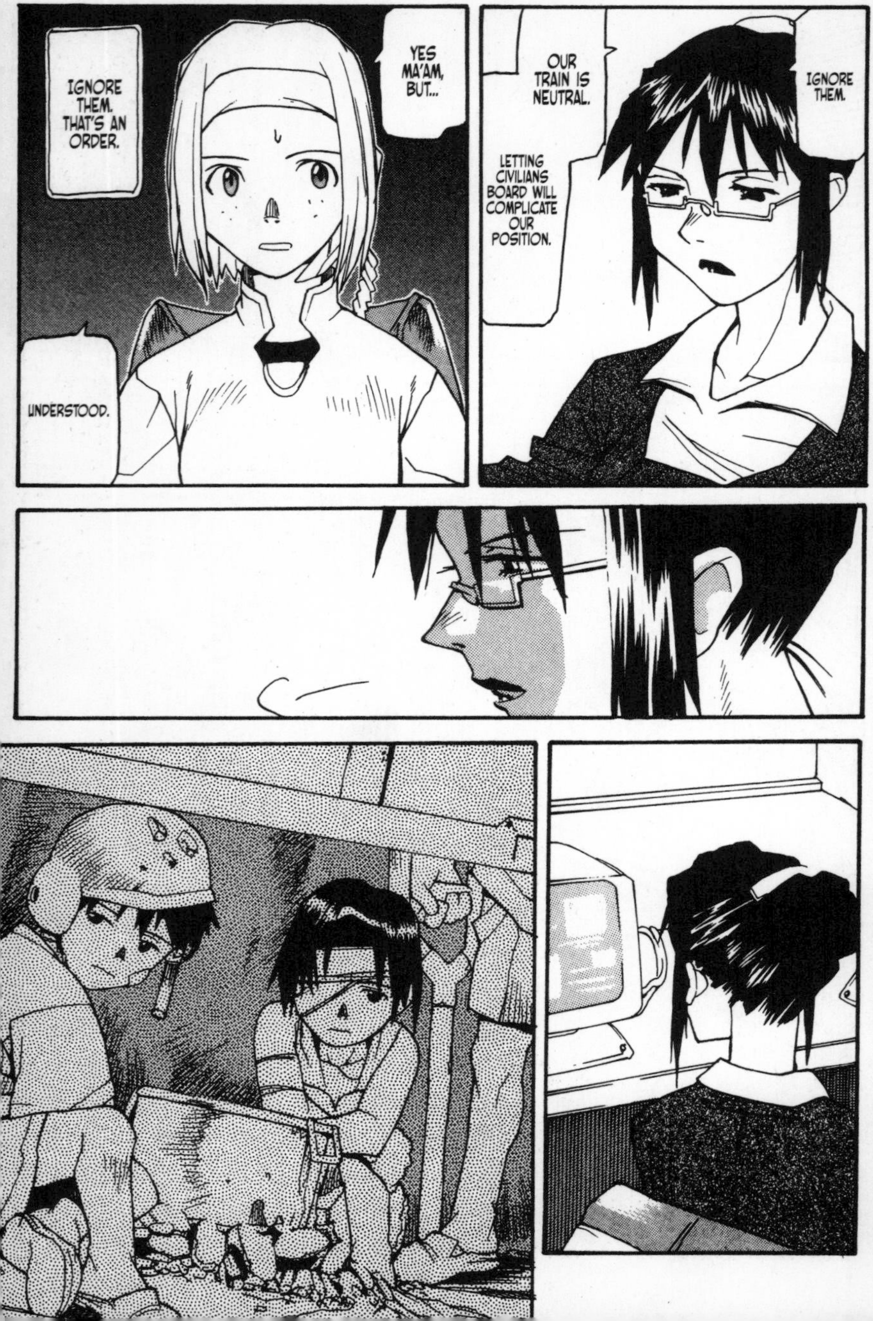
IGNORE THEM.
OUR TRAIN IS NEUTRAL.
LETTING CIVILIANS BOARD WILL COMPLICATE OUR POSITION.
YES MA'AM, BUT...
IGNORE THEM. THAT'S AN ORDER.
UNDERSTOOD.

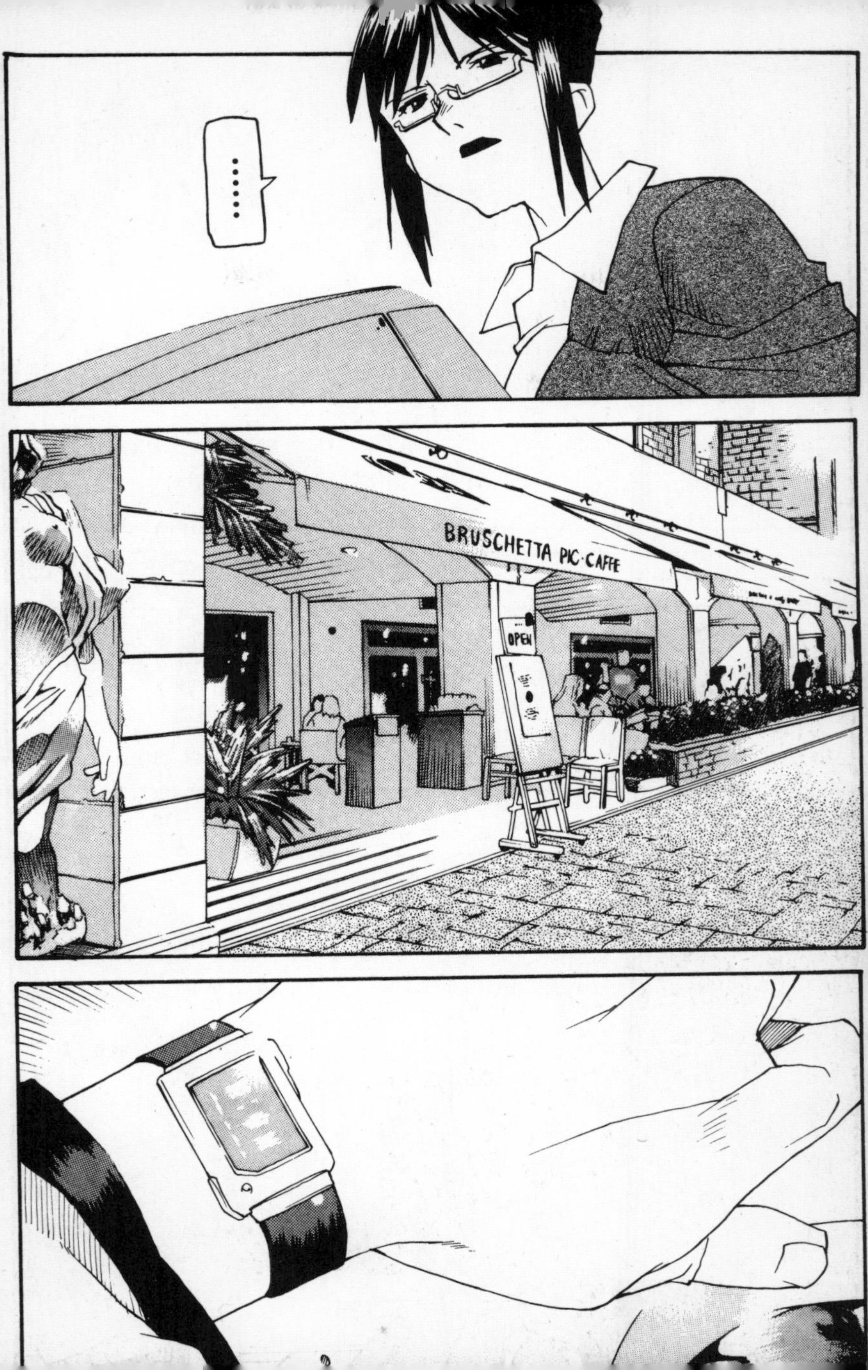
……
BRUSCHETTA PIC·CAFFE
OPEN

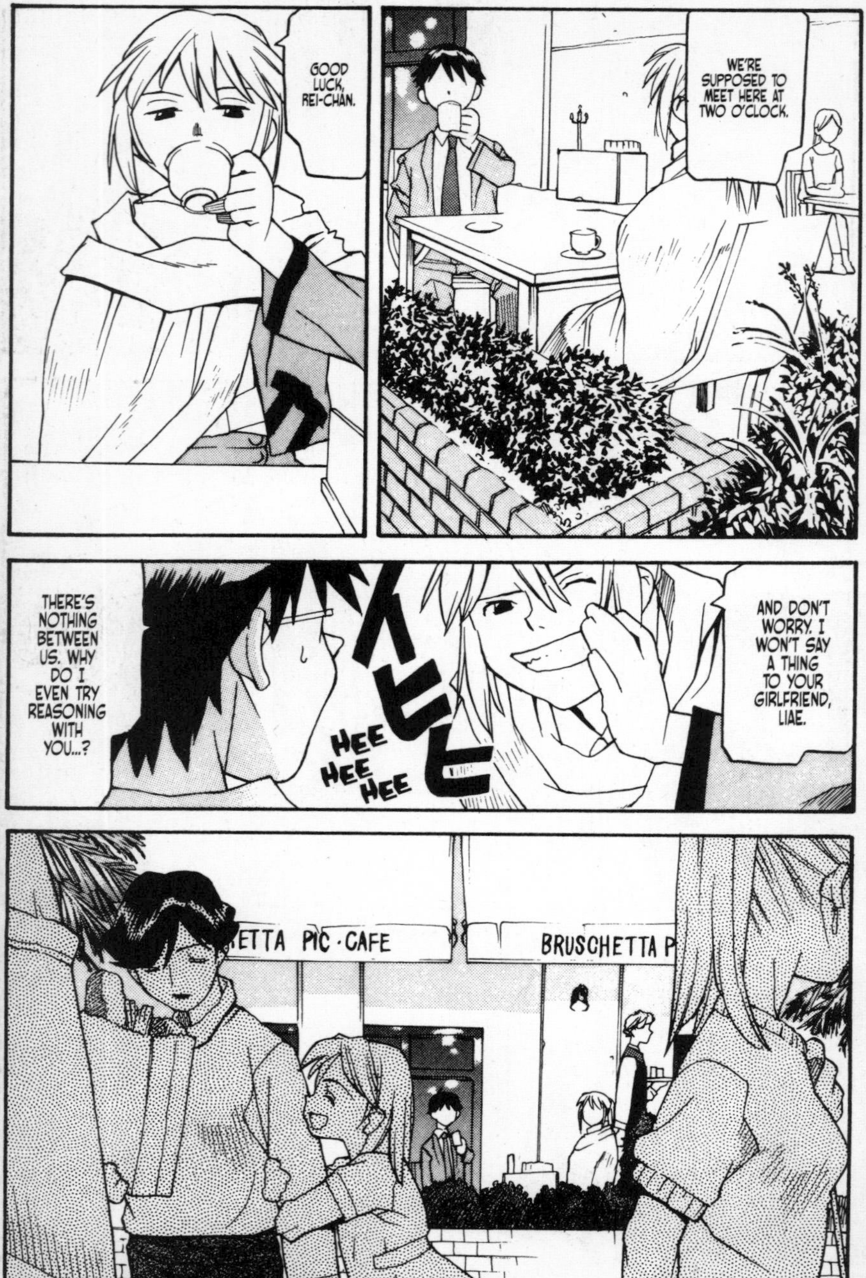
WE'RE SUPPOSED TO MEET HERE AT TWO O'CLOCK.
GOOD LUCK, REI-CHAN.
AND DON'T WORRY. I WON'T SAY A THING TO YOUR GIRLFRIEND, LIAE.
HEE HEE HEE
THERE'S NOTHING BETWEEN US. WHY DO I EVEN TRY REASONING WITH YOU...?
BRUSCHETTA P
ETTA PIC · CAFE

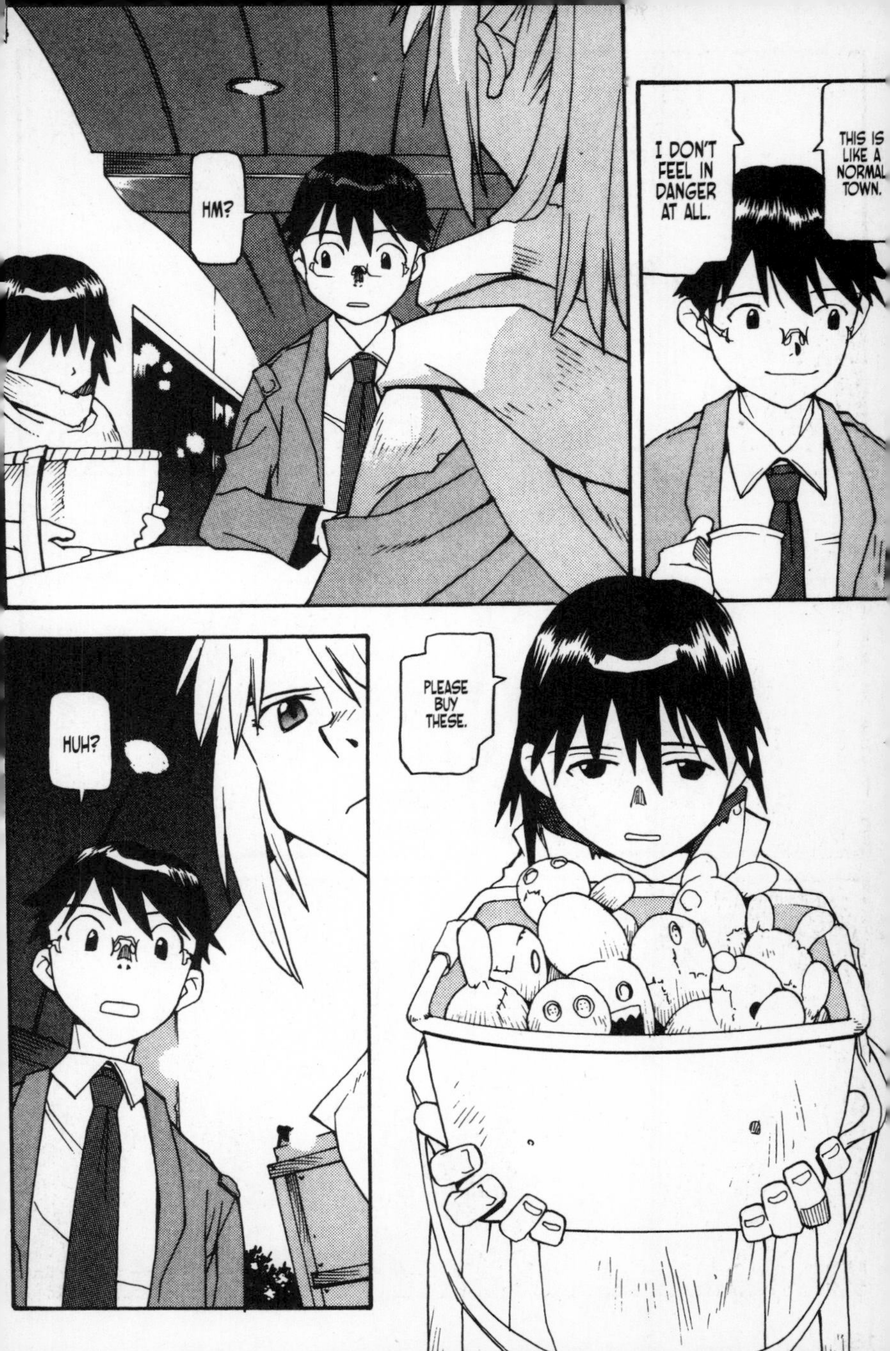
THIS IS LIKE A NORMAL TOWN.
I DON'T FEEL IN DANGER AT ALL.
HM?
PLEASE BUY THESE.
HUH?

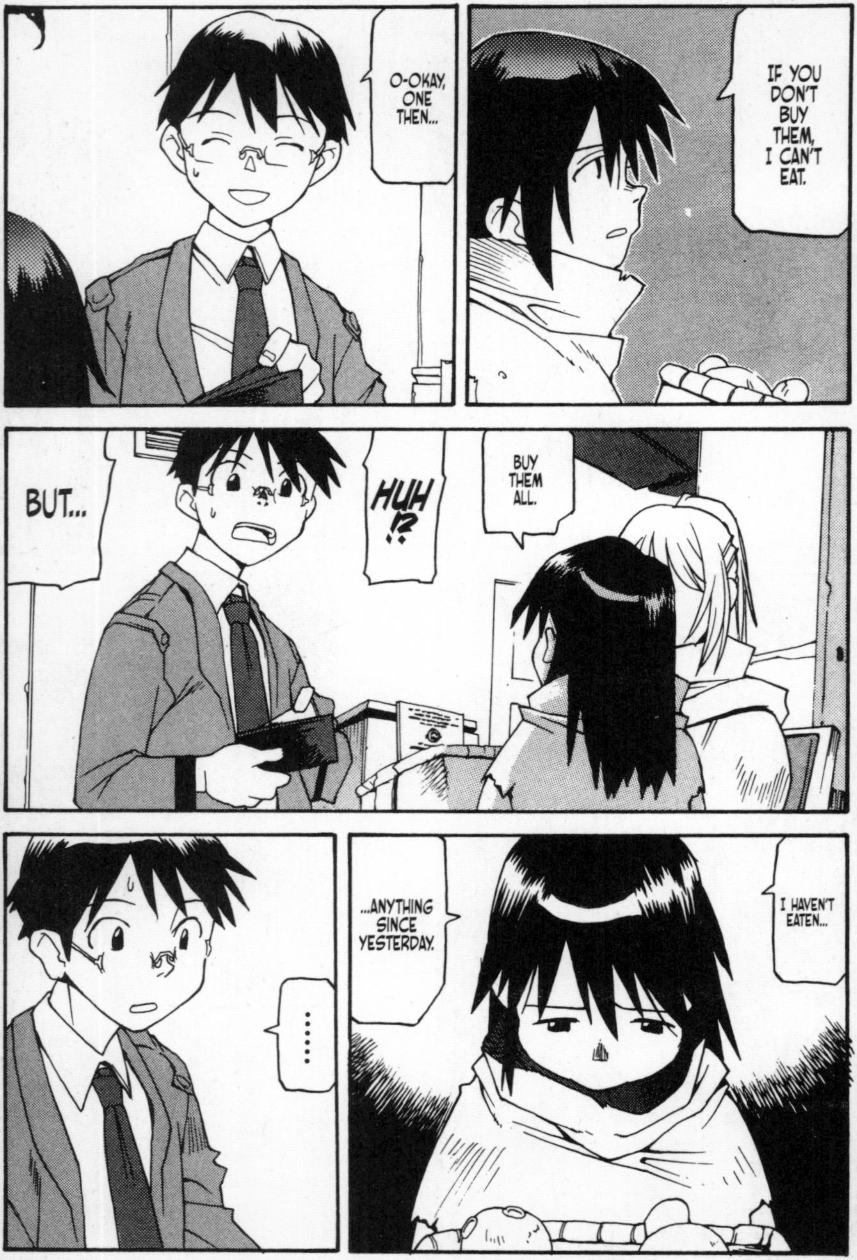
IF YOU DON'T BUY THEM, I CAN'T EAT.
O-OKAY, ONE THEN...
BUY THEM ALL.
HUH !?
BUT...
I HAVEN'T EATEN...
...ANYTHING SINCE YESTERDAY.
......

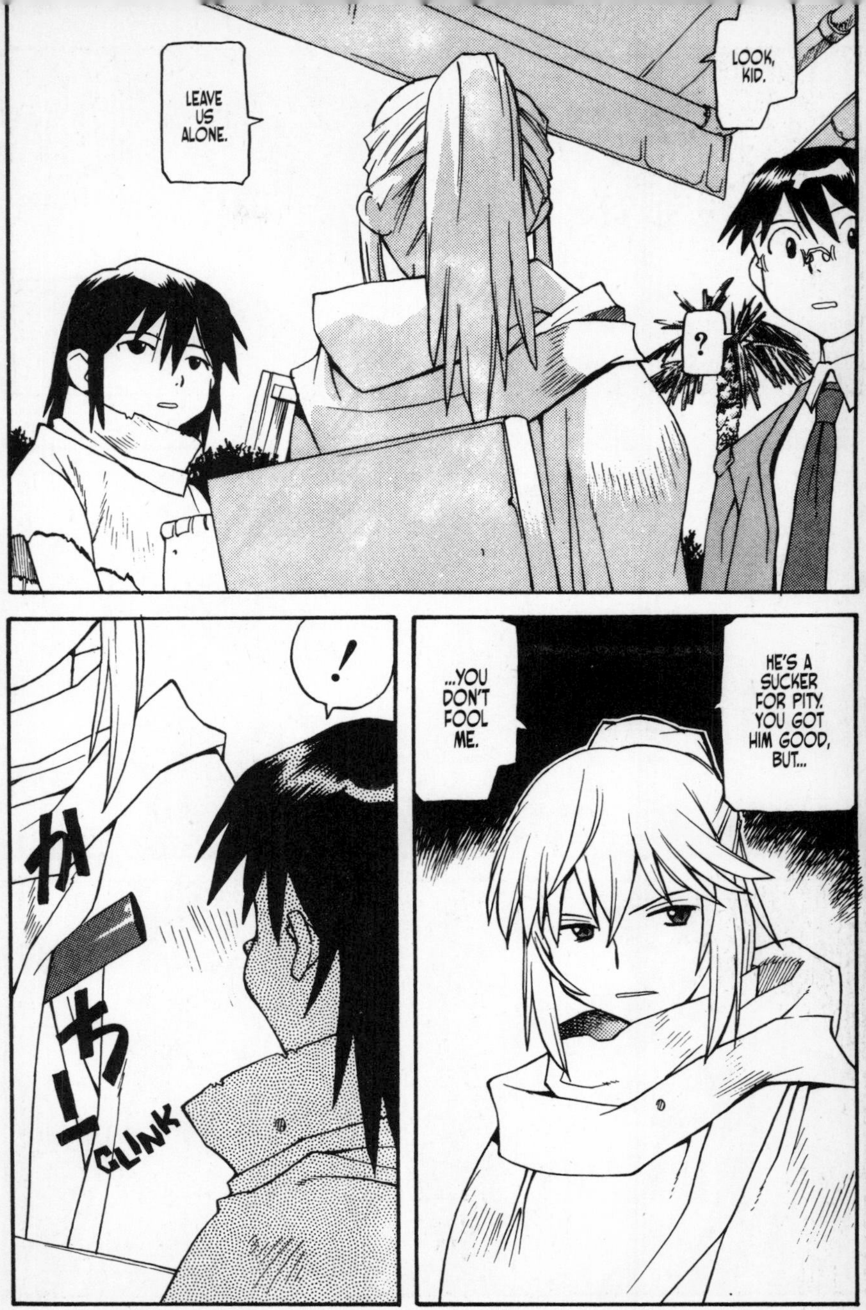
LOOK, KID.
LEAVE US ALONE.
?
HE'S A SUCKER FOR PITY. YOU GOT HIM GOOD, BUT...
...YOU DON'T FOOL ME.
!
GLINK

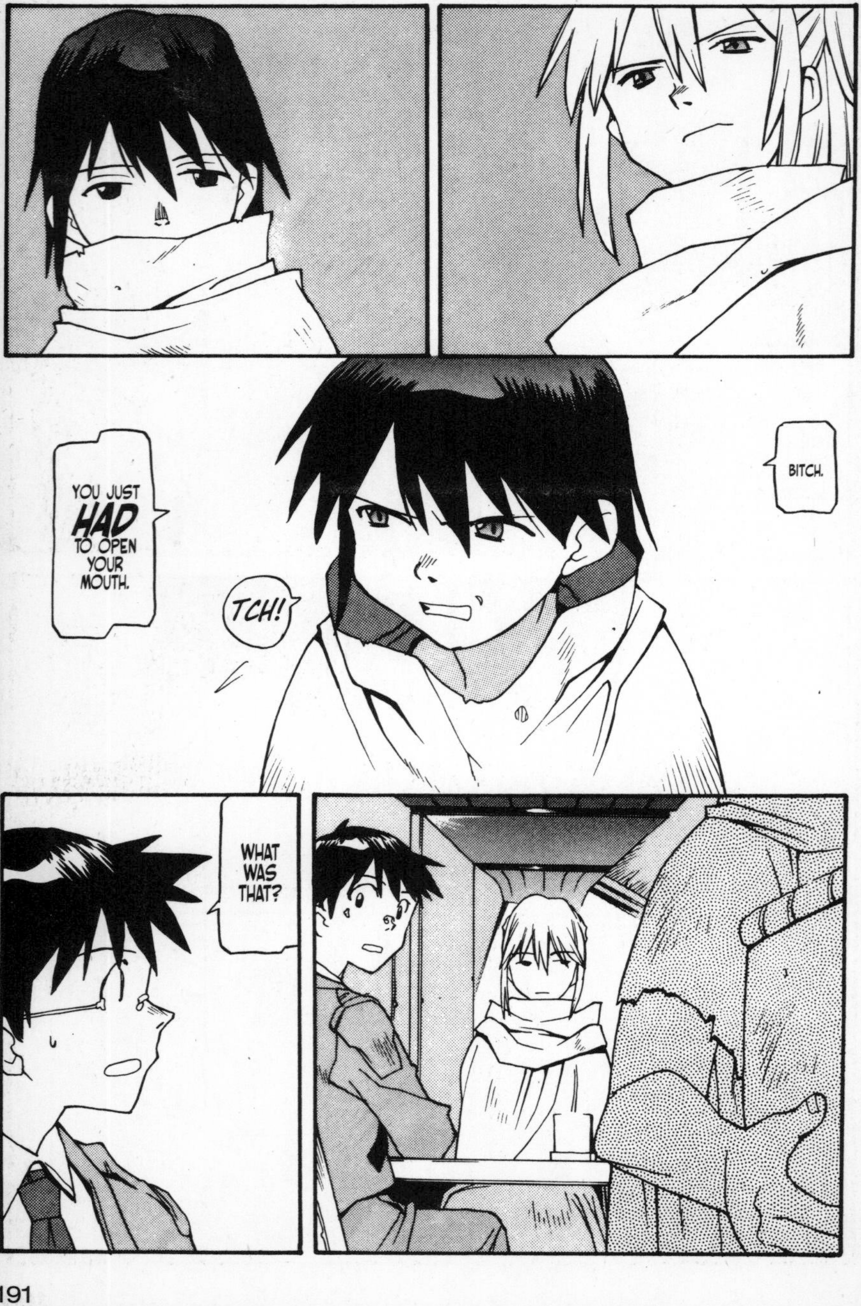
BITCH.
YOU JUST *HAD* TO OPEN YOUR MOUTH.
TCH!
WHAT WAS THAT?

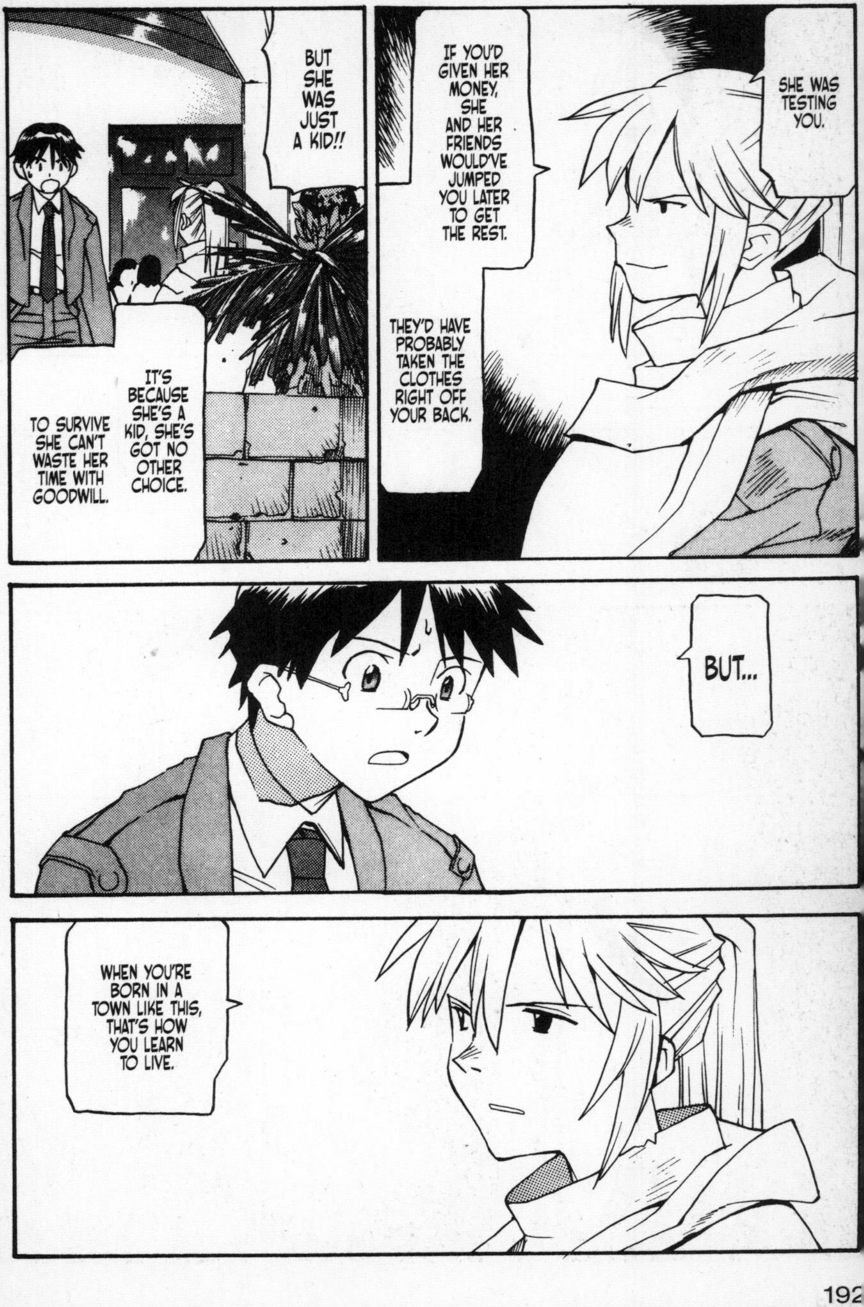
SHE WAS TESTING YOU.
IF YOU'D GIVEN HER MONEY, SHE AND HER FRIENDS WOULD'VE JUMPED YOU LATER TO GET THE REST.
THEY'D HAVE PROBABLY TAKEN THE CLOTHES RIGHT OFF YOUR BACK.
BUT SHE WAS JUST A KID!!
IT'S BECAUSE SHE'S A KID, SHE'S GOT NO OTHER CHOICE.
TO SURVIVE SHE CAN'T WASTE HER TIME WITH GOODWILL.
BUT...
WHEN YOU'RE BORN IN A TOWN LIKE THIS, THAT'S HOW YOU LEARN TO LIVE.

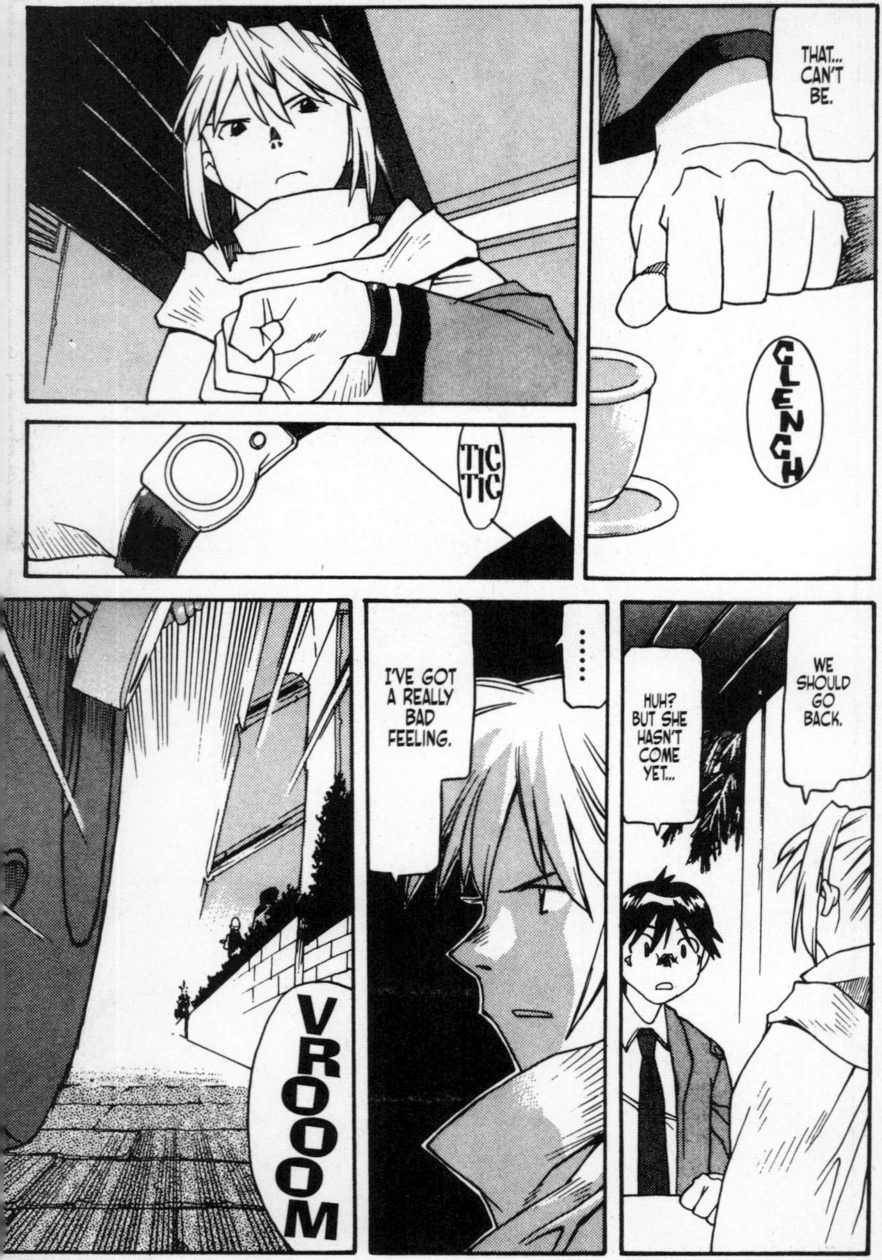
THAT... CAN'T BE.
CLENCH
TIC TIC
WE SHOULD GO BACK.
HUH? BUT SHE HASN'T COME YET...
......
I'VE GOT A REALLY BAD FEELING.
VROOOM

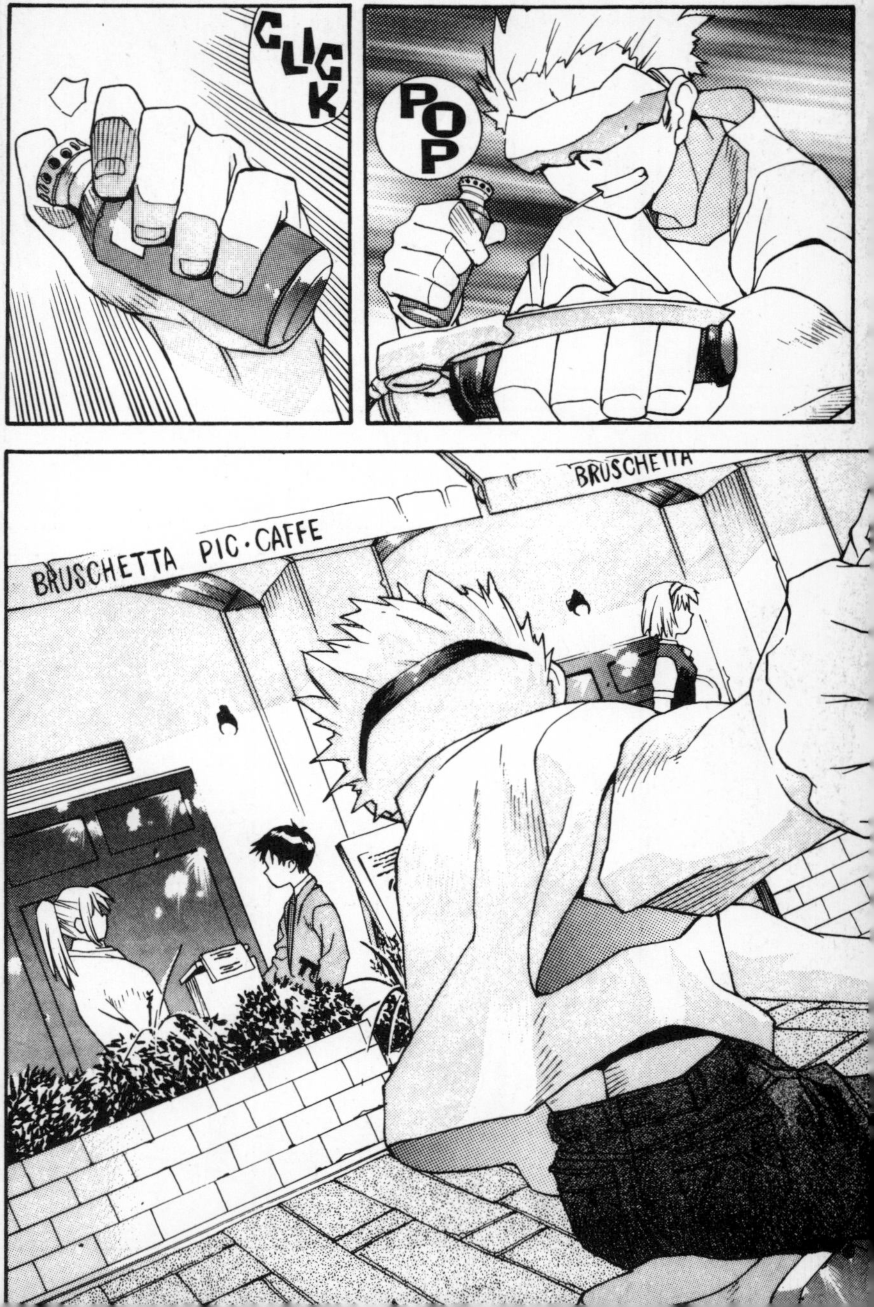
POP
CLICK
BRUSCHETTA
BRUSCHETTA PIC·CAFFE

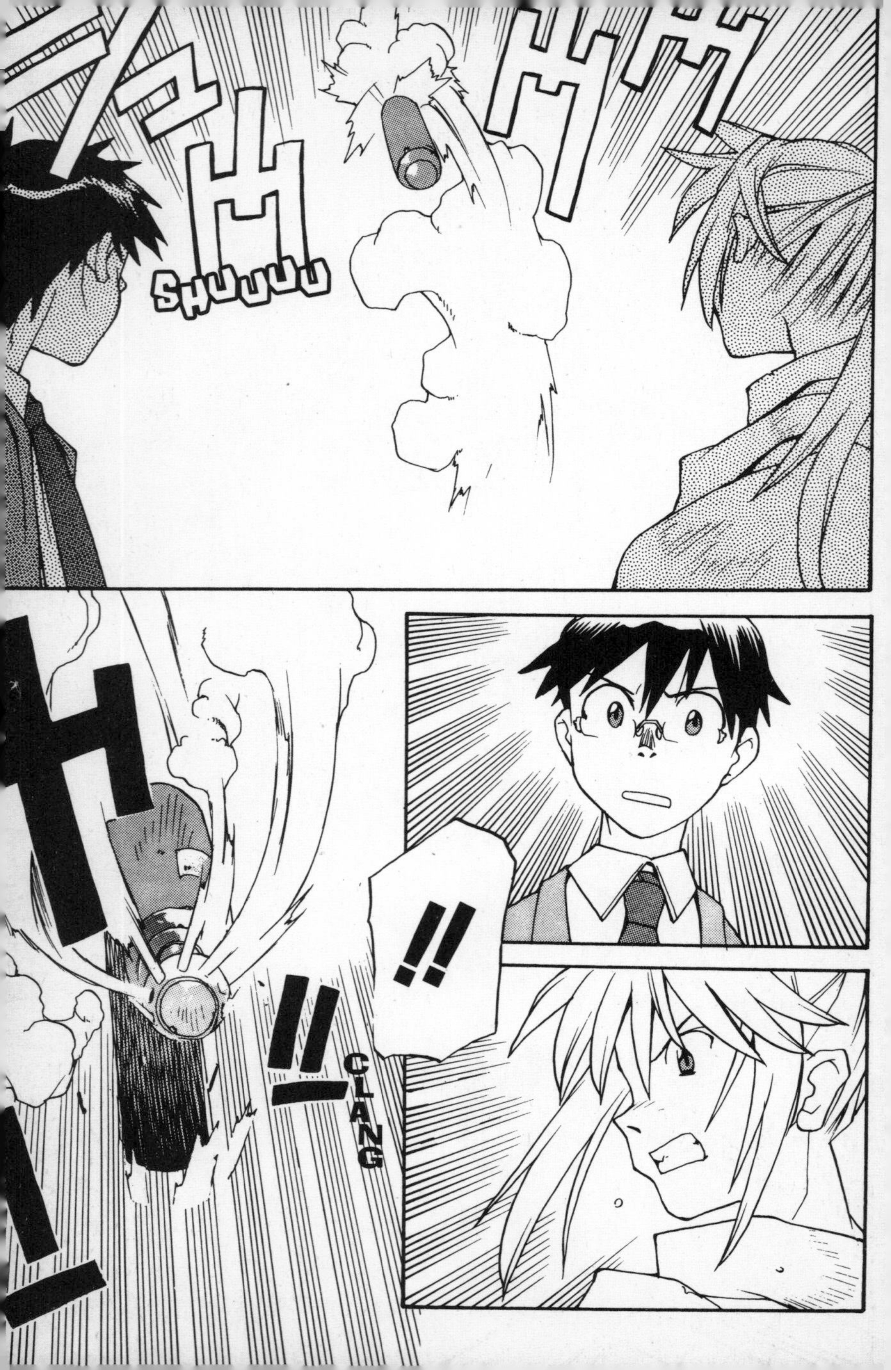
SHUUUU
!!
CLANG

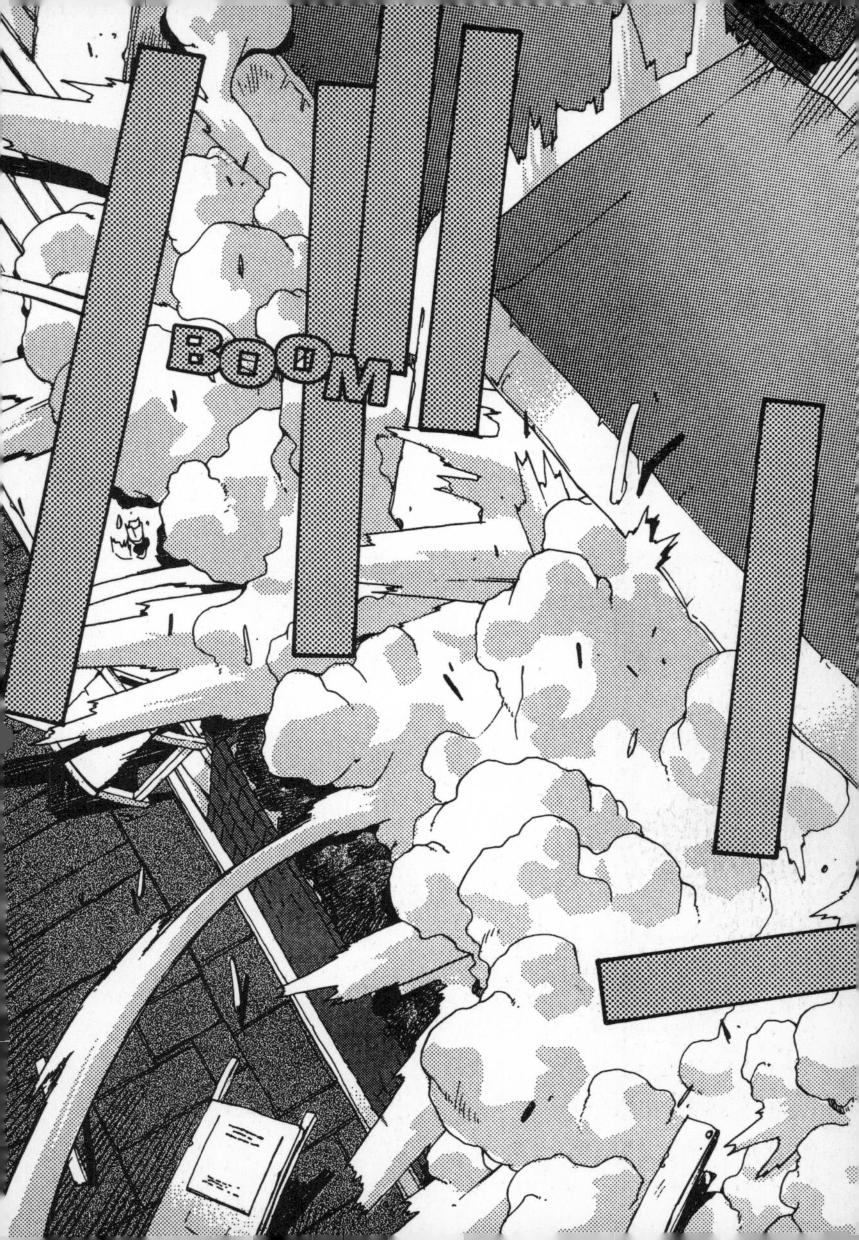
BOOM

SISTER LOU

TRAIN + TRAIN PROT WRITERS NOTE
FILE NO. 005

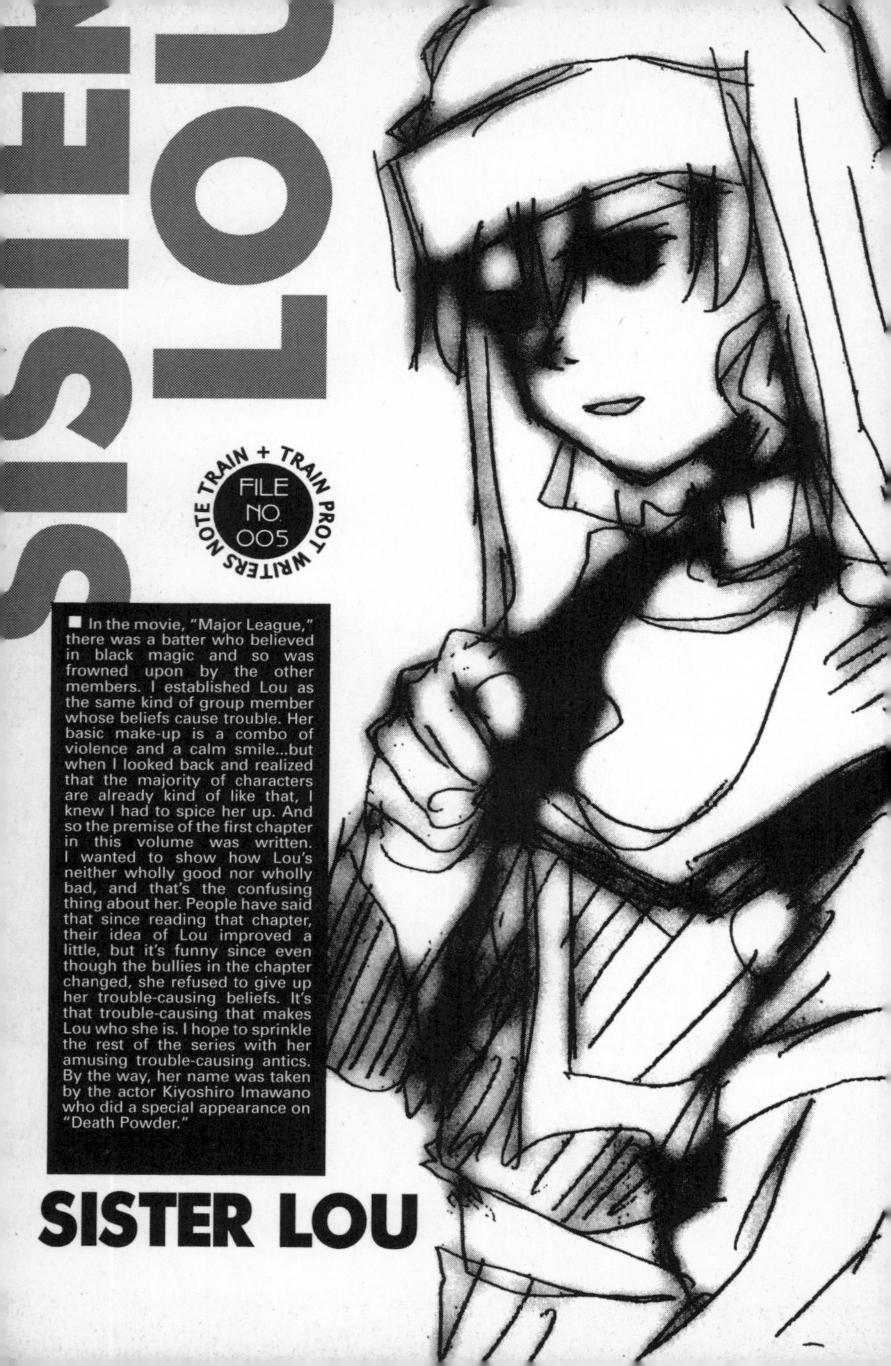

■ In the movie, "Major League," there was a batter who believed in black magic and so was frowned upon by the other members. I established Lou as the same kind of group member whose beliefs cause trouble. Her basic make-up is a combo of violence and a calm smile...but when I looked back and realized that the majority of characters are already kind of like that, I knew I had to spice her up. And so the premise of the first chapter in this volume was written. I wanted to show how Lou's neither wholly good nor wholly bad, and that's the confusing thing about her. People have said that since reading that chapter, their idea of Lou improved a little, but it's funny since even though the bullies in the chapter changed, she refused to give up her trouble-causing beliefs. It's that trouble-causing that makes Lou who she is. I hope to sprinkle the rest of the series with her amusing trouble-causing antics. By the way, her name was taken by the actor Kiyoshiro Imawano who did a special appearance on "Death Powder."

SISTER LOU

In volume 4 of TRAIN + TRAIN

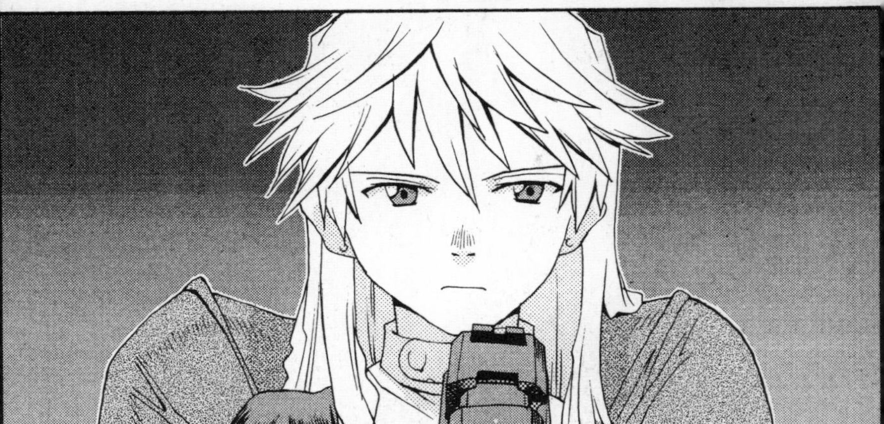

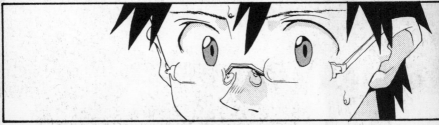

Some tests only have one right answer.

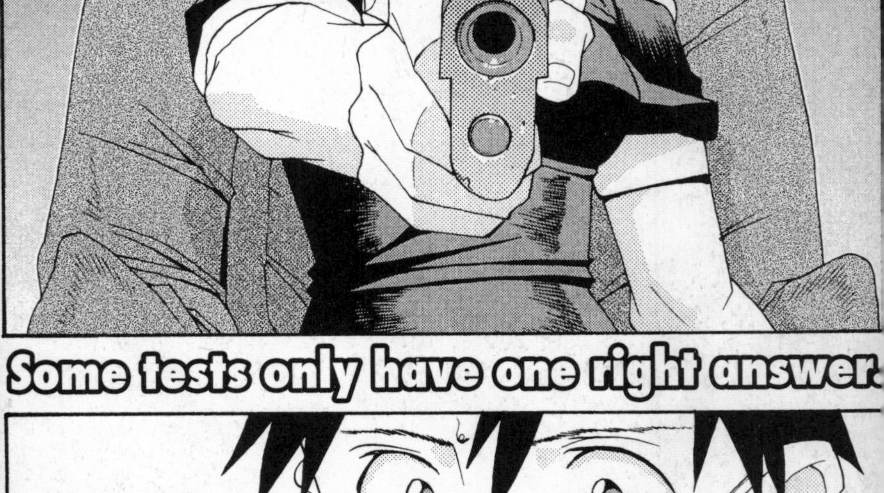

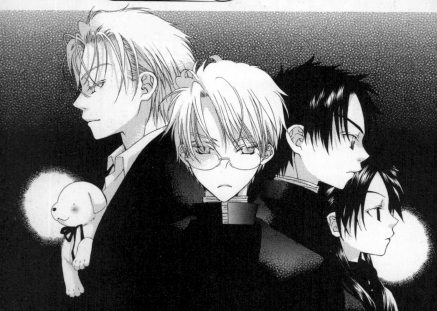
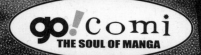

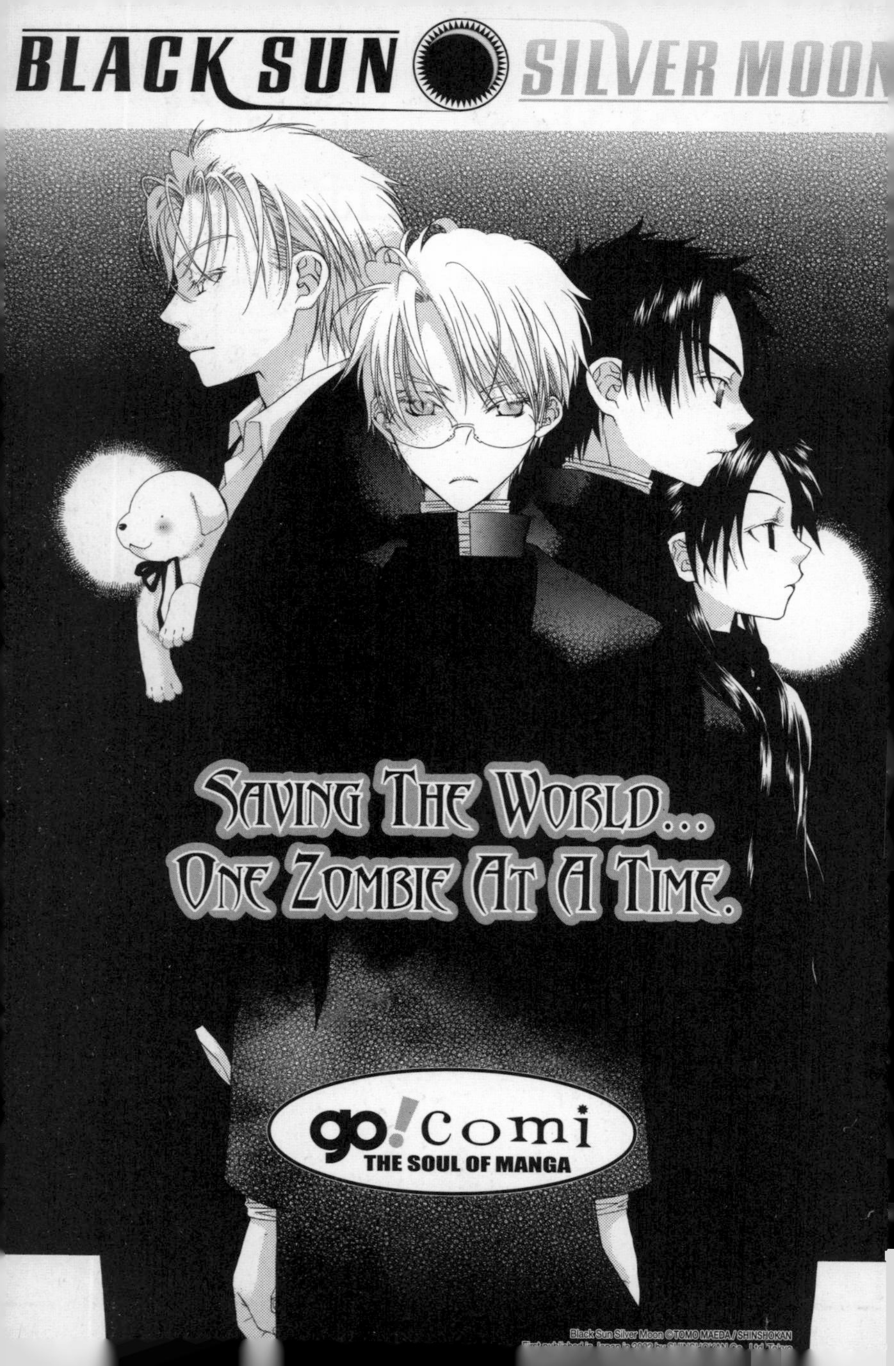

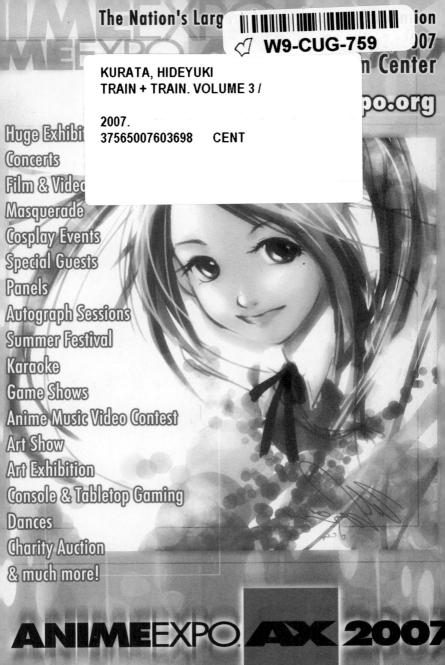

illustrated by Zelda C. Wang